T0314278

THE FLETCHER JONES FOUNDATION
HUMANITIES IMPRINT

The Fletcher Jones Foundation has endowed this imprint to foster innovative and enduring scholarship in the humanities.

The publisher gratefully acknowledges the generous support of the Fletcher Jones Foundation Humanities Endowment Fund of the University of California Press Foundation.

*Technology and the Search for
Progress in Modern Mexico*

Technology and the Search for Progress in Modern Mexico

Edward Beatty

UNIVERSITY OF CALIFORNIA PRESS

University of California Press, one of the most distinguished university presses in the United States, enriches lives around the world by advancing scholarship in the humanities, social sciences, and natural sciences. Its activities are supported by the UC Press Foundation and by philanthropic contributions from individuals and institutions. For more information, visit www.ucpress.edu.

University of California Press
Oakland, California

Library of Congress Cataloging-in-Publication Data
Beatty, Edward, author.
    Technology and the search for progress in modern Mexico / Edward Beatty.
        p.   cm.
    Includes bibliographical references and index.
    ISBN 978-0-520-28489-0 (cloth : alk. paper)
    ISBN 978-0-520-28490-6 (pbk. : alk. paper)
    ISBN 978-0-520-96055-8 (ebook)
    1. Technological innovations—Mexico—History—19th century.   2. Technology transfer—Mexico—History—19th century.   3. Technology transfer—United States—History—19th century.   4. Technology transfer—Europe, Northern—History—19th century.   I. Title.
    HC140.T4B43   2015
    338′.064097209034—dc23   2014036981

Manufactured in the United States of America

24   23   22   21   20   19   18   17   16   15
10   9   8   7   6   5   4   3   2   1

In keeping with a commitment to support environmentally responsible and sustainable printing practices, UC Press has printed this book on Natures Natural, a fiber that contains 30% post-consumer waste and meets the minimum requirements of ANSI/NISO Z39.48–1992 (R 1997) (*Permanence of Paper*).

CONTENTS

ILLUSTRATIONS

FIGURES

TABLES

ACKNOWLEDGMENTS

I am deeply grateful for the generous support of a large number of friends, colleagues, and organizations in the research and writing of this book. Much of the initial research was funded by the National Science Foundation, NSF Award #0217001 (with special gratitude for the advice of Bruce Seely), supplemented over the years by generous research support from the Kellogg Institute for International Studies at the University of Notre Dame (with special gratitude to Scott Mainwaring and Sharon Schierling). Bibliographers and archivists at numerous libraries and archives have offered their own generous and expert help and advice over the years, including Dr. Sergio Antonio Corona Páez of the Archivo Histórico at the Universidad Iberoamericana Laguna; Barbara Floyd of the Canaday Center at the University of Toledo; Walter Brem at the Bancroft Library; the late Scott Van Jacob and more recently, David Dressing, at Notre Dame; and the many professional staff at the Archivo General de la Nación and the Condumex archive in Mexico City, the Library of Congress, the US Patent Office, the Wisconsin Historical Society, and the Benson Latin American Collection at the University of Texas at Austin. I owe special thanks for permission to reproduce photographs to Ricardo Espinosa and Cecilia K. Peimbert in Mexico. Both the Kellogg Institute at Notre Dame and the Instituto de Iberoamérica at the Universidad de Salamanca, in Spain, have offered congenial settings for writing and critique.

I have received valuable feedback from audiences at the University of Chicago, Michigan State University, Notre Dame (at the Kellogg Institute and especially the Mexico Working Group), Yale University, the University of California, San Diego, the Colegio de México, the Department of Economics at the Universidad de Salamanca, Georgia Tech University, and the Universidad Nacional Autónoma de México. Numerous friends and colleagues have offered their time and insight to read and critique one or more chapters of this book. These include John Deak, Bill French, Susan Gauss, Aurora Gómez-Galvarriato, Patricia Graf, Guillermo Guajardo, Anne Hanley, Ian Inkster, Herb Klein, Elisabeth Köll, Moramay López-Alonso, Graciela Márquez, Jeremy Mouat, David Nye, Paul Ocobock, Emily Osborn, Alma Parra, Jaime Pensado, Yovanna Pineda, Gabriela Recio, Jaime Ros, Patricio Sáiz, Steve Samford, Angela Vergara, Rick Weiner, Mikael Wolfe, and John Womack Jr. The project has benefited immensely from their wisdom and knowledge, while any shortcomings and errors remain very much my own. This work benefits from the continuing influence of Stephen Haber and the careful readings of Richard Salvucci and Alan Knight; I cannot overstate their contributions and my own gratitude for their generosity and wisdom. All errors and omissions are of course my own. At the University of California Press, Kate Marshall, Stacy Eisenstark, and Elisabeth Magnus have been wonderful guides over the past year.

Many research assistants have contributed to this work over the past ten years: Manuel Dávila, Valeria Sánchez Michel, Eva Garon, Brittany Proffit, Stuart Mora, Marcela Monsalve, Toni Otokunrin, Lara Mancuso, Laura Garcia Meléndez, Kathryn Schilling, and Billy Smith. I owe particular thanks to the recent superb work of Carolina Gutiérrez, Esther Terry, Susy Sánchez, and Courtney Campbell.

Finally, this book is dedicated to my father and to my mother.

South Bend, Indiana
August 2014

ONE

Introduction

DURING THE 1970s and 1980s, "dependency" provided a common paradigm for Latin America's condition, and "dependency theory" dominated much of the scholarship on the region. The dependency approach argued that Latin America's development was adversely conditioned by the economic and political power of the industrialized world. Deeply entrenched unequal relations between the Latin American periphery and a European and US core constrained local development paths, producing poverty, inequality, authoritarian politics, and underdevelopment.[1]

By the late 1980s and 1990s, however, new scholarship marked the sharp decline of dependency's influence as an explanatory paradigm.[2] Empirical studies failed to support some of dependency's central claims, and a new generation of scholars moved in other directions: many historians turned to cultural and local studies, while many social scientists took up the study of national institutions and actors in search of local explanations for political and economic outcomes in Latin America. Since then, both historians and social scientists have explicitly or implicitly dismissed the notion that Latin America "depended" on the industrialized core, centered in the North Atlantic, and have often emphasized local agency within the region. *Dependency* has become a word that most Latin American historians have assiduously avoided for nearly two decades. Nevertheless, the story of technological change in nineteenth-century Mexico is fundamentally one of dependence. Through Mexico's nineteenth century and into the early twentieth, nearly every local effort to innovate, to adopt new ways of doing things in mining, agriculture, and manufacturing, critically depended on access to imported hardware (tools, machines, and parts) and imported technical knowledge and expertise (know-how) from the countries of northern Europe and the United States. Examples of Mexican expertise, ingenuity, and technological capabilities were not altogether absent from the nineteenth-century experience: they were most famously centered in Monterrey but were also present in individuals and firms throughout the country. However, these were isolated and exceptional across a broader landscape in which growing interest and investment in new technologies focused overwhelmingly on the well-publicized availability of global goods: new machines, processes, and expertise developed in and exported from England, France, Germany, Belgium, and the United States—what I will refer to as the "North Atlantic." In this, Mexico's experience differed little from that of many other countries around the globe.

This book argues that dependence on imported machines and know-how was the defining trait of Mexico's history of technology in the nineteenth century and that dependence would remain an important legacy into the twentieth. Built on a broad survey of innovation across the Mexican economy and several detailed case studies, the book examines the nineteenth-century origins of that dependence. In contrast to the assumptions implicit in the more iron-clad nature of the older dependency approach, however, this dependence was not structurally determined by an unequal relationship of exchange between Mexico and the United States and Europe. Nor was it uniformly prescriptive: individuals, firms, industries, and even regions could and did develop independently, with substantial local capacities for technological creativity. Dependence was not hegemonic or inevitable but rather contingent on conditions within Mexico. The particular course of technological development in nineteenth-century Mexico made persistent dependence a likely but not inevitable outcome in the twentieth.

Mexico's technological dependence arose in the gap between *adopting* new technologies and *assimilating* new knowledge and expertise. On one hand, importing, adopting, and using new technologies from the countries of the North Atlantic proved relatively easy, at least after 1870. Over the previous half century (ca. 1820–70), persistent economic malaise and low consumer demand in Mexico had consistently discouraged investment in new machines and expertise, with some important exceptions. After about 1870, however, more propitious social and economic conditions in Mexico combined with a dramatic increase in the availability of new machines and knowledge in the North Atlantic as the country reintegrated into an expanding Atlantic economy. Together with gradual social and cultural changes in Mexico, these conditions increased incentives to invest in innovation by adopting machines, tools, and production systems as well as new technical knowledge and expertise embodied in print materials and in people themselves. The result was a massive wave of technology imports between roughly 1870 and the outbreak of revolution in 1910. New technologies, in turn, pushed further social change, increased productivity, and underlay economic growth.

However, it proved far more difficult for individuals and firms working in Mexico to *assimilate* the knowledge and expertise embedded within new technology imports. Most Mexicans were effectively excluded from opportunities to engage with new technologies in ways that might yield learning. Even for the relatively few with access to technical education and economic opportunity, the obstacles to learning and mastering new knowledge proved substantial. Because individuals and firms had only rarely adopted the technologies of the first industrial revolution before 1870, Mexico possessed an accumulated deficit of local experience and capabilities when faced with a flood of technology imports thereafter, ranging from iron, steam, and mechanized production techniques to the new advances in chemical, metallurgical, and electrical science and technologies of the second industrial revolution. By late century, then, the gap between Mexican capabilities and the North Atlantic technological frontier had widened considerably. Few in Mexico had the particular kinds of human capital necessary to assimilate the knowledge and expertise embodied in technology imports. As a result, both entrepreneurs and policy makers found it cheaper and quicker to import hardware and expertise from abroad than to develop it at home. Dependence on imported technology meant that there would be little demand for domestic sources of technology, and little stimulus to local technological capacities. There would be, in other words, relatively little pressure to invest in the local development of human capital, high-wage skills, and the local production of machines, tools, and their parts. This would depress the potential for both economic development and social opportunities in the long run.

Ironically, the origins of technological dependence are found in Mexicans' aspirations for economic independence. Throughout Mexico's first full century of independence (1820–1911), the country's political and economic elites largely agreed that that *el progreso material*—material progress, focused especially on new technologies—was crucial to the nation's future. Although they vigorously debated whether that future should be primarily agrarian, extractive, or manufacturing, most argued that acquiring and using new technologies would increase productivity and production, thereby generating new wealth. This view of the "inevitable law of progress" and the "enrichment of the nation" became especially vigorous and nearly unchallenged in the second half of the nineteenth century, when, with few exceptions, Mexican investors and public officials focused on *adopting* new technologies from abroad rather than *inventing* and developing them at home.[3]

In this view, national wealth no longer simply lay in Mexico's untapped natural resources, in the country's soil and minerals and geographic diversity that Alexander von Humboldt had famously extolled at the beginning of the century. Instead, progress and wealth lay in the knowledge, skills, labor, tools, and capital required to extract and transform those resources.[4] Nearly ubiquitous references to "material progress" offered a positivistic reference to the physical manifestations of economic progress—new buildings, new infrastructure, and especially the most modern machinery—that could drive the mechanization of economic activity, from the extraction, processing, and transportation of raw materials to the local manufacture of products in new factories. Though partly a vision of an imagined national future, this view also reflected a more concrete and immediate imperative. The alternative was clear: without material progress, Mexico risked succumbing to the threat of North Atlantic and especially US expansion, whether military or economic, and becoming dependent (or, as they put it, "tributary," or even "enslaved") to the country's northern neighbor. By midcentury and after, most observers fervently believed that without the generation of new wealth derived from the productive capacity of newly adopted technologies, Mexico would remain as weak and vulnerable as it had been over its first half century of independence (ca. 1820–70).[5] Even the iconography of national wealth had become increasingly mechanical by century's end: the railroad, the anvil, and the factory, as we can see in the frontispiece to Justo Sierra's magisterial *México: Su evolución social* (1902–5) (figure 1), in Ireneo Paz's celebratory *Álbum de la paz y el trabajo,* published on the occasion of the country's 1910 centennial, or in the iconic landscape-with-railroad paintings of José María Velasco. In other words, *el progreso material* essentially captured what we think of as economic growth: a sustained increase in productivity and production, driven by the adoption of new technologies and measured in increased aggregate output and the generation of new wealth, both public and private.

Support for material progress came not only from Mexico's entrepreneurs, intellectuals, and government officials but also from across much of the social spectrum in direct and indirect ways. The pursuit of progress in Mexico was essentially an elite project and ideology, driven by a search for profit and for national improvement understood in both economic and cultural terms.[6]

FIGURE 1. Representations of *el progreso material*. Frontispiece from Justo Sierra, ed., *México: Su evolución social,* vol. 1 (1902; repr., Mexico: Miguel Angel Porrúa, 2005), original in color. Reproduced with permission from Cecilia K. Peimbert and Editorial Miguel Ángel Porrúa. See also the illustrated section headings in vol. 1, book 2, p. 417 (science) and vol. 2, p. 99 (industry).

Mexico's public men valued the "precision," "calibration," and large-scale productive potential of new technologies, as well as the moral attributes of progress, arguing that modern factories equipped with new technologies would become "august temples for the regeneration of men through work."[7] At the same time, however, many tens of thousands of Mexicans entered those temples of progress as both workers and consumers over the last decades of the century. Although slow and uneven, the expansion of consumer markets for goods and services created new incentives to invest in technological innovation. As ordinary Mexicans bought more ready-made clothing, for example, women and garment manufacturers bought sewing machines. As more Mexicans drank beer instead of pulque, Mexican investors faced new incentives to establish domestic breweries and mechanized glass bottle factories. As global demand for gold, silver, and industrial metals rose, foreign capital brought a host of new machinery and refining processes to Mexican mining camps. And this demand was self-reinforcing as well: as new production technologies lowered the production costs of cloth, clothing, beer, bottles, and precious metals (for example), consumption rose still further.

The actual "consumers" of new technologies—those who responded to rising demand for technology's products—ranged from the women and men who bought sewing machines, to entrepreneurs who built new factories to brew beer or manufacture glass bottles, and to foreign investors and mining engineers who pushed a more scientific and industrial approach to mining in Mexico. By 1910, hundreds of thousands of Mexicans worked with or in close proximity to industrial technologies, including roughly thirty-two thousand in textiles, five thousand in cigarette manufacturing, perhaps eighty thousand or so in mining, ten thousand in the electrical industry, over twenty-five thousand on the railroads (and another five thousand for the Compañía de Tranvías de México alone), and at least three hundred thousand sitting regularly or occasionally at sewing machines.[8] New technologies, imported from the countries of the North Atlantic, had become deeply integrated into the social and cultural lives of many Mexicans.[9] In factories, mines, public works, haciendas, and ranchos, as well as in many households, people increasingly substituted new machines, processes, tools, and products for traditional ones: steam and then electricity for the motive power of men and mules, reinforced cement for stone, dynamite for black powder and shovels, beer for pulque, glass bottles for ceramic jugs, and ready-made clothes for home-stitched apparel, to name just a few. These consumers, workers, engineers, entrepreneurs, and government officials were the primary agents of technological change in a society that embraced, contested, and endured material progress— what historians have often vaguely labeled "modernization." Although this book focuses narrowly on technologies used to mechanize economic activities, these were intimately linked to the broader needs, ambitions, dreams, and frustrations of Mexicans across the social spectrum.

Machinery and tools shipped from North Atlantic ports were unloaded on Mexico's docks and railway platforms; some were stored in local warehouses while the rest were reloaded onto branch railways or wagons or mules or the backs of men and boys and shipped to the interior.[10] Print materials were packed in bags and pouches and sent onward to cities, offices, homes, and mining camps. Investors, engineers, supervisors, and young men (nearly all men) just out of college—"technicians" in one way or another—stepped off ships and railcars and traveled to the national capital, to provincial cities, or to haciendas, factories, and construction sites. Then the vast majority of these three types of technology imports disappear from our sight. Historians can glimpse bits and pieces of the inundation in the monthly and yearly reports of trade ministries on both sides of the Atlantic, or newly installed in some corner of the country: in almanacs and advertisements and aging photographs, in newspaper notices and travelers' accounts, in government surveys and sometimes in court cases, and ultimately as rusting relics of another age. We can observe the impact of technological change in new sources of employment, in the displacement of traditional livelihoods, in social dislocation and outbursts of protest, in changing relative prices, and—at least in some activities—in rising labor productivity. Indeed, it was the extensive adoption of technologies from the North Atlantic that made possible rapid economic growth in Mexico from the 1870s to 1910, at just over 4 percent per year. However, we have little understanding of the experience of adoption and diffusion of new technologies in Mexico, little clear sense of what differentiated typical from atypical experiences, and even less about the long-term consequences for the twentieth century.

This book traces the contours and patterns of technological change in nineteenth-century Mexico in order to better understand the sharp contrast between the scarcity of innovation before 1870, rapid technological modernization thereafter, and persistent dependence on imported knowledge and expertise into the twentieth century. It examines those factors that encouraged and facilitated the adoption of new technologies, as well as those that limited innovation—that delayed adoption, constrained diffusion, impaired their effective use, and sometimes prevented adoption altogether. Some machines and forms of technical expertise were widely embraced and became deeply integrated into Mexican society and culture, while others barely gained traction. Experiences of adoption varied widely across firms, sectors, industries, and regions. Scholars have until now focused on a handful of industrial settings or anecdotal accounts: the largest, best-connected firms, or industries and activities with the most dramatic change, or the least. In contrast, this book explores a set of representative cases ranging from everyday technologies to larger industrial-scale projects. From railroads, steam power, and iron to sewing machines, glass bottle manufacturing, and silver refining, it identifies central trends and patterns across the Mexican economy. Finally, it explores the apparent paradox of high *adoption* and low *assimilation* in Mexico. Despite the widespread adoption of new technologies after 1870, few Mexican engineers, mechanics, and workers were able to assimilate new knowledge and expertise. Technical expertise and human capital were already scarce in Mexico, opportunities for direct learning and interaction were few and jealously guarded, social networks that might have diffused new knowledge were weak, and government policy tended to favor imports over local learning. In other words, a massive investment in technology imports was not matched by investment in local capabilities, and this was an opportunity lost. As a result, twentieth-century Mexico would inherit relatively weak local capacities to absorb new technical knowledge and to generate sustained technological innovation, independent of foreign expertise and imports. The book sets Mexico firmly within the Atlantic world in order to present a Mexican history of global technologies. It directly addresses the broader challenges of "late development": the challenges faced by people and countries around the globe as they sought wealth, economic growth, and even national survival in the wake of the early North Atlantic industrializers.

MEXICO AND THE CHALLENGE OF LATE DEVELOPMENT

Technological innovation—adopting and using new ideas and tools and machines—originates in inventive activity or in the borrowing of others' inventions (and often in a combination of the two). This has been the history of industrialization—the mechanization of production—over the past two centuries. Early industrialization in the United States and western Europe was itself heavily based on imported British machinery, British ideas, and émigré technicians.[11] This first generation of relatively late industrializers imported and commercialized new textile machinery, steam engines, transportation technologies, and metallurgical skills—the core technologies of the so-called first industrial revolution. Within a generation or two, however, this group of countries moved from initially adopting, imitating, and depending on foreign technologies to becoming technologically innovative in their own right, centers of industrializing inventive activity. By the second half of the century, the countries of the North Atlantic were producing the vast majority of global patents and new tools and machinery, from steam engines to plows to sewing machines. Japan would soon become the canonical case of successful late development, as would South Korea nearly a century later. The global list of relatively wealthy nations in the late twentieth century provides an effective count of those who achieved sustained economic growth and wealth through first *adopting* and using the technologies of others and then *assimilating* technological know-how, deepening their own capabilities to manufacture capital equipment and to generate inventive activity, technological creativity, and sustained economic growth at home.[12]

The point is not to compare Mexico's development path with those of the United States and other North Atlantic countries but to place Mexico within a global context. To extract Mexico from its Atlantic context would be anachronistic, denying Mexico a central part of its historical experience. Three issues stand out. First, Great Britain and the United States have been technology producers and exporters for two centuries. As a result, scholars' primary research questions inquire into the origins and determinants of inventive activity. But Mexico, like much of the world, has long been a technology importer, and the vast majority of imported technologies came from the North Atlantic. All mechanizing and modernizing firms in nineteenth-century Mexico bought from or competed against exporters in North Atlantic countries. The markets they confronted went well beyond Mexico's borders. Second, investors, intellectuals, and policy makers in Mexico explicitly conceived of their country and its future in direct and intimate relation with the economic (and military) powers of the North Atlantic. Mexico's public men aspired to the sovereignty and wealth—both public and private—that they saw in "Germany, the United States, France, and England . . . the four nations that march at the front of civilization."[13] They could not conceive otherwise, given the dramatic and competitive expansion of the North Atlantic economies through the nineteenth century. Their obsession with the North Atlantic was of course exacerbated by Mexico's own not-so-distant experience with foreign interventions. Finally, however, North Atlantic countries should not provide scholars with the normative model for relatively later developers like Mexico. As economic historians have recently argued, the British and US paths were exceptional. Among other factors, the first industrializers had faced a very different international context between 1750 and 1850. It would be far more instructive to place Mexico's experience in relation to other relatively late industrializers: southern or eastern Europe, Scandinavia, Russia, Egypt, the larger economies of South America, and of course Japan. All were technology importers, and all sought to join, in some fashion, the confraternity of the North Atlantic.

For entrepreneurs and government officials around the world in the nineteenth century, the prospect of simply adopting new machines and tools from the earliest industrializers in the North Atlantic appeared quicker and easier than investing in the slow, expensive, and uncertain process of invention. The choice was simple and obvious to Mexico's federal deputy Ramón Esteban Martínez de los Ríos in the 1820s: "Foreigners have better machines than ours."[14] Estevan de Antuñano observed in 1837 that western Europe "owed all its wealth to fortunate inventions of machinery."[15] "Many times," noted a Mexican official in 1843, "imported technology can be more useful than [our own] invention."[16] A generation later, Miguel Lerdo de Tejada agreed and pushed his government to support investors' efforts to introduce "the improvements [in tools and machines] that are daily made in other nations."[17] As Gilberto Crespo y Martínez argued in 1897, Europe and the United States had achieved wealth and "civilization" exactly because of their technological expertise: their "better capacity to know and superior ability to execute."[18] Mexican interest in acquiring "the most modern" technology from the North Atlantic would endure as an economic, cultural, and ultimately political imperative well into the twentieth century.[19] Mexico was not alone. Adopting technologies from the North Atlantic became the globally dominant practice, little different in nineteenth-century Mexico, Brazil, and Argentina than in parts of Europe, Egypt, Russia, and Japan.

From the vantage point of the late twentieth century, economists have generally agreed. Economic theory has long seen technology—knowledge—as a public good that can flow easily between users and between countries. In this view, the nineteenth-century wave of inventive activity in England, the United States, and other North Atlantic countries provided a global stock of knowledge from which others could readily pick and choose. Countries outside the North Atlantic could reap this technology spillover without bearing the substantial costs and uncertainty of research and development, of inventing new machines and systems from scratch. By quickly adopting new technologies from the global leaders, poorer countries would "catch up" and eventually "converge" with industrialized nations.[20] For development economists and international development agencies in the second half of the twentieth century, so-called "technology transfer" occupied a central place in addressing issues of underdevelopment and poverty.[21]

Economic historians of nineteenth-century industrialization have also long embraced this linear view. In his classic 1962 study of "economic backwardness," Alexander Gerschenkron argued that "industrialization always seemed the more promising the greater the backlog of technological innovations which the backward country could take over from the more advanced country."[22] A generation later, Sidney Pollard (1981) noted that once new technologies were adopted, "nothing appeared to be able to prevent the region concerned from 'taking off.'"[23] Similarly, Robert Allen (2009) has recently written that late developers discover "that it pays to leap over many stages of technological development and go directly . . . to the latest . . . technology. Catch-up is very rapid—a great spurt. The Industrial Revolution spreads around the globe."[24] Each of these scholars, focusing on a handful of successful cases, believes that less industrialized countries should be able to catch up by adopting new technologies from the earlier industrializers, resulting in relatively faster rates of productivity growth and an eventual convergence in per capita income.

Nineteenth- and early twentieth-century elites in countries like Mexico thought along remarkably similar lines. For them, "catch-up" and "convergence" translated as "material progress" (*progreso material*) and "national wealth" (*riqueza nacional*) as they sought to attain the economic wealth, cultural prestige, and political sovereignty enjoyed by countries like Britain, the United States, France, and Germany. Although the language and labels differed, today's concept of convergence through technology-driven economic growth is not anachronistic. It was the lifeblood of nineteenth-century national aspirations.

Around the world in the nineteenth century, observers marveled at (and sometimes feared) the material manifestations of North Atlantic progress: the rapid appearance of new technologies and the resulting industrialization, increasing wealth, and corresponding concentration of economic, political, and of course military power in that one corner of the world. London's Crystal Palace exposition of 1851 presented this model decisively on the world stage, and subsequent world's fairs continued to dramatically display the technological basis for North Atlantic industry and wealth. Mexicans visited international expositions and wrote about "the ingenious and powerful inventions" on display.[25] Juan Nepomuceno Adorno, inveterate promoter of Mexican invention, lamented from Europe in 1858 his own country's "dependence on foreign countries" for skilled workers and machines.[26] Half a century later, a visitor returning from the 1904 St. Louis Exposition extolled "the fruit of the genius and talent of men, never seen until now," and worked energetically to bring much of what he saw to Mexico.[27] Most of Mexico's public men measured their country's status against the standard set by North Atlantic technologies, "the marvels of North American invention."[28] As they saw it, Mexico could overcome its "backwardness" (*atraso*) only by adopting new machines and processes from the economies of the North Atlantic, those "manufacturing nations . . . that have made the most astonishing industrial progress."[29] Elites around the globe sought to capture the economic wealth of the early industrializers by adopting the technological basis of industrialization first developed in the North Atlantic, bridging local societies and global possibilities.[30]

New technologies thus constituted the central and most visible manifestation of Mexico's search for material progress. Simultaneously with the private endeavors of many entrepreneurs, Mexican officials sought to remake the country in the North Atlantic image, both materially and culturally. As consumers of North Atlantic progress, they envisioned, as vice-minister of development Manuel Fernández Leal explained in 1891, placing Mexico "in that admirable group of countries that . . . march united at the vanguard of progress."[31] When the federal government opened Mexico's own Museo Tecnológico Industrial in 1903, now-minister Fernández Leal announced (with mixed ambition and naïveté) that "the country is entering a period clearly industrial, a period that seems to be the perfect state of most civilized nations."[32]

This focus on technology imports did not mean that domestic sources of inventiveness were wholly ignored or absent. Mexican artisans, mechanics, engineers, and scientists actively worked to assimilate European science, to develop new techniques, and to modify old ones. Mexico's new patent laws of 1890 and 1903 aimed to awaken the "inventive genius" of potential Mexican inventors.[33] Indeed, several thousand Mexicans applied for and received patent rights from the federal government between 1840 and 1910, and some made notable contributions to technical advances in certain fields.[34] But few in governing circles had much faith in the potential of local inventors, at least in the short run.[35] With human capital notoriously scarce and highly concentrated, only a small percentage of the population had ready access to scientific and technical knowledge. After midcentury, Mexico's newspapers frequently commented on the increasing importance of "applied science" in the global economy and lamented Mexico's "scientific backwardness."[36] From the perspective of Mexico's political and economic elites, the alternative to local invention seemed the far more logical choice: to import new machines, processes, ideas, and personnel from the North Atlantic, where they had already been invented and developed, and where machinery manufacturers and suppliers anxiously sought buyers in every corner of the world. This was of course a vision of Mexico in the North Atlantic mirror, one that equated mechanized technologies with European accomplishments, cultures, and peoples. With little faith that most Mexicans could effectively engage new industrial technologies, entrepreneurial efforts sought overwhelmingly to acquire new machinery and expertise from abroad, and government policy consistently aimed to facilitate those efforts.[37]

By the 1870s, then, Mexican interest in material progress dovetailed with rapidly expanding global flows of capital, machines, people, and other forms of embodied knowledge.[38] The end of the Civil War in the United States inaugurated a long period of industrial expansion in the North Atlantic, led by the United States and Germany. This "second industrial revolution" or era of globalization brought new wealth and power to the North Atlantic that both enticed and threatened the rest of the world.

This was a world divided between a small set of technology exporters in the North Atlantic and everyone else, technology importers. Machines, tools, production systems, engineers, and print materials carrying technical specifications and formulas spread outward from the global center of invention and manufacture in the North Atlantic, along with rapidly expanding flows of investment capital and migration. This was part spillover from industrial growth in western Europe and the United States, part imperialist project, and part the explicit objective of national governments and investors in importing countries like Mexico.

Across the globe, the impact was both transformative and profoundly dislocative. However, few societies then or since have proven able to translate ready access to global knowledge into sustained economic growth and independent technological creativity, despite the optimism of nineteenth-century observers and twentieth-century economists. While a small number of countries over the past two centuries have built growth, development, and sustained technological creativity on top of an early dependence on imported technology—Japan is the classic case—most have not, despite roughly similar access to new technologies and knowledge in the international market. As a result, nearly two hundred years of massive global trade in machines and knowledge has not yielded a globally balanced distribution of wealth and welfare. This was as true for many in the late nineteenth century as it has been for much of the postcolonial world in the second half of the twentieth. One historian of the subject labels technology transfer "that which normally fails."[39]

Why has adopting technologies and assimilating technological knowledge proven so challenging when economic theory assumes it should be so easy? Efforts to adopt new production technologies and to assimilate new knowledge and expertise frequently face significant obstacles. This is especially true when technologies cross borders and when there is a large gap in the level of technical knowledge, capabilities, and experience between the exporting and importing countries—exactly the situation of Mexico (and many others) in the late nineteenth century. Crossing borders implies the likelihood of operating in a context very different from that within which the technology originated.

Historians of technology have argued that technologies are a collectivity of knowledge conceived, designed, manufactured, and used within a particular social and economic context. New ideas and ways of doing things are shaped not only by technological antecedents, demographic pressures, and economic markets, constraints, and incentives but also by their social, cultural, and political environments: values, tastes, and habits; commercial practices; legal standards and requirements; political institutions and organizational structures; and the characteristics of and relations between social groups. Technology is not exogenous to society but emerges out of and is embedded firmly within a social context. It is socially constructed rather than autonomous and deterministic.[40] Yet this approach to understanding technological change has largely evolved through studies of invention and innovation *within* societies and has not frequently been applied to the movement of technologies *between* societies. Indeed, context, or a "distinctive production ecology," becomes all the more important when technologies that are invented, developed, and designed in one place are then adopted for use somewhere else.[41] If society and technology are mutually constitutive, then moving knowledge across borders—*adopting* new technologies and *assimilating* new know-how—cannot be a frictionless process.

Machines, ideas, and people are highly portable, and borders generally porous.[42] But adopting and using technologies from abroad typically requires more than simply acquiring a machine or blueprint, picking it off the global shelf, and installing it in the new (e.g., Mexican) setting. Such "turnkey" operations, in the language of development economists, were the exception rather than the rule in the nineteenth century. The list of practical challenges to adopting and using imported technologies only begins with the most general kinds of requirements for successful use: to acquire, install, operate, maintain, repair, troubleshoot, and perhaps modify.[43] Each of these "production capabilities" requires a level of technical knowledge and experience as well as substantial research, information gathering, feasibility studies, and management skills, depending on the size and complexity of the technology in question. New factory systems typically demand, for instance, that investors and managers invest substantial effort to acquire information regarding a wide range of new machines and ancillary systems, as well as to identify and access new markets for skilled labor, raw materials, and intermediate inputs.[44] Even small-scale product technologies, like stationary steam engines, agricultural implements, sewing machines, and hand tools, were sold and used in settings that posed substantial new demands, as both sellers and users in Mexican mines, farms, and homes could attest. Adopting new technologies frequently entails tacit and local knowledge—an understanding of the technology, of the know-how embedded in it, and of its intimate relationship to a local ecology of necessary and complementary inputs and activities that cannot be codified in blueprints or explicit instructions. To adopt and use new technologies, workers must negotiate the challenges of adapting technologies to new conditions or, conversely, of adapting the context to fit the requisites of the new technology.

But this kind of knowledge and expertise is typically scarce in preindustrial societies, like Mexico in the nineteenth century. There, at the very moment when the importance of scientific and technologically informed human capital expanded dramatically in the North Atlantic, it remained scarce and highly concentrated. If those individuals or firms who want to invest in imported technologies cannot locate production capabilities locally, they must turn abroad. This choice depends on the relative level of technical competencies available in local and foreign markets, on the relative cost of both alternatives, and on cultural preferences. Figure 2 maps the situation facing those interested in adopting and using new technologies from abroad, beginning with the space between the distant origin of new technologies and

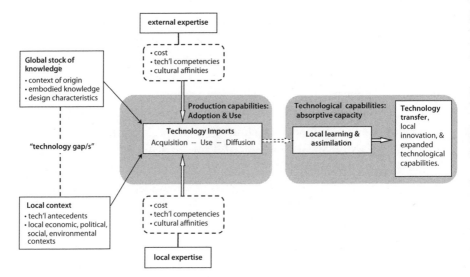

FIGURE 2. The relationship between technology imports, capabilities, and transfer.

the local context for adoption (the "technology gap"). It highlights the need to acquire technological expertise ("production capabilities") locally or from more distant sources.

In the late nineteenth century, the rapidly widening distance between scientific and technical know-how in the North Atlantic and the rest of the world meant that new investors in the latter context typically purchased production capabilities in the person of foreign engineers, technicians, and skilled workers. As one shareholder in a porcelain factory in Puebla put it as early as 1844, modernizing local production depended on hiring foreign experts who would "bring [to] us their skills and secrets."[45] Fifty years later, from Monterrey's new glass bottle plant to factories producing beer, cement, steel, cigarettes, textiles, and chemicals, as well as to slaughterhouses, packing plants, railroads, and mining operations, it was foreign expertise that installed and managed the first generation of industrial-scale production systems in Mexico. Even so, however, these men had to navigate the multiple obstacles to adopting technology imports, obstacles that were implicit in the distance and difference between the North Atlantic context of origin and the Mexican context of adoption. While some obstacles proved relatively malleable, others were more intractable and help explain the varied experience of technology imports across the Mexican economy: rapid adoption, or delays, impaired use, limited diffusion, and occasionally outright failure.

"Technology imports," however, are not the same thing as "technology transfer." *Transfer* denotes not just successful *adoption* and commercial use but also the local *assimilation* of the knowledge and expertise necessary to troubleshoot, repair, modify, adapt, and perhaps replicate imported technologies. Such technological capabilities (the second shaded box in figure 2) can stimulate and sustain local creativity, invention, and innovation.[46] Technology transfer thus depends on human capital, on a process of *learning*, or the ability of locally based managers, engineers, mechanics, workers, and consumers—all "technicians," in a sense—to absorb or acquire the critical knowledge, expertise, and capabilities through sustained engagement and interaction with technology imported in the form of machinery, people, or print materials.

Initial reliance on imported technology was the norm for all late developers in the nineteenth century, exacerbated by the context of late development. In Mexico, for instance, a fifty-year delay in adopting railroad, steam, and iron technologies meant that when adoption became widely viable after about 1870, local production capabilities were exceedingly scarce. This history made late-century reliance on imported expertise almost unavoidable. But initial reliance on imported machines and expertise could lead in several directions. It might stimulate local capacities by exposing local workers and technicians to new knowledge, generating learning, and facilitating the spillover of new know-how to local society. Conversely, early dependence might be self-reinforcing. If local workers, engineers, and managers do not have the opportunity to engage and interact with imported technologies, learning is not likely to occur, and the gap between technological expertise in exporting (e.g., North Atlantic) versus importing countries only widens. In the late nineteenth century, countries like Mexico faced a local scarcity of technological capabilities relative to their relative abundance in the North Atlantic. Bridging this gap would require substantial learning, but learning, absorbing, or assimilating new know-how would depend on several factors: (1) the size of the technology gap, itself a path-dependent function of previous experience; (2) opportunities for interaction between local workers and imported knowledge embodied in machines, in print, and in people; (3) local levels of human capital and especially of scientific and technical education; (4) the diffusion of new knowledge and skills through networks, organizations, and communities of technicians; and (5) incentives provided by government policy. Building skills and acquiring expertise is a cumulative, complex, and contingent process that revolves around the relationship between local technicians and imported technologies. By implication, successful adoption does not easily lead to assimilation.

In the short run, Mexico's reliance on imported human capital facilitated technology imports, the establishment of large-scale mechanized production facilities, and rapid economic growth through the late nineteenth century. Investors, entrepreneurs, and consumers adopted new machines, processes, and products that became deeply integrated into local cultures of production and consumption. In the long run, however, persistent reliance on external expertise undermined the potential for local learning, with just a few intriguing exceptions, most famously centered on the northern city of Monterrey. The historical record suggests that while short-term economic growth can result from *adopting* new technologies, long-term development depends on the ability to learn from and to *assimilate* new knowledge.[47] Efforts to import and adopt new technologies in the particular context of nineteenth-century Mexico encountered obstacles that often delayed projects or constrained operation and diffusion. But for the most part, those individuals and firms that sought to adopt new technologies were able to acquire production capabilities from abroad in the form of skilled workers, technicians, and engineers. These men helped navigate obstacles to adoption that proved more often than not relatively malleable. The barriers to local learning, however, proved substantially more intractable and would bequeath a prevailing though not universal legacy of technological dependence to the twentieth century.

HISTORY AND HISTORIOGRAPHY

Mexico's nineteenth century provides an ideal frame for a study of innovation and learning in the context of late development. Before the 1870s, substantial obstacles discouraged efforts or undermined most attempts to adopt new technologies across Mexico's economic landscape. The story is well known. A debilitating, self-reinforcing cycle of political instability and economic stagnation followed Mexico's extended independence conflict (1808–21), weakening incentives for investment across the economy while discouraging most governmental attempts at institutional reform and economic promotion.[48] Transportation was costly and dangerous. The only financial institutions were notaries, pawnshops, and the church. Policies governing economic activities were largely unchanged from colonial Hispanic norms, save for the critical dismantling of Spanish mercantilism and tax policies.

Property rights were often insecure. No national market existed save for high-value products like silver and silk. Most production and commerce happened locally in villages, valleys, regions, or urban areas and their hinterlands, except for the long reach of demand generated by the larger mining centers. Incomes for most Mexicans were too low to sustain a consumer market of sufficient size to justify investment in anything more than artisanal and home production. Mexico's oft-lamented weak consumer markets (*falta de consumo*) were only partly the result of a large rural subsistence economy. They were also a function of markets constrained by costly transport, low productivity levels, and high taxes. For all these reasons, demand for new production technologies remained weak for decades.

Persistent economic malaise meant that Mexico largely missed adopting the core technologies of the first industrial revolution, which had been developed and diffused in the North Atlantic countries during the early decades of the nineteenth century. Railroad construction, essential to overcoming Mexico's topographical barriers to expanding markets and new investments, famously lagged for over half a century after the first commercial lines in Britain and the United States, and decades after the initial rail concession in Mexico. Equally important and less well known was the long delay in Mexico's adoption of steam power, part of a larger story about the impact of natural resource endowment on the critical transition from animate to inanimate sources of power. Local capacities to produce and transform iron and steel into tools and machine parts also remained scarce, with major implications for Mexico's long-term technological capabilities. Although there were a handful of cases of important innovation between 1820 and 1870, these were exceptional and isolated stories.

Mexico's economic recovery began in the late 1860s and early 1870s, predating the *pax porfiriana*, and—in the absence of reliable GDP figures—can be traced clearly in rising levels of foreign trade.[49] New investment in transportation technologies slowly began to stitch together regional and national markets and linked Mexican resources to a rising North Atlantic demand. Renewed investor interest in export activities from mining to commercial agriculture began to expand production with the first stirrings of foreign capital investment, itself pushed by the expansion of the North Atlantic economies after the US Civil War. These new infrastructure- and export-oriented enterprises purchased increasing amounts of supplies from abroad, especially capital equipment, and Mexican imports grew at about 6 percent per year while exports grew at nearly 7 percent annually over the next decade or so.[50]

In large part, Mexico's economic expansion after about 1870 was spillover from a rapidly expanding Atlantic economy that generated demand for Mexican resources and increasing flows of capital, entrepreneurship, and technology to Mexico and elsewhere across the globe. At the same time, newfound political stability under the governments of Benito Júarez (1867–72), Sebastián Lerdo de Tejada (1872–76), and Porfirio Díaz (beginning in 1876) established favorable conditions through a combination of personalistic and institutional initiatives in which long-standing interest in material progress could gain real traction. Gradual institutional reform through the 1880s and 1890s did much to encourage investment across the economy, the political backdrop for Mexico's rapidly rising levels of technology imports, early industrialization, and economic growth. Our "about 1870" watershed does not, of course, represent a clean break of before and after. Interest and investment in mechanized industry date to at least eighteenth-century and especially Bourbon modernization projects. At the same time, nonmarket practices and traditional, hand-based production technologies survived well into the twentieth century.

Despite the scope of material progress between 1870 and 1910, the history of technology in Mexico has received little attention from historians. We have glimpses of technological change in the secondary literature, many anecdotal accounts, and several broad assertions but very little systematic examination.[51] None of the recent major works on Mexico's economic history treat technology in any explicit manner, despite its centrality to any explanation of economic growth and development.[52] We have few firm-level studies that focus carefully on technology choices, and even fewer at the household level.[53]

Lack of research has not, however, kept historians from offering a wide variety of assertions. They have frequently suggested—often implicitly and sometimes wrongly—that most Mexicans did not fully embrace newly imported technologies, which consequently (in their telling) remained largely superficial rather than deeply transformative. The adoption of foreign technologies, in one articulation of this view, was more about Mexican elites and the middle class *emulating* foreign culture than about adopting and internalizing new productive capabilities. In other words, foreign technologies and ideas and norms amounted to little more than a facade, without altering foundational structures.[54] At the same time, others argue that foreign technologies were often *resisted* by many Mexicans, especially by the majority who lived in rural towns and villages.[55] As a consequence, rural Mexico was famously depicted as a land of "machineless men."[56] Similarly, foreign technologies have typically been portrayed as fundamentally *disrup-*

tive, clashing with traditional norms, weakening existing social networks, or exacerbating inequalities.[57] Or newly introduced technologies were primarily a *political instrument* of Mexican elites, the *científicos* and others who sought to better manage society, build a state, and present a modern nation to the world.[58] Recently, some historians have explored the *cultural* consequences of technological change in nineteenth- and twentieth-century Mexico, arguing for a significant depth of embrace and integration.[59] Some economic historians have characterized imported technologies as *inappropriate* to the Mexican context in their technical complexity or productive capacity.[60] And development economists have long seen foreign technologies as isolated *enclaves*, or islands of modernity, with few links to local markets and society.[61] Finally, historians have frequently argued or implied that Mexicans lacked both the interest and the capacity to engage in important forms of inventive or innovative activity.[62]

Nineteenth-century travelers from the United States and Europe would not necessarily have disagreed with much of this. It was the exotic and traditional that consistently drew their attention in Mexico. Although their hosts were typically white skinned, multilingual, and cosmopolitan, travelers' writings are filled with Indians, viewed through travelers' own cultural blinders: huarache clad or barefoot, stooped over digging sticks (*coas*) in the fields, stoic, tough, but not always hardworking, resistant to innovation—the antithesis, in other words, of modern culture.[63] Mexico, by extension, came to exemplify a country resistant to North Atlantic technologies, to mechanization, and to progress. A generation later, these representations of sharply contrasting "civilization" and "backwardness" were sometimes restated by the first wave of anthropologists working in rural, largely indigenous villages. As with nineteenth-century travelers, it was the world of the villages—islands dense with culture—that drew their attention.[64] Development economists in the 1960s and 1970s would also focus on Mexico's dual economies and cultures, often emphasizing the preponderant weight of the traditional sector as a fundamental and structural brake on economic development.[65]

These perspectives suggest that imported technologies left only a weak imprint on Mexico. They posit a country sharply divided between a relatively small modern sector and a large, mostly static, traditional sector. They focus on a deep chasm between foreign technology and Mexican culture, between elite visions and common experiences, between urban and rural Mexico, between industrial and artisanal practices, between a *México moderno* and an essentialized *México profundo*.[66] Yet each dichotomy also posits a space between. This book examines that space, how broad it was, and whether our current conceptions fit the historical evidence.

. . .

This book examines how Mexicans sought global goods and technologies to meet local needs and aspirations. Its primary focus is on those machines and processes that were developed in the North Atlantic and that were, in some fashion, adopted in Mexico to facilitate transport, power, and production in mining, agriculture, and manufacturing—technologies of production. There is much it leaves out: technologies of sanitation, of entertainment and pleasure, of communication, or of marketing, for example. It pays less attention to inventive activity than to the adoption of imported technologies. Although its objective is to identify and explain the central patterns and tendencies of technological change across Mexico's economic landscape, coverage is uneven. The canonical advances of the North Atlantic industrial revolution receive special attention in chapters 2 and 3 (railroads, steam power, and iron), while textile production, agricultural techniques, and others receive somewhat less. Three detailed case studies dominate the middle of the book—sewing machines, glass bottle manufacturing, and the use of cyanide to refine precious metals—because they represent broader categories and types of technology in manufacturing and mining. This book provides context but not a substitute for a wide range of sorely needed, more narrowly focused and finely grained studies of particular technologies, individual firms or industries, and local experiences.

Part I of the book's three sections surveys Mexico's technological landscape over the nineteenth century, from independence to revolution, and lays out the stark contrast between relative stasis before about 1870 (chapter 2) and rapid adoption thereafter (chapter 3). Following independence in 1821, economic malaise meant few incentives to adopt new production technologies. Nowhere was this more evident than with the canonical technologies of Europe's first industrial revolution: railroads, steam power, and iron. With the exception of the textile industry and some regional innovation in commercial agriculture, this was the case across most of the economy. As a consequence, Mexican workers and technicians had few opportunities to assimilate new knowledge, and by midcentury Mexico's intellectuals and officials increasingly referenced Mexico's backwardness (*atraso*) relative to the North Atlantic economies. Beginning shortly after the restoration of republican government in 1867, however, new technologies embodied in machines, people, and print began to pour into Mexico from the United States and Europe. Their adoption altered both production and people's lives by substituting mechanical methods for what had previously been homemade, handmade, and locally made. By 1910, many Mexicans found work in the new industries, consumed the products of new factories, and saw their lives affected in powerful ways—the decisive and often socially dislocative beginnings of Mexico's material modernization.

Part II of the book presents three case studies to better illustrate the local dynamics of adopting new technologies and assimilating new knowledge. Each case represents a broader type of technology to better understand trends across the Mexican economy. Sewing machines (chapter 4) represent a class of small-scale, multiuse technologies, typically sold as products themselves and integrated into production systems in households, workshops, and factories. Sewing machines arrived quickly in Mexico and by the 1870s had diffused widely across urban and rural Mexico to become nearly ubiquitous by century's end. They were adopted by tens of thousands of women in their homes and by men in workshops and new clothing factories. They made possible a rapidly growing ready-made clothing sector, marketed to middle-class Mexicans in department stores across the country. But this was a fragile diffusion. Adoption was highly sensitive to economic downturns, and machine use was dependent on difficult access to spare parts and repair expertise. Consumers quickly mastered the ability to use sewing machines, but learning did not extend to a ready ability to repair, modify, and replicate.

The automated mass production of glass bottles (chapter 5) represents a broader range of large-scale, factory-based production systems that were brought to Mexico between 1890 and 1910. In response to rising domestic demand for beer, Mexican investors acquired the patent rights to the new Owens automatic glass bottle–blowing machine shortly after its development in the United States. However, unexpected obstacles to financing, installing, and operating this novel technological system delayed commercialization for over a decade and required adaptations to both the technology itself and the Mexican context for critical production inputs. Sustained effort by a group of Mexican investors and managers yielded substantial local learning to both use and modify the technology, a significant exception to the general trend of low assimilation. These abilities would, in the decades after the Revolution, lay foundations for one of the country's most innovative and successful firms.

Meanwhile, miners and metallurgists working in Mexico introduced the use of cyanide to separate gold and silver from ores (chapter 6), representative of a broader set of processing technologies within the export sector. Though cyaniding was quickly applied in gold mines, efforts to adapt it to Mexico's predominant silver ores proved much more difficult. Sustained experimentation eventually yielded the necessary adaptations, and by 1906 or so the cyanide process dominated precious metal refining. As with glass bottles, the multiple challenges of adoption created many opportunities for substantial learning. However, in mining it was foreign workers, engineers, and managers who accrued new expertise, and most would leave Mexico during the Revolution. Mexican engineers and skilled workers, who had played prominent roles in the industry a generation earlier, had been largely squeezed out.

Part III steps back from the case studies to broadly examine those factors that constrained the adoption of new technologies and the assimilation of new knowledge and expertise. Despite the centrality of technological change after 1870, it was not universal, uncontested, or unilinear. Technology and investment capital spilled over Mexico's borders and washed across the landscape: in some places this inundation settled and pooled; in other places it evaporated and left few marks. Chapter 7 examines the obstacles to technological change: those factors that *delayed* the adoption of new technologies, that *impaired* their use or productive capacity in Mexico, or that *prevented* their adoption altogether. Yet the central paradox of economic growth in Mexico is the contrast between a tidal wave of technology imports—adopted and sometimes widely diffused—and a stubbornly persistent dependence on foreign know-how and hardware. Technology imports may alter the nature of work, boost productive output, and yield new sets of winners and losers, but they do not necessarily lead to the effective transfer of skills and knowledge. Chapter 8 examines the gap between *adoption* and *assimilation* by focusing on those factors that limited learning and the assimilation of technical know-how. In late nineteenth-century Mexico, opportunities for learning, interacting with, and engaging with global technologies were unequally distributed, with predictable results. In the short run, widespread adoption of new technologies made possible a dramatic transformation of the country's productive potential. In the long run, they did little to contribute to the development of domestic capabilities among Mexico's engineers, mechanics, and workers.

PART ONE

Narrative

TWO

Technology and the Emergence of Atraso, *1820–70*

MEXICO'S RENOWNED MINING COLLEGE LAY nearly in ruins by the late 1820s. Established in 1792 as the first technical school in the Western Hemisphere and housed in Manuel Tolsa's grand building, it was the crowning achievement of Bourbon efforts to inject new scientific and technical expertise into the colonial economy. In the aftermath of Mexico's independence in 1821, however, its facade had begun to crumble around the edges, and "the walls and staircases [were] cracking." Lectures and courses had nearly ceased, its mineral collection lay "in the worst order possible," and a lone professor gave occasional lectures, "his auditors now reduced to two or three solitary pupils, and the gloom of the vast apartments in the interior corresponds too well with the dilapidated state of the building without."[1] The next generation brought little change. One visitor in 1840 found it "all miserable and ill kept," and a US diplomat in 1842 described the school's equipment as "miserable; the collection of minerals utterly insignificant; the pupils few; and, among the wastes and solitude of the pile, wanders the renowned [Professor Andrés] del Río—one of the most learned naturalists of this hemisphere."[2]

The dilapidated state of the Mining College after Mexico's independence largely mirrored conditions across the nation—arguably a nation in name only, as Mariano Otero famously noted.[3] Economic production had fallen sharply since the peak of late colonial growth, at least in the commercial economy. Silver production—long the engine of the colonial economy—was half what it had been just two generations earlier. Mining was not alone, and across Mexico's fractured economic landscape productive activity in commercial agriculture and in artisanal workshops had been severely disrupted by over a decade of violence and instability. Per capita wealth apparently fell by over 20 percent in the tumultuous decades between 1800 and 1820, although our data are sketchy. And by most accounts, little changed through the next several decades. For nearly half a century after independence, individuals and firms working in Mexico made relatively few significant or successful efforts to adopt new production technologies.

At the same time, however, independence brought with it a wave of optimism among Mexico's political and economic elites, buttressed by modest recovery of investment in the 1820s and 1830s in mining, commercial agriculture, and textile manufacturing. Yet this optimism collapsed by the late 1840s, when Mexico suffered invasion by the United States (1847–48) and the loss of half the national territory, descended into full civil war (1857–59), and was invaded and occupied by French troops who supported a foreign monarch on a fragile Mexican throne (1862–67). Observers attributed the new nation's economic crisis to the trauma of nearly two decades of political strife, "the melancholy effects produced by years of civil war and unsettled government."[4] Through midcentury, Mexico's acutely fragile economic and political circumstances eroded early optimism, and many Mexicans increasingly focused on how their country lagged behind the industrializing North Atlantic. Explicit references to "backwardness" (*atraso*) increasingly appeared in public discourse.

The timing of Mexico's economic malaise could not have been worse. Between 1800 and 1870 the economies of Britain, the United States, and the North Atlantic became global centers for the invention and use of mechanized technologies in transportation, mining, agriculture, and manufacturing. Building on the gradual expansion of commerce, consumer culture, and scientific thought over preceding centuries, inventors and entrepreneurs in the North Atlantic generated a sustained wave of technological innovations through the late eighteenth and early nineteenth centuries, conventionally labeled the first industrial revolution.[5] Centered on new advances in power (water, and then the coal-burning steam engine), in transportation (steam applied to rails and ships), in metalworking (the production and precise working of iron and steel), and in the textile industry, new inventions, new investments, and early industrialization transformed production, labor, and social relations in Britain, the United States, and parts of continental Europe.

Mexico's public men were well aware of these developments in the North Atlantic—in "those nations that have made in their industry the most astounding progress."[6] They engaged in ongoing debates about the nature of their own country's material wealth, labeled alternately "national wealth," "prosperity," or (later in the century) "material progress." Free traders like José María Luis Mora, Lorenzo de Zavala, and others hewed closely to the liberal doctrine of comparative advantage, locating Mexico's potential wealth in its natural resources and advocating their exploitation and trade in the Atlantic economy. At the same time, protectionists like Lucas Alamán and Estevan de Antuñano sought to remake Mexico in the emerging North Atlantic industrial image, locating national wealth in the transformation of resources by applying capital and labor to industrial activities. All, however, agreed on the importance of adopting new technologies from the industrializing North Atlantic in order to increase productivity in agriculture, mining, or manufacturing.[7] Mexico needed, they believed, those "ingenious and powerful inventions" rather than "the simple and imperfect machines" of its own colonial past in order to locate "the inexhaustible source of prosperity."[8]

Yet Mexico would remain largely isolated from the main currents of technological change in the North Atlantic through the first half or so of the nineteenth century. The technological basis of production across the Mexican economy in the early 1860s remained little changed from the late colonial era, with just a few exceptions. Most striking, and most consequential, was relative stasis in the foundational technologies of the first industrial revolution: transportation, the use of inanimate power, and iron working. Scarce technological change meant little productivity change, and Mexico's per capita GDP remained largely flat, in relative terms falling from about half of the North Atlantic average to less than a third. The gap in technological capabilities between Mexico and the North Atlantic, less easily measured, grew similarly large. As some historians have argued, by missing the first industrial revolution, Mexico quickly "fell behind" the North Atlantic.[9]

This chapter examines technology in Mexico's postindependence economy, circa 1820 to 1870. After a brief survey, it turns to the foundational technologies of the first industrial revolution: transport, power, and iron. Not only did Mexico's long delay in adopting these technologies illustrate a broader pattern of stasis, but their absence also undermined the local development of technological capabilities by limiting opportunities for learning through the rest of the nineteenth century. Early in the century, Estevan de Antuñano and others had called for the local development of tool and machine factories "to contribute to our national wealth and power" and to "give occupation to our carpenters and blacksmiths."[10] After midcentury, the widening gap between technological capabilities in the North Atlantic and those in Mexico meant that entrepreneurs and public officials turned instead to foreign tools and machines—those "invented and perfected in other countries"—rather than advocating their local production.[11] Few responded to Antuñano's *grito*, and such calls, scarce to begin with, were not frequently repeated through the century. Even if they had been, the technical skills of tool and machine making were too scarce to support local manufacture. When the opportunity to adopt new technologies on a large scale finally came after 1870, entrepreneurs and policy makers would find it much easier to import know-how and expertise from abroad than to develop it at home.

TECHNOLOGY AND MEXICO'S POSTINDEPENDENCE DEPRESSION

Over its first half century of independence, Mexico suffered the entwined maladies of endemic political strife and prolonged economic depression. Barely born in 1821, Mexico very nearly fell apart; of its industry, nearly "all had disappeared."[12] That, at any rate, has long been the conventional wisdom, often summarized but little researched—its technological contours even less so.[13] Persistent economic depression provided few incentives to invest in new technologies. Without innovation, growth was constrained and depression lingered in a self-reinforcing cycle. Historians commonly reassert that the technologies of production in Mexico changed very little between 1800 and 1870, a view often repeated in textbook histories.[14]

Mexico's long fall from Spain's most prosperous colony to an impoverished independent state affected nearly all sectors of the economy. Ties with Spain disintegrated almost completely, and Spanish institutions quickly became the object of intense political debate. Like José María Luis Mora, many in Mexico lamented "our misfortunes."[15] Weakened political institutions and social dislocation after independence bred a sharp increase in banditry, which burdened travel and transportation, already costly over rugged terrain and unmaintained roads. Credit markets had never reached much beyond wealthy relations, the church, and pawnshops, and capital became increasingly scarce after independence. Chronic state penury and political competition undermined most attempts at institutional reform until mid-century or after, further discouraging investment. Economic stagnation and political instability reinforced each other in a vicious circle: instability discouraged productive investments and undermined economic growth, which in turn bred persistent political conflict over limited resources and hence more instability. All the while, neither the state nor the private sector proved able to invest in new infrastructure or human capital.

Most Mexicans lived close to the subsistence economy. Both agricultural *peones* and unskilled urban workers typically earned under two *reales* per day, or about twenty-four cents, roughly the individual subsistence level. Even regular laborers' wages in Mexico City bought little more than the basic necessities for an average urban household—and those who held regular wage-earning jobs were among the laboring elite.[16] In the countryside, where most Mexicans lived, cash incomes were substantially lower and sometimes nearly nonexistent. By one recent estimate, the majority of Indians and mestizos in rural Mexico purchased goods in the cash market on average only 1.5 times per year.[17] Juan Adorno noted that "there are villages which do not see the face of a half *real* of silver in a year."[18] Most Mexicans may well have been better off after independence—they paid less taxes, for instance—and agriculture production proved sufficient to avoid the food crises that had plagued Mexico in the late eighteenth century. But they were still unable to buy the kinds of goods and services that, given greater demand, might have induced investment in new production technologies: clothing, furniture, transportation, processed foods and beverages, tools and utensils, and the like. Those few who had access to cash bought from abroad or from local artisans. A much-lamented "lack of consumption" (*falta de consumo*) underlay stagnant investment across the domestic economy. Low incomes and local markets meant that production remained small scale, artisanal, and generally home based.

Although reliable data on Mexico's early nineteenth-century economy are notoriously scarce and sketchy, we can trace the general tendencies through three subperiods.[19] First, Mexico's economy clearly suffered a contraction in per capita production between the peak of colonial growth and the culmination of independence, roughly 1800 to 1820. The next generation, from 1820 into the 1840s, witnessed some modest recovery from the depredations of the independence conflicts. What recovery happened, however, did not last, and all evidence suggests significant economic challenges and contraction in per capita wealth through the middle decades of the century, roughly 1848 to 1867, when Mexico suffered two major foreign invasions and civil war. Overall, the Mexican economy saw no net gain in per capita production and likely a modest decline for the full period running sixty or seventy years from the end of the colonial era until about 1870, during which economic output did not keep pace with modest population growth. This was true for both the export sector and the domestic economy: Mexico's exports-to-GDP ratio remained the same in 1870 as in 1820.[20]

What we know about wages and prices in postindependence Mexico reinforces this general portrait. Daily wages for urban construction workers stayed at about forty-four centavos (3.5 *reales*) from the 1820s until the mid-1840s before settling at about thirty-eight centavos through the 1850s and 1860s. Prices for basic foods like maize, flour, frijoles, and beef also changed very little from the 1820s to the 1860s.[21] Stagnant prices for labor and basic goods during this era of slow population growth imply that there was little underlying change in production technologies. As a result, Mexicans were on average a bit poorer in 1870 than they had been in 1810.

However, this does not mean that there was no investment in production technologies. From the late 1820s to the mid-1840s, new investments and modest recovery came to some activities and some regions. By 1843, government reports tentatively compared the country's "rapid growth" with "the complete ruin" of the 1820s.[22] But modest recovery was just that: modest, local, and with little long-term impact on the technologies of production in mining, agriculture, and manufacturing.[23]

In mining, British investors quickly took advantage of the first opportunity to invest directly in Mexico's old silver districts, pumping several millions of pounds sterling into a half-dozen new companies in the 1820s and 1830s.[24] These enterprises—the Real de Monte in Pachuca chief among them—brought managers, engineers, and hundreds of Cornish miners to Pachuca, Guanajuato, and Zacatecas. At great expense and effort, the British installed Mexico's first steam engines to pump water from the flooded mine shafts, they worked where possible to install mule-drawn railcars to carry ore from mine to refinery, and they experimented with several alternatives to Mexico's traditional patio amalgamation refining method. These investments yielded some revival in silver production, but by the late 1840s the British firms were largely bankrupt. Their efforts to identify and adopt more efficient ways to extract and refine Mexico's deeply buried and complex silver-bearing ores had not succeeded. Although Mexican investors successfully took over most of the British properties in the 1850s, steam power remained rare and Mexico's traditional mercury-based refining system continued to dominate silver production.

A similar story played out in commercial agriculture. Gradual urban growth in the 1830s and 1840s induced hacendados in some parts of the country to expand their cultivated acreage and to invest in new irrigation projects, grain storage, and milling facilities.[25] In Puebla, flour shipments into the city grew steadily. In Jalisco, the average size of haciendas increased as entrepreneurial hacendados with deeper pockets bought up neighboring lands. In Michoacán, the average sale price of haciendas had recovered late colonial levels by the mid-1850s, though it would collapse again over the next decade. In Veracruz, cotton planters introduced the first few mechanical cotton gins. And in Morelos, a handful of sugar planters invested modestly in new crushing and refining equipment from Europe. The available data suggest that overall increases in food production did not much exceed population growth, although the new investments were apparently sufficient to prevent the kinds of recurring food shortages that had repeatedly plagued New Spain in the late eighteenth century. Most of the modest growth in food production came from putting land and labor that had been abandoned during independence back into production. On haciendas and in rural villages, agriculture continued to be characterized by low-productivity techniques.[26] Local officials in the village of Tulancingo (Hidalgo) reiterated in 1844 what was common through the nation: "Farming tools are those common and well known in our nation, and the method of cultivation is ancient, with no advances."[27] Because food production occupied roughly two-thirds of the national population, persistently low productivity levels meant that most Mexicans were poor, had few possibilities for economic improvement, and constituted only a weak consumer market for manufactured goods.

Finally, manufacturing activities also remained small scale and artisanal through the postindependence decades, with one notable exception.[28] Imports of cheap cotton cloth from Britain had for several decades undermined the artisanal spinning and weaving activities that occupied thousands of Mexicans during the eighteenth century, and spelled the death knell for the colonial *obraje* workshops, already in decline. In response, a vigorous artisanal lobby and their allies in government pushed for increased tariff protection during the 1820s and 1830s. They were joined by early proponents of modern manufacturing, most famously Lucas Alamán and Estevan de Antuñano. Tariff protection and direct government financing through the Banco de Avío (1830–42) gave investors incentives to establish Mexico's first modern textile factories in Orizaba, Puebla, Mexico City, and Guadalajara, importing thousands of mechanical spindles and looms from the United States, England, and France. By the 1860s some fifty-two new textile factories employed over ten thousand workers, equipped with 162,000 mechanized spindles and 4,400 looms. Newly mechanized production pushed cloth prices down by almost 50 percent in one generation.[29] These textile factories provided virtually the only enduring site for the adoption of new production technologies during Mexico's first half century.

Aside from modest and localized investments in mining, agriculture, and textile manufacturing, we have little evidence of significant technological change in Mexico between 1820 and 1870. Farmers, workers, technicians, and entrepreneurs undoubtedly worked to modify the tools of their trades or to develop new processes and products. Perhaps they were inspired by new ideas gleaned from neighbors, or pushed by necessity, or simply prodded internally by an innovative disposition. But whatever the extent of such small-scale microinvention and quotidian tinkering, it left virtually no footprint for historians to track. Neither local and contemporary accounts nor national histories pick up traces of domestic invention.[30] Mexico offered patent protection to domestic inventors under the laws of 1820 and 1832, but patentees numbered barely five per year over this half century, and nearly two-thirds of these represented foreign introductions.[31] By all accounts, inventive activity was exceptional and, when present, largely isolated from the broader economy.

Nor did Mexicans import many new technologies from abroad. Between 1825 and 1870 Mexico imported just over 17 million dollars of iron and steel manufactures, fully half of this only after 1860.[32] Machinery constituted less than 20 percent of this amount. In an economy that produced virtually no iron or steel or tools or machinery of its own, machines and tools manufactured in the North Atlantic offered the only available supply of looms and spindles, steam engines and boilers, iron plows and cotton gins, diverse machine parts and castings, and even basic hammers, saws, files, iron bars, and nails. Figure 3 illustrates the dramatic contrast between extremely low levels of iron and steel imports before about 1870 and steeply rising levels thereafter.

How low were Mexico's imports of iron and steel manufactures before the 1870s? For a typical year in the mid-1830s, they made up only 0.5 percent of Mexico's total imports, less than 0.1 percent of GDP, or an investment of less than one centavo per capita. Over the seventeen years running from 1829 to 1846, the value of Mexico's total imports of iron and steel amounted to less than a quarter of the total expenditures of just a single mining firm, the Real de Monte, during the same years.[33] Machinery purchases from just one source—the federally funded Banco de Avío—account for over 15 percent of the nation's total iron and steel imports, and likely a majority of total machin-

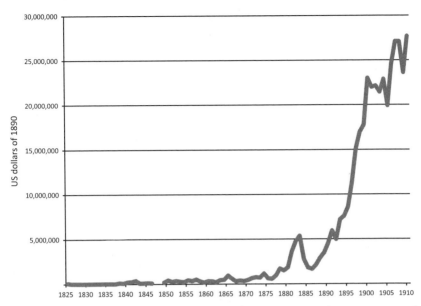

FIGURE 3. Mexican imports of iron and steel manufactures, 1825–1910. Sources: commercial publications of the United States, Great Britain, Germany, and France; see Appendix 2 for details.

ery imports.[34] Despite the rapidly rising production of iron and steel manufactures in North Atlantic countries, very little found its way to Mexico.

The general trend of Mexico's iron and steel imports through this half century reinforces our earlier narrative of Mexico's postindependence economy. Figure 4 uses a logarithmic version of figure 3 to illustrate the trend in the growth of imports of iron and steel manufactures through three distinct periods. In the first, following a one-time surge in machinery imports, driven mostly by British mining investments around 1825, Mexico's annual iron and steel imports remained low for the next decade. Imports then climbed into the early 1840s, with modest investments in mining, commercial agriculture, and textile manufacturing. However, their absolute level, as we saw in figure 3, remained very low. The second period begins with the end of growth in the crisis of 1847–48, and imports remained nearly flat through the troubled years of the 1850s and into the late 1860s, with sharp fluctuations. Growth reemerged just before 1870 and increased at a strong and steady pace through the rest of the century.[35] These trends in iron and steel imports likely provide a good proxy for trends in fixed capital investment and in economic activity generally over Mexico's long nineteenth century.

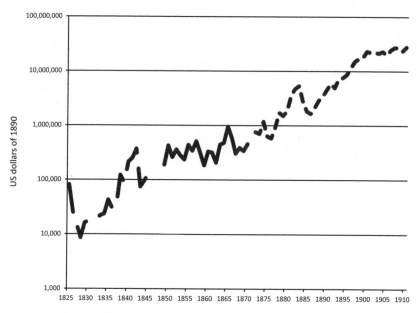

FIGURE 4. Growth of Mexican imports of iron and steel manufactures, 1825–1910, logarithmic scale. Sources: commercial publications of the United States, Great Britain, Germany, and France; see Appendix 2 for details.

If imported machine hardware was scarce in postindependence Mexico, so too was technical knowledge and expertise embodied in print materials and people. Imports of books and other print materials, for instance, averaged only about 6,000 dollars annually from the United States. Patent applications from outside Mexico carried specific information about new technological advances in the North Atlantic, and Mexico boasted one of Latin America's first national patent laws, adopted in 1832, modeled on the Spanish law of 1820.[36] Like all patent systems, Mexico's offered temporary monopoly protection to inventors of new technologies and products; like many nineteenth-century systems, it also offered protection to anyone who simply introduced new techniques or economic activities to Mexico. But between 1832 and 1870, Mexico conferred under two hundred patents. Of these just over one hundred were claimed by foreign applicants, and about one-third represented patents of introduction. Averaging under five patents per year, this was a tiny number over almost half a century. Spain, not known as a center for technological innovation, granted 3,786, or about one hundred yearly, with the same patent system. Meanwhile, northern European countries conferred some 286,000, and the United States issued over 110,000 (in the context of a much more restrictive system). These North Atlantic patents represented technologies—new knowledge—available for innovation, but only a tiny percentage of these found their way to Mexico.[37]

The same can be said for immigrants and workers from North Atlantic countries. Although we lack quantitative data on the comings and goings of foreigners in Mexico through this period, the numbers were small. Several hundred British technicians and Cornish miners arrived in the late 1820s and early 1830s to work in Pachuca and other mining centers. The new textile and paper mills funded by the Banco de Avío hired European managers and mechanics to oversee their operations, and a handful of hacendados also hired foreign managers and mayordomos. A number of foreign patentees during these years resided in Mexico, either as temporary workers or as long-term immigrants. And by the 1850s, commercially oriented immigrants from France and Germany played a growing role in wholesale trading. But the foreign-born population in Mexico never rose beyond a very small percentage during these decades, and Mexico received less than 0.5 percent of all European immigrants to the Americas through the long nineteenth century. A stagnant economy with few opportunities, persistent xenophobia, and recurring political talk of curtailing foreign business ownership effectively discouraged immigration from 1820 to 1870.[38] Modest immigration was counterbalanced by several periods of significant out-migration: thousands of Spaniards expelled in the 1820s, and smaller numbers of foreign residents and workers during the tumultuous years of 1847–48 and 1857–67. Although many of those who did come to Mexico brought with them important skills and knowledge, their numbers were small and their impact was localized until the last third of the century.

．　．　．

In postindependence Mexico, nearly all efforts to adopt new technologies were plagued by the same obstacles that had long constrained colonial production—the high cost of transportation, an uncertain and often unsupportive institutional environment, and a fractured economic landscape of local markets, built atop a weak foundation of consumer demand. As a result, innovation remained exceptional and did not coalesce into a national phenomenon. With the partial exception of the textile industry, where a handful of modern mills appeared in the 1830s and survived midcentury crises, few early investments in new technologies had a lasting impact on Mexico's economic development. The anonymous author of an 1830 pamphlet noted that "it is impossible to profitably manufacture here, and no one will do things that lose them money."[39] Mexico, in other words, was unable to engage the first wave of technological innovation sweeping across the industrializing North Atlantic. Nowhere can we see this more clearly than with the canonical technologies of the first industrial revolution: transportation, steam power, and iron.

TRANSPORTATION

Nature "has denied us," lamented Lucas Alamán in 1843, "all means of interior communication."[40] Costly transportation, he explained, dictated small markets, low levels of consumption, and few incentives to invest in large-scale or mechanized production. Mexico is a country forged from a stunning but rugged topography. The jagged landscape left the central plateau, home to most Mexicans, isolated from oceanic trade and internally fragmented. Lateral profiles of Mexico taken at the twenty-fifth, twenty-third, twenty-first, and nineteenth parallels vividly illustrate the challenges facing any cross-regional transport effort (figure 5). Regional autarky, as a result, had long been the norm.[41] Roads in colonial New Spain had been notoriously poor for generations, often little more than rough paths trod by foot and hoof. Viceregal authorities invested very little in road construction and maintenance after the first peak of mining activity in the sixteenth century. Outside towns and cities, carriages and wagons could navigate only a handful of well-traveled and less precipitous routes. Even where carts and wagons could travel, roads were typically so rough and unmaintained that vehicles had to be built especially solid. The classic Mexican mule-drawn transport cart, or *carro*, had just two wheels, each of heavy wooden timbers, rimmed with wood or iron, of large diameter to navigate the rocky, rutted paths. Most cargo traveled on animals, or on human backs. Before 1520, in a land without draft animals, thousands of men (*tamemes*) passed their lives carrying heavy loads on their backs, bent forward with tump lines taut across their foreheads. Although human cargo carriers would survive into the twentieth century as auxiliaries off the rail grid, most colonial and nineteenth-century cargo traveled on mules, from silver bars moving out of the Sierra Madre to the grain, cotton, charcoal, and other merchandise trucked into urban markets. Mules were an extensive technology, each carrying up to one hundred

Perfil del territorio mexicano en el paralelo de 25°

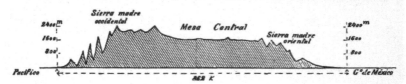

Perfil del territorio mexicano en el paralelo de 23°

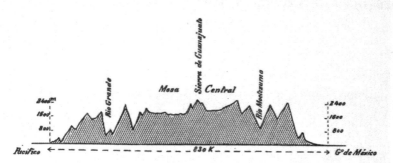

Perfil del territorio mexicano en el paralelo de 21°

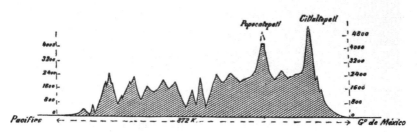

Perfil del territorio mexicano en el paralelo de 19°

FIGURE 5. Four lateral profiles of Mexico, taken at the twenty-fifth, twenty-third, twenty-first, and nineteenth parallels. Reproduced from Justo Sierra, ed., *México: Su evolución social,* vol. 1 (1902; repr., Mexico: Miguel Angel Porrúa, 2005), 11, with permission from Cecilia K. Peimbert and Editorial Miguel Ángel Porrúa.

kilograms or so, moving slowly, about twelve to fifteen miles a day depending on the terrain. The 426-kilometer trip from Veracruz to Mexico City typically took twenty days. Mule trains of many hundreds of animals were not uncommon; an estimated sixty thousand regularly worked the northern *camino real.*[42]

By the early nineteenth century, New Spain's roads were in desperate need of repair, and even the central arteries of colonial commerce, like the heavily traveled route from Mexico City to Veracruz, could not be traversed by wagons or carts for much of their length. Slow deterioration meant that by independence wagons were exceptional, and mules and men hauled most cargo across the Mexican landscape. Running constant deficits, federal spending on public works never exceeded 10 percent of the federal budget through the first decades. Most road proposals never materialized, like the 1831 effort to improve the road from the Pacific coast in Oaxaca across to Veracruz, which never broke ground because of lack of funds.[43] Several early efforts to build railroad lines also went nowhere.[44] Neither roads nor rails provided cost-effective transport alternatives for those interested in doing business beyond local regions. As a result, even in the relatively wide-open terrain of the Bajío, for instance, freight rates for transporting grains from haciendas into León or Guanajuato typically doubled the market price of the food.[45] Moving heavy tools and machinery proved especially difficult and expensive, often simply impossible. Oceanic shipping typically added about 20 percent to machine acquisition costs, while overland rates could push this two or even three times higher.[46] Most investors simply didn't try. Machinery ordered by the British mine managers in Pachuca sat for months in Veracruz, waiting for mule trains to transport it, at great cost, up the eastern escarpment. New papermaking machinery ordered by José Vicente Gutiérrez in 1841 faced freight charges that doubled its acquisition cost. Estevan de Antuñano lost several shipments of textile machinery, lamenting that oceanic and overland transport of machinery always "requires great risk, cost, and delay."[47]

Little changed into midcentury, and in 1879 Matías Romero still identified transportation costs as the "greatest obstacle to the import of machinery to Mexico." Mexico, he argued, "cannot attain to [*sic*] the future . . . without the construction of railways to facilitate the transportation of machinery, tools, and necessary effects to [*sic*] increasing production."[48] There had been little public investment or private interest over the preceding half century; only two patents issued in Mexico before 1870 concerned transportation of any kind. The tyranny of terrain continued to dictate the economic logic of production: markets for goods were nearly always local, small scale, and artisanal; much of the national territory was "almost inaccessible."[49] Only high-value, low-bulk products like silver, gold, and sugar could withstand long-distance cargo costs to reach national or export markets. Nearly all basic manufactured and processed goods were made and consumed within local markets, by hand and on small scales. Without expanding markets, there was little incentive to invest in more economical long-distance transportation. Without more efficient transport, markets would remain local. Every effort to adopt new machine-based technologies faced the persistent disincentive of high transport costs.

POWER

If low-cost transportation constituted one necessary but missing requisite for the adoption of new technologies, inanimate sources of power offered another. At independence, the power to move goods across the Mexican landscape, to haul rock and water out of mines, to pulverize ore, to grind grain, to crush sugarcane, to cut wood, and to spin and weave thread came overwhelmingly from animate sources: mules, horses, oxen, and the labor and sweat of men, women, and children. Entrepreneurs interested in expanding productive capacity could do so only extensively: by increasing, for instance, the number of mules and *malacates*—those hoists and whims and turnstiles that had constituted the common machinery of mechanical power in Mexico through the colonial era (figure 6).[50] Water provided the only viable alternative. Windmills were not unknown in Mexico but were scarce enough to warrant almost no mention in the historical sources. Spanish settlers had established water-powered grain mills in central Mexico beginning in the mid-sixteenth century. By 1800, water turned the millstones of dozens of grain mills across New Spain, as well as the machinery of the larger sugar *ingenios* in Morelos, the fulling mills (*batanes*) associated with some woolen mills (*obrajes*) in Puebla and Guadalajara and in a small handful of paper mills and sawmills around Mexico City.[51]

But Mexico's geography and climate posed sharp limits to the adoption and diffusion of water power. Water power is always and everywhere site specific, dependent on water's abundance and verticality, often induced with millponds or low-head dams. In Mexico, surface water was scarce and highly seasonal across the central plateau where most people lived and worked.

FIGURE 6. Old Mexican *malacate*, or horse-whim, at Guanajuato. Note the opposing beams where the man leans, moved by horses or mules. Reproduced from T. A. Rickard, *Journeys of Observation* (San Francisco: Dewey, 1907), 196.

There, water scarcity had long constrained the diffusion of water power. As Fausto de Eluyar, founder of Mexico's Royal Mining College, noted in 1807, "Water scarcity ... only rarely permits the application of water wheels."[52] Chronic water scarcity provoked frequent concern and motivated early efforts to economize. José Antonio Alzate developed a new mill design in 1795, specially adapted to regions of water scarcity. Many large-scale enterprises in New Spain, like the Casa de Moneda, the Real Fábrica de Tabaco, and most mineral refineries, relied on animate power instead.[53] Water scarcity proved an obstacle to new economic activities before and after independence. When new textile factories sought suitable locations for their mills in the 1830s, the best sites, already scarce, had mostly been taken, and new investors had to buy out existing grain mills. Water litigation between mill owners, municipalities, and hacendados littered provincial courts. Even with access, the seasonality of rain and water flow meant that the textile mills shut down or turned to animal power for half the year or more. Of the several dozen new textile factories established in the 1830s and 1840s, a quarter relied entirely on animate power, while most of the rest used animals to compensate for the irregularity of local water flow. Dependable year-round water power was rare in Mexico and largely explains, for example, Orizaba's long dominance in the textile industry.[54] Alongside costly transport, Mexico's endemic water scarcity presented another major obstacle to early mechanization.

By the late eighteenth century, steam engines promised to liberate miners and manufacturers from the constraints of both animate and water power, in Mexico as in the North Atlantic.[55] New Spain's miners first sought steam technology early in the eighteenth century as they tunneled deeper into the earth and groundwater flooded their shafts. The traditional mule-driven whims and hoists proved inadequate to drain mine works, even with design and scale improvements. In the deeper mines they quickly "show their limitations," lamented Alzate in the 1790s.[56]

In 1728, Don Isidro Rodríguez, a wealthy mine owner in Pachuca, hired Miguel López Dieguez to go to London to investigate the "fire device" that he had heard was pumping large quantities of water from the River Thames. Rodríguez instructed López to acquire two scale models, "absolutely exact," of this Newcomen engine; to bring back two samples of every piece of the machine made from bronze, copper, or iron; to contract someone "who understands everything about this device and who can teach our workers"; to commit to paper a detailed description of the machine; and to solicit in Madrid an exclusive privilege to use the engine in New Spain, Peru, and Guatemala for thirty years.[57] After eighteen months in Europe, traveling to London, Paris, and Madrid, López returned to Pachuca with most of what Rodríguez had requested. He advised, however, against building the Newcomen engine. Expensive to install (some of its pieces weighed up to 36 *quintales,* or 3,600 pounds, and were "untransportable"), the machine, López argued, could not efficiently raise water the necessary height in Rodriguez's mines.[58] He worried also that without a local capacity to manufacture parts for repair, mining operations would be plagued with repeated closures and would remain in "permanent dependency on England."[59] Instead, López encouraged Rodríguez to install simpler hoisting mechanisms that he had observed in Europe, some powered by animals, others by a large water wheel. They would be built largely of wood, and construction would require only "a minimally skilled boat builder."[60] Armed with the know-how he had gathered in Europe—"In me resides the key to this business"—López worked to install several of these novel designs, along with an English smelting furnace.[61] But as he had predicted, iron pieces proved difficult to acquire and expertise even more so; the capital requirements quickly ran to over 20,000 pesos, with few results. A generation later, José Antonio Alzate again raised the possibility of adopting steam power, predicting that steam engines would replace "two hundred men or forty horses: it is undeniable that this machine will be not only useful, but necessary."[62] But necessary or not, López and Alzate and others in the eighteenth century ultimately had little confidence that steam power could be adopted in New Spain, and they continued to focus their attention on modifications to existing hoist designs. At the end of the century, *malacates* continued to dominate mine drainage, and miners continued to search for more powerful means to remove water.

By then, however, improvements in the efficiency of European steam technology coincided with a deepening crisis in New Spain's mining as production levels stagnated and rising water levels increasingly threatened operations. In 1803 New Spain's viceroy José de Iturrigaray offered to subsidize the introduction of steam power, noting its recent success in European mines. Fifteen years later, Viceroy Juan Ruiz de Apodaca repeated the call, offering a prize for the first mine owner to install a steam engine, "one of the most fortunate discoveries."[63] In November 1818 Tomás Murphy, a British miner working in Pachuca, responded by asking for a ten-year exclusive privilege to introduce steam engines to his mines, together with "the foreign technicians needed to install them."[64] New Spain's Tribunal de Minería advised against granting Murphy a monopoly that might discourage others' efforts but proposed a shareholding company that could oversee acquisition of steam engines and expertise for all New Spain's mining districts. In Guanajuato, Catorce, Zacatecas, Pachuca, and Sombrerete, miners applauded the idea, noting "the great desirability" of steam power, but none proved willing or able to contribute to a common enterprise, given the political uncertainties and depressed conditions of the moment.[65] Meanwhile, New Spain's technocrats continued arguing the relative merits of steam in the 1810s and early 1820s. Lucas Alamán, traveling in Paris, sent back a detailed report on the efficiency of steam power. In Mexico City, Fausto de Elhúyar was substantially more pessimistic about the possibility of introducing steam, while Simón Tadeo Ortiz lobbied in favor. Traveling in the United States, Lorenzo de Zavala lyrically touted the advantages of steam engines: they are "more a living being than a machine."[66] Although Elhúyar recognized the great capacity of steam power, he repeated long-standing concerns about the great cost of acquiring, installing, and maintaining steam engines, especially in Mexico's fuel-scarce environment.[67]

British mine investors finally introduced the first steam engine to Mexico in the late 1820s. By 1830 they had installed several engines in the Real de Monte mines in Pachuca and several more in Fresnillo by the mid-1830s, all pumping water from deep shafts. At the same time, several of the new textile mills financed by Lucas Alamán's Banco de Avío worked to install steam engines to complement seasonally scarce water power.[68] These efforts, however, yielded few results. By the late 1840s the British mining companies were nearly bankrupt. Their new Mexican owners worked assiduously to maintain the technical innovations undertaken by the British, including steam power and experiments with new refining methods. They did not, however, undertake new efforts to import costly engines or to adopt major innovations.[69] The Banco de Avío projects likewise left a limited long-term legacy. Many funded projects did not survive, and most of the new textile factories relied primarily on animals or water power. One 1843 census of forty-seven textile mills counted just three that had adopted steam power; fourteen years later, another census of thirty-seven mills reported that none used steam.[70] Mexico's annual imports of steam engines averaged under 4,000 dollars annually well past midcentury, sufficient to cover only two or three machines yearly.[71]

By the late 1860s, only a small handful of steam engines operated in Mexico; in some districts, "not a machine exists."[72] A quarter of Mexico's scarce steam capacity could be found in the Yucatán, where installation did not entail high overland transport costs.[73] Even Guanajuato, Mexico's oldest and largest mining center, boasted just one old steam engine, imported in 1825 but abandoned until repaired in 1857. Otherwise, all the power to dig and extract rock, draw water, and crush and refine ore came from men and mules. Seven thousand mules, for instance, worked the crushing mills around Guanajuato, consuming 24,500 arrobas of straw each week and 2,600 fanegas of corn.[74] The same held true in manufacturing. For a full half century following independence, incentives to adopt steam technology were not strong enough to overcome the substantial obstacles posed by the high cost of the machines themselves, further encumbered by the cost of overland transportation, technical expertise, and fuel. Fuel wood was perennially scarce, and domestic sources of coal were as yet unexploited. The constraint before the 1870s was not so much lack of capital as the relative cost of steam against the status quo. Without reliable inanimate power, the muscles of mules and men continued to power most economic activity, mechanization was scarce, and both mining and manufacturing activities remained small scale and artisanal.

As with railroads and steam power, iron's importance to the nation's national wealth (*riqueza nacional*) was not lost on Mexican observers. Antuñano called it "the base material for all industry," and Alamán described iron as "the necessary element for all the others . . . and [the material] that makes the machines which all use."[75] A congressional committee argued in 1845 that the nation's economic progress depended on iron "flowing among us like water in the desert," an odd but compelling metaphor.[76] Iron's durability, versatility, and malleability made it indispensable to the production of nearly every new implement and machine for mechanized production.

In colonial New Spain, farmers, hacienda peons, construction workers, and artisans typically used rudimentary instruments in their trades, more often made of wood than metal. By all accounts, iron itself and metal tools like hammers, saws, chisels, shovels, and axes were scarce, although not entirely absent. In the eighteenth century, for instance, moderately prosperous farmers (*rancheros*) and entrepreneurs might own a limited range of metal tools and implements. Near Guadalajara, a small-scale sugar planter named Nicolás Méndez Vallesteros left at his death in 1758 a modest horse-operated sugar mill and a number of agricultural tools, including several hoes and other implements. In the same region, two middling farmers who died in the 1770s listed various carpentry tools in their wills, "as this was my trade," one of them noted.[77] They were not alone, and artisans across New Spain acquired and used metal tools in their crafts. Overall, however, metal-edged tools were "scarce and defective" through the colonial era and well into the nineteenth century.[78] The vast majority of households at every level of society owned few tools beyond ordinary kitchen items like a mortar and pestle to grind grain, a comal on which to cook tortillas, and a pot or two, usually ceramic, sometimes copper. Even nails were scarce, practically absent, so there was little need for hammers. The omnipresent and multipurpose machete served to cut and carve wood in place of saws and axes. Farmers in the village economy might own an iron hoe but more commonly relied on wooden implements, especially the traditional *coa*, or digging stick, or perhaps a single-handled wooden plow.[79]

Metal tools were scarce because they were expensive. Nearly all iron had to be imported, and at high prices. Colonial importers advertised "iron and steel from Spain, brass and iron wire, . . . iron bars . . . sledgehammers, iron hoops, pails, picks, axes."[80] But with the heavy freight charges of Atlantic and overland shipping, imported tools easily cost more than the yearly wage of an ordinary laborer. High metal prices meant that New Spain's blacksmiths were often kept busy modifying older equipment for new uses or fashioning minimal metal parts on wooden tools. Juan Serrano, directing the *desagüe* of the Central Valley in the eighteenth century, ordered six hundred wooden bars and four hundred wooden spades, with their working edges reinforced by a thin metal sheathing.[81] When Isidro Rodríguez sought to acquire the Newcomen steam engine in the late 1720s, he knew that all metal parts would have to be imported, given the lack of local iron and iron-working expertise.[82] Those who could afford iron implements paid high import prices or bought from local blacksmiths who had themselves paid dearly for imported iron.

Blacksmiths (*herreros*) had worked in New Spain since Hernán Cortés sent for "two blacksmiths with all their bellows and tools and lots of iron" to help build boats and armaments for his final assault on Tenochtitlán in 1521.[83] Within a generation, men like Alonso Hernando, Bartolomé González, Francisco Gutiérrez, and Juan García arrived from Spain to establish blacksmith shops in Mexico City, forging hammers, chisels, files, pliers, scissors, nails, horseshoes, and other iron tools. Through the colonial era, local blacksmiths continued to establish new forges, working small quantities of local iron or more expensive imported metal. Some acquired significant expertise. In the smithy of the Real Casa de Moneda in Mexico City, blacksmiths fabricated lathes of local design to shape and finish silver coins. One of the more skilled smiths, Pedro María Bernard, presented in 1787 a new design for the mint's forge bellows, operated by one man instead of five. Although his efforts were initially discouraged, within a few years the mint boasted "seven mechanical bellows for the ovens, made by a skilled blacksmith."[84] About the same time, indigenous metalworkers in the region of Tlapujahua, Michoacan, developed a local capacity to manufacture parts for their sugar *ingenios*, although their efforts were undercut when the crown allowed the importation of similar machines from Spain.

New Spain's mines consumed large quantities of metal-tipped bars, shovels, sledges, chisels, and other tools. Other large enterprises also collected large tool inventories, like the sugar *ingenio* in Xochimincas in 1647, owned by the Jesuit Colegio de San Pedro y San Pablo.[85] The workshops of the larger mines, the sugar *ingenios*, the *obrajes*, and Mexico City's Casa de Moneda were capable of constructing, repairing, and modifying a wide variety of metal tools and simple machine parts. In the blacksmith shop of the Royal

Mining College, Gerónimo Antonio Gil produced machines and parts for instructional use in its courses. In Puebla, Juan de Palafox y Calva Gálvez designed and built a "new instrument to grind wheat" in order to increase the productivity of local mills, "an instrument like a clock to measure distance," and, most usefully, "a new instrument to make and sharpen files," perhaps the first metal-based machine tool devised in Spanish America.[86]

But these were isolated accomplishments and did not yield a dependable supply of instruments, tools, and machinery for productive use. Without a domestic source of cheap iron, blacksmiths' work remained expensive and their activity limited. Isolated examples of tool and machine construction never formed the basis for a domestic toolmaking industry in New Spain, and the vast bulk of iron and tools used in the colony were imported from Europe, always at high cost.[87] It was not native abilities that constrained local workmen but their limited access to materials and the low demand for their product. As a result, by the start of the nineteenth century New Spain could boast only a very modest level of iron-working expertise.

After independence, incentives to invest in the domestic production of tools and machine parts grew only slowly.[88] When European war interrupted the supply of imported iron after 1804, New Spain's most prominent metallurgist, Andrés del Río, established an iron foundry (*ferrería*) in Coalcomán, Michoacán, though it closed operations within a year. The next effort to produce domestic metal did not come until the 1830s, with investments in two new blast furnaces. Neither succeeded, although several smaller operations using older Catalan furnace designs in Real de Monte (Mexico), Atotonilco (Jalisco), Chalco (Mexico), and Oaxaca achieved limited production for local markets. In 1831 the Banco de Avío supported efforts by the Zacualpa de Amilpas Ironworks in Cuautla to erect a blast furnace near local iron deposits, with close access to the Mexico City and Puebla markets, but it too was soon abandoned. Congress took up the pressing issue in the mid-1840s, noting the "backwardness" of Mexico's few iron foundries and suggesting increased government support. The Banco de Avío also helped fund the foundry La Biscaina in Puebla. After many difficulties, it settled into steady production under American management and was soon joined in Puebla by three smaller foundries. According to Guy Thompson, these firms "fully" satisfied the regional demand for iron products, ranging from simple ingots, railings, balconies, spurs, and stirrups to an intriguing forty-six power looms, copied from British models.[89] Mexico's first successful blast furnace (*alto horno*) reportedly began production in the early 1850s with steam-driven bellows, a water-powered rolling mill, and a full machine shop. By the mid-1860s three firms ran blast furnaces, though production in each was still limited by high operating costs, low capacities, and substantial transport costs.[90]

Despite these establishments, the domestic production of iron and iron tools and machine parts satisfied only a very small portion of national demand.[91] Estevan de Antuñano noted in 1837 that "the scarcity of good tools is nearly absolute" and argued for their local manufacture in order to support "mechanical and rural industry."[92] Six years later, Lucas Alamán described the "*atraso*" of the iron industry and called for legislation to "protect and develop" national iron production, arguing that "the lack of iron will be injurious to all industrial efforts."[93] A special commission established by the Cámara de Diputados reported in 1845 that "of our established ironworks, some have closed, others are on the verge of the same fate, and even the best produce little iron, poor iron, expensive iron, iron that cannot be sold except with protection against foreign products; our inability to produce and our forced dependence on foreign supplies are the result."[94] By the mid-1850s a national survey reported just five iron foundries, two of decent size but the others employing just ten workers.[95] Even with the new blast furnaces, national iron production in the 1860s did not likely exceed a very modest five thousand tons annually.[96] With scant domestic production, high-priced imported iron and tools continued to satisfy the majority of national demand.[97]

By the 1860s, the scarcity and high cost of iron tools motivated one group of lobbyists to urge a reduction of import tariffs on iron.[98] Whenever possible, toolmakers substituted wood for iron. One visiting mine engineer observed that most tools in the industry were "constructed absolutely without iron; one does not find even a single iron nail."[99] New investments had made only a small dent in the country's near-complete dependence on imported iron manufactures. Obstacles abounded: no reliable source of high-quality iron ore had yet been located; new foundries always faced the high cost of construction materials, skilled labor, and especially fuel; and the government could do little to protect domestic iron workers from imports, given their absolute necessity for economic activities across the country.[100] Iron's high cost handicapped all efforts to adopt new tools and machines, whether manufactured at home or imported from abroad. Without affordable transport, inanimate sources of power, and affordable tools, consumers could buy only abroad or from local artisans.

Mexico's economic "backwardness" (*atraso*) was not a concept invented by development economists and economic historians in the latter half of the twentieth century.[101] In the 1820s, references to *atraso* are difficult to find in Mexico's public sphere. By the 1840s, however, intellectuals and officials in Mexico increasingly referenced their country's *atraso* relative to the North Atlantic. Their concerns were clear and well grounded. Free traders worried that the early British investments to revive Mexico's silver mines had yielded only frustration and little growth, while the Banco de Avío, the great hope of industrial promoters and protectionists, had been shut down after barely more than a decade of operation. Mexican observers of the North Atlantic world plainly understood the direct equation between wealth and power, *riqueza* and *poder*. On both sides of the great economic debates of the day, Mexicans knew that the economic and political gap between Mexico and the North Atlantic yawned wider every year.[102]

Although the articulation of a highly competitive, Darwinian race between nations would not fully emerge until the last third of the nineteenth century, soon after independence writers across the political spectrum began to lament Mexico's poor economic showing in a comparative Atlantic context. Mexican observers vividly saw the economic power of Britain in the increasing flow of cotton imports that threatened the livelihood of thousands of artisans in Mexico. Governors from Puebla, Jalisco, Querétaro, Oaxaca, Mexico, and San Luis Potosí bemoaned the loss of artisanal jobs in the 1830s, and pamphlets by "*el artesano oprimido*" clamored for protection.[103] "The nation will perish," worried the authors of one congressional report, "in the face of foreign competition," while another writer lamented Mexico's ongoing "dependence" on foreign sources of skilled workers and machines. "We are left," noted Juan Nepomuceno Adorno in 1858, "with only a fictitious industry."[104] The strongest critique of Mexico's material progress relative to the North Atlantic came from Estevan de Antuñano, Lucas Alamán, and other promoters of domestic industry. They clearly identified "industrial independence" as key to closing this gap. "The Mexican nation cannot be peaceful, rich, strong, and civilized," Antuñano wrote, "however great its natural assets and national independence may be, as long as it does not also consummate its industrial independence."[105] There was no more important frame of reference for Mexicans at midcentury than the industrializing countries of the North Atlantic—"the most fortunate of the universe," as viewed from the South—whose rising power compelled the search for material progress in Mexico.[106]

But political liberals were also concerned about the challenge posed by North Atlantic industrialization and economic power. Tadeo Ortiz lamented in 1832 that Mexico had already "lost time in the race of civilization," and Lorenzo de Zavala and others marveled at the industrial advances in Lowell, Massachusetts, and elsewhere in the North Atlantic.[107] Through the 1840s and 1850s Mexican liberals wrote with increasing frequency about foreign industrial models and warmed to the use of moderate tariff protection to induce local industry.[108] The liberal press warned of the dangers of "backsliding" after the modest progress of the 1830s and argued that the protection of industry was the only way to avoid becoming "tributary," or "a slave to other nations."[109] They viewed Mexico within an explicitly competitive international context: the ability to produce "its food, its clothing, and its arms" constituted the "economic and military independence" of every nation; thus the "obligation of every legislator" was to promote strategies to "preserve the existence and liberty [of the nation]."[110] By midcentury prominent liberals were echoing Estevan de Antuñano's earlier *grito* for economic independence, understood primarily as industrial or manufacturing independence. By 1855 this view had found an institutional home in the new Ministerio de Fomento, where its director, Manuel Siliceo, noted the office's mission to "ensure . . . *industrial independence,* without which *development* is absolutely impossible" (emphasis added).[111] Economic independence—and economic progress in general—had become an explicitly comparative norm, and through midcentury England was "unquestionably the first ranked industrial nation in the universe."[112]

By midcentury Mexico's press regularly and explicitly referred to the country's backwardness relative to a North Atlantic model of modern, civilized, and progress-oriented nations. *El Monitor Republicano* in 1846 moaned, "So backward is our scientific knowledge," noting the "backwardness of our industry" in the context of an explicit comparison between "less industrial peoples" and "their skilled neighbors."[113] Similar references occur repeatedly in *El Siglo XIX* and elsewhere through the 1840s and early 1850s in phrases like "the backwardness in industry," "the backwardness that is ours," and "the perpetual backwardness of our nation."[114] One congressional commission lamented Mexico's *atraso*—"We have lost confidence in ourselves, and faith in our future"—and wondered aloud whether Mexico would return to a "colonial" status.[115] Just a year before his death, Lucas Alamán noted that the sanguine views of the 1820s "seem ridiculous to us [because now] events are moving rapidly and decisively toward the supremacy of the United States and the collapse of Mexico's illusions."[116] Miguel Lerdo de Tejada tried to put a positive spin on the country's progress since the 1820s but continued to worry that domestic production was "far from flattering."[117] The pessimism implicit in such views at midcentury contrasted sharply with the more hopeful views of the 1820s. While these new fears did not entirely exclude more sanguine visions of Mexico's economic future, they did increasingly focus government policy toward a more balanced view of engaging the Atlantic economy while at the same time promoting and protecting a more diverse domestic economy—arguably an incipient developmentalist state.[118] Through the second half of the century, the opposite of *atraso* would become *el progreso material*, at the center of which lay the adoption of modern technologies.

. . .

When Benito Juárez triumphantly returned to the presidential palace in Mexico City in July 1867, French troops were gone from Mexican soil, Maximilian was dead, his army was vanquished, and his Conservative allies were politically cowed. Juárez and his ministers, however, faced daunting challenges: an empty treasury, no access to foreign credit, a highly contested political arena even within the victorious liberal camp, and a stagnant economy. Nevertheless, there were early signs of economic renewal. Investments by local entrepreneurs in mining had resulted in several new bonanzas and a sharp uptick in silver production through the 1860s. French investment during the Second Empire resulted in several new textile factories, outfitted with newly imported looms and spindles. More importantly, the economies of the United States and other North Atlantic countries were poised for a sustained period of dramatic growth following the end of the US Civil War in 1865. Juárez and his successors proved quick to respond, sending public signals abroad that Mexico would welcome foreign investors to give "life to our anemic market," and they did not have to wait long.[119] Their first priority was investment in railroad technology to connect Veracruz with Mexico City, then north toward the US border, a Tehuantepec rail crossing, and other major trunk lines. Within a decade, the governments of Juárez, Lerdo de Tejada, and Porfirio Díaz would sign contracts with US and British rail investors to begin construction on these lines and others. At the same time that railroads were lowering transport costs within Mexico, oceanic freight rates were falling to a fraction of their previous level because of North Atlantic advances in ship design and steam power.[120]

Mexico, in other words, would soon have unprecedented and nearly unfettered access to new production technologies from the North Atlantic: machines and tools by the crateful, but also new knowledge and expertise embodied in print and in people. For four decades after 1870, investors and consumers in Mexico would import and adopt vast quantities of new technologies in all three forms. Both transformative and dislocative, this inundation would lift a rising tide of economic growth and provide the foundation for subsequent twentieth-century development, although it would also yield increased social inequality and a higher concentration of economic and political power in the short run.

But none of this was yet evident in 1867. After nearly half a century of fragmented and frustrated efforts, Mexico boasted only one hundred kilometers of railroad track, barely a handful of operating steam engines, and little domestic capacity to produce iron or to manufacture iron tools and machine parts. Mexico's total imports of machinery and hardware over its first half century of independence amounted to less than what they would be in the year 1900 alone. Likewise, total patents issued over the same half century were surpassed in a single year by the mid-1890s. If measured by technology imports, Mexico's postindependence depression had been sustained and deep. One stark consequence of low levels of investment in technological innovation was that productivity—average output per person—was lower in 1867 than it had been fifty or even seventy years earlier.

As Mexican officials and investors eagerly awaited the arrival of foreign technologies in the late 1860s, they were aware only of the promise of the material progress that they saw embodied in the North Atlantic. The direct consequences of Mexico's experience over the preceding half century were painfully obvious to contemporary observers: high transport costs posed a nearly insuperable barrier to any supralocal economic activity, mules and men continued to power all economic activity, and the country depended overwhelmingly on imported iron and steel. As a result, it used little. They tended to agree with Estevan de Antuñano's observation a generation earlier: "We are very backward in our mechanical arts," lacking both "*maestros y máquinas*"—masters and machines.[121] As a result, Mexico remained highly vulnerable to foreign domination. Less visible but perhaps more consequential in the long run were the indirect effects of Mexico's long delay in adopting the technologies of the first industrial revolution. Railroads, steam power, iron, and mechanization remained unknown quantities for the vast majority of Mexicans. Absent these foundational technologies of the first industrial revolution, workers, mechanics, and engineers in Mexico had had few opportunities to acquire critical knowledge and expertise at the very moment when the frontier of technological innovation in the North Atlantic had moved toward the application of steel, chemicals, and electricity in the so-called second industrial revolution. With scant adoption of new technologies before the 1870s, Mexicans had few opportunities to assimilate new technical knowledge. The scarcity of technical know-how in Mexico, of "skilled men who possess both theoretical and practical knowledge," as one report noted, had changed little by the time that Juárez rode triumphantly into Mexico City in 1867.[122]

THREE

Technology and the Imperative of Progreso, *1870–1910*

BEFORE CLOSING ONE EVENING IN early 1879 on Calle Espíritu Santo in Mexico City, employees of Roberto Böker's hardware store arranged several Singer sewing machines on the central display counter. These had just arrived on the train from Veracruz—then the only operating rail line in the country—and had been carried from the station to the store on mule-drawn wagons. Over the next few weeks, Casa Böker would quickly sell these machines to women and men who bought them, primarily for home use, paying ten pesos up front, the rest in ten-peso monthly installments, the machines delivered to city addresses on the backs of porters. These were just a few of the roughly 3,200 sewing machines shipped to Mexico that year by Singer and other manufacturers in the United States and Britain. They constituted an even smaller fraction of the large volume of new machines, tools, and parts that arrived at Mexican ports and found their way inland to homes, haciendas, workshops, and mines. Mexico's total machine imports for 1879 reached over half a million US dollars, then just 2.5 percent of the country's total import bill, but already over seven times above the level of machine imports a decade earlier.[1]

Thirty years later, Calle Espíritu Santo boasted electric tram cars and lighting, although Casa Böker had moved to a grand new building several blocks away, just off the Zócolo, and the Singer Company had by then established its own headquarters on Calle de Manrique in Mexico City. Late that year—1909—railcars laden with heavy steel machinery crossed the Mexican border at Nuevo Laredo as part of a much longer cargo train, bound for Monterrey and a factory site there, still under construction. Two large machines, recently designed and manufactured in Toledo, Ohio, filled one car nearly to capacity. These were the Owens automatic glass bottle–blowing machines, series AE, that would constitute the technical core of the Compañía Vidriera Monterrey's new automated glass bottle factory. At the same time, not far to the southwest in one of Chihuahua's remote mining camps, an American mining engineer watched eleven "mountain Indians" carry bulky sewing machines on their backs down a zigzag trail leading to the small community.[2] Mexico's sewing machine imports had by now grown to some fifteen thousand units annually, marketed to consumers well beyond urban areas. Investment in new factories, in mining equipment and mineral refining plants, and in myriad small-scale product technologies like sewing machines continued to push Mexico's total imports of machine hardware upward, now accompanied by thousands of foreign technicians and skilled workers. Although in 1909 the effects of recession in the Atlantic economy had already cut into the peak of Mexico's machinery imports, they had expanded an astounding two hundred-fold since the late 1870s, accounting for over 10 million dollars annually. Machinery now made up 10 percent of all imported goods, and total iron and steel manufactures took fully 20 percent of all Mexican imports.

Over the four decades from roughly 1870 to 1910, individuals and firms working in Mexico purchased a vast and steadily increasing quantity of new technologies from the countries of the North Atlantic. Physical artifacts—technological hardware in the form of machines, tools, implements, and their parts—made up only one big part of this flow. So too did new processes, new forms of organization, and new ideas and skills embodied in print materials and in people themselves. This flood of machines and print and people swept through Mexico's ports of entry and washed across the landscape, seeping into daily lives by transforming production, labor, and consumption for Mexicans at all social levels, in many corners of the country.

This unprecedented wave of technology imports should not be seen as a *cause* of social change. Instead, investment in technology imports responded to gradual social changes in Mexico, to slowly rising demand, to new market opportunities, and to political incentives. First in rail transportation and silver mining, then in industrial metals, in commercial agriculture, and, after 1890, in domestic manufacturing, new investment drove economic growth at an impressive annual average of roughly 2 percent per capita for roughly four decades, circa 1870 to 1910.[3] Built on a foundation of imported machines, tools, ideas, and expertise, this era of growth offers a stark contrast with the preceding half century. Before about 1870, net economic growth had been zero for fifty years at best, and there is little evidence that people and firms in

Mexico adopted new technologies: machinery and tool imports were small, domestic abilities to manufacture them scarce, foreign patent applications almost nonexistent, and immigration numbers low.

This chapter traces the magnitude of the spillover of technology from the North Atlantic to Mexico. Beginning about 1870, economic expansion in the North Atlantic countries—the so-called second industrial revolution— created the international context for Mexico's technology imports as European and US manufacturers sought overseas markets for tools and machinery. After a brief survey of this experience, the chapter takes up the foundational technologies of the first industrial revolution: railroads, steam power, and iron. If firms and investors in Mexico had only rarely adopted these technologies before 1870, the story changed quickly thereafter. Within a generation, investors working in Mexico had built an extensive national rail system, imported thousands of steam engines, and established new iron foundries and the first integrated steel plant in Latin America. All mani-fested both the spirit and the accomplishments of material progress.

On one hand, the scale and transformative nature of this experience illustrate the supposed advantages of late development. As Alexander Gerschenkron argued a half century ago, efforts to industrialize in the wake of the first industrial revolution faced the happy prospect of simply adopting new technologies from the industrial leaders in the North Atlantic, rather than relying on the expensive, slow, and uncertain process of local invention.[4] Latecomers thus enjoyed substantially lower costs of innovation. Relatively easy adoption and innovation would yield rapid economic growth—exactly what Mexican investors and officials hoped, and exactly what many develop-ment specialists have predicted since Gerschenkron's early insights.[5] And exactly, it seems, what transpired in Mexico after about 1870 in a neat equa-tion: imported technology yielded rapid economic growth, which under-wrote thirty-five years of enforced peace and stability—the so-called *pax porfiriana.*

On the other hand, however, Mexico's experience of rapid technological change in the late nineteenth century also reveals the limits to the advantages of relative backwardness. First, despite the adoption of rail, steam, and iron capabilities after about 1870, none proved a panacea to the multiple challenges facing the Mexican economy. Off the rail grid (and even on it), transportation costs remained high and the source of constant complaint. Use of steam power remained out of reach for many potential users because of the persistent scarcity and high cost of fuel. The vast majority of iron and steel used in Mexican mines, cities, and factories continued to come from abroad rather than from domestic sources; machine construction remained nearly absent. As we will see in chapter 7, the adoption of new technologies from abroad was not always an easy and frictionless endeavor.

More importantly, the delayed adoption and limited diffusion of these and other technologies carried substantial opportunity costs for the development of technological capabilities in Mexico. Between 1800 and 1900 inventors and entrepreneurs in the North Atlantic countries dramatically transformed the leading edge of production technologies in nearly every aspect of economic activity. What had been novel in the early decades of the century (steam power, mechanical looms and spindles, railroads, and the standardized production of tools and machines, for instance) was by the last third of the century commonplace. By then, the technological frontier in the North Atlantic had moved toward more fully automated large-scale production systems and the industrial production and application of steel, chemicals, and electricity. Mexico's relative isolation from the technologies of the so-called first industrial revolution meant that by the 1870s and after, when the conditions for massive technology imports became favorable for the first time, Mexican engineers, mechanics, and skilled workers had little accumulated experience working with production technologies from the North Atlantic. The capacity of Mexican technicians to engage North Atlantic technologies of production—to install, operate, troubleshoot, repair, modify, and perhaps replicate—had been low in the 1820s, and there were few opportunities to acquire this expertise over the next half century. When the floodgates opened after 1870, the gap between local capacities in Mexico and the challenges represented by cutting-edge North Atlantic technologies of the second industrial revolution had grown much wider. Learning was not impossible, as we will see in the chapters that follow. But it was exceptional. As a result, firms, individuals, and policy makers who sought to adopt new technologies had little choice but to turn quickly toward foreign sources of both hardware *and know-how*—the tools and machinery of industrial production as well as the human expertise necessary to install, adapt, and operate new production systems. As Estevan de Antuñano remarked in the 1830s, "We are very backward in our mechanical arts," lacking both "*maestros y máquinas,*" masters and machines.[6] Little had changed by the 1870s or the 1890s. Mexican firms would be able to import both with relative ease through the last decades of the century, but whether this imported know-how would spill over to local, Mexican capabilities would be a different question, one that we will examine more closely in chapter 8.

. . .

Industrialization spread steadily in Europe and the United States through the nineteenth century. But the decades around 1870 mark a clear watershed in the volume of international trade and investment. Rapidly expanding trade was driven by demand from and the production of new industries across the North Atlantic, facilitated by significant decline in oceanic and overland transport costs. The end of civil war in the United States (1865) and the unification of Germany (1871) prefigured the so-called second industrial revolution, characterized by growing industrial production of machinery and increasing investment in chemical, electrical, and precision instrument industries. After about 1870, the Atlantic economy entered a new phase, accruing wealth and power to Europe and the United States that would underwrite a new age of imperialist expansion.

At the same time, in Mexico, the Liberal victory over Maximilian and the restoration of Republican government in the late 1860s enabled President Benito Juárez and his successors to open Mexican markets and attract foreign investment. And investors both foreign and domestic responded to new opportunities: to transport goods or information, to extract minerals from the earth, to process raw materials, or to manufacture bottles or clothing or construction materials. In the North Atlantic economy, Mexican firms could increasingly access a vast reservoir of new ways of doing things, an exogenous supply of new knowledge generated by the late-century wave of invention, innovation, and economic growth. What did the resulting spillover of new technologies look like? For the historian, Mexico's massive importation of capital equipment is easiest to observe: locomotives, electric dynamos and motors, steam engines, hydroelectric plants, sewing machines, diverse factory machinery, chemicals, scientific instruments, and of course simple tools: hammers and saws, screws and nails. Artifacts like these physically embodied new knowledge, new ways to undertake productive processes, or new ways to extract, manipulate, and transform raw materials that contemporaries observed "being introduced in many parts of the country."[7] The figure for Mexico's total imports of technical hardware provides one rough measure of fixed capital investment and the productive capacity of the Mexican economy through this era of rapid late-century growth.[8]

Mexico's machinery and hardware imports between 1870 and 1910 totaled roughly 215 million dollars out of a total import bill for all manufactures of iron and steel of about 273 million. This is a striking amount, nearly a third of the country's total import bill over the same period.[9] Mexico's machinery imports grew far more quickly than any other single class of goods in the country's import trade, and faster than the average annual growth of machine imports in any other Latin American country at a striking annual average of nearly 11 percent per year over four decades.[10] Figures 3 and 4 in chapter 2 presented the dramatic shift in the volume of capital equipment imports before and after about 1870, mirroring the same pattern in Mexico's total foreign trade. From the 1870s to the 1910s, the US share of Mexico's capital equipment imports grew from 39 percent to 66 percent, while Britain's share fell from 53 percent to just 14 percent (figure 7). France, which had supplied 8 percent early on, nearly disappeared, while Germany, absent at first, captured 17 percent by 1910, mostly in tools and hardware.[11]

Machinery constituted the largest portion of Mexico's total iron and steel imports, at 55 percent by 1900 to 1910. Table 1 illustrates the growth of machinery imports in relation to other categories of iron and steel manufactures.[12] Although disaggregating this massive import flow is difficult, we can glean some detail from the import records. Agricultural implements, for instance, expanded from an annual average of 22,300 dollars in the 1870s to an annual average of 400,770 dollars yearly in the decade after 1900. However, they were quickly dwarfed by growing imports of mining and manufacturing equipment: agricultural implements made up 14 percent of all machinery imports in the early 1870s but barely 4 percent by the turn of the century, despite their growing volume. Likewise, steam engines and boilers captured 11 percent of machinery imports in 1870 and grew by 10 percent yearly to 1910 but took just 5 percent of all machinery imports after the turn of the century. Sewing machines constituted a massive 52 percent of all machinery imports in the 1870s but despite consistent growth fell to just 5 percent after 1900 as other classes expanded more quickly. Meanwhile, investment in textile machinery grew by nearly 200 percent between 1879 and 1910.[13] In other words, substantial growth in agricultural implements, steam engines, and sewing machines (for instance) was dwarfed by even more massive growth in industrial mining machinery, new factory-scale manufacturing equipment, and electrical machines and apparatus. Table 1 illustrates the large contribution of mining and electrical equipment after 1900, together taking over half of all machine imports.

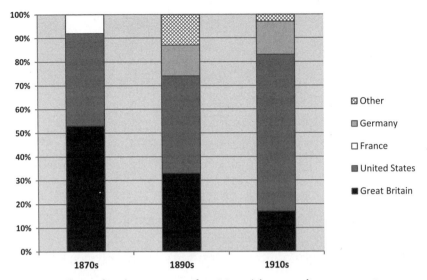

FIGURE 7. Shares of machinery imports from Mexico's largest trading partners, 1870–1910. Derived from Sandra Kuntz Ficker, *El comercio exterior de México en la era del capitalismo liberal, 1870–1929* (Mexico: El Colegio de México, 2007), 160, table 3.4.

TABLE 1 Disaggregation of Iron and Steel Imports to Mexico from the United States, 1870–1910

	1870–1880	1900–1910	Annual Average Growth Rate (%)
	SHARE OF TOTAL IRON AND STEEL IMPORTS (%)		
Basic forms	5	24	14.3
Tools and hardware	22	7	9.8
Machinery	38	55	14.3
All other	35	14	
	SHARE OF TOTAL MACHINERY IMPORTS (%)		
Agricultural	14	4	9.1
Steam and boilers	11	5	10.5
Sewing machines	52	5	5.1
Mining machinery*	na	25	
Electrical**	na	28	

*Covers 1907–10 and not disaggregated previously.

**Covers 1903–10. See Appendix 2 for sources and discussion.

Beyond machinery, basic forms of iron and steel made up fully a quarter of the total by the turn of the century, up from just 5 percent in the 1870s: bars and sheets and rods and hoops of iron and steel, iron and later steel rails for the railroads, castings of machine parts of all sorts, and endless spools of wire. Tools and hardware ranging from saws, edge tools, and files to cutlery, locks, hinges, and nails, for instance, expanded by nearly 10 percent over the period but fell from 22 percent of all iron and steel imports to just 7 percent in the face of rising volumes of machinery and basic forms.

North Atlantic firms that manufactured machines, tools, and metal forms aggressively sought buyers in Mexico, as they did across the globe, advertising extensively in international journals and in the Mexican commercial press. They established offices in Mexico City and agencies throughout the country, struck deals with local retailers like Casa Böker to market their wares, sent sales agents on regular trips, and maintained a steady correspondence with businessmen in Mexico, distributing catalogs and sending detailed product descriptions.[14] They partnered with American consuls to sponsor machinery exhibitions in public spaces, like the one held in the old Mining College in 1879 (figure 8). Mexican technology buyers had little difficulty selecting and purchasing machines and tools off a North Atlantic supply shelf. Mining hardware that could be acquired in places like Leadville, Colorado, or Grass Valley, California, in 1900 could be acquired with nearly the same ease in most Mexican districts, though with added transport costs. The same held true for factory and farm machinery. As a result, the southbound cross-border rail traffic in machinery grew to tremendous proportions. In just one week in the summer of 1907, at the very height of the investment boom, some 3,200 railcars loaded with an "enormous cargo" of machinery and hardware headed south through Ciudad Juárez.[15]

New knowledge came to Mexico embodied not only in machine hardware but also in software, captured in print and in people. Print materials carried technical knowledge codified in blueprints, textbooks, trade journals, instruction manuals, sales catalogs, and patent applications, arriving in luggage or through the mail and into the hands of readers across Mexico. Though it is more difficult to quantify than hardware, we have some rough indications of the magnitude of this current. Mining suppliers in Mexico City sold textbooks and journals and pamphlets on the newest mining methods, metallurgy, mineral chemistry. In January 1908 the offices of the *Mexican Mining Journal* in Mexico City offered forty-one technical titles for sale, include six texts on the new cyanide refining process, ranging from three to twenty-five

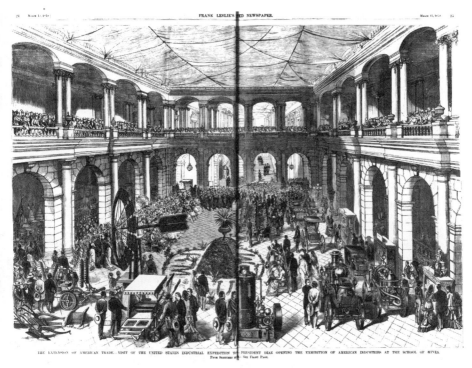

FIGURE 8. The extension of American trade: President Díaz opening the exhibition of American industries at the School of Mines, 1879. Reproduced with permission of the Library of Congress Prints and Photographs Division, Washington, D.C.

pesos each, while "The Book Exchange," opposite the Hotel Iturbide in Mexico City, offered a long list of texts on mechanical engineering, surveying, irrigation, and other technical topics.[16] Several libraries in Mexico's largest cities built collections of foreign technical volumes, including the library of the Sociedad Mexicana de Geografía y Estadística, which held several thousand scientific and technical titles, including the *Annual Reports* of the US Patent Office.[17] American mining publications circulated widely through Mexico's mining districts. Each shipment of supplies that arrived in mining camps via train or mule carried editions of *Mining and Scientific Press* or the *Engineering and Mining Journal,* and US mining engineers in Mexican camps were frequent (and timely) contributors. Managers of new factories regularly received issues of their industry trade journals from the United States or England.[18] The bookstores of Calle Donceles in Mexico City still held in the 1990s shelves of dusty manuals, trade journals, and technical texts from the turn of the previous century. As in all other venues for technology imports, Mexico's international trade in books and print materials had been virtually stagnant from 1825 to 1870 but grew rapidly at an average rate of about 9 percent per year thereafter. At the same time, Mexico experienced its own explosion of print culture, and hundreds of local and national newspapers contributed to the broader exchange of information and ideas.[19]

Patent applications provided another vehicle for the transmission of technical knowledge from the North Atlantic to Mexico. Mexican patent law required that applicants present technical descriptions and drawings, effectively detailing new technical developments at the global frontier.[20] Like other patent systems, Mexico's offered inventors temporary private monopoly in exchange for making new knowledge available to the public. Although patent applications may represent transformative technological breakthroughs, they also may represent minor advances or even frivolous or fraudulent claims. Nonetheless, they offered Mexicans the single largest source of direct and detailed information on cutting-edge inventive activity in the North Atlantic.[21] Entrepreneurs in Mexico valued patent rights: they invested millions of pesos in acquiring, advertising, trading, and defending them. Patents became the constant subject of commentary in the Mexican press by late century: as emblems of novelty and quality, as legal strategies to protect market share, as property rights with real economic value, and as symbol for the most modern technology.[22]

Five North Atlantic countries constituted the global center of inventive activity, producing 86 percent of all global patents before the First World War: the United States, Great Britain and its dependencies, France, Germany, and Belgium (figure 9). Countries outside Europe and the North Atlantic took less than 2 percent of all global patents. In Mexico, patent applications had been scarce before the 1870s but then rose quickly through the rest of the century, growing tenfold between 1880 and 1890, and tenfold again by 1905. Most of this growth came from North Atlantic inventors and firms. By 1910, Mexico had conceded roughly ten thousand patents to foreign applicants compared to about four thousand to Mexicans. These foreign patent applications provide one rough indication of the scale and scope of new technical knowledge available to investors and consumers in Mexico—Gerschenkron's so-called advantage of late development.

Finally, new technical knowledge also came to Mexico embodied in people, from many dozens of investors to tens of thousands of engineers, foremen, technicians, and skilled workers. Across the economy, the adoption and commer-

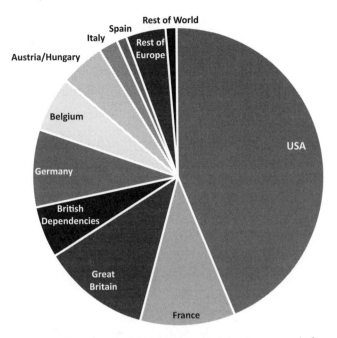

FIGURE 9. Distribution of world patents by originating country before 1912. Derived from Ian Inkster, "Patents as Indicators of Technological Change and Innovation—An Historical Analysis of Patent Data, 1830–1914," paper presented at the Meeting of the Newcomen Society, London, 2002.

cialization of new production technologies came courtesy of the know-how in the heads and hands of specialists from the North Atlantic. Some of these men (mostly men) were highly trained and experienced engineers who came to build new enterprises or were sent by their employers in the United States and Europe to install new plants and machinery. But most were young men just beginning their careers, recently graduated from US mining schools, attracted to the "magnet" that was Mexico, and encouraged to cut their teeth for a few years south of the border.[23] Hundreds flooded Mexico City, provincial centers, and especially the mining districts, knocking on doors, replying to advertisements, looking for work, and quickly taking positions as "mine engineer" or "metallurgist" or "assayer" or "superintendent" in the mining camps that dotted the Sierra Madre or as supervisors and consultants in new factories. They came in search of opportunities and experience and advertised their presence any way they could. They posted hundreds of classified "job wanted" or "services available" ads in the daily editions of Mexican newspapers: "Experienced cyanide man, open to accept position at once. Can erect plant and take full charge. Speaks English, German, and some Spanish. Good references" or "Cyanide chemist, working, desires superintendancy, mining, milling, lexiviation, assaying. Spanish."[24] They sent letters of inquiry to mine managers across the Sierra: "Will do anything," twenty-six-year-old Harold Lane wrote to Colonel Daniel Burns at San Dimas, Durango, "for a good chance higher up."[25] Mining firms also posted ads, typically in English: "Wanted—First class cyanide chemist and mill man; must be sober and furnish good references . . . ." or "Wanted—good mining men to take charge of the development and operation of a number of mining properties in the state of Oaxaca . . . young single men preferred."[26]

These men brought with them extensive technical knowledge and a deep faith in new machines and processes. Tens of thousands of American (and some European) miners, engineers, and technicians found employment in the mining camps of Guanajuato, Zacatecas, Sonora, San Luis Potosí, and Hidalgo, just as they did in dozens of new factories and work sites throughout the country. They constituted, in the words of one, "a strong piece of mental machinery for industrial development."[27] Mining engineers predominated, but US consuls and commercial agents encouraged aspiring "young men" of all professions to seek their fortune in "a new field, a new market such as Mexico."[28]

Virtually all efforts to adopt technologies in Mexico depended on imported managers and technicians to install, operate, and oversee new machines and production systems, regardless of whether firms were controlled by foreign or national capital. This had also of course been true in the 1820s and 1830s, when efforts to adopt steam technology in the mines and to build new textile and paper factories required sending abroad for "the foreign technicians that we need" in order to "attend to the construction and installation of the machinery."[29] When foreign technicians were unavailable, imported machinery might sit unused in warehouses.[30] This remained true after the 1870s, when "all and every one . . . has needed to resort to foreigners to install" and operate new machinery and production systems.[31] The founders of the Cervecería Cuauhtémoc, for instance, hired Joseph M. Schnaider of St. Louis to oversee its brewing operations, along with a core of US technicians and workers, while the Fábrica de Vidrios y Cristales, the Cervecería de Toluca y México, and the La Cruz Blanca brewery all hired Germans to head subdepartments within their firms. The manager of a new glass factory in Puebla traveled to France to find expertise that he could not find in Mexico. The Toledo Glass Company sent two technicians to oversee installation of automated machinery at the Compañía Vidriera Monterrey, while Singer provided its own technical assistance to those who bought their machines. Imported foreign expertise played critical roles in steel, beer, cement, cotton textile, petroleum, and all other new establishments: from the designers of buildings to the installers of machines, to all managers and supervisors and to the technicians and workers who had daily and direct interaction with new machines and processes. At the Fundidora Monterrey, foreign technicians managed and staffed every department: Belgians, Hungarians, French, English, Italians, North Americans, "and even Irish."[32] Across the board, new technology imported from the North Atlantic was inevitably accompanied by foreign expertise to install, operate, troubleshoot, and repair, substituting for the local scarcity of skilled labor and technical expertise.

Human vectors of imported technological know-how were abundant, especially in Mexico City and the nation's mining districts, but also in nearly every corner of the country. By 1910 some forty thousand US citizens lived and worked in Mexico; they had been coming at a rate of several thousand per year since the early 1890s.[33] Thousands more immigrants hailed from Europe, many in the first or second generation of naturalized families. The Barcelonnettes formed a classic immigrant stream from France: several thousand young men, funded by relatives and friends, who had gradually built a set of tightly knit and successful business groups, most notably in dry goods and then in the textile industry around Puebla and Guadalajara.[34] Significant numbers of German immigrants moved into the hardware trades in Guadalajara and elsewhere, as well as to new coffee and ranching enterprises in the far South.[35] The governor of Sonora reported in 1900 almost 3,000 foreign residents: 1,453 from the United States, 825 Chinese, 150 French, 113 Germans, 101 Spanish, 78 British, 60 Italians, and 123 of unknown nationality. Two thousand Americans lived in the city of Chihuahua.[36] Mexico's 1900 national census counted over sixty-two thousand foreigners resident in the country—600 percent above an 1855 census!—three-quarters of whom came from the United States, Spain, France, England, and Germany.[37] Although Mexico received just a small fraction of the vast late-century immigrant flow from Europe to the Americas, and less than 1 percent of Mexico's population was foreign born, "technicians" were especially prominent among those who did come.[38] Some came as short-term employees and worked in Mexico for weeks, months, or a few years. Others, like Ricardo Honey or Juan Brittingham, built careers and established their families in Mexico for the long term, adopting Hispanicized names in the process. Cultures of innovation often centered on immigrant "colonies," each with its own associations and networks. These included the American, English,

Spanish, Barcelonnette, and German communities in Mexico's larger cities, as well as more isolated groups like the Mormons of Chihuahua, who introduced new farming and ranching techniques that reportedly "transformed agricultural practice in the region."[39] Whether large investors, small farmers, mechanics, railroad workers, salesmen, or mining engineers, most brought with them an accumulated familiarity with new technological developments in the North Atlantic. Ready access to this highly mobile global movement of technicians—skilled, trained, and experienced—greased the wheels for the commercialization of new production technologies in Mexico. It would also weaken incentives to develop local sources of technical expertise.

. . .

Economic malaise had delayed the adoption of rail transport, steam power, and iron capabilities through Mexico's first half century. This was also the case, of course, for nearly all types of production technologies newly available in the North Atlantic. Before 1870, the demand for technological innovation in the Mexican economy was simply too low to overcome the substantial costs of adoption. But the long delay in adopting railroads, steam, and iron capabilities had even greater significance for Mexico's economic development. The absence of affordable transportation and power mandated local markets and artisanal production methods. Without any significant capacity to produce and work iron and steel, nearly all tools and machinery were imported, costly, and scarce. And Mexican technicians had few opportunities to work with and learn from new machines and production processes. Beginning in the 1870s, however, new investments came rapidly to the canonical technologies of the first industrial revolution. By the end of the century, Mexico boasted an integrated national network of rail lines, thousands of steam engines, and a nascent iron industry with the first integrated steel mill in Latin America. Indicative of the wide range of production technologies that flooded Mexico between 1870 and 1910, these experiences illustrate the transformative extent of late-century technological change but also begin to suggest its limitations.

RAILROADS

Almost four decades after the Mexican government awarded the first railroad concession in 1837, British investors completed Mexico's first major line in 1873 between Veracruz and Mexico City. Over the next fifteen years, the full package of financial, managerial, and technological expertise spilled quickly over the Mexican border as US rail investors looked aggressively for new markets to link with the just completed US transcontinental lines. They had constructed Mexico's main trunk lines by the late 1880s, supported by substantial federal subventions, and over the next two decades extended branch lines to dozens of mining, manufacturing, and agricultural districts. By 1910, the country boasted nearly twenty thousand kilometers of railways.[40]

Designed to link Mexico's natural resources with the Atlantic economy, railroads also decisively broke down barriers to interregional trade. Most of the commodities carried by Mexico's railways were in fact destined for domestic markets.[41] In the positivist discourse of the day, railroads had "crossed deserts, abysses, and frontiers . . . stimulating the great latent energies of an organism craving for life," although their socially dislocative impact was also substantial.[42] For the first time in the century, cargo transport costs fell low enough to allow the movement of a wide range of consumer and producer goods across the landscape, including imported machinery as well as technical information embodied in print and people. As a result, expanding markets provided incentives for investment in the technologies that would increase the scale and efficiency of production. Quite simply, nearly all of Mexico's economic expansion between 1890 and 1910 would have been impossible without rail transport. Railroads' advantages of low transport costs, reliability, speed, and bulk capacity generated high savings over any plausible alternative.[43]

While Mexico's rail network constituted an essential precondition for the waves of technology imports that followed, it did relatively little to directly stimulate local technological capabilities. First, freight costs remained a subject of constant concern for mineral refiners and new industrialists. Intensely preoccupied with production costs, plant managers wrote frequently to railroad officers and government officials seeking redress from what they saw as unnecessarily high rates.[44] Off the rail grid, transport costs would remain high until roads and the gasoline engine pushed into Mexico's more remote regions after the 1920s. At the height of the railway age, mules and *arrieros* remained essential to get goods to and from rail terminals. Some five thousand mules worked constantly at the turn of the century, for instance, on the sixty-mile trail between the Jesus María mines of Chihuahua and the nearest railroad terminal, at sixty dollars per ton transported, in a scene replicated across the country.[45] Freight rates continued to increase the cost of adopting new machinery in Mexico by between 20 and 50 percent.[46] This was also the case for shipping goods from farm and village and mine and factory to rail stations in every state of the country. A large percentage of the national population still lay beyond the reach of Mexico's new railroad grid.

Second, although Mexico's rail network generated a massive demand for materials as well as human expertise, demand did little to stimulate the development of local, Mexican supplies. Nearly all inputs were imported, "from individual nails to complete stations."[47] Steel rails, for instance, were the most basic component of the vast capital equipment needs of the rail system, and until 1903 every rail extending roughly sixteen thousand kilometers came from iron and steel plants in the United States or Britain. Over just four years, the Ferrocarril Central Mexicano alone imported over one hundred thousand metric tons of rails. Even after Mexico's first steel mill, the Fundidora Monterrey, began domestic production of rails in 1903, imports continued to supply between 70 and 90 percent of demand, in part because of significant quality advantages over the Fundidora's products.[48] In 1908, railroad companies imported another one hundred thousand metric tons of rails with a price tag of 3.5 million dollars.[49] Locomotives lay at the other end of the technical spectrum, at about 10,000 dollars per engine. US manufacturers like the Baldwin Works in Philadelphia sent nearly 1,300 engines to Mexico between 1870 and 1910, valued at over 13 million dollars, more than four-fifths of Mexico's total locomotive imports.[50] Steel rails and locomotives together accounted for 60 percent of all railroad inputs, the rest comprising rolling stock, parts, and diverse machines and tools, also imported.

The technological requirements for constructing and operating a national rail system included not only capital equipment like rails and locomotives but also the personnel who conceived, planned, engineered, constructed, managed, repaired, and operated the system. Nearly all these, to a man, were "imported" from the North Atlantic by the companies that received government concessions. Though foreign workers made up just 10 percent of all railway workers (and there were twenty-six thousand employed by the Mexican National alone in 1910), they held nearly all managerial and skilled positions.[51] Railroads offered Mexican engineers, mechanics, and skilled workers only limited opportunities for technological learning. There are some very modest signs of new opportunities in the last years of the Porfiriato. A few Mexicans begin to appear as engineers, firemen, brakemen, and machinists on the major rail lines, and the Gran Liga Mexicana de Empleados de Ferrocarriles, established in 1903, represented the interests of an increasingly skilled group of Mexican rail workers.[52] The repair workshops (*talleres*) of the major railroad companies offered perhaps the most promising venue for technological learning; some thirty-nine were scattered along the major trunk lines from Chihuahua to the Yucatan, together employing thousands of workers. All worked to repair equipment, from rolling stock to switches, and some—like the Central's well-equipped facility at Aguascalientes—assembled cargo cars from wheels, axles, and other materials shipped from the United States.[53] Although the larger workshops were fully equipped with foundries, furnaces, blacksmith's forges, lathes, and other metalworking machines, there is little indication that Mexican workers acquired experience that might have translated into independent technical capabilities. On one hand, as Guillermo Guajardo has argued, the workshops proved a space in which Mexican railroad workers learned new, industrial work habits along with opportunities to acquire more specific forms of technical knowledge and expertise. On the other hand, these opportunities do not appear to have led to a sustained accumulation of technical skills by railroad workers as a group. Shop-floor opportunities were not supported by effective formal training programs, skilled workers enjoyed few interactions with engineers, and they faced regular obstacles in their relations with US managers and mechanics.[54] Even after nationalization of major rail lines in 1907, Mexico's rail network remained largely an extension of a North American system, and what skills accumulated to local workers in the workshops were largely dispersed during the revolutionary years of 1910–20. Productivity in the workshops remained extremely low in the 1920s. In the end, neither the railroad workshops nor independent metal factories in Mexico would provide a major source for railroad inputs beyond steel rails until the 1950s.

Mexico's railroads were not, however, classic economic enclaves. Employing many thousands of Mexican laborers, at wages generally higher than those available in other sectors, railroads decisively broadened markets for consumer goods throughout the country and contributed significant savings in transport costs over the four-hoofed alternative. Railroads were indispensable to Mexico's late-century economic growth because they provided the skeletal infrastructure for a national economy and an essential requisite for technology imports and thus economic growth. But the railroad companies spent nearly 40 percent of their operating costs on foreign technology inputs through this period, and in 1910 alone—long after the completion of the major trunk lines—imported supplies still totaled 21.4 million pesos, or over 10 percent of Mexico's total import bill for that year.[55] In other words, railroads' backward linkages were meager: their demand for steel rails, freight cars, fuel, parts, and (perhaps most critically) human expertise did not stimulate substantial investment in supplying those goods within the country.

POWER

High costs also long undermined the adoption of steam power in Mexico. First, investors faced the high cost of purchasing the machine itself, typically no less than that of building a water mill in the early nineteenth century.[56] Second, until railroads dramatically lowered transport costs, Mexico's poor roads and rugged geography stymied most efforts to introduce heavy iron machinery into production centers within the Meseta Central. Third, steam technology required skilled workers to install, operate, and maintain, and skilled labor was perennially scarce and expensive. Together, these three factors posed high barriers to the adoption of steam power until the 1870s or after. They help explain why fully a fourth of Mexico's steam power was located in the Yucatan, within a short distance of ocean ports. Thereafter, however, each of these barriers fell substantially. Capital flowed quickly into Mexican markets while manufacturing conditions in the North Atlantic pushed steam engine prices to only a tenth of earlier levels.[57] Mexico's new railroads carried heavy machinery to previously remote regions, and thousands of young engineers and skilled workers from the North Atlantic sought employment opportunities in Mexico.

As a result, Mexican firms began importing large numbers of steam engines from the United States and Britain. Imports rose tenfold from the 1870s to the 1880s, tripled into the 1890s, and doubled again by the first decade of the twentieth century. Mining and mineral-refining operations purchased 40 percent or more of all stationary steam engines. By the turn of the century, however, adoption by manufacturing firms was not far behind, at roughly 30 percent of the total, with the remainder in commercial agriculture.[58] Mexico's textile mills increasingly used steam power in some capacity, although only about a fifth used steam alone for motive power, and these were the smallest among the hundred or so in Mexico by 1890.[59] Dependable water power, when available, remained cheaper than steam in Mexico's fuel-scarce environment. By 1900, however, most new manufacturing plants throughout the country powered their machinery with steam, a few in con-

junction with hydropower and increasingly with electricity. Many hacendados also invested in steam power to turn grain mills and sugar *ingenios,* or to
pump water for irrigation, although many grain mills remained tied to
hydropower, like four of the six largest mills in the Chalco district south of
Mexico City.[60] All told, Mexican firms imported something on the order of
twelve thousand new steam engines between 1870 and 1910, generating an
estimated aggregate capacity of about 577,000 horsepower.[61]

Yet the diffusion of steam power in Mexico came only at the very end of
the global steam age. By the last decade of the century, electricity had slowly
begun to replace water and steam as the principal source of motive power in
the Mexican economy, as it did throughout the North Atlantic. Investors
brought electricity first to a few Mexican mines, factories, and cities in the
late 1880s, and its reach slowly spread as companies installed their own coal-
fired electrical generating plants, initially to power isolated pieces of machinery.[62] In 1893, the Santa Ana mine of San Luis Potosí became the first to use
electric power for both power and lighting; two years later, the Hercules
textile mill in Querétaro connected its machinery to electric power, only a
few years after the inauguration of electrical power in the United States.[63]
Over the next fifteen years new hydroelectric companies like the Mexican
Light and Power Company, the Guanajuato Power and Electric Company,
the Northern Mexican Power Company, and the Compañía Hidroeléctrica
e Irrigadora de Chapala emerged to provide regional electrical power.[64]
Electricity carried multiple advantages. Most importantly, it cut power costs
by 50 percent or more over both hydropower and steam.[65] This meant lower
production costs as well as the ability to supply greater amounts of power to
large-scale production machinery. Electricity also freed production from the
locational constraints of water and steam: fractional electric motors could be
placed nearly anywhere at mine sites, refineries, or in factories. For both reasons, electricity was an absolute prerequisite for adopting many of the new
production technologies of the late nineteenth and early twentieth century,
from the powerful tube mills necessary for cyanide reduction in gold and
silver mining to the hundreds of sewing machines within new clothing factories. Electricity enabled mines and manufacturing plants to reorganize
production processes to increase efficiencies; it also enabled relatively smaller
firms to adopt mechanical power for the first time, partially countering the
late-century trend toward increasing industrial concentration. By 1910, electrical machinery of all sorts had captured over 28 percent of Mexico's
machinery imports. Fuel oil and gasoline engines also began to capture some

of the power demand of Mexican industry, although the major expansion of domestic petroleum production did not come until 1908–9, and gas engines were not commonplace in transport or in production until after the Revolution.

But it was steam that primarily powered Mexico's early adoption of mechanized, industrial-scale production in mining, manufacturing, and agriculture in the late nineteenth century. Steam provided the critical transition between the limitations of animate and water power—dominant before 1870—and the widening possibilities of electrical power into the twentieth century. Yet despite the dramatic late-century adoption of steam power, its impact on mechanization and technological capabilities remained limited, as we will see in chapter 7. The dominant story of steam power in nineteenth-century Mexico is one of delayed adoption before 1870 and constrained diffusion thereafter. The costs of steam power remained relatively high in Mexico because of the high cost of fuel in an environment without abundant wood or coal. Miners and manufacturers complained bitterly, and only widespread access to electrical power would solve this long-standing obstacle to the adoption of mechanized production.

IRON

Mexico's capacity to produce iron and to manufacture iron tools and machine parts had been virtually nonexistent through the first half of the century, and imports of iron and iron manufactures also remained small. There was simply not sufficient economic demand to generate significant investment in either local metalworking capabilities or high-priced imports. By the late 1860s, however, the first stirrings of new investment in the Mexican economy began to push demand for iron and steel manufactures upward. Absent a domestic capacity to produce iron or steel, or to manufacture structural forms, machine parts, and tools, investors imported nearly all that they needed. Mexico's imports of iron and steel manufactures rose rapidly through the next decades, at 11 percent yearly, faster, in fact, than any other import class in Mexico's foreign trade.

Rising demand also began to stimulate new investments in Mexico that would establish a modest but important iron and steel sector by 1900. Before midcentury, Mexico's blacksmiths worked imported iron, or small quantities of low-grade local material. Mexico's first iron foundries dated from about midcentury, clustered around iron deposits in Hidalgo, Jalisco, and Puebla, producing for local blacksmiths. Several of these expanded gradually through the 1860s and 1870s, installing the first furnaces to produce pig iron and utilizing water or steam power to run their forges. The Fundición de Apulco in Hidalgo was likely the largest of these, although the evidence is thin. Its blast furnace (*alto horno*) produced about two tons of pig weekly in the mid-1860s under the management of one Emilio Boudoüin, a civil engineer from France.[66] Also in Hidalgo were several foundries operated by the Sres. Jecker & Compañía, who claimed their own steel process, protected by a 1859 patent.[67] Ricardo Honey, a Cornish miner who arrived in Pachuca in the 1860s at age twenty-two, began investing in Hidalgo's iron foundries by the 1880s. He acquired the Apulco foundry and several others, and by the turn of the century controlled at least eight, including the Apulco, Encarnación, San Miguel, Comanja, Guadalupe, and Los Reyes foundries.[68] By 1883 the Piedra Azul ironworks near Durango also boasted a blast furnace with a daily capacity of nearly three metric tons.[69] Some of these early foundries produced iron in traditional catalan forges, or pig iron (*arrabio*) in new blast furnaces. Some produced basic forms like bars, rods, or sheets in furnaces and rolling mills. Most of the business for finished iron came in pieces for balconies and parts for construction or carriage work. Some, however, produced cast parts for machines or simple tools and implements, and a few could produce small amounts of cast steel in their forges, primarily for edge tools.

Rising domestic demand for iron and steel manufactures continued to induce investment in new foundries and forges through the 1890s. One report noted between twenty and twenty-five foundries in 1903, another reported thirty-nine in 1905.[70] Most of these were small operations, producing pig and simple metal forms for local or regional consumers, often for decorative work. But large-scale foundries also began to appear around the turn of the century. Best known is the Compañía Fundidora de Fierro y Acero de México, S.A. (the Fundidora Monterrey), established in 1903 as a massive, fully integrated steel plant that included blast furnaces, open-hearth furnaces, a Bessemer converter, and rolling mills—the first integrated steel plant in Latin America.[71] Though extraordinary in its scale and sophistication, the Fundidora was not as unique as many historians have suggested.[72] The Consolidated Rolling Mills and Foundries Company (La Consolidada) bought pig iron from the Fundidora and produced steel alloys and castings. The Compañía Industrial Mexicana, in Chihuahua, produced wrought iron and some steel and bronze, specializing in valves, and holding a patent for a valve design.[73] The Fundición de Fierro y Bronce in Aguascalientes produced pumps and some agricultural machinery. The Monterrey Foundry and Machine Company produced cast machine parts and worked toward manufacturing steam engines. Ricardo Honey headed the Compañía Nacional Mexicana de Hierro y Acero, which controlled his iron foundries in Hidalgo. And the Fabrica de Clavos de Alambre de Monterrey, S.A., made nails using imported wire, as did a company in Veracruz.[74]

Most of the evidence we have regarding Mexico's iron and steel capabilities during this period is anecdotal and still very limited. We know, for instance, that the major railway companies established workshops to repair rolling equipment and to manufacture basic metal parts, most notably at the Mexican Central's *taller* in Aguascalientes and the International Railroad's facilities in Ciudad Porfirio Díaz (now Piedras Negras).[75] The larger mining companies also had their own metal shops, employing blacksmiths capable of skilled work to manufacture replacement parts and repair machinery. Las Minas de Tajo in Sinaloa boasted "an iron foundry annexed to the workshop, with the capacity to produce all kinds of machinery parts up to a weight of two tons," while the El Oro mines in Michoacan soon gave up on importing expensive metal lining plates for their tube mills and began manufacturing their own to specifications that met local conditions.[76] The diffusion of cyaniding plants after 1900 created a large new demand for huge steel tanks that some of Mexico's newer iron and steel mills could supply.[77] The federal government also ran its own metal foundry to produce armaments at its facilities in the Ciudadela, in Mexico City. By the late 1880s it was producing metallic shells for the army's Remington and Mauser rifles and cannon barrels for its artillery, with a reputation, apparently, for the "skill and dexterity of [its] operatives."[78] A number of the smaller or midsized firms, including the Apulco foundry in Hidalgo, produced structural shapes as well as parts and sometimes, apparently, full machines for Mexican industries. The Apulco foundry, for instance, advertised "cast iron and machinery parts of all kinds and sizes, piping, agricultural implements, columns, sledges for mines, pins for cars, bars, etc., etc., etc."[79] Several other firms made agricultural implements and machines, such as the sugar mill recently on display in the courtyard museum of the Palacio de Cortés in Cuernavaca, manufactured at the Fábrica Nacional de Maquinaria Emeterio Garza, which specialized in "general machinery for agriculture and industry."[80] As early as 1893 *El Comerciante Mexicano* reported that the American-managed Monterrey Foundry and Machine Company produced large metal parts for new mining equipment, as well as several horizontal steam engines of between twenty and twenty-five horsepower each, and boilers.[81] More intriguing are scattered reports that other firms developed specialized machine construction capabilities. The Compañía Industrial Mexicana apparently had the capacity by 1910 to manufacture machines "of every description" for mining and commercial agriculture, including, reportedly, Corliss steam engines. Their "machinists, pattern makers, and skilled labor" were all Mexican, showing "the most remarkable aptitude for the intricacies of mechanical work."[82] To the south, in Torreón, "Los Talleres de Hornos" boasted a general machine workshop to repair and build machinery, complete with an eight-hundred-pound steam-driven forging hammer and milling machine. All their workers were reportedly "born in the area . . . instructed and trained by the young business owner D. Claudio Juan Martínez."[83]

Among those firms with significant metallurgical and machine-building capabilities, the Fundición de Sinaloa stood out. Established in Mazatlán in the mid-1870s under the direction of Alejandro Loubet, a French-trained engineer, and partly financed by Joaquín Redo, a Sinaloan sugar planter and entrepreneur, the Fundición developed the capacity to manufacture steam engines, boilers, stone crushers, air compressors, and other machinery for regional mining and sugar-refining firms (figure 10).[84] By the early 1880s the company had manufactured the first steam engines and boilers ever made in Mexico, successfully imitating foreign designs. Although several other foundries managed or attempted to manufacture machinery, the Fundición de Sinaloa represents the only sustained successful effort. Between 1891 and 1906 it manufactured at least 243 steam engines and boilers, averaging about forty horsepower each (table 2).[85] This early success, noted *El Minero Mexicano,* meant that "the state of Sinaloa and its surrounding areas will have no need to resort to the United States with regard to machinery."[86]

However, the combined production of all these foundries and machine shops—including the massive Fundidora Monterrey—remained relatively small through the period, barely a percentage point or two of total imported machinery. Although *The Mexican Year Book* noted in 1912 that "iron foundries are numerous in the Republic" and that some were beginning to produce "finished articles of the highest grade and character," *numerous* is a relative term.[87] There were likely no more than several dozen iron foundries in the country, and most were small operations with just a handful of employees. If the Fundidora Monterrey produced about 50,000 metric tons of pig iron yearly by 1910 (with an installed capacity of at least 110,000 tons), the

FIGURE 10. Horizontal double-acting cylinder steam engine manufactured by the Fundición de Sinaloa. Reproduced courtesy of the Archivo General de la Nación, with special thanks to Miguel Angel Aviles-Galan.

TABLE 2 Steam Engines and Boilers Manufactured by the Fundición de Sinaloa, by Sector of Final Sales, 1891–1906

Sector	Number	Total hp	Av. hp	% hp
Mining	48	2,313	48	24
Industry	56	2,372	42	24
Agriculture	27	1,247	46	13
Maritime	5	139	28	1
Warehouse	34	1,206	35	12
Navy	39	1,562	40	16
Export	3	169	56	2
Not elsewhere specified	31	793	26	8
Total	243	9,801	40	100

SOURCE: Derived from Arturo Carillo Rojas, *Los caballos de vapor: El imperio de las máquinas durante el cañedismo* (Culiacán, Sinaloa: Colegio de Bachilleres del Estado de Sinaloa, 1998), 177–78; also Miguel Angel Aviles-Galan, "'A Todo Vapor': Mechanisation in Porfirian Mexico Steam Power and Machine Building, 1891–1906" (PhD diss., University of British Columbia, 2010).

remaining foundries apparently only matched this quantity, for a national total of roughly 100,000 metric tons or so of iron per year.[88] This represented only a small fraction of Mexico's imported iron and steel, and domestic products could not compete with imports on a quality basis.[89] The domestic price for pig iron stood around thirteen dollars per ton in 1907, which would place the annual value of national iron production at about 1,300,000 dollars, or not quite 5 percent the value of Mexico's total imports of iron and steel manufactures.[90] Mexico would remain heavily dependent on iron and steel imports for everything from simple sheets, bars, plates, beams, wire, and nails to tools and diverse machinery well into the twentieth century.

. . .

Mexico's imports of machinery and other hardware provide one measure of the level, growth, and direction of total fixed capital investment. Imported hardware constituted the physical infrastructure for the country's rapidly expanding productive capacity in mining, agriculture, and manufacturing because domestic firms could not supply local needs. From iron and steel forms to nails, tools, sewing machines, and complex factory machineries, imports reshaped both production and working lives across the economy. New machinery combined with similarly large imports of new knowledge embodied in print and in people to constitute a veritable flood of technology imports. Rapid adoption and diffusion of the core technologies of the first industrial revolution after 1870—railroads, steam power, and iron and steel production—provided crucial elements of this experience, which spread rapidly across much of Mexico's economic landscape. These and other imported technologies underwrote Mexico's early and tentative transition from a labor- to a capital-intensive economy and made possible the rapid expansion of productivity and productive capacity. Technology imports yielded an early process of import substitution in consumer goods (like textiles, clothing, some processed foods, cigarettes, matches, shoes, etc.) and in some intermediate inputs (like cement and, to a much more limited extent, iron and steel products).

The rapid and widespread adoption of imported technologies between 1870 and 1910 demonstrates the relative ease with which investors and entrepreneurs could pursue a developmentalist vision of material progress. With the critical support of imported expertise, embodied in thousands of foreign engineers and mechanics, they navigated the obstacles to adoption and acquired the capabilities necessary to install and operate new technologies that were readily available in the North Atlantic. The next section of this book turns to three case studies that provide more detailed portrayals of what adoption looked like on the ground. Each case represents a larger class of technologies. Sewing machines stand in for small-scale, multipurpose product technologies; automated glass bottle machinery represents large, complex, factory-scale production systems; and the cyanide process for separating gold and silver illustrates the challenges facing a broader set of resource processing technologies. As we have noted with railroads, steam, and iron, however, these three case studies also illustrate the contrast between relatively rapid adoption and significant limits to the ways in which adoption stimulated local technological capabilities—as well as exceptional experiences of technological learning. After looking at the three cases, we will return to examine those limits more closely in chapters 7 and 8.

PART TWO

Case Studies

FOUR

Sewing Machines

IN THE SUMMER OF 1902, Mexico City's *Diario del Hogar* published a poem by Luis Tablada, written specially for the newspaper's semiregular publication of cultural pieces. As the poem begins, the father of a working-class family has just died. The mother, despairing of feeding their young baby, comes across an old sewing machine in her husband's workshop, "as if provided by God." As "the wheel on its axis spun," she sees her way to remunerative employment and soon can buy food in the market, "which her work had found." Tablada ends by addressing the machine itself, which has now taken the place of the father in the home, providing "to the poor woman / Bread, help, and protection / Blessed be your invention / Oh sewing machine!"[1] Others, however, were not so ready to give their blessing. Labor activists also held up the widowed mother with young children, forced to turn to the sewing machine to survive but, in their view, still unable to "earn enough to buy bad food, to have dismal housing, or to dress with decency." The "unhappy women" at sewing machines worked long hours just to earn a "paltry salary; but what work! . . . Few jobs are more contrary to a worker's health."[2]

Whether the sewing machine was a blessing or curse, two generations earlier all needlework was done by hand; peasant and townsperson and elite alike wore clothing either home-stitched, sewn by local tailors, or imported as a luxury good from the United States or Europe, where it too had been stitched by hand. Yet through the second half of the nineteenth century sewing machines swept across Mexico, as they did worldwide. What began as a trickle in the 1860s soon became an accelerating stream of imports. Manufacturers in the United States alone shipped 10.3 million dollars' worth of machines to Mexico between 1870 and 1910. Adding imports from Britain and Germany, total machines exceeded 325,000 individual units. By 1910 it was possible that nearly one in every seven Mexican households owned a machine. By then, clothing imports had fallen sharply, hand-stitched clothing was increasingly exceptional, and Mexicans at most social levels increasingly bought and wore ready-made clothing, most of it now sewn domestically. This early expansion of mechanized clothing production created new opportunities for employment and enterprise and moved more and more women into low-paid workshop and factory jobs at the same time that it squeezed out (but never entirely displaced) both home production and imported apparel.

From the 1870s into the early twentieth century, economic growth provided just enough disposable income for many in Mexico's slowly expanding middle and working classes to commit monthly payments of ten pesos, while foreign companies like Singer aggressively marketed their new products. As a result, tens of thousands of Mexican women (and fewer men) acquired machines and integrated machine sewing and ready-made clothing into their economic and cultural lives. The sewing machine did not cause social change. Agency lay in the interests and efforts of those in Mexico who bought machines and in the foreign companies that marketed them. Social change made widespread adoption possible, and with adoption came further social change. Adoption of mechanized sewing was not frictionless, however, and both sellers and consumers had to navigate obstacles in the new Mexican context. These included Mexico's social geography, its still developing transportation system, its small and fragile consumer markets, and, at times, local environmental conditions. Nevertheless, adoption proceeded nearly as quickly as household incomes would allow, and the machines soon made possible the first generation of Mexico's ready-made clothing industry.

Across the country, women young and old learned quickly to operate sewing machines, sometimes instructed by sewing machine company agents, sometimes by local women hired by those companies or by their employers in workshops and factories, and often by neighbors and relatives in their homes. But local assimilation of the technological capabilities associated with sewing machines proved substantially more difficult. Like many product technologies, sewing machines were a black box: relatively easy to operate but more difficult to troubleshoot, repair, or replicate in whole or in part. Acquiring assistance and spare parts could stall operation and delay repairs, especially for users in rural towns and villages. No domestic firm appeared until the second half of the twentieth century to produce parts and supplies for the machine, from its complex inner workings to assorted bobbins, spools, finely wound thread, and needles. For users in Mexico's cities, access to expertise, parts, and new machines proved relatively easy through foreign agents. Furthermore, the government's policy of duty-free machine imports offered few incentives to develop local capacities. As a result, it proved cheaper to continue importing machines, parts, and supplies from the United States and Europe. As with other examples of small-scale, multiuse technologies, widespread adoption did not generate substantial opportunities for backward linkages that might have stimulated more extensive technological learning and capabilities.

. . .

During the last decades of the nineteenth century hundreds of young men came to Mexico and other Latin American nations from the United States and Europe with a particular mission. They were dressed neatly and conservatively and traveled on a budget from town to town, often on foot. They were neither missionaries nor government agents but sewing machine salesmen, and from Mexico's largest cities to small mestizo towns like San José de Gracia in Michoacán and even more distant mining camps they appeared perhaps as often as the priest, for whom children sometimes mistook them.[3] These salesmen were, as the Singer Sewing Machine Company boasted, "peacefully working to conquer the world."[4]

This was just the image that the foreign sewing machine companies wanted to cultivate: the sewing machine as the very symbol of a modern, productive people, and—because of its scale and relative affordability—of an industrial and democratic spirit within reach of both urban and rural households. In Argentina as early as 1868 President Domingo Sarmiento was captivated by just this image as he wrote of "that republican spirit; that feeling of government itself; the sewing machine that makes its sweet trick-track sound in every village of the civilized world."[5] The whirring and clicking of the machine often elicited more comments than the machine's productivity or its often elegant design. In 1874, the editor of Mexico's *El Monitor Repúblicano* described a governor's speech as "how a Singer sewing machine sings," and "the machine sang" to the destitute mother in Luis Tablada's poem.[6] The distinctive sound of the pedal-driven sewing machine seemed to be everywhere to many travelers in Mexico, heard during the lull of afternoon siestas or even after midnight before major fiestas.[7]

Between 1850 and 1900 the sewing machine galvanized attention across the globe. Karl Marx famously saw in its work forces that impoverished workers and deepened class conflict. "The fearful increase of death from starvation during the last ten years in London," he argued, "runs parallel with the extension of machine sewing."[8] In Mexico, newspapers like *El Socialista* and *La Convención Radical Obrera* would pick up this argument as they drew attention to the plight of poorly paid female clothing workers.[9] In stark contrast, the media organs of the expanding capitalist class viewed this first, mass-produced consumer durable quite differently. *Godey's Lady's Book* argued that this "Queen of Inventions" would "effectively banish ragged and unclad humanity from every class," while the *New York Times* asserted that it was the "best boon to woman in the nineteenth century."[10] And in Mexico, poems, articles, and advertisements sang its praise. *El Correo de Chihuahua* described women's sewing machine labor as "almost intellectual, guiding the cloth with minimum effort . . . finding here their future, and saved from the horrors of misery."[11] The sewing machine either threatened to subordinate or promised to liberate women. All agreed its impact was revolutionary.

From the perspective of new manufacturing companies in England, Germany, and especially the United States, the global diffusion of the sewing machine might be seen as an imperialist project. These companies, Singer foremost among them, worked to identify, capture, control, and profit from newly opened foreign markets. Singer, the world's first true multinational firm, pushed global diffusion during the decades before the First World War and commanded a massive 90 percent market share outside the Western Hemisphere.[12] For investors and consumers, from industrialists to tailors and housewives across the social spectrum, the machine was an emblem of the modern, mechanized, North Atlantic world as well as a novel tool to enhance productivity, transform work, and generate income. Estimates for the labor savings generated by machine over hand sewing in the late nineteenth century are fairly uniform: the machine allowed a labor savings of between 70 and 90 percent over hand methods, an extraordinary leap in productivity over the previous state of the art.[13] As the sewing machine spread globally it undermined but did not wholly eliminate hand-stitching trades and provided a new means by which managers in the clothing business could extend control over women's labor through direct employment in workshops as well as through outworking arrangements. While women's "sweated" labor antedated the machine's introduction, the sewing machine enabled its survival and expansion through the twentieth century.[14]

Mexico's early history with the sewing machine was a globally shared one. Once commercial production of the machine began in the 1850s, it found ready consumers in the United States, Britain, and parts of continental Europe. As machine prices dropped over the following decades and the major manufacturing companies—led by Singer—introduced installment plans and aggressive marketing strategies, global markets expanded exponentially. The United States, Britain, France, Germany, Russia, Central Europe, Japan, Latin America, India, and the Middle East all witnessed the rapid, trans-formative, and often socially dislocative adoption of sewing machines.[15]

. . .

Mexico's first sewing machine was probably brought into the country some-time in the mid-1850s, unloaded on the docks of Veracruz, and carried inland by mule or oxen.[16] By the early 1860s manufacturers in the United States were shipping machines to retail stores in Mexico City. Advertisements taken by hardware and general stores for sewing machines began appearing with fre-quency in the mid-1860s.[17] Singer, for instance, initially worked through an exclusive sales agreement with the commercial outlet of Reichmann and Holder, which would soon become the famous hardware retailer Roberto Böker y Compañía. Also in Mexico City, G. Lohse y Compañía sold La Nueva Americana machines, while the Uhink y Compañía agency at No. 3 Calle de Ocampo advertised itself as "the only agency for the whole Republic with the excellent and legitimate Horve [sic] sewing machines, of the famous ELIAS HORVE JUNIOR [sic], inventor of the sewing machine."[18] In Puebla, the Gran Ciudad de Londres store served as an early Singer agency, and sewing machine sales offered a major new market for retail outlets in provincial cities across the country; in Mexico City, they underwrote Roberto Böker's rapid expansion into the city's most important commercial establish-ment.[19] Sewing machine sales surged nationwide, and as early as 1880, Matías Romero, Mexico's secretary of finance, could write (with only modest exag-geration), "It can be assured . . . there is not a family in Mexico, whose circumstances permit them the expense of a sewing machine, which does not use one."[20]

Intense competition dominated sales markets as firms like Singer, Wheeler & Wilson, New Howe, Standard, Union, Grover & Baker, Davis, Domestic, Household, White, and others fought aggressively for shares of the Mexican market.[21] They advertised widely, vied for brand and trademark recognition, and pushed their machines through networks of brokers and sales agents (figure 11). "Probably every sewing machine manufactory in the world has

FIGURE 11. Wheeler & Wilson Sewing Machine advertisement, *La Sociedad*, July 30, 1865.

agents in Mexico," reported one salesman.[22] Most of these were American, but German and some British firms also competed vigorously. The German firms, like the British and smaller American manufacturers, marketed their machines through existing local commercial outlets, and German and British machines held nearly a quarter of the Mexican market around the turn of the century.[23]

Early on, however, the Singer Company moved to directly control the marketing and sales of its machines worldwide. In 1882, they established a central office in Mexico City with regional offices and sales agents throughout the country. Men like C. W. Whittemore, L. O. Harnecker, and R. L. Gregory built the company's central office capacity over several decades and eventually established over a dozen regional offices throughout the republic. These branches oversaw dozens of subagencies and hundreds of salesrooms and traveling salesmen both in urban districts and across the countryside.[24] Singer's agents pushed their machines in cities and towns and "through all the routes of rural geography," "flitting in and out of house after house," often (though not always) doing a "thriving business."[25]

By 1887 Singer's agent in Mexico City was pushing the central office in New York to increase exports, as "all the men in the territory [are] howling for machines."[26] A year later the Mexico City manager reported that the growth of the business was "getting to be enormous and I am getting afraid of it."[27] By the early 1890s, however, the peak of this hypercompetitive phase had passed—undercut by extended drought in Mexico and the Atlantic recession of 1892–93—leaving the Singer Company with a dominant market share, in large part due to its tightly controlled system of agencies and sales agents. Yet none of the firms selling in Mexico had much trouble finding customers and moving their inventory, as their agents throughout the country continued to turn over dozens of units each month.[28] By 1902 Singer boasted over five hundred salesrooms in Mexico and an extensive system of regional offices, agents, and salesmen. Singer's advertisements were no longer those of one firm among many but dominated newspapers like *El Pais, El Imparcial,* and *Diario del Hogar,* reflecting a market share of at least 75 percent. Singer's success in Mexico generated a public fascination with the company and its founder, and local papers published pieces about Singer's wife, his children, and his fortune.[29]

By the early 1870s Mexico's annual sewing machine imports had already reached about 52,000 dollars annually.[30] Over the next decade machine imports grew rapidly, expanding eightfold and reaching an early peak of over 400,000 dollars annually by 1882. The competitive nature of this period is evident in the Singer Company's internal correspondence; by 1879 Singer's New York office pushed its Mexican agents to redouble their efforts, as imports from other companies were "exploding."[31] The sewing machine market weakened briefly from 1882 to 1885, coinciding with sharply reduced sales of sewing machines throughout the world, and the 1882 sales levels were not reached again until about 1901.[32] Imports then redoubled quickly, reaching a prerevolutionary annual peak at just over 1 million dollars in 1907. By then Mexico furnished the fourth-largest market for sewing machines manufactured in the United States, after Britain, Germany, and Australia.[33]

How many sewing machines were shipped to Mexico before 1910? Trade records tell us only import values, not the number of units, so we have to divide import values—totaling about 14 million dollars between 1870 and 1910—by machine prices to get unit numbers. Through the 1870s, the average unit price of new machines lay in the seventy- to ninety-dollar range.[34] In 1877–78, however, the US patent pool that controlled sewing machine technology expired just as manufacturing firms were producing ever more machines, more efficiently, and unit prices fell rapidly. By 1892, reports on the value and quantum of total machine sales from several of Singer's regional offices in Mexico yield average prices ranging from twenty-five to forty dollars.[35]

Affordability was bolstered by new payment plans. Led by Singer's innovative marketing strategies, most companies used the hire-purchase or installment plan. This typically required ten to fifteen pesos up front and subsequent monthly payments of ten pesos, which incorporated an implicit interest rate. In Singer's contracts, full legal ownership of the machine transferred to the customer only with the final installment, although customers did not always understand this nuance—or sought to take advantage of it by reselling or pawning the machines before they were fully paid for.[36] Sewing machines could be even more affordable in secondary markets. Advertisements for used machines appeared with frequency in Mexico City's daily newspapers, with prices running well below those for new machines, often between twenty and fifty pesos by the 1880s. One early advertisement asked seventy-five pesos for a Singer machine "in good condition," noting that "you can see it at No. 1034 Espíritu Santo at any hour of the day."[37] Secondhand machines could also be found in Mexico City's pawnshops, at similarly low prices.[38]

If households, workshops, and factories spent 14 million dollars on sewing machines between 1870 and 1910, then Mexico imported at least 328,000 individual sewing machines.[39] Annual import levels grew rapidly from the 1860s to an early peak in 1882–83, coinciding with a generalized boom in capital equipment investments in those years. After a short and sharp decline through 1886, steady growth resumed and became especially steep between 1900 and 1907. If the average household in Mexico contained five people, then the roughly 328,000 machines meant that one in every seven households could boast one, or 2.6 percent of the national population.[40] Globally, no country matched the rate of diffusion in the United States, where 10 percent of the population owned machines by 1875. Only Great Britain and Australia reached this level before the First World War, and only just.[41] By 1914 most European countries fell somewhere in the 4 to 7 percent diffusion range, with Italy and Russia just below. Under the Mexican 2.6 percent diffusion level lay the Ottoman Empire and the Balkans, which reached 1.5 percent by 1910, and the Philippines, which crossed the 2 percent threshold in 1917. Further below Mexico lay India, where fewer than 1 percent of all households could have had machines in 1916.

Where did roughly 328,000 sewing machines go? Who bought and used these machines, and in what contexts? Across the world, sewing machine consumers fell in two general categories. First, men and especially women bought the majority of sewing machines for home use. Some of these were purchased by wealthy upper-middle-class families, but most went to middle- and working-class homes as investments to boost income through work as independent tailors or seamstresses or, more commonly, through paid outwork in the garment industry. Second, investors in small to midsized workshops and new, larger clothing factories purchased new sewing machines by the dozen. In most countries, household purchases constituted the majority of all sales, perhaps up to 90 percent, with the rest going to centralized workshops and factories.[42]

In Mexico, women dominated the household sewing machine market and constituted the largest share of overall demand. Sewing machine advertisements in Mexico as elsewhere consistently identified women as the primary users of new machines across a range of socioeconomic levels (recall figure 11). Among Mexico's economic elite, however, family machines were relatively rare: "Sewing machines are everywhere . . . [in Mexico, but] more commonly in the poor man's hut than in the rich man's mansion," noted one observer in 1892.[43] Yet many wealthy homes and haciendas possessed a machine, typically used, however, by hired help. In the *casa grande* of one elegant hacienda near Aguascalientes, the "yankee sewing machine" that a visitor observed in the sewing room was likely used by the *empleada*.[44] This was not always the case, however, and an anonymous Mexican photographer captured an older gentleman in tie and hat quietly working at a machine set just outside the door to his home (figure 12).

Advertisements for sewing machines appeared regularly in nearly every newspaper in Mexico, outnumbering those for any other single product

FIGURE 12. "Lino con su máquina." Reproduced with permission from Ricardo Espinosa.

except patent medicines. The principal audience for newspapers like *Diario del Hogar*, "periódico de las familias," was the middle class.[45] At the upper end, this urban social group included the wife of the Poblano artist Daniel Dávila (1843–1924), painted daydreaming at her sewing machine in his evocative *Soñando*.[46] Professional middle-class families often contracted out sewing (or bought ready-made clothing in the city's new department stores). Many, however, purchased sewing machines for family use or to supplement household income. Yet the number of urban professionals, managers, affluent shopkeepers and artisans, and public sector employees made up a relatively small percentage of the national population. Instead, the principal middle-class market for sewing machines reached further down the social scale. These consumers—"whose circumstances permit the expense"—could be found more broadly dispersed across the socioeconomic landscape: in Mexico's cities, in provincial towns, in mining camps, and in rural villages.[47]

Just how large was this market, and how far down the socioeconomic pyramid of Mexican society did sewing machine consumption reach? A household's ability to save at least ten pesos monthly constituted the critical threshold. In Mexico City, the minimum cost of living around the turn of the century was just over three pesos weekly.[48] Households typically pooled money from multiple earners to support living expenses, including investment in productive capital like the sewing machine. Assuming a three-peso weekly subsistence cost of living, any household with an aggregate income just over one peso per day could potentially put aside forty-one centavos daily, or ten pesos monthly. In 1895, this threshold reached well below the professional middle class and included not only the emerging lower-middle-class market (small shopkeepers, neighborhood service providers, and skilled workers, for instance) but also the larger and rapidly increasing number of laborers working on wage contracts in the modernizing sectors of the Mexican economy: in transport, construction, manufacturing, mining, and services. A pooled family income threshold of just over one peso per day likely meant that the potential market for sewing machines included the many tens of thousands of workers who earned not much more than a peso for a day's ten- or twelve-hour shift (*jornada*).[49] We should not be surprised, in other words, that sewing machines diffused quickly and broadly in both urban and rural Mexico.[50]

For many consumers, a sewing machine offered a means to increase family income, to raise living standards—perhaps out of poverty—and to aspire to a better life. Sewing machines enabled some women to undertake commercial production independently, typically serving friends and neighbors on an informal and irregular basis. Their machines, set up in patios or on the sidewalk just outside their doors, were quickly integrated into neighborhood cash and barter networks and became centers of gossip—akin perhaps to community wells—and provided a means to increase family income in the informal sector.[51]

But most women who used sewing machines to create income-generating work did so within the more circumscribed relations of commercial outwork or "sweated" labor. Across Mexico's cities, women had long undertaken piecework from their homes for local tailors and garment merchants, sewing precut cloth or shoe parts by hand. Ready access to sewing machines allowed this practice to expand and take on a more intensive form in Mexico, as it did in the North Atlantic. Women turned many household machines in Mexico's cities to commercial use, and by 1921 an estimated ten thousand women and men in Mexico City alone did commercial sewing out of their homes.[52] Outwork enabled garment merchants to transfer risk to the female workers, who usually bore the cost of the capital equipment themselves. This arrangement also mitigated labor management and oversight costs for the largely male cloth merchants and garment manufacturers. Female outworkers remained highly vulnerable to extremely low wages and irregular piecework. By 1899 this image had become almost cliché, and the *Vocabulario de Mexicanismos* noted skeptically that although the "golden dream of poor women is to acquire a sewing machine," most fell victim to creditors and descended back into poverty.[53]

Sewing machines, however, were not just an urban technology in late nineteenth-century Mexico. They were also quickly adopted in villages and hamlets throughout the countryside. The *National Geographic* noted in 1919 that "Yankee sewing machines" were found in the average home in both urban and rural Mexico. Nor did they escape the observant eyes of the American journalist John Reed as he traveled with Pancho Villa's troops across the Chihuahuan desert in the early months of 1914. Even in the most modest single-roomed, dirt-floored homes, he reported, there sat a sewing machine in a place of honor, "as in every other house I saw in Mexico."[54]

Though perhaps overstated, Reed's observation was not far off the mark. Since the early 1870s, Singer's system of agencies, subagencies, and local salesmen had spread its tentacles across the countryside, and many machine companies had been shipping to regional ports since the 1860s. As early as 1870, for instance, two hundred machines were shipped and sold in Mazatlán within twelve months, many staying in the city, but others bought by residents of inland villages and mining camps. A Singer agent in Oaxaca reported sales of 410 machines during an eighteen-month period in 1888 and held 350 more in inventory. By 1892 the regional office in Tampico reported regular monthly sales of 30 to 40 machines; agents working Chihuahua and Zacatecas reported selling about 40 machines per month; and the Puebla office reported over twice that, averaging 95 per month and peaking at 123 monthly. In 1893 Singer's Mexico manager thought of sending an agent to "explore" the states of Tabasco, Campeche, and Yucatan, which he believed would "offer a splendid field for a profitable business."[55]

Once away from the central ports of entry in these far-flung regions, serviced by ships or trains, marketing the sewing machine depended on multiday journeys on hoof or foot over rugged terrain. Central office managers frequently complained to New York about the difficulty of extending markets, of reaching new customers, and generally of doing business in Mexico beyond the extent of the rail lines, where "the distances are so great and the larger part of the territory so difficult to reach."[56] Singer's subagency in Chilpancingo, Guerrero, required mule transport over 175 arduous mountainous miles to reach an area "so sparsely settled the towns so far apart that our subagents have to cover large areas and consequently there are many points which they can only visit once in three or four months."[57] Some regional agencies were entirely cut off from the central office for months at a time. "Mr. Patterson is so far away from railroad communication," reported central office manager Oscar Graham in 1887, "[that] during the rainy season which is now on and likely to last for the next two months, [he is] almost inaccessible."[58] As Graham explained, "There are no horses and wagons, nor any need for any, as transportation of merchandise is made on the backs of donkeys and Indians."[59]

While thousands of machines arrived in Mexico from the United States via train and steamboat, sewing machine importers proved able to push the machines well beyond the reach of the rail lines. In the high remote mountains tucked into the far southwestern corner of Chihuahua, an American mining engineer one day watched eleven men carrying bulky packs on their backs down a long zigzag trail toward the mining camp. Each of these "mountain Indians" had been loaded for the ten-mile journey with a Singer machine, to be sold for fifteen pesos down, ten a month thereafter, at the mining camp's company store.[60] "Enter an adobe or thatch house having a dirt floor, no windows, and one hole for a door," observed another visitor, "and you will find a sewing machine."[61] Just after the turn of the century, the German photographer Hugo Brehme recorded an indigenous family in their thatched one-room home in Tehuantepec, in the photograph partially reproduced on the cover of this book. With ceramic pots on the floor, woven baskets on a shelf, they carefully posed next to a treadle-operated Singer machine, under which sat their son, crosslegged, a chicken in his arms.

The machines could be found, reiterated another observer, "in many huts made of bamboo and thatched with palm leaves."[62] And in the village of San José de Gracia in Michoacán one salesmen sold five treadle machines, which arrived a week later along with a young lady from the town of Jiquilpan to demonstrate their use.[63] Even after ten years of dislocative revolution, the anthropologist Robert Redfield observed in the 1920s that "the sewing machine alone, among modern machines, has become part of the general Tepoztecan material culture; it is found in all parts of the village and in houses otherwise Indian in character."[64] The acutely observant Diego Rivera notably included a sewing machine in his 1926 portrayal of an idealized campesino tableau on the walls of the third floor of the Secretaría de Educación Pública.

Tens of thousands of sewing machines diffused widely to many corners of the country because of their perceived productive potential, durability, ease of use, and affordability. This would have been impossible, of course, without the lower shipping costs made possible by rail transport. Sewing machines became deeply integrated into Mexican society and culture, testament to the interest and ability of Mexicans living in villages, towns, and cities to invest exceedingly scarce resources in the adoption of a novel modern technology.

If most sewing machines found their way into households, used there for some combination of family and commercial labor, thousands were also installed in centralized work sites for the manufacture of ready-made clothing. As in the United States and Europe, sewing machines propelled the growth of the ready-made clothing business in Mexico; they were also used widely in other trades that involved stitching, including shoe and hat manufacturing.[65] Ready-made clothing production in Mexico began to cut sharply into both traditional household production and the import trade, which by 1910 had fallen to less than a fifth of its earlier levels in a dramatic process of import substitution.[66] Sewing machines were used in "all the tailor, shoe, hat, belt, and other workshops of the city" by the 1880s.[67]

Investors in Mexico's new garment factories bought sewing machines by the dozens and employed growing numbers of full-time seamstresses. Sewing quickly became the largest single occupation for women in Mexico City, where seamstresses made up a remarkable 35 percent of the workforce.[68] By 1910, thousands of women sat at machines in new factories and workshops like La Sinaloense or La Tampica, or the shop in the San Antonio Abad neighborhood where one recent migrant from the countryside found herself in 1910. These were not unlike the one pictured in figure 13 (note the electrical lighting, the cramped quarters for the treadle machines, the women sewing on the mezzanine, and of course the men observing at the back of the room). She later recalled, "I did not know how to sew, but this man paid well and only hired poor yet honorable people, right? He paid two people who taught us; that was how I learned to sew pants, jackets, soldiers' uniforms . . . [and] I remained a seamstress until I married."[69] As one social historian of Mexico City has noted, the city's downtown at the turn of the century "was filled with upscale dressmaker shops, clandestine sweatshops jammed into old

FIGURE 13. Men observing women working in a sewing workshop, ca. 1915, Mexico City. Casasola archive, © 5499, CONACULTA-INAH-SINAFO-FN-MEXICO.

buildings, and small living quarters where a woman might sew for relatives and acquaintances."[70] Younger, single women typically worked in the centralized shops, while married women or single mothers more often undertook outwork in their homes.

Most of the ready-made clothing business in Mexico, as elsewhere, first developed within small to midsized enterprises, organized either as outwork or in modest workshops. Some began as cooperatives, like the Sociedad de Sastres in Mexico City with a dozen machines in 1874, and others as private enterprises that had grown out of earlier artisanal businesses.[71] Before the introduction of electricity in the 1890s, steam engines provided the only centralized power source for the sewing machines, and even then economies of scale in clothing production were limited, especially given the unusually high cost of fuel and steam power in Mexico. Large clothing factories were the exception and smaller workshops or sweatshops the norm until electrification made centralized power affordable around the turn of the century. Electricity substantially lowered power costs, and variable-speed, decentralized, and small-scale electric motors proved well adapted to shops with large numbers of sewing machines. By the late 1890s larger clothing enterprises began to appear in Mexico, motivated by the demand generated by a growing middle- and working-class urban population and the availability of the sewing machine.

Investors responded to new urban markets for ready-made clothing and began to establish clothing manufactories in and around Mexico City, Orizaba, Chihuahua, and other cities. Enrique Tron quickly became Mexico's leading clothing manufacturer, at the head of a group of French and Mexican investors who established garment enterprises that employed over six hundred seamstresses, retailing their products through their Palacio de Hierro department stores. In 1887 the first large-scale clothing factory powered by steam opened in Chihuahua; by 1892 it had become La Paz, owned by Federico Sisniega of the extended Terrazas clan and running 40 machines. With access to electricity by 1902, it had expanded nearly sixfold to 225 machines and several hundred workers; it would soon open its own electricity-powered subsidiary in Mexico City to compete against garment makers in the national capital.[72] Also in Chihuahua, seven shoe factories together employed about two hundred men and women, though most as outworkers.[73] Sewing machine salesmen themselves pursued opportunities in the clothing industry. H. W. Ford, formerly an agent with the Davis Sewing Machine company, sought to open a shirt factory with fifty machines in 1891, requesting machine estimates from the Davis, Wheeler & Wilson, and Singer companies.[74] L. O. Harnecker, Singer's general manager in Mexico City, also dealt in steam engines. In 1893 he sold several to clothing manufacturers in Chihuahua and Guadalajara to power dozens of sewing machines in each location.[75] The Mexican military provided a reliable source of demand for clothing manufacture. New workshops and thousands of seamstress jobs depended on government procurement contracts, in the process becoming prime targets for labor activists.[76]

By the turn of the century electrification had increased economies of scale in the industry and thus increased incentives for large-scale investments. At the same time, new fashion houses and department stores like the Palacio de Hierro, Liverpool, El Puerto de Veracruz, and El Centro Mercantil pushed for ever larger supplies of relatively low-cost, ready-made clothing.[77] In photos of the era, store-bought overalls, pants, and shirts begin to appear on working-class men on city streets. As a result, jobs for seamstresses rose by a third nationally, while the number of dressmakers in the capital nearly tripled between 1885 and 1910.[78] Most workers in the sewing trade were unskilled, working under difficult conditions, for low wages, often on a piecework basis. New clothing enterprises provided employment for thousands of women—mostly young and single—many of whom previously lived in rural settings and who sought livelihoods in Mexico's expanding cities, where immigration drove population growth averaging over 5 percent annually. The mechanization of sewing created new kinds of remunerative work for women and increased cash income in urban households but probably did little to increase women's welfare.[79]

Despite these developments, the production of ready-made clothing in Mexico's expanding garment industry lagged behind the expansion of the nation's textile industry, but not by much. The decentralized nature of garment manufacturing means that we have no reliable data on national production as we do for cotton cloth in Mexico's textile mills. But clothing imports declined at a time of expanding markets at home—a clear indication of the industry's growth. Between the late 1870s and 1910, Mexico's ready-made clothing imports from the United States and Europe fell dramatically as domestic production expanded behind a protective tariff wall that added between 40 and 100 percent to the price of imported clothing.[80] The textile industry employed some thirty-two thousand workers, while the number of self-employed (artisanal) tailors had fallen to just a fifth of 1870s levels.[81] Mexico was not yet the global center of garment production that it would become later in the twentieth century, but the introduction of the sewing machine and its rapid diffusion to factories, workshops, and households provided the technological foundation for an early process of effective import substitution and transformed the social lives of thousands of Mexican women.

• • •

By 1910 sewing machines could be found virtually everywhere in Mexico: in garment factories, in the shops of seamstresses and tailors, and in the homes of Mexicans at nearly all levels of society. "There is hardly a village in Mexico," reported the US consul general in 1897, "where [the] sewing machine may not be found."[82] Women had long been deeply engaged in the culture and commerce of sewing and moved with relative ease from hand sewing to commercial machine sewing. Nor was there any widespread public opposition to the adoption of sewing machines in Mexico, although efforts by employers to cut the pay of seamstresses provoked frequent protests against labor contractors and cloth merchants through the 1880s and 1890s. Women workers in the newly mechanized sewing trades organized to lobby and strike for better working conditions. But these actions focused less on factors intrinsic to the new technology than on the nature of management and remuneration. In contrast to workers in the textile industry, seamstresses in the clothing trade tended to see new technology as a source of income and employment and identified their employers as the immediate source of low wages or difficult working conditions. To escape the latter, for instance, one group organized its own "Sewing Agencies" independent of clothing contractors in order to arrange direct marketing to clients.[83]

Nor is there evidence that Mexicans were disinclined to use sewing machines for cultural reasons. There were some exceptions, of course, including those at the highest socioeconomic levels who could afford to buy imported clothing and have their home sewing done by high-end tailors, and who shunned manual labor themselves (like elites across the globe). Nevertheless, they bought machines and installed sewing rooms, and their husbands and fathers and brothers advocated technological modernization in the public sphere. At all social levels, sewing machines represented something powerfully symbolic, as "emblems of superiority and riches."[84] But were they simply "emblems," whose mimetic value outweighed their utilitarian and pecuniary value? John Reed's observations might make us wonder: "the inevitable sewing machine . . . converted into a sort of an altar by a tiny embroidered cloth upon which burned a perpetual . . . flame before a tawdry color print of the Virgin."[85]

But there was nothing uniquely Mexican in the way the sewing machine conveyed powerfully symbolic meanings.[86] And there is little evidence in the United States, Mexico, or elsewhere that the symbolic meaning of the machine trumped or otherwise diminished interest in its capacity as a productive tool. In one rural Mexican village, a visitor noted that eleven newly purchased Singer machines were in constant use, "centers of gossip" to be sure, but also run hard and shared almost communally by "the owners, their friends, and all the neighborhood."[87] There is little in the wide array of anecdotal evidence on sewing machine use in Mexico to indicate that rapid and widespread adoption of sewing machines did not quickly yield a transformation of productive work in a manner very similar to that experienced in the United States, Europe, and elsewhere.

Nevertheless, the adoption of the sewing machine in Mexico was a fragile experience, vulnerable to the weak nature of Mexico's incipient consumer market. On one hand, sewing machines' low cost meant that they were accessible to many wage-earning Mexicans in the commercial economy. On the other hand, monthly installments lay at the very margin of many consumers' ability to pay, and defaults were frequent. Singer's office in Mexico City quickly became expert on the relationship between weather and agricultural conditions in nearly every state of the nation and regularly reported local rainfall and corn harvest data to the company's New York headquarters. Even short-term, localized drought meant low corn yields on family farm plots, and those with sewing machines quickly fell behind in their monthly payments. When drought was sustained and regional in scope, the impact on national sewing machine sales (and the number of repossessed machines) increased quickly. Drought conditions were especially severe, for instance, from 1891 to 1893. "Business is very poor here just now," Singer's central office reported in June 1892, "and if rain does not fall soon, the sales for this year will materially decrease as money is exceedingly scarce and the people in many districts are in abject misery."[88] Nearly a year later conditions were still bad in the North, where the "business will largely be influenced by this season's rainfall as the greater part of the section has suffered from drought for three years and the land has therefore remained untilled so that the agricultural districts have practically been closed to us."[89] Low rainfall not only affected crop yields but also could shut down mines because of "the high price of fodder and corn," affecting machine sales and collections in those districts.[90]

In the early months of 1893, a national typhus epidemic compounded the effect of extended drought, hitting especially hard in urban areas where open sewers depended on rain to wash away refuse and human wastes. Singer's Mexico boss, L. O. Harnecker, noted that deaths in Mexico City ran at nearly one hundred per day, with "endless funeral processions"; the sick included Singer's chief clerk, its bookkeeper and cashier, the manager of the city department, two of his clerks, the machine account clerk, and several canvassers. By January, Harnecker was pleading with his New York bosses for a transfer out of the country.[91]

As drought, poor harvests, and illness cut incomes, sales plummeted and purchasers quickly fell behind in their monthly installment payments. By mid-1892 Singer's agents were repossessing about as many machines as they sold, although many customers tried to evade repossession by pawning their machines for quick cash. Used machines could be hocked for between twenty-five and fifty pesos. "We have been in the criminal courts almost daily with cases of machines pawned on trial," complained the Mexico City office at the height of the crisis. "The Judge gave us an order to search all the pawnshops in the city and . . . we have visited so far twenty-eight pawnshops and taken the numbers of 309 of our machines . . . . Fully two fifths are either leased or have been pawned by parties who had them on trial; this is a criminal offence."[92] Similarly, during the major textile industry strikes of 1906–7 in Orizaba, many workers reportedly returned their machines to local Singer offices, recouped a portion of their payments, and left the area in search of more stable employment.[93] Even in good times Singer faced the problem of customers pawning not-yet-paid-for machines, leaving delinquent accounts and frequently no traceable address. At one point Singer's central office complained about the "hundreds of our machines" to be found in the city's pawnshops; customers had paid Singer ten pesos down and then pawned the machines for twenty pesos, costing the company "endless litigation and expense."[94] Sewing machines may have diffused widely in Mexico, roughly on par with diffusion levels in eastern Europe and above those in India, but many who bought them did so at the absolute margin of their ability to pay.

At the same time, widespread adoption had a decidedly mixed impact on technological capabilities in Mexico: many thousands learned to use the machine, but troubleshooting and repair skills were scarce, and local capacities to manufacture parts or the machine itself remained undeveloped until the second half of the twentieth century. The machines' internal complexity meant that the technical requirements of operation could be substantial, from negotiating normal use (pedal operation, needle threading, bobbin replacement, fabric manipulation, variation of fabric and thread weights, etc.) to the occasional demands of troubleshooting (unjamming moving parts, replacing broken components, etc.) and more substantive repair. Importers and sales agents vigorously advertised the "simplicity and durability" of their models.[95] As agents chose which models to market in Mexico, they sought these qualities. "It is the simplest machine," wrote Juan Brittingham in explaining his recommendation, "and will stand lots of hard work and hard knocking."[96] Indeed, rapid and widespread adoption testifies to the relative ease with which women in homes and workshops were able to operate sewing machines. Salesmen from Singer occasionally complained about buyers' abilities, but otherwise Mexicans across socioeconomic levels quickly became proficient, including "scores of native women" who became "expert operators."[97]

Sewing machines were typically sold with a quick lesson from the sales agent. Those buyers who lived in towns and cities could easily get ongoing technical support from regional offices, and Singer often sent a technician or trainer to follow in the wake of their provincial salesmen, instructing "the people in the manner of operating machines and their advantages."[98] Oral histories of women who worked in the early clothing factories indicate that a few short lessons were sufficient for them to begin steady work involving long hours toiling at the machines.[99] Training was also a social welfare project undertaken by charitable organizations like the Mexican Philanthropic Society (Sociedad Filantrópica Mexicana). Through the 1890s and 1900s, these societies purchased machines and set up sewing workshops for those without "the means to purchase their own machine," giving instruction in operation and, they hoped, providing a new livelihood for the poor.[100]

Beyond basic use, however, developing the technological capabilities associated with machine sewing proved more difficult, including basic troubleshooting and repair, access to spare parts, and modification, replication, and manufacture of the machine itself. Sewing machines did of course break down in the course of work, and costly access to parts and repair expertise could prevent productive use.[101] In Mexico's cities, demand for repair services for consumer durables like sewing machines would eventually lead to the rise of a new class of largely self-employed artisanal mechanics—"something much needed here" in the late nineteenth century.[102] By the mid-twentieth century, nearly every neighborhood in Mexico's cities would boast a general-purpose repair shop, where the proprietors and a worker or two sat amid piles of used and broken machines, tinkering, repairing, jury-rigging, and fashioning makeshift parts to keep machines running. One measure of the ubiquity of these small operations can be seen in a later commercial census of Jalisco, where 525 so-called "machine shops" averaged just 3.47 workers apiece.[103]

But local repair expertise was rare and as yet undeveloped before 1910, even in cities. There had been little opportunity for technically minded Mexicans to become familiar with and learn from mechanical technologies generally, and precision-engineered metal parts in particular, and there was not yet a critical mass of mechanical technologies that demanded services of repair and adjustment. Singer's Chihuahua office asked New York headquarters to ensure that all machines were "adjusted and tested" in the factory, "as we have no one at Chihuahua who knows anything about these machines."[104] In more remote areas, access to repair and parts could be more difficult. In some cases, broken machines were "stored inside the house as souvenirs" when there was no local access to repair expertise.[105] An American mining engineer, traveling by mule for four lonely days into the mountains of eastern Sinaloa, ate lunch one day in a simple adobe home along the road. Before he left, his hostess brought out a Singer machine that would not work, asking if the engineer understood machinery. He worked at the moving parts, poking and prodding, and before long a stream of baby cockroaches poured from the interior of the machine. "The movement was frozen, but a little force broke it, and by rocking, I could get a little motion which gradually increased . . . . The more motion, the more roaches, the more roaches, the more motion. They ran all over the table top . . . so fast that they couldn't stop at the edges, but fell off. Chickens . . . were quick to take note of the new food supply. Their cackling brought the whole flock out and I had chickens all over my feet, and roaches on my hands."[106] The engineer asked his hostess to boil some chicken fat, which he used to oil the machine and "it began to run smoothly."

The obstacles to a local ability to modify, adapt, replicate, and manufacture the machine were greater than simple troubleshooting. Government policy provided no incentive. Without tariff protection, no one would try to manufacture machines or parts as long as supply links to the United States remained open. Even so, Mexico's metallurgical and machine-tooling capabilities could not have supported the manufacture of the small-scale, finely calibrated parts that made up the technical core of the sewing machine's design. It was one thing for the Fundición de Sinaloa in Mazatlán to manufacture the large parts of steam engines, but something else altogether to manufacture the more intricate components of sewing machines.

There were, however, several intriguing hints of potential. Mexico's exhibit at the Paris Exposition of 1889 included a "Mexican" sewing machine displayed and apparently constructed by Leandro Ramírez, about whom we know nothing more.[107] In the summer of 1900 Timoteo Saucedo wrote from San Luis Potosí to the Singer Office in New York, noting that he had recently read of the company's interest in undertaking the manufacture of sewing machines in Durango or Monterrey. He offered his services as agent and intermediary if the company would consider his city instead.[108] Almost two years later, notices appeared in several Mexican newspapers that Singer was exploring the possibility of opening a factory in Mexico to manufacture sewing machines for the Central and South American market. The factory would be located in Mazatlán—perhaps not coincidentally home to the country's most successful machine manufacturer—and the media took note when a "director de trabajos" was named in 1902.[109] Neither of these projects, however, ever materialized.

. . .

Nearly as soon as sewing machines appeared in the United States, manufacturing firms and commercial intermediaries sought to advertise and sell them in Mexico. Durable, simple to use, and affordable, they quickly found an eager market. The slow trickle of machine imports in the late 1850s and 1860s became a steady flow after 1870. Households throughout the country and at nearly every socioeconomic level purchased machines on the installment plan. Without any significant economies of scale, diffusion depended on consumer demand, on household incomes across urban and rural Mexico. Businessmen also purchased thousands of machines to set up workshops and, with the availability of electricity in the late 1890s, larger clothing factories. The adoption and diffusion of mechanized sewing in Mexico quickly expanded the country's productive capacity, increased income opportunities for families, fundamentally altered the occupational lives of thousands of women, and transformed the culture of clothing consumption. Even advocates for Mexico's growing working class declared it "a marvel," although *El Socialista* argued that the sewing machine shifted bargaining power in favor of employers and away from "the unhappy seamstress."[110] Working women in Mexico would continue to invest in sewing machines and other labor-saving devices for decades to come. Individual decisions to invest nearly 14 million dollars in imported sewing machines before 1910 represented the carefully considered adoption of a new means of production.

Here was a society highly receptive to a new technique, a machine that promised a revolutionary leap in productivity and output. Large numbers of families and households became accustomed to mechanized production through the sewing machine, which could stimulate a kind of learning by doing if not learning by seeing. The future mechanic, agricultural innovator, general, and president Alvaro Obregón reportedly received his first lesson in mechanical technologies by watching his mother sew on their family's machine.[111] But obstacles to adoption were present, and to assimilation even more so. First, the market for sewing machines was a fragile one, vulnerable to any erosion in the cash-earning capacity of Mexican households. This was true not just in rural regions and villages but in cities as well, where agricultural crises rippled through economies in less direct ways. Second, widespread adoption did not imply that the know-how embedded within the machine's design and manufacture transferred easily. Indeed, neither Mexican investors nor the companies that controlled the marketing and distributing of sewing machines in Mexico had any incentive to promote the local assimilation of knowledge and skills. Just the opposite. Mexican innovators and manufactures could certainly get their hands on codified descriptions, blueprints, old patent specifications, or the machines themselves to reverse-engineer. Perhaps a few highly skilled men (like Leandro Ramírez) might manage to construct a unique model in their workshops. But the gap between the know-how embedded in sewing machine construction, on one hand, and Mexico's metalworking and machine-tooling capacity, on the other, was too great to bridge, at least in the short term. Despite the introduction of hundreds of thousands of sewing machines, Mexico did not develop the capacity that might have supported—at a minimum—repair and maintenance tasks and—at a maximum—the machines' modification and replication.[112]

FIVE

Beer and Glass Bottles

DESPITE RAPIDLY EXPANDING DEMAND FOR glass bottles in the Atlantic world over the last decades of the nineteenth century, in 1900 bottles were still largely blown by hand. Highly skilled, specialized, and high-wage glass blowers produced hundreds of bottles daily to contain milk, fruits, vegetables, patent medicines, and of course the emerging intoxicant of choice for the burgeoning working class in Europe and the Americas: beer. Mexico would eventually become the world's largest beer exporter in the early twenty-first century, and the roots of this industry are found in deep social and economic changes of the late nineteenth century, dependent on imported brewing know-how.[1]

In Mexico as in the United States and Europe, rising consumer demand for beer meant rising demand for glass bottles. However, bottle-making techniques remained little changed from previous centuries, and bottle producers could not keep up with rising demand. Brewers and other bottle users felt this tension acutely throughout the North Atlantic. Since the 1870s, inventors and mechanics on both sides of the northern Atlantic worked to develop machinery to automate part or all of the delicate hand-blowing process, but with only limited success. Not until 1903 in Toledo, Ohio, was a fully automated glass bottle–blowing machine built that would prove commercially viable. Michael Owens's system quickly became the foundation for the modern glass bottle industry in the United States, Europe, Mexico, and beyond.

To say that the Compañía Vidriera Monterrey successfully adopted the Owens bottle technology in Mexico is to oversimplify. Between 1903 and 1910 nearly a dozen independent investors within and outside Mexico sought to adopt the new Owens system. All, however, confronted a series of major obstacles, and it would take a decade of effort, investment, and repeated dead ends before one group of investors succeeded in commercializing the technology in Monterrey. The details of this story illustrate both the magnitude of obstacles facing the adoption of new factory-scale production systems from the North Atlantic and the payoffs to negotiating those obstacles. Other new, large-scale enterprises like the Fundidora Monterrey, Cementos Hidalgos, and La Jabonera La Laguna as well as the breweries themselves faced similar—though still under-researched—challenges. In the case of the Vidriera Monterrey, nearly a decade of effort produced substantial local learning about glass making, automated bottle technology, and management of large-scale production operations. Moreover, the Vidriera's management worked to ensure that this know-how accrued to domestic technicians and employees. As a result, the Vidriera would become one of twentieth-century Mexico's most economically successful and technologically innovative firms. In this case, the substantial challenges of adoption eventually yielded local learning, assimilation of know-how, and the development of locally grounded technological capabilities.

Owens's glass bottle–making machine was, however, a very different beast from the sewing machine. The Mexican market could support the adoption of hundreds of thousands of sewing machines across individual households and clothing shops. The small scale and affordability of sewing machines meant that it was consumer demand that drove—or at times limited—diffusion, rather than the supply from manufacturers and marketers. In contrast, however, the tremendous scale of the Owens technology meant that the domestic market could support only a relative handful of machines, despite rapid growth in beer consumption. The large scale and high fixed costs of adopting the Owens system meant that its adoption and diffusion were driven by questions of supply—of cost and scale; these were the questions that Mexican investors wrestled with for a decade. Sewing machines were everyday product technologies; the Owens machine (and other factory production systems) decidedly were not. The irony is that the wide diffusion of the sewing machine provided greater potential for the accumulation of skills, among more people, but it was the challenges of commercializing the Owens machine that yielded an earlier, deeper, and arguably more transformative experience of technology transfer.

· · ·

Beer provided the fastest-growing source of demand for glass bottles in Mexico, as elsewhere in the late nineteenth-century Atlantic world. As late as 1890 bottled beer was a scarce and expensive drink throughout the country. It was, in the words of one observer, an "aristocratic beverage" drunk by foreign expatriates and relatively few Mexicans, mostly in the northern states.[2] Until then, existing breweries were small-scale, specialized affairs catering to the tastes and pocketbooks of a narrow social group, and the vast majority of the country's very limited beer consumption was imported from the United States, Germany, and Britain, its cost often tripled by freight and duties. A bottle of beer cost between five and ten times a mug of pulque, the traditional fermented product of the maguey plant, and pulque remained the intoxicant of choice for the vast majority of Mexicans, as it had for centuries.[3]

Yet a mere decade and a half later Mexico's common alcohol culture had transformed, especially in urban areas and in the North. By 1907 national consumption of bottled beer had increased dramatically, from barely two to over fifty million liters annually, marketed aggressively and competitively by a half-dozen large breweries in Mexico's largest cities. If it was only the wage-earning and salaried men of these cities who increasingly chose to drink beer instead of the traditional and cheaper alternative, this would amount to nearly four hundred pints per person per year.[4] Changing tastes reflected changing attitudes, and as the editors of one Monterrey newspaper suggested, it was beer, not pulque, that brought men "comfort and happiness, and open[ed] the way to a higher civilization."[5]

Mexico's beer consumption rose dramatically in just under a generation, but imports of beer from the United States and Europe fell to under 20 percent of their previous level as modern, large-scale breweries (cervecerias) opened through the 1890s in Monterrey, Chihuahua, Toluca, Guadalajara, Orizaba, Mazatlán, and Mérida to supply the domestic market behind protective tariffs. In each case, investors contracted the expertise of foreign brewers and engineers from the United States or Germany. In 1890, national beer production lay somewhere in the neighborhood of just two or three million liters; by 1902 the new breweries were turning out about twenty million liters, and by 1910 national production reached nearly fifty million liters per year—satisfying an astounding 99 percent of national demand.[6] About 88 percent of all imports came in bottles, and consumers' preference for bottles over draft from barrels meant that it was "more difficult to sell a glass at fifteen cents than a pint bottle for 31 cents."[7] Like ready-made clothing, Mexican beer presents a classic import-substituting story: entrepreneurs identified an expanding market that was supplied by imports and, with the

FIGURE 14. Artisanal workers in a Mexican glass factory, ca. 1905. Casasola archive, © 5765, CONACULTA-INAH-SINAFO-FN-MEXICO.

support of increased government protection and contingent on their ability to hire technical expertise and hardware from abroad, opened local production facilities that successfully replaced imported goods.

But Mexico's new breweries faced a common constraint in the 1890s, as did their counterparts in the United States and Europe. The bottles to put the stuff in were either imported or blown locally by hand, and most Mexican breweries hired their own small force of émigré glassblowers, who invariably could not keep up with demand (figure 14).[8] Moreover, the breweries' glassworks were frequently plagued by the high cost of skilled workers. Mexico's largest bottle producer, the Fábrica de Vidrios y Cristales, S.A., associated with Monterrey's Cervecería Cuauhtémoc, shut its doors and sent its glassblowers home in 1904 after only a year in operation because of the high wages demanded by skilled workers.[9] The great expense of hand blowing meant that imported (though still hand-blown) bottles supplied nearly 80 percent of Mexico's demand.[10] Reliance on imports and limited local production meant high bottle prices for everyone and a persistent "shortage of bottles for beer," as one Monterrey distributor lamented.[11]

Inspired by rising consumer demand, Mexico's brewers and potential bottle investors were confident of four basic preconditions. First, they believed that the rapidly expanding domestic market for beer and thus for glass bottles was sufficient to justify substantial investment in large-scale mechanized domestic production. Indeed, by 1907 total national beer consumption in Mexico could have kept at least a dozen Owens machines busy. Second, bottle manufacturing enjoyed substantial tariff protection. Before 1890, bottle tariffs were essentially prohibitive and served federal revenue needs as well as the interests of skilled glass artisans. The major tariff revision of 1891 considerably reduced import duties on bottles in relation to beer, creating high levels of effective protection for brewers. It is no accident that the 1890s witnessed the first major wave of investment in Mexican breweries. The new tariff schedule of 1905, in contrast, recognized that breweries were now well established and thus sought to focus investors' interest in bottle production by increasing duties on glass bottles relative to beer. After 1905, glass bottles enjoyed a roughly 100 percent ad valorem protection against imports.[12] Third, potential glass manufacturers were confident that they could acquire the necessary raw materials, at reasonable cost. Indeed, they noted, artisans and traditional manufactories had been making glass in Mexico for centuries, using local sources of silica, alkali, lime, and fuel.[13] Fourth, competition between regional breweries drove down beer prices through the 1890s and increased the incentives of each brewery to gain advantage over its competitors by finding a solution to persistently high bottle costs. In 1901 Monterrey's Cuauhtémoc brewery entered the Mexico City beer market, which had been dominated by the Cervecería Toluca y México. The introduction of refrigerated railcars on the major trunk rail lines in 1902 placed national markets within the potential reach of all large breweries. Within a couple years, the big breweries in central Mexico (Toluca y México and the Moctezuma brewery in Orizaba—see figure 15) responded by selling aggressively in the Monterrey market. The Cuauhtémoc had also opened distribution agencies on the northwest coast, contesting the market there with the Cervecería Sonora, and others established warehouse facilities in regional centers like Puebla, Mexico City, Celaya, San Luis Potosí, Torreón, and Guadalajara.[14] By 1904 rapidly growing consumer demand, substantial tariff protection, confidence in input markets, high levels of competition among Mexican brewers, and the high cost of imported or locally hand-blown bottles combined to create powerful incentives to invest in new mechanized bottle technologies. Whether these conditions would be sufficient to actually commercialize this

FIGURE 15. The Cervecería Moctezuma, Orizaba, Mexico. Photograph by Charles B. Waite. Reproduced with permission from the DeGoyler Library, Southern Methodist University.

new technology, and whether commercialization would yield local learning, remained to be seen.

. . .

In the late nineteenth-century Atlantic world, growing divergence between rising demand for bottles (and lamp chimneys and electric lightbulbs) and the traditional, hand-blown nature of all glass container production created a supply bottleneck and persistently high prices.[15] Hand-blown techniques depended on artisanal skill, painstakingly acquired through long apprenticeship and work. Translating the delicate art of bottle blowing to an automated process proved extremely difficult, and the big breakthrough did not come until after 1900. Michael J. Owens worked for Edward Libbey in his Libbey Glass Company of Toledo, Ohio.[16] In 1890 the Libbey Company won a contract to make lightbulbs for Edison General Electric. When the boys who raised and held the molds for the glassblowers went on strike the following year, Owens developed a device that performed this action with a mechanical foot pedal, eliminating the demand for child labor in the glass plant. In 1894 Owens patented a semiautomated process in which skilled workers began a blowing process that was completed with compressed air, further boosting workers' productivity. In 1895 Libbey, Owens, and several Ohio-based investors organized the Toledo Glass Company to market the patent rights to these new devices and to support further research and development. By 1898 Owens had made the first step toward the mechanization of bottle blowing with the development of an experimental handgun that reversed the traditional process: instead of blowing molten glass into a hollow mold, by hand, a vacuum drew the molten glass from a tank into the mold. Over the next five years Owens and his assistants doggedly worked through a series of technical obstacles. By 1903 he had developed and patented a fully automated machine that, with one tender, could make eighteen thousand bottles daily.[17] This "Owens machine" represented a revolutionary jump over the prevailing hand methods in the North Atlantic bottle industry. As Edward Libbey reported, the audience of glass men who gathered for the machine's first public demonstration in October was "thunderstruck with the machine."[18]

Toledo Glass received their US patent for the new technology in early 1903, and by 1904 had applied for numerous foreign patents, including one in Mexico.[19] Interest spread rapidly, and the Toledo Glass Company developed a marketing strategy based on the machine's scale and cost. The machine's initial output ran to roughly 5.5 million pint bottles per year, and this figure more than doubled through constant design improvements by 1910. The price tag was steep, however, and only large, well-financed firms could afford one.[20] As a consequence, Toledo Glass followed a restrictive marketing strategy, offering use licenses to a limited number of firms. In the United States, they licensed the Owens machine to manufacture a specific kind of bottle (milk, medicines, beer) in exchange for payment in cash and stock and a continuing stream of royalty payments based on annual production levels.[21] For the European market, Toledo Glass set up the independent "Owens European Bottle-Machine Company" to market their use rights. They established a demonstration plant in Manchester, England, and shortly thereafter licensed and installed machines in Rheinahr, Germany, later selling the right to sublicense the machine to a syndicate of European manufacturers for 12 million German marks.[22]

By late 1904 there existed a fully automated machine that would in short order revolutionize the bottle industry in the North Atlantic. One firm held the US and foreign patent rights and sought to market these rights to bottle producers or middlemen around the world. The productive capacity of even one Owens machine represented a dramatic leap in productivity over previous hand methods, and within less than a decade the Owens machine accounted for over 50 percent of US bottle production and had forced a

40 percent contraction in the wages of the remaining skilled glass workers. Bottle costs also dropped dramatically relative to general price inflation. Average bottle costs in 1919 lay at less than half what they had been in 1899, and labor costs per unit would fall by fully 94 percent by the 1920s.[23] The Owens machine's scale also meant that the Toledo company would issue only a limited number of licenses for its use, conferring effective monopolies on a small number of firms, and the bottle industry worldwide would become increasingly consolidated. Everyone else had to find other ways of surviving: by dramatically cutting the wages of traditional skilled blowers; by adopting cost-saving, partially automated machines; or by focusing on a distinctive niche within the larger bottle market. In the years following 1903, there was little reason to believe that a similar story would not play out in foreign markets where sufficient demand for bottles suggested the possibility of locally adopting the Owens technology.

Mexican entrepreneurs quickly became aware of the productive promise of the Owens machine. Motivated by the growing, everyday preference for beer among tens of thousands of Mexicans, and hopeful of increased tariff protection, they sought to bring automated production to Mexico. To their dismay, however, the combination of rapidly growing domestic demand and readily available technology did not yield quick adoption. Recurring obstacles would delay the commercialization of the Owens system for almost a decade, and successful innovation would ultimately depend on protracted entrepreneurial efforts to negotiate the fit between the Owens system and a new context.

. . .

No one in Mexico had more motivation to acquire the new Owens machine than the owners of the Cuauhtémoc brewery in Monterrey, the largest of Mexico's half-dozen or so new large breweries. Established in 1890, by 1901 it controlled roughly 28 percent of the national market.[24] Isaac Garza, founder and president, had been interested in the Owens machine since early 1904.[25] In June of 1905 Garza and his partner Tomás Mendirichaga traveled by train north to Ohio to meet with the managers of the Toledo Glass Company. To their dismay, however, they discovered that they were not Toledo's first visitors from Mexico. Only days before their arrival, Juan Terrazas and Juan Brittingham—shareholders in the rival but much smaller Cervecería Chihuahua—had been in Toledo and had signed an option to purchase the

Mexican patent rights to the Owens machine.[26] Juan Brittingham first came to Mexico from the United States in 1883 at age twenty-four to visit his college friend Terrazas, heir of the wealthy Terrazas family of Chihuahua. This initial visit turned into an extended stay and eventually a lifetime committed to a wide range of business activities while Brittingham was raising a family in the twin northern cities of Gómez Palacio and Torreón.[27]

That Brittingham had heard of the Owens machine in the first place is not surprising. Over the course of his career in Mexico he operated as a one-man clearinghouse for information on business opportunities in northern Mexico and on new technological developments abroad. Brittingham corresponded extensively with investors, engineers, and plant managers in the United States. He traveled almost yearly in the United States, touring factories and meeting with businessmen. He received trade journals and machine catalogs in the mail and would frequently follow up news of foreign developments by writing directly to machine manufacturers in the States, seeking technical details and prices and sometimes exploring the possibility of serving as a sales agent in Mexico.[28] South of the border, he passed all this information on to friends, partners, and business acquaintances, and he proved adept at discussing and debating detailed technical issues regarding a wide range of new developments. His daily correspondence—sometimes reaching several dozen letters—reveals an entrepreneur closely attuned to developments and opportunities on both sides of the border and dedicated to aggressively pursuing them in Mexico.

Brittingham first saw the Owens glass bottle machine when he visited the International Exposition held in St. Louis in the fall of 1904. That August, he arranged with the president of the Mexican Central Railroad to reserve a special car, and in early October he packed his family on board for what would be a typical working vacation. In his letters from St. Louis to his friends Juan Terrazas and Enrique Creel (then governor of Chihuahua), Brittingham raved about what he saw: "So grand, superior, and extraordinary [that ...] one cannot describe this exposition but must see it in all its detail."[29] He urged Terrazas and Creel to visit on their own, "because undoubtedly it is one of those accomplishments, the fruit of the genius and talent of men, never seen until now." With a bit of chagrin and perhaps more than a touch of pride, Brittingham explained that in order to "dedicate [himself] exclusively to a detailed study of the exhibits" he had missed all the clubs and theaters of the city, instead retiring to his hotel between nine and ten each night so as to be "fresh and ready" to continue his "campaign" through the exhibit halls the next morning. Amid all the marvels of the exhibit halls, the Owens machine captured Brittingham's attention. Within days of returning to Gómez Palacio in late October he sent a detailed description of the Owens machine and its capabilities to Creel, which he followed up with a series of letters touting the business opportunity it presented.[30]

Initially, Brittingham's reports generated little enthusiasm among his associates. Creel was distracted by his gubernatorial duties, and Juan Terrazas had little initial interest in venturing alone into new commercial territory—at least without the support and assurance of his "oldest friends." To Brittingham he candidly admitted his "suspicion of any new invention."[31] The contrast between Terrazas's and Brittingham's attitudes toward innovation could not have been greater. Where Brittingham raved about the technological advances he saw in St. Louis and was constantly encouraging investment in new machines, Terrazas was much more cautious, reserving judgment and expressing suspicion, and refusing to invest "even a penny" without some kind of contractual guarantee of success.[32] Yet by early March 1905 Brittingham's badgering persuaded a reluctant Terrazas to arrange an exploratory trip to Toledo—on the condition that Brittingham accompany him. The two benefited from a serendipitous connection. Arthur Fowle, the American technical manager at a glycerin plant affiliated with their regional soap factory La Jabonera La Laguna, was first cousin to Edward Libbey, founder and president of the Toledo Glass Company.[33] Through Fowle, Terrazas and Brittingham obtained a special invitation from the managers at Toledo Glass to view the Owens machine in operation.

But Isaac Garza and his Monterrey partners had also been communicating with Toledo, as had many others: the Toledo Company received at least ten independent inquiries concerning their Mexican patent rights.[34] Beer and glass men in both the United States and Mexico were well aware of Mexico's rising beer consumption, the bottle supply constraint, and the opportunities this juncture represented. Brittingham and Terrazas knew that if they did not act quickly their competitors could shut them out of any participation in the automated bottle business, and to their delight the connection with Fowle quickly yielded preferential treatment.[35] "The news we get from Toledo," reported Brittingham on the eve of their trip north, "is that we should be ready to make a [financial] commitment. [As] Isaac Garza will have preference *after* us. . . . I fear we will have to take immediate action."[36]

Brittingham and Garza's race to Toledo in the early summer of 1905 was a reflection of their personal entrepreneurship as well as of the competitiveness of the Mexican beer industry. But this race was also shaped by the particular marketing strategy adopted by the Toledo Glass Company and the political institutions governing foreign patents in Mexico. Mexican patent law offered exclusive rights for twenty years to both domestic and foreign inventors.[37] Toledo Glass had solicited and received the Mexican patent rights in 1903, as it had in foreign markets around the world. The company then sought to sell the monopoly rights outright to business groups who would either use the machine or license its use rights to bottle manufactures within national and multinational boundaries. For Mexico, this meant that one and only one bidder would receive the Toledo Company's monopoly right to exploit the Owens technology, and this is what both Brittingham and Garza sought that June. Each feared that their failure would give a competitor significant advantage in the main field: Mexico's rapidly expanding and increasingly lucrative beer market.

In Toledo, Brittingham and Terrazas signed an option that gave them until September to make an initial payment of 50,000 dollars, with two remaining annual installments of 25,000 dollars each. By September, back in Mexico, they formed the Owens Mexican Bottle Machine Company ("La Owens de México").[38] Their contract with Toledo Glass obligated the American company to supply two Owens machines and the necessary technical support to install them at any time within a four-year period.[39]

Thus the contractual requisites for the transfer of the technological hardware and expertise embedded in the Owens system were complete by September 1905. The Chihuahua group's initial victory in this effort did not follow from their prominent position in Mexico's beer or glass industries; they were only a minor player in the former and absent in the latter. Instead, it resulted from their international connections and from the particularly transnational context in which Brittingham operated. Nor was their decision to acquire the Owens system founded on a detailed study of the economics of bottle production in Mexico. Most importantly, they had not yet gathered any information on whether the new system could profitably compete against imported bottles in the Mexican context. They had not investigated supplies of raw materials or fuel, thought through distributional possibilities, or even established the best location for a new factory. Their decision was based primarily on entrepreneurial enthusiasm and the dynamics of a highly competitive and rapidly expanding beer industry. How readily that decision would translate into commercial viability would require a far more careful consideration of the particular Mexican environment for glass and bottle production.

Moreover, the Chihuahua group's relatively minor status in Mexico's beer industry meant that they were not well placed to directly commercialize the new technology themselves. Substantial challenges faced Brittingham and his partners in the fall of 1905.

. . .

Acquiring the Mexican patent rights to the Owens machine represented the smaller of two necessary investments. Raising sufficient capital to actually establish a glass factory would eventually double or triple the initial 100,000-dollar investment.[40] For Brittingham and his partners, deciding whether to make that larger investment required resolving two central questions. The first was largely a question of business strategy: Would they establish an Owens-based bottle factory on their own, or would they seek to license the patent rights to other groups? The second question involved the economics of bottle production in Mexico: Could any domestic producer actually compete with foreign bottle manufacturers, assuming both utilized the Owens system? For Brittingham, determining production costs and competitive price levels—identifying markets, raw materials, fuel, labor and management concerns, transport costs, ancillary technology choices, and tariff protection—was worth pursuing only if his group chose to directly invest in a new bottle plant. Thus far they had spent little time addressing these issues, despite committing 100,000 dollars to the future of the Owens system in Mexico. Although both Juan Terrazas and Francisco Belden favored direct investment, Brittingham's own instincts lay in the opposite direction. Over the next two years he would lead efforts to license the system to other parties.[41]

Brittingham preferred the licensing option because the Cervecería Chihuahua was not big enough alone to absorb the productive capacity of even one Owens machine, and Brittingham feared that their competitors would refuse to buy Chihuahua-made bottles. Any Owens-equipped bottle factory would need access to Mexico's largest beer markets in Monterrey and central Mexico. But these markets were dominated by the country's largest breweries—the cervecerías Cuauhtémoc and Toluca y México. "They know," he wrote William Walbridge at Toledo Glass, "[that] we would not risk to put up a large glass works because we could not count on their bottle consumption, except at their price."[42] The Cervecería Chihuahua could not do this alone, and Brittingham knew it.

Almost immediately upon returning from the Toledo trip Brittingham and his partners began to aggressively pursue possibilities. Francisco Belden opened negotiations with Tomás Mendirichaga and Isaac Garza of the Cervecería Cuauhtémoc in Monterrey, while Brittingham asked Juan Terrazas to write letters of introduction to a Mr. Wiechers of the Cervecería Toluca y México and to Julio Limantour, a director of the Moctezuma brewery in Orizaba (and younger brother of Mexico's finance minister).[43] These brewing interests and others were, at the same time, pursuing their own strategies to buy into the Owens system.[44]

Mexico's large brewers were not the only ones interested in the Owens Mexico patent rights. Several US investors had also inquired after Toledo's Mexican rights. J. A. Bolton of Montclair, New Jersey, had developed fairly detailed plans to establish a modern bottle factory on Mexican soil.[45] Others sought ways to capture a share of the Mexican bottle market through exports. As Walbridge warned Brittingham early on, "I believe today that [these American companies] will make an effort to obtain the Mexican [bottle] trade and any glass factory in Mexico not equipped with the Owens machines might just as well close its doors."[46] The competitive threat to nonadopters was obvious. Among these US interests was Adolfo Busch, president of the Anheuser Busch Company of St. Louis, in this case representing his subsidiary interest in the large American Bottle Company. Busch had begun talks with Toledo Glass in early 1905 about the Mexican patent rights and protested strongly against the option acquired by Brittingham that summer.[47] Although Brittingham's clear preference was to strike a deal with the larger Mexican breweries, he felt that the American company offered a "safety valve" in case the Mexican options broke down entirely.[48]

Yet licensing the rights to the Owens machine in Mexico ultimately proved impossible. As Brittingham and his partners aggressively pursued licensing deals with three different firms through 1905 and 1906, royalty payments quickly emerged as an intractable obstacle. Despite the technology's promised ability to overcome the bottle supply constraint, uncertainty about whether an Owens-equipped Mexican factory could compete successfully against bottle imports on a price basis, even with substantial tariff protection, was widespread. The specter of royalties on top of high operating costs turned this uncertainty into deep pessimism.

Negotiations with the Cervecería Cuauhtémoc rapidly degenerated into mutual frustration and stalemate. Following the Toledo company's practice in the United States, Brittingham offered to license the Owens patent rights at cost in exchange for royalty payments on annual bottle production. Brittingham's royalty offers through this period ranged from fifty to fifty-five cents (gold, or US dollars) per gross of bottles, but Isaac Garza in Monterrey insisted on a royalty of no more than fifty cents (silver, or Mexican pesos) per gross, exactly half Brittingham's asking price.[49] Garza argued that Monterrey held the upper hand. An Owens-based factory, he asserted, could survive only with the business of Mexico's largest brewery—the Cuauhtémoc. "The weapon they are holding over us," complained Brittingham, "is that we cannot establish a glass factory of our own because we will then lose the consumption of bottles used by the Cuauhtémoc Brewery, the biggest plum on the Mexican tree."[50] On the other hand, Brittingham was confident that Monterrey's brewing interests would ultimately be forced to use Owens-produced bottles, either as the products of their own factory, as imports from American manufacturers like the American Bottle Company, or as purchases from a Brittingham-controlled bottle plant. "I told [them] I was sure they would [buy from us]," he reported to Belden in late December, "because they would have prices so low that they wouldn't be able to match anywhere else."[51] Brittingham hoped that the Monterrey people were not as indifferent as they sought to appear: "I know from our friend Belden that Mendirichaga and Garza believe the machine will be the salvation of their bottle factory."[52]

Nevertheless, neither side showed much interest in finding a middle ground through 1906, and the royalty issue proved intractable. Privately, Brittingham expressed little tolerance for Monterrey's hard line. To his partners in Mexico and to Walbridge in Toledo he voiced his "great disappointment" in Garza and Mendirichaga's negotiating efforts. By December 1905 he was condemning their "threats," their "intrigues," their "constant menacing," and their efforts to "put the screws to us."[53] He viewed their counteroffer of fifty cents silver per gross as "a complete joke" and by March 1906 had all but abandoned negotiations in frustration.[54] "We are getting tired of these people," he admitted to Walbridge as he asked the Toledo Company to more actively encourage negotiations with Busch and the American Bottle Company.[55] By July, communications between Gómez Palacio and Monterrey had been abandoned altogether.

In September, the American Bottle Company presented an alternative way out for Brittingham and his partners, although they saw this option as decidedly second best. A deal would at a minimum recoup their investment in the Owens patents and perhaps net them a profit. But the long-term intentions of American Bottle remained uncertain. Mexico's brewers feared that American Bottle, the largest manufacturer in the world, sought the Mexican Owens rights only to secure an additional export market by ensuring that no other firm could adopt the Owens machine and produce competitively south of the border. Indeed, in 1906 they were accused of "dumping" large quantities of their bottles on the Mexican market at below-cost prices.[56] In March 1906 Brittingham's growing frustration with the Monterrey group led him to authorize Walbridge to offer the American Bottle Company the same patent transfer deal that Brittingham had received from Toledo.[57] By July, several directors of the American company were pressing hard to consummate a deal with Brittingham, but they apparently lacked unanimous support among their own board. By September it was clear that the opposition within the American company had won, despite Brittingham's last-minute appeals to his intermediaries in Toledo.[58]

The last of the three sustained attempts to license the Owens machine came closest to fruition. In February of 1907, W. D. E. Negovetich and Luis Roever approached the Toledo Glass Company to inquire about the Mexican rights.[59] They claimed a long interest in the Mexican bottle business, connections with European bottle makers, and sufficient financial backing to establish a Mexico City bottle plant with an annual capacity of ten million pint bottles. All they lacked was the Owens machine. Toledo Glass responded to their query with technical and production details on the Owens machines but otherwise referred them to Brittingham. Although Brittingham initially viewed these men as "simply promoters . . . and [patent] speculators," he met with Roever in Gómez Palacio later that month to begin negotiations, but royalties again proved divisive.[60] Brittingham raised his earlier demand and now asked for sixty-five cents (gold) per gross on annual production under a million gross and fifty cents (gold) on annual production over a million gross. Given the size of the Mexican market, the effective offer was the former. Roever countered with a willingness to consider seventy-five cents (silver), barely over half of Brittingham's request. Roever also wanted an exclusive license, which Brittingham refused unless Roever's firm agreed to pay royalty on all bottles *consumed* in Mexico, not just on their factory's eventual production.

On the royalty issue Roever and Negovetich found an ally in the Toledo Company. Increasingly anxious to see their machines installed in Mexico, Walbridge urged Brittingham to reconsider his initial position. Royalties charged by the Toledo Glass Company, Walbridge explained, were based on the relative cost of production and tariff levels in different countries. While relative costs and protection levels allowed the Toledo Company to charge fifty cents gold or higher per gross in the United States, conditions in Germany and Canada permitted royalty levels of only 70 percent those charged to American companies (at thirty-six and thirty-five cents gold respectively).[61] Walbridge argued that the Mexicans needed to consider tariff protection and the likelihood of higher raw material costs, and therefore royalties should fall closer to those charged in Canada and Germany.[62] Finally convinced by this argument, Brittingham accepted a new figure of seventy-five cents silver (or thirty-seven-and-a-half cents gold) per gross and lamented that "we could have induced both Monterrey and Toluca to go into the business from the start; both were willing but we held out for 50 cents gold, citing your contract with the American Bottle Company."[63] Through May and June of 1907 Brittingham worked closely with the lawyers of Toledo Glass to draw up a licensing contract with Roever and Negovetich. By August, however, negotiations had again bogged down. Both Toledo and Brittingham remained opposed to transferring exclusive rights, and the general economic contraction that began in 1907 tightened possibilities for financing new ventures in both Mexico and the United States, fatally undermining the deal.[64]

In each of these three cases, high royalties combined with the uncertainty of production in a new market drove negotiations toward failure and slowed Brittingham's efforts to commercialize the technology. Not until the Toledo company presented evidence of the wide variance in their licensing contracts with firms in the United States, Canada, and Germany did Brittingham retreat from his initial royalty position. By this point, however, it was too late. Furthermore, it was not at all clear to potential Mexican investors that the Owens machine would produce bottles at a cost sufficiently low enough to compete with foreign imports. Indeed, most observers believed that production costs in Mexico would be substantially higher than in the United States, at least initially. The burden of royalty payments had only made them more uncertain and less willing to invest.

. . .

Repeated failures to license the Owens patent rights pushed Brittingham's group toward the other alternative. Terrazas and Belden had long felt that "in the end, we will probably have to establish a glass factory ourselves."[65] This meant, however, that they would have to directly navigate the economics of bottle production in Mexico. This effort would consume another six years before they would be ready to place the machines in commercial operation, haltingly, in 1912.

Foreign competition constituted the central challenge. Investment in local production made no sense without the ability to undersell imports, even with the "valuable" opportunity offered by monopoly rights to the powerful Owens machine. "Bottles made by your machine," complained Brittingham to Toledo in 1906, "can be imported into this country about as cheap as they can be made here," even with the burden of substantial transport costs.[66] Potential Mexican producers enjoyed, of course, the de jure protection of Mexican tariffs and the de facto protection of transport and breakage costs on imports. Nevertheless, it became increasingly clear that the uncertainties of domestic bottle production would be substantial, and questions about the cost and accessibility of raw materials, fuel, and transportation services quickly occupied the attention of Brittingham and his partners.

Initially Brittingham had "great confidence" in finding reliable and proximate sources of the most important production inputs. After all, nearly all Mexico's cities boasted glass workshops or manufactories; "We have already studied [these]," he wrote to Belden and Terrazas in early 1906.[67] This early optimism, however, proved severely premature and turned quickly to a more plodding uncertainty and frustration. Locating low-priced, high-quality sources of raw materials and fuel proved substantially more difficult in Mexico's relatively undeveloped economy than Brittingham had initially calculated.

"The most difficult problem to resolve," he reported in October of 1906, was the most obvious: sand.[68] At first, Brittingham had believed that "it would seem impossible that we could not find in this country sand and pure silica that are so abundant in Europe and the United States," but time and again his searches ended in frustration.[69] Brittingham's correspondence through 1907 reveals exhaustive efforts to locate raw material deposits of sufficient quality that could be shipped to a factory site at reasonably low cost. Sand from both the Chihuahua River and the Médanos de Samalayuca (the infamous desert of dunes across which the Camino Real passed in the eighteenth century) contained too much iron, a problem that plagued most inland sources.[70] Coastal sources tended to be purer but entailed high transport rates, making the final delivered cost prohibitive on this high-bulk, low-value material. The closest noncoastal domestic white sand deposits near rail lines were reported to be in Michoacán, also far enough to make transport costs excessive.[71] Sources north of the border proved equally discouraging. Good white sand could be had at Alamogordo in New Mexico, but again freight rates would likely push costs too high for competitive production. Brittingham also gathered information on the cost of grinding sand from local sandstone, as well as grinding mined quartz, but again found the fuel-intensive grinding costs plus freight rates discouraging.

While sand made up roughly three-fourths of the final product by weight, chemical ingredients accounted for the largest cost share among the raw materials.[72] Various alkali chemicals could work, but sodium sulfate or carbonate were most commonly used. Although many observers believed these were "abundant" through northern Mexico, finding the right supply at the right cost bedeviled investors through late 1910.[73] Again, several regional sources were considered and rejected. In 1906 Brittingham explored the possibility of purchasing bisulfate of soda from a local explosives firm; several months later he pursued several leads for exploiting the natural soda deposits of the Pacific Coast.[74] Neither option proved viable, and the chemicals were eventually imported from England at high cost.

Even more important to final production costs was the price of the fuel used to melt raw materials and to power the automated bottle machine and ancillary equipment. Indeed, the economic geography of the US glass industry had been fundamentally shaped by fuel costs for a century.[75] In Mexico, fuel costs had long been a "grave obstacle" to all fuel-intensive activities, according to Finance Minister José Yves Limantour and many other observers.[76] This was increasingly the case in the nineteenth century as forests near industrial and mining regions thinned and as the power demands of new large-scale automated technologies exceeded the caloric capacity of wood-based fuels. "The fuel question is really the most serious to be properly answered," advised George Dithridge, experienced in the glass business.[77] At one point Brittingham estimated that between 80 and 90 percent of the final cost of glass bottles would be fuel costs—hence the desperate need to shave every cent from its price.[78] The coal mines of Coahuila provided one obvious fuel source. These—the only large coal deposits in Mexico—were proximate to the northern industrial centers and thus presented the cheapest fuel source available, but doubts about its quality were commonplace. "Salinas coal is not of the first quality," admitted Dithridge (who had initially recommended its use), and he quickly advised Brittingham to explore imported coal or fuel oil instead, noting that the electric power plant in Parral, Chihuahua, ran on coal imported from New Mexico.[79] But imported coal quickly ran up against high freight rates on the railroads, and this exacerbated the "difficult problem in the expense of the [raw] material."[80] To address this issue, Brittingham engaged in a strenuous and lengthy campaign with the major railroads to obtain lower rates, lobbying railroad presidents as well as Finance Minister Limantour and President Díaz himself.[81]

While the price and quality of sand and soda and fuel were largely out of Brittingham's control, the freight rates on these inputs delivered to a factory site could be negotiated and quickly became the target of much of Brittingham's correspondence from late 1907 through 1909. Requesting rate information from the relevant US and Mexican rail lines, he was repeatedly frustrated by what he saw as "absurdly high" quotations.[82] Mexico's consolidation of the National Railroad lines in early 1909 only exacerbated these frustrations, as rates for most classes of freight increased, threatening the viability of the entire project. "Freight rates on coal are now $3.19 ton and will go to $3.90 ton and we cannot have more than $2.50 ton and compete with foreign imports," Brittingham wrote to Isaac Garza.[83] At one point he tried to play one rail company off another by suggesting that the factory's location (and thus which rail line would receive the company's business) would depend on the rates they could offer.[84] But he received little satisfaction, and the fuel question remained unresolved into 1909.

As Brittingham continued to investigate the troubling question of production costs, he returned to the strategic issue of accessing Mexico's main glass bottle markets. He remained convinced that a sales commitment with the brewers of Monterrey or those of central Mexico was essential. In 1908 he sought to organize a combination of Mexican brewing interests to jointly undertake an Owens-based bottle enterprise.[85] In March he renewed contact with Isaac Garza in Monterrey for the first time since 1905, exploring a "mutually convenient" arrangement for a joint enterprise.[86]

This time, negotiations between Gómez Palacio and Monterrey through the summer and fall of 1908 displayed considerably more "expressions of fine courtesy and friendship" than they had three years earlier.[87] What was different this time? Other options had repeatedly failed, but more importantly, royalties no longer posed an obstacle to investment. Now Brittingham and Garza sought a path toward commercialization that would combine the patent rights of Brittingham's group and the consumer market commanded by Garza's group, avoiding the burden of royalties altogether. By October 1908 the deal was inked, leaving only several important but tractable issues to

FIGURE 16. The Owens automatic glass bottle machine, ca. 1910. Reproduced with permission of the Canaday Center, University of Toledo, Ohio.

negotiate.[88] One year later, they official constituted the Compañía Vidriera Monterrey, S.A., capitalized at 1,200,000 pesos. The Monterrey group contributed the facilities of their old glassworks, and Brittingham's group contributed the Owens patent rights.[89] Construction on the new factory began in late 1909 under the direction of an American engineer, a Mr. Wilcox from the Arbuckle Ryan engineering firm of Toledo, who came highly recommended as "one of [the] best erecting engineers" by the management at Toledo Glass.[90] Two Owens machines crossed the Mexican border on railcars sometime in midwinter, one brief moment in the long saga of this story of technology adoption (figure 16). By February 1910 the new factory neared completion, and its investors hoped that it would begin producing bottles by August.[91]

Again, however, early optimism proved misplaced. Recurring obstacles would delay operation for yet another three years. Despite the adoption of a technological package well tested and firmly established in North Atlantic factories, with machinery delivered ready to install from Toledo along with experienced American technicians and glass engineers to erect the new Mexican plant, its directors and managers continued to face a host of choices in commercializing the Owens system in the new Mexican context. The largest of these challenges centered on fuels, skilled labor, and adapting the technology itself to a novel input mix.

Glassmaking placed great pressure on fuel choices because it required exceptionally high temperatures in the melting furnaces. Not just any fuel would do, and gas burned hotter than coal. Most US glass plants used gas to fire their ovens, many producing their own gas from anthracitic or bituminous coal. By March 1909, however, Brittingham and Garza had concluded that Mexican coal was not of sufficient quality to burn directly or "adequate to produce gas."[92] Increasingly, then, the most attractive alternative appeared to be gas processed from crude petroleum, obtained from newly opened oil fields on Mexico's Gulf coast. Brittingham spent several weeks in July in the United States visiting the Toledo Company and several glass factories that were experimenting with different fuel arrangements. He reported to Garza that some had success using a mixture of petroleum and oxygen to fuel their ovens, obviating "the need to invest in a gas plant that is so costly."[93] By early August, Garza had gathered information on the use of fuels by other Monterrey industries (notably the textile mill "La Leona"), had located diesel motor suppliers (the German "La Siemens Schuckertwerke de México"), and had obtained delivery prices from the Waters Pierce Oil Company via Tampico. He reported to Brittingham that at current prices using fuel oil would cost just under 1.25 centavos per horsepower per hour: "This is high, but secure, and more economical than the use of coal, and will resolve our problem."[94] Nevertheless, the company would begin its operation with coal but switch to petroleum before finally settling, a decade later, on natural gas imported from Texas.

In contrast, labor posed little initial concern to Brittingham and his new partners, even though labor problems had long made the glass industry "an unholy business for all who have entered it."[95] Most informed observers in Mexico viewed the scarcity of skilled labor as a "serious hindrance," and it had reportedly been the downfall of Monterrey's first bottle company.[96] But the Owens machine radically reduced the need for skilled labor in the production process. José Yves Limantour warned Brittingham in 1908 that the labor issue had been "the true cause of all failures" in the glass business, but the Owens system would "eliminate [this] great anxiety."[97] Production would depend only on a permanent manager, a technical director, and several machine operators.

Skilled workers proved easy to find but not inexpensive. Brittingham and Garza could pick from the steady stream of young and experienced American men who traveled to Mexico seeking new opportunities. Word of the new Mexican operation also passed quickly through regional networks of American businessmen and, more broadly, through international glass circles. In the early months of 1909 Brittingham received over a half-dozen job inquiries from experienced glass men in the United States, Mexico, and Europe.[98] Initially, all skilled positions at the plant were filled by foreign technicians, who provided critical if costly expertise in navigating early technical adaptations. When the American engineers at the Vidriera Monterrey temporarily fled north during the civil unrest of May 1911, Roberto Sada complained to Brittingham that the plant was left without "sufficient experience to operate the Owens machines."[99]

The Owens system also reduced the need for unskilled labor. Instead of the old ratio of two or more assistants for each skilled blower, the automated system required only a handful of semiskilled machine tenders and a few common laborers, principally to assist the technicians and machine tenders and to facilitate the flow of raw materials and final products through the factory. The firm's total payroll covered just over one hundred employees during these early years of operation. By 1923 this number had fallen by 50 percent as a result of mechanization in ancillary processes surrounding the Owens machine, despite a doubling of installed capacity.[100] Labor costs fell to a fraction of their traditional level, as they had in the United States. Most of the Vidriera's workers were local laborers performing unskilled and semiskilled jobs through the factory.

Adjusting the American-designed Owens system to the new Mexican context proved the final difficult challenge. When engineers heated the furnaces to melt the first batch of ingredients in early September 1910, the resulting glass looked good, but the tube between the melting furnace and the supply tanks quickly clogged with solidified material. This "frozen throat" problem forced the American engineers to spend weeks cleaning the pipes and months to run a series of "extremely costly" experiments to find a solution to the problem.[101] November found them still working when technicians at the Toledo Company suggested that the problem lay in the interaction between the raw materials and the design of the technology. Monterrey's furnace, they explained, had been designed for materials similar to those used in the United States. The silica used in the Monterrey plant cooled more quickly, however, and thus created the flow problem. "If we had known

[this]," they wrote, "we should have designed a . . . style of furnace such as we built for the factory at Rheinahr [Germany]."[102] Although the "frozen throat" posed the biggest technological challenge in adjusting the Owens system to the new Mexican setting, a host of other issues also plagued start-up efforts. Experimental production runs conducted through the fall of 1910 led to a lengthy list of minor adjustments to the system and its ancillary parts, and the entire operation remained "unsuccessful" through 1911.[103] If this was supposed to be a "turnkey" operation—easily installed and operated—reality proved far more difficult. The "fit" between technological components of the system and constituent parts of the Mexican context—principally but not limited to raw materials—proved the most persistent problem. The Toledo engineers thought that Monterrey sand was the principal obstacle. "You may be able to use these materials someday," they advised Monterrey's managers, "but with your present tank we must continue to advise American materials."[104] For the Monterrey directors, however, using American sand was out of the question given the additional burden of transport costs. The American engineers at the Monterrey plant had also learned this lesson, and their work to adapt the Owens system to Mexican materials took another full year of experimentation. Further delays came while they waited for parts and materials from US suppliers and for a consulting visit by Michael Owens himself in September 1911.[105]

By early 1912 the problems that had plagued innovation of the Owens technology for the better part of a decade had largely been solved. On-site engineers had successfully redesigned the connection between furnace and tank to work with Mexican materials. Although the timing coincided with increasingly pervasive violence and civil conflict in Mexico, and the company paid no dividends to shareholders until 1918, the success of early production runs led the company to expand its capital by 300,000 dollars in late 1912, primarily to acquire two additional Owens machines from Ohio.[106] The Vidriera's production began at 40,000 bottles per day—twice the hand-blown level—and within a decade rose to nearly 150,000 per day or roughly fifty million per year.[107] Although this was still well below the plant's capacity, it represented a major share of national demand and largely displaced imported bottles in the Mexican market.

The 1910s and 1920s continued to present challenges to the operation of the Owens system at the Vidriera Monterrey. The company switched fuels in 1913, requiring further changes to ancillary machinery in the factory, they continued to search for better quality and lower-cost raw materials, and on numerous occasions they faced significant troubleshooting and adjustment challenges on the shop floor. By the mid-1920s, however, the Vidriera Monterrey was poised for several decades of what would be extraordinary growth. Under the leadership of the Garza-Sada ownership team, the company aggressively reinvested profits to expand and modernize the plant, undertook an internal research and development program to improve machine and glass process techniques, Mexicanized the technical workforce, and provided opportunities for learning and upward mobility (though at the same time undermining workers' efforts to assert autonomy). The company vertically integrated into raw material and intermediate input supplies and developed new businesses to produce crystal and flat glass. By the 1930s La Vidriera was producing in house all the plans and blueprints for new and expanded facilities and had developed the internal capacity to design and manufacture its own glass machinery—the epitome of effective technology transfer. Eventually, the firm's R&D facilities generated new machine and process inventions that it marketed internationally, holding numerous foreign patents by the 1970s. By then, the Vidriera Monterrey had become the center of the vast Grupo Industrial VITRO, by the 1990s reportedly the third-largest bottle manufacturer in the world.[108]

. . .

Technological innovation in glass bottle production came to Mexico at the turn of the twentieth century because more and more Mexicans had switched from drinking pulque to drinking beer. Although pulque producers sought to discover techniques to preserve and bottle Mexico's traditional low-alcoholic drink, all efforts failed until much later in the twentieth century.[109] North Atlantic brewers, in contrast, had already solved the technical problems of pasteurizing and bottling beer. And in Mexico, beer consumption rose steeply between the 1880s and 1910, part and parcel of social changes that accompanied urban and industrial growth as Mexico gradually integrated into a globalizing Atlantic economy. This is evident, for instance, in the correlation of beer drinking with other symbols of modern, urban life: ready-made suits, railroads, and middle-class professionalism generally (figure 17). Beer consumption still lagged behind pulque, but after 1890 new domestic breweries successfully challenged beer imports in regional markets. By the 1930s, breweries would stand in the top rank of Mexico's national industries.[110]

FIGURE 17. Men, beer, and railroads: "Celebrating the arrival of the Mexican Central, ca. 1911." Casasola archive, © 32022, CONACULTA-INAH-SINAFO-FN-MEXICO.

Beer's success created a new demand for glass bottles and provided entre-preneurs with incentives to replace hand-blown or imported bottles with large-scale, mechanized production. Imported bottles from the United States offered the default solution, but the implicit protection of overland transport provided incentives for domestic production, and the Díaz government upped the ante by doubling bottle tariffs in 1905. By then, the automated technology could be readily purchased in the North Atlantic, and glassmaking, all assumed, was a fairly uncomplicated activity that had long been practiced in Mexico. For investors and their partners in Mexico's brewing industry, adopt-ing automatic bottle production on a large scale seemed a simple matter, what development economists would later call a "turnkey" operation.

In many ways, acquisition of the Owens machine hardware, the legal rights to use it in Mexico, and the expertise to install and manage it proved relatively straightforward. Economic incentives were favorable, information about new technologies flowed easily across the border, initial investment capital was forthcoming, Mexico's patent institutions facilitated contracting, and tariffs favored domestic bottle production over imports.

But the obstacles to successfully commercializing the Owens system proved both persistent and quotidian, as they were for many new factory-scale technological systems in the late nineteenth century. All of Mexico's new industries had to compete against imported products from experienced and highly efficient firms in the North Atlantic, operating within well-developed supply and distribution markets. In contrast, Mexico's new manufacturing firms had to navigate a context of relatively undeveloped markets and a scarcity of local expertise. Early investors and their managers had to locate raw materials and other inputs of sufficient quantity, quality, and cost; acquire skilled and unskilled labor, again of sufficient quality and cost; and arrange transportation of both materials and products when, even with railroads, costs still ran high. Many found the challenge of reducing production costs low enough to undersell competing imports significantly more difficult than they had expected, even with tariff protection. This was the case for the Vidriera in its early development stages, of the Fundidora Monterrey during its first decade of operation, and of many other new industrial firms where profits did not often meet expectations. It also explains why so many new manufacturing firms sought to secure monopoly positions within their industries.[111] If royalty payments were part of the cost equation, investors might pull out altogether.

Luis Roever had suggested in 1907 that any new glass firm in Mexico would "have to experiment at first, as is only natural, and this experimenting will cost us some money."[112] The expatriate glassman George Dithridge concurred that a new factory "would require a period of uncertainty," one that he linked primarily to the training of Mexican workers.[113] Once construction of the Vidriera Monterrey's plant had begun in late 1909 and the necessity for constant troubleshooting and modifications became evident, its managers recognized that their anticipated production costs would be realized only at some point down the line, when operations had "gotten down to a good smooth running basis."[114]

Negotiating these kinds of classic "infant industry" challenges cost substantial money and time, but this experience also produced substantial opportunities for local learning. The directors of the Monterrey's new Vidriera eventually proved able to internalize the new knowledge and expertise about automated glass and bottle production and a range of ancillary activities. As Isaac Garza and others took over management from Juan

Brittingham, their entrepreneurial focus shifted from acting as a technical intermediary to engaging in local learning. Absorbing the technological know-how necessary to operate the Owens system in Mexico had begun in 1904. The transition to Isaac Garza, Roberto Sada, and their Monterrey-based group only heightened this dedication to assimilating the technological capabilities inherent in the Owens system.

SIX

Cyanide and Silver

EFFORTS TO EXTRACT GOLD AND SILVER from the earth faced an international crisis in the last quarter of the nineteenth century: at the very moment when demand for the metals increased in a booming Atlantic economy, miners around the world found it increasingly difficult to extract them from recalcitrant rock. Easily accessible, rich, and refinable gold and silver ores had become globally scarce, and the dominant refining system of previous centuries proved inadequate to profitably refine low-grade ores on a scale demanded by an expanding world market. This was true in Mexico as in many of the world's mining centers. The challenges facing miners were not new, but the pressures to resolve them were more acute than ever. A new technological system emerged in the 1890s that largely solved this problem and it would dominate precious metal mining through the twentieth century. Between 1890 and 1910, the cyanide process spread rapidly in the global mining community as one part of a broader late-century technological revolution. In Mexico, one local engineer noted, "Its introduction caus[ed] a true revolution in the metallurgical industry."[1]

The widespread adoption of cyanide processing rejuvenated precious metal mining in Mexico after the turn of the century. Like the Owens bottle technology, however, adapting the cyanide process to Mexican ores and conditions proved challenging, costing miners ten years of experimentation and great expense. Originally developed in British laboratories to refine gold-bearing ore, Mexico's predominantly silver-bearing rock proved especially recalcitrant to cyanide's charms. However, a decade of persistent experimentation by mining engineers yielded a body of new knowledge and the techniques necessary to successfully apply cyaniding to silver ores. The result was a revolution in output and productivity. Gone were the days of local bonanzas of high-paying ores, of Mexican miners and mining engineers long experienced in the northern mining camps—the rule-of-thumb men for whom following underground veins and refining ore was more practiced art than calculated science. Instead, a flood of foreign capital, technical hardware, and expertise accompanied cyanide to Mexico between 1890 and 1905, and cyaniding became one basis for industrial-scale mining and refining operations in Mexico's gold and silver districts, now resolutely scientific in approach, managed by US engineers carefully trained in chemistry and mineralogy.

The adoption of cyaniding generated substantial learning and new knowledge, but very little of this accrued to Mexican mining engineers and workers. Mexican mining experts had effectively managed excavation and refining technologies in one of the world's leading production centers for three centuries. As recently as the 1870s and 1880s, Mexican miners had dominated management and technical positions in the industry. By the end of the century, however, it was foreign mining engineers and technicians, mostly American, who monopolized nearly all managerial and skilled positions in the industry and who oversaw the adaptation of cyaniding to Mexican ores. As a result, the adoption of the cyanide process in Mexico yielded little local learning and had little impact on Mexico's long-term technological capabilities. Given the region's long tradition of mining history and expertise, this was tragically ironic. Since the mid-sixteenth century Mexican miners had proudly defended their expertise against Europeans. In Pachuca in the sixteenth century, Bartolomé de Medina developed the mercury amalgamation system, which would process much of the world's silver for over three centuries, and through the colonial period New Spain's miners proved adept at adapting European techniques to local conditions. When Spain's Bourbon reformers tried to impose new European methods in the 1780s and 1790s, colonial miners and scientists rose in vigorous and successful defense of the superiority of their local methods. The Royal Mining College, established in 1792, provided an institutional foundation for the development and defense of local expertise, and its graduates played major roles in mining and other fields through the nineteenth century. When the British investors and mining technicians who had come to Mexico in the 1820s left in the late 1840s, Mexican engineers and managers and workers reclaimed the region's mines and refineries and oversaw the industry's expansion through the 1860s and 1870s. But when foreign capital brought new, large-scale scientific and industrial methods to bear on the problem of low-grade ores in the

1890s, Mexico's miners found themselves squeezed out. With little access to the technical knowledge underlying the application of chemistry, electricity, and civil engineering to mining's challenges, and with no local tradition of developing or building the necessary heavy equipment, Mexican technicians could not participate. The mining boom of the turn of the century was wholly dependent on global knowledge and expertise, and Mexico's mining engineers would have a hard time catching up through the twentieth century.

. . .

For millennia, human desire for gold and silver had been largely satisfied by finding metals on or close to the earth's surface. There, exposure to water and air oxidized and isolated these metals from the mineral compounds with which they were bound. As a consequence, loose, or easily loosened, free, and inert nuggets, flakes, and dust of pure, or "native" gold and silver could be readily collected through relatively simple panning or sluicing methods, most commonly where nuggets lay in the alluvial gravels of existing or ancient streambeds, already freed from their host rock. But, by the 1870s or so "The cream of the known alluvial deposits had been skimmed off the surfaces of the world's goldfields, and the auriferous quartz veins running deep into underlying bedrock scorned the simple tools and techniques of sluicing."[2] What was left was hard to get to and hard to refine.

In Mexico, miners had long faced this challenge. Before the arrival of the Spanish in the early sixteenth century, indigenous miners collected small amounts of free gold and silver from alluvial deposits, surface outcroppings, and shallow pits, using simple smelting furnaces to facilitate the separation of precious metal from other minerals.[3] Early Spanish prospectors, keen to discover the source of Aztec treasure, quickly discovered that surface and alluvial deposits were scarce, and by the 1540s they were following silver-bearing veins deeper into the earth in Zacatecas, Pachuca, Guanajuato, and elsewhere.[4] Deeper underground, however, below the waterline, gold and silver remained bound in chemical compounds with sulfur, arsenic, and other minerals. These unoxidized or "refractory" ores posed a major challenge to Spanish miners. Smelting in furnaces offered one solution, but it would be centuries before furnace-building and smelting technologies could handle large volumes, and smelters of any size were always burdened by high fuel costs in Mexico's high-elevation, semiarid, and wood-poor regions.

FIGURE 18. The patio system at the *hacienda de beneficio* La Purísima Grande, Pachuca, Hidalgo. Photograph by J. Bustamante Valdés. Reproduced courtesy of the Benson Latin American Collection, University of Texas at Austin.

In 1554, Bartolomé de Medina, a Spaniard working in Pachuca, developed a mercury-based amalgamation system to separate silver and gold from their ores. Amalgamation mixed finely ground rock with a soupy mix of water, mercury, salt, and copper sulfate (*magistral*), then agitated this *torta* for several days until the mercury had fully combined with the precious metal. Flushing off the ground waste rock with water, workers boiled off the mercury in ovens, leaving pure metal. This patio process, as it was known in Mexico after the broad patios where the mixing typically took place (figure 18), constituted a new and enduring technological system for the large-scale refining of refractory silver and gold ores—those that were difficult to separate by simple grinding and sluicing, or uneconomical to separate by smelting.[5] Its central characteristics included animate or human power to excavate, haul, crush, and mix the ore, as well as practiced, artisanal judgment in the assessment of ore, the sorting of milled rock, and the management of the amalgamation process by the *azogueros* (mercury men).[6] The patio system and its classic *hacienda de beneficio* dominated Mexican mining centers from the mid-sixteenth to nearly the end of the nineteenth century; by the late eighteenth century, it had diffused to Europe and beyond.[7]

In the 1880s and 1890s, new investments in Mexican mining brought a flood of new technologies to extract and refine minerals.[8] Mining companies aggressively sought and acquired novel technologies as they became available in the North Atlantic market: dynamite, pneumatic drills, and more powerful steam engines and pumps, among many other new machines and processes.[9] They also experimented with modifications of the old amalgamation process, as well as new refining systems such as chlorination and lixiviation.[10] However, the introduction of new capital, equipment, and methods did not yet represent a transition to a novel technological system. As long as mining depended on the discovery of new bonanzas and the extraction and refining of high-grade ores, these innovations tended to be localized modifications to the dominant system, adaptations to the peculiarities of a particular ore and location. The challenges facing miners who sought gold and silver at ever greater depths, in more recalcitrant rock, and in lower concentrations remained substantial.

Deeply buried, low-grade ores constituted the defining challenge in extracting and refining precious metals in late-century Mexico and many other global mining districts. The precipitous fall in the global price of silver after the 1870s only exacerbated the challenge. Laboratory assays told mine managers that valuable metal lay buried in deep veins, as well as in the vast piles of tailings that stretched below their mine works—the waste rock accumulated from centuries of extraction and refining. Because the patio method often extracted less than 70 percent of an ore's silver, towering piles of waste rock still contained valuable metal.[11] The tailings dump at Real de Monte, Pachuca, for instance, had an estimated value in low-grade ore of 3,710,000 dollars, while the Guanajuato Reduction and Mines Company estimated two million metric tons of ore in their dumps and another one and a half tons as stope fillings, almost an "unlimited amount" of unrealized profit.[12] Miners also knew that "the amalgamation system wasn't applicable to those ores" because it could not extract metal from low-grade, recalcitrant ores at low cost.[13] As the leading North American mining journal put it in 1890, "How to treat low grade refractory ores is the most interesting problem [in mining] today."[14] A Mexican analyst concurred: the problem had become "no longer finding the mineral, but extracting it abundantly and cheaply, and refining it at the lowest possible price."[15]

In Guanajuato, where typical ores had been valued at 35 to 100 pesos of precious metal per ton of ore in the late eighteenth century, assessed values had fallen to just 6.50 to 7.00 pesos per ton in the 1880s; mine after mine increasingly faced "great quantities of very poor ores."[16] At the legendary Valenciana mine, annual production had fallen from 15,456 metric tons in 1884 to under 2,000 metric tons at century's end.[17] Even with the introduction of new drills and pumps and pans and concentrating tables, as well as innovations in the patio process and experimentation with new systems, refining costs per ton quickly exceeded production values. By the 1890s patio refining was more efficient than it had ever been, but at a cost of roughly 8 to 12 pesos per ton, it simply did not pay to process most of the ore available to miners.[18] Mexico's traditional mining centers like Guanajuato, Pachuca, and Zacatecas had fallen into a state of "almost complete stagnation" at the turn of the twentieth century.[19]

Silver's dramatic price depreciation in the world market further undermined what profitability remained for most Mexican miners under the old system. Although Mexican mines and *haciendas de beneficio* produced both gold and silver, Mexico was a silver country and gold had long been a relatively minor by-product. By the late 1890s, silver's fall had cut the value of mining companies' product by a full 50 percent since the early 1870s. Miners quickly found that the old calculus of costs and benefits using the amalgamation process no longer held. It had become nearly "impossible to mine ore for silver alone."[20] The challenge presented by low-grade ores, whether newly excavated or in tailings piles, was painfully obvious to officials in the Mexican government. A congressional decree in mid-1887 authorized the executive to procure any refining process for silver or gold that would recover at least 98 percent of assayed metal at a cost per ton not to exceed three pesos.[21] Low-grade ores, the high costs of amalgamation, silver's depreciation, and the market power of the large industrial smelters all worked to undermine the traditional technological system within *haciendas de beneficio*. Mexico's oldest districts, like Guanajuato, Pachuca, and Zacatecas, presented "a series of abandoned refineries, and the appearance of desolation and death."[22]

· · ·

Meanwhile, British scientists working on the gold extraction problem for the Cassel Gold Extraction Company in Glasgow, Scotland, developed in 1887 a method that used a diluted cyanide solution to dissolve gold and thereby separate it from its host ore.[23] In general terms, the cyanide process worked by mixing finely crushed or ground ore ("sands," or even finer "slimes") with potassium or sodium cyanide solutions at very low concentration (under

0.5 percent). When these materials were placed in large tanks, mixed, and agitated, the cyanide selectively dissolved the gold. The gold-bearing solution was decanted or filtered, and the gold was finally extracted by precipitation over zinc shavings.[24] These basic components of the process stood relatively constant from the 1890s well into the twentieth century. In practice, however, mining engineers developed multiple variations that reflected the inheritance of local practice, adjustments to local ore characteristics, and mill managers' constant efforts to increase yields and decrease costs. The Cassel Company quickly patented the "MacArthur-Forrest" cyanide separation process, taking patents throughout the world and establishing subsidiaries to market and manage their cyanide rights in the world's gold mining centers. By 1891 cyanidation was well established in South Africa's Transvaal gold districts, by 1894 in New Zealand (and with a bit more delay, in Australia), and by the second half of the decade in the gold mines of the western United States.[25]

Cyaniding, its historians agree, "rescued [gold mining] from the doldrums into which many sections of the industry had sunk after the late 1870s" because refining costs fell dramatically and extraction rates rose from roughly 55 percent to 95 percent.[26] World gold production doubled between 1890 and 1900, and doubled again by 1910. Cyanidation would be the centerpiece of the technological system that defined gold mining worldwide through the twentieth century. Mexico, however, had been a silver country for over three centuries. Mexico's mines had always produced some gold, but the yellow metal remained a minor by-product of Mexico's silver districts.[27] While cyanide's relevance to Mexican gold production would quickly become apparent, its application to silver remained highly uncertain.

First notice of the MacArthur-Forrest cyanide process in Mexico came in March 1890, when *El Minero Mexicano* reported on an article published in the *Engineering and Mining Journal* the previous December. "This procedure" the paper noted, "which has only been in practice for a little more than a year," would reduce the cost of refining "the most stubborn minerals" from fifteen to twenty dollars per ton to about five dollars.[28] The article gave a brief description of the process and predicted that it would produce "a revolution in the current system of reducing metals."[29] They were absolutely right: whereas in 1890 the patio process still dominated the refining of gold and silver ores, by 1910 it had virtually disappeared from the Mexican mining landscape, replaced by cyanidation. The impact on Mexico's mining production was tremendous; its impact on Mexico's technological capacities, however, would be far weaker.

In 1891 the Cassel Company sent the mining engineers Bertram Hunt and W. H. Trewartha-James to tour important mining centers in Mexico with a portable cyanide testing kit. Although Hunt later recalled positive results from initial tests on silver ores, their efforts received little attention in Mexican and North American mining circles.[30] In 1893 the Cassel Company received the Mexican patents to the process and over the next several years continued to send agents to Mexico, testing ores and looking for investment opportunities.[31] Cassel transferred its Mexican patents to the Mexican Gold & Silver Recovery Company, Ltd. (hereafter MGSRC), establishing a central office and laboratory for assaying and testing ore in Mexico City, with field offices and agents in mining districts around the country.[32] The MGSRC would be, its parent company hoped, the chief agent for the introduction and diffusion of the MacArthur-Forrest process in Mexico, providing a steady stream of royalty payments to the home office in Britain, complemented by sales of the cyanide compound itself, which Cassel produced for world markets.

Early efforts to introduce the MacArthur-Forrest process in Mexico focused on a handful of districts where gold was already the dominant product: the El Oro–Tlalpujahua region on the state border between México and Michoacán, and several sites far to the northwest in the Sierra Madre Occidental of Sonora and Sinaloa. In 1894, MGSRC's James B. Haggin worked to introduce the process first at the El Oro mills, and several years later at nearby Dos Estrellas mines in Tlalpujahua. Installation of the necessary cyaniding tanks and accessories began in late 1894, and the plant was operational within a year. The initial refinery was small scale, designed as an adjunct to the existing amalgamation process, treating gold-bearing ore from the mine's large tailings piles.[33]

Meanwhile, new gold strikes and growing American interest in Sinaloan and Sonoran mines provided a second focus for early cyaniding efforts. New investment through the 1880s made the Sierra Madre the most active mining district in Mexico.[34] In 1893 the Anglo-Mexican Mining Company bought several existing gold properties in Sinaloa and invested to improve and expand mining and milling facilities; two years later it hired James E. Mills to experiment with ways to economically treat their tailings. His small-scale tests with gold ores and the cyanide process looked promising, and the company brought in Henry R. Batcheller of Boston to expand these efforts, later overseen by E. A. H. Tays. By 1898 they had a cyanide plant capable of treating 1,500 tons per month operational at the Guadalupe y Anexas mines at

San José de Gracia.[35] At about the same time, several other companies erected modest cyanide facilities in Northwest gold camps. In the Hermosillo district of Sonora, the MGSRC erected a forty-ton cyanide plant at the Cerro Colorado mines; the Minas Prietas mines under the Creston-Colorado Mining Company sent their low-grade ores and tailings to cyanide treatment, perhaps as early as 1898; while the Charles Butters company completed a cyanide plant shortly after 1900 to process the tailings of the Gran Central mines. The Pan-American Mining Company erected a one-hundred-ton mill about the same time, as did Palmarejo and Mexican Goldfields Ltd., just across the Sierra divide in Chihuahua.[36]

By 1902 cyanidation was firmly established in Mexico, and independent assay offices in Mexico City had, for several years, advertised that they could conduct cyaniding experiments "on a practical scale."[37] However, cyanide remained restricted to districts where gold was the dominant mineral product.[38] Even there, cyanide treatment was often still an auxiliary to amalgamation rather than a central component of the refining system. None of the mills mentioned above were primarily registered as cyanide plants in the 1897–1900 *Memoria* of the Secretaría de Fomento.[39] Nevertheless, the results were stunning. Mexico's gold production had already exploded, reaching by 1902 ten times its level of just a decade earlier. But gold production remained less than a third of national silver output in value, and the latter remained untouched by the early cyanide revolution.[40]

Most miners and metallurgists around the world assumed that gold-dominant ores constituted the only effective and affordable target for cyanidation.[41] Despite experimentation in Mexico's silver camps by Hunt and Trewartha-James in the early 1890s, all the initial adoptions came in gold districts. These cyanide plants always yielded some silver, but far less efficiently than they yielded gold. At the Palmarejo plant in southwest Chihuahua, for instance, cyanidation in the first years extracted 95.5 percent of the assayed gold value of mined ores but only 52.5 percent of the silver value, well below the typical yield in amalgamation plants.[42] Until 1902, Mexico's leading mining paper, *El Minero Mexicano,* discussed cyanidation only in relation to gold ores, though that was about to change dramatically.

. . .

Over a decade after news of the MacArthur-Forrest process first reached Mexico, most miners and metallurgists remained skeptical about the viability of the cyanide process for refining silver-heavy ores. For John Southworth, who visited perhaps more Mexican mining camps than any other man at the time, the application of cyanide to silver ores "presented an apparently insurmountable problem."[43] Mexican silver companies continued to build, expand, and modify their *haciendas de beneficio* based on mercury amalgamation. In the old Pachuca camps, for instance, companies invested heavily in new mining and milling facilities into the early 1900s, including a 30,000-dollar amalgamation facility at the Hacienda Progreso and later an entirely new amalgamation plant at Loreto.[44] Cyaniding experts continued to focus almost exclusively on gold, advising as late as 1904 that "the greater the proportion of gold, the more manifest the advantage of cyaniding."[45]

At the end of 1903, Mexico's production of silver in cyanidation plants totaled only a small fraction of national production.[46] Not until January 1902 did *El Minero Mexicano* publish on the possible application of the cyanide process to silver ores. Their reprinted article from the *Transactions of the Institute of Mining and Metallurgy* (London), written by the chief chemist of the MGSRC, Walter H. Virgoe, offered a detailed chemical treatise on what he presented as a continuing challenge to the industry.[47] The general view toward the cyanidation of silver ores was still largely skeptical, "scarcely heard of," according to one advocate.[48] As late as 1903 the MacArthur-Forrest laboratory in Mexico City remained focused on gold ores. This skepticism was not just a Mexican phenomenon but characterized views on cyaniding and silver throughout the global mining industry. There had, in fact, been little serious attention to the cyaniding of silver ores worldwide. One of the first British textbooks on the process only begins to discuss the treatment of silver ores in its fourth edition, in 1906, still warning readers, however, that "the weak point in the present treatment of these ores is the low extraction of silver."[49]

That little had changed on the refining end of the silver business is evident in John Southworth's magnificent 1905 compendium of Mexico's mines, *Las Minas de México,* based on his extensive travels and reports from mining districts over the preceding years. He noted that Mexico's major silver regions still lay in deep recession and relied heavily on traditional methods. In Pachuca, only the two new *haciendas de beneficio* were working. In Guanajuato, most of the major mines remained underwater, with nearly three-quarters of the hundred-plus shafts entirely abandoned. Throughout the country, cyaniding of silver ores was still rare, amalgamation was the norm, and the industry was depressed.[50]

Cassel's agents in Mexico had experimented with silver ores through the 1890s. In 1891, Hunt and Trewartha-James noted that by using a stronger cyanide solution on more finely ground ore (stronger and finer, that is, than what MacArthur and Forrest used for gold ores), they could obtain a higher extraction of silver.[51] In 1896 Francis J. Hobson, a chemist employed by the MGSRC, conducted experiments on ores bearing significant quantities of both gold and silver in the state of Sinaloa, using a highly diluted cyanide solution and closely matching the earlier results, though he did not cite them. Hobson soon erected a small cyaniding plant, and two years later he reportedly oversaw the installation of a cyanide plant in Durango, followed shortly by another mill.[52] Over the next two years a few more small cyanide plants were erected in silver districts, including the first that was not simply an annex to existing silver amalgamation or lexiviation plants.[53]

Transition from experiment to large-scale application came first in the great silver district of Guanajuato, inaugurating a dramatic period of major investments across the country. The San Francisco cyanide mill of the Guanajuato Consolidated Mining and Milling Company, in operation by February 1905, was (according to its designer) "the first complete and successful cyanide plant for the treatment of silver ores" in Mexico.[54] It was certainly the first large-scale, fully integrated cyanidation plant and thus set the standard for all those that followed. Major investments in rejuvenating the Guanajuato mines had begun in 1898 with the organization of the Consolidated Company, which initially had erected a new amalgamation mill. Within several years, however, high production costs and low-grade ore led the company's management to realize "that the future of the company depended on finding some process that would make a higher recovery and operate more economically than . . . amalgamation."[55] What happened next is subject to competing and contradictory accounts by the leading participants. They agree, however, that E. M. Hamilton had conducted promising experiments with cyaniding Guanajuato ores around 1902 but that subsequent tests conducted by the MGSRC lab in Mexico City discouraged interest. By 1904, either Hamilton or Bernard MacDonald replicated the successful tests with weak solutions and fine grinding, yielding silver close to or above 90 percent of the assay. Quickly thereafter, the Guanajuato Consolidated Company, and soon many others, invested heavily in new cyaniding plants based on that approach.[56]

New US companies quickly bought up large numbers of the district's mines.[57] Investing heavily in rail transport, electrification, and a wide range of

new techniques to pump, dig, and process ore, one company after another followed the Consolidated's first adoption of the cyanide process. Each hired cyaniding experts and erected new plants to process low-grade ores and tailings: the Bustos and Flores mills of the Guanajuato Reduction and Mines Company; the Jesús María mill at La Luz of the Guanajuato Amalgamated Gold Mines Company; and the Perigrina, Pinguico, Nayal, and San Próspero mills of the Guanajuato Development Company (figure 19).[58] By August of 1906 the district was, for the first time in a century, "again in boom conditions," as a local paper observed; Guanajuato had undergone "a complete transformation."[59] As one of the principal consulting engineers boasted, "Thus a new era of silver metallurgy has been ushered in and firmly established."[60]

Meanwhile, most of the rest of Mexico's silver mining industry, "after watching Guanajuato," followed that district's example, although Guanajuato's mills would retain the lead in adopting improvements in silver cyaniding.[61] The Pachuca district lagged slightly behind but followed quickly after 1906. Although their amalgamation plants had been fully redesigned barely a decade earlier, Real de Monte, La Blanca, San Francisco, and other mines quickly installed new cyaniding plants.[62] Pachuca was not alone, as several dozen mining companies around the country worked to build new cyaniding plants between 1906 and 1908. The only important district that remained relatively untouched by the diffusion of cyaniding was Zacatecas, where in early 1907 "as yet little has been done."[63]

Transformation in Mexico's gold and silver industry was nothing short of revolutionary. "Up to two years ago," explained one editorial in 1906, "the patio process was all that was known."[64] Until then, the major silver districts remained in a state "of almost complete stagnation," as they had been for several decades.[65] Yet by 1906, local Mexican newspapers spoke of the inauguration of a wholly new technological system, "a complete transformation ... changing systems established for many centuries" with the adoption of cyaniding, electrification, pneumatic drills, dynamite, and other innovations.[66] The industry's leading North American journal noted a year later that "the cyaniding of low grade ores and the old dumps is no longer an experiment; the profits on $30 ore have been raised to about $22, where formerly they were less than $3."[67] Profits rose dramatically because cyaniding pushed yields to over 90 percent of assay values and at the same time substantially reduced costs. Where costs at cutting-edge amalgamation plants ran about eight pesos per ton, new cyaniding plants cut this in half or more. High yields and low costs meant that it was now profitable to process silver ores that assayed at only nine pesos or less per ton.[68] By 1907 cyanide capacity in Mexico reached over five thousand tons daily, and amalgamation was "almost totally abandoned," as its operating costs were higher than the value of the metal contained in the available ore.[69] By one count, amalgamation accounted for barely 2 percent of national production in 1907, while cyaniding had expanded to over 30 percent (and in Guanajuato nearly 90 percent).[70] Most of the rest came from the large smelters, the subject of a different technological story. By 1910 cyanide had made the local refining of gold and silver ores economically viable again, and this "enormous technological leap" injected new life into Mexico's precious metal districts (figure 20).[71]

. . .

But this story of cyanide's diffusion in Mexico obscures the extensive work necessary to adapt the process to Mexico's recalcitrant silver ores. Extensive experimentation, adaptation, innovation, and learning made adoption possible and pervaded the Mexican experience. "Constant experimentation" by mine managers and engineers was in fact the norm throughout both Mexican and world mining camps at the turn of the century.[72] As cyaniding matured,

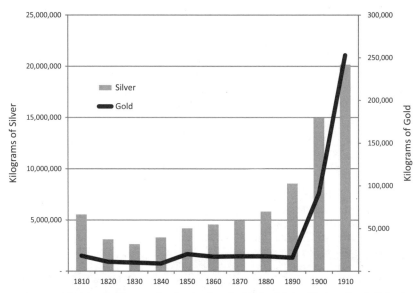

FIGURE 20. Gold and silver production by decade. Derived from Christopher J. Schmitz, *World Non-ferrous Metal Production and Prices, 1700–1976* (London: Frank Cass, 1979), tables 12.20 and 5.18; compare with Marvin D. Bernstein, *The Mexican Mining Industry, 1890–1950: A Study in the Interaction of Politics, Economics, and Technology* (Albany: State University of New York Press, 1964), 128, table 7, and Juan Manuel Romero Gil, *La mineria en la noroeste de México: Utopía y realidad, 1850–1910* (Mexico: Plaza y Valdés, 2001), 199–200.

some mills continued to amalgamate ores at the stamping stage or added pan amalgamators; some amalgamated and ran the ore over concentrating tables between stamping and treating, using a wide variety of classifiers and tables and crushers and grinders, altering the specifications of the cyanide process itself: strength of solution, number of washes, length of wash, size and design of tank, type of agitation, and on and on. The constant goal of all experimentation was to increase the extraction rate, to push the yield as close to or above 90 percent of the assay value as possible, all the time keeping a close eye on production costs. The scope of possible variations is evident in the dozens of published descriptions of the ever changing state of the art. From the entry in figure 21, a portion of the table of contents of a 1901 London text on gold milling, one can get a sense of the possible permutations of what—at this still early stage—looked like a relatively simple process:[73]

Innovation in cyaniding was driven by the compelling economic logic of profitability. Profits in the first decade of the twentieth century came only for those companies that discovered new bonanza ores (a very small subset of the

CHAPTER X.

CYANIDATION.

Chemistry—Equations; Action of KCy on Base Metals; Selective Action; Sources of Oxygen; Temperature; Loss of KCy; Applicability— Testing Ores: Neutralising, Analyses, Laboratory Guidance, Impediments; Testing Solutions; Testing Water; Estimating Oxygen in Liquors; Wet *v.* Dry Milling. Leaching Plant—Accommodation; Vat Dimensions; Ranging Vats; Shape of Vats; Materials of Vats; Wooden Vats; Steel Vats; Masonry Vats; Vat Filters; Vat Doors; Vat Foundations; Vacuum Apparatus; Agitators. Charging and Discharging Vats—Delivery: Traction, Conveying, Pumping, Tailings Wheels; Filling: Classification, Distributors, Intermediate, Direct; Concentration; Sampling; Discharging. Storage and Circulation of Liquors—Stock Tanks, Settling Tanks, Pipe Lines, Pumps. Leaching —Preliminary Washes, Strong Liquors, Weak Liquors, Final Washes: Examples. Treating Pyritic Ore—Percolating, Agitating; Oxygenating, Bromo-cyanidation; Roasting. Treating Slimes—Coagulation, Decantation; Lime Process; Agitation: Barrels, Mechanical Stirrers, Pumps, Pneumatic; Filtration: Presses, Continuous Filters. Precipitation—Clarification; Zinc, Lead-Zinc, Zinc fume, Lead, Iron, Charcoal, Aluminium, Stannous Chloride, Cyano-amalgamation, Copper Sulphide. Clean-up—Zinc shavings, Zinc dust, Lead, Charcoal. Arrangement of Works. Working Results: Costs and Extractions in Australia, India, New Zealand, Transvaal, United States. Poisoning . . . 473–686

FIGURE 21. Cyaniding by the book: table of contents for chapter 10 from Charles George Warnford Lock, *Gold Milling: Principles and Practice* (London: E. & F.N. Spon, 1901), xiii–xiv.

total) and for those who successfully lowered mining and milling costs through the adoption of new techniques. Nearly all faced the common challenge of making low-grade ores pay.[74] This was especially true for Mexico's *antiguas*, the older mines whose bonanzas had played out long ago and which sat on huge tailings dumps, the accumulation of decades, or sometimes centuries, of crushed ore that still held valuable metal. At the same time, the catastrophic fall in the price of silver in the world market loomed over Mexico's silver miners.

"Practically all over the republic," mines and refineries undertook efforts "for the reducing of the cost of handling their materials . . . to get the operating expenses reduced to the lowest possible figure."[75] As one mining engineer wrote, "The low value of the ore treated [in Mexico], by stimulating economy, is the cause of the great progress which has been made within the last year in the treatment of silver ores."[76] No longer would the business of mining be what Matías Romero had earlier called a "game of chance," dependent on experience, judgment, and lucky strikes.[77] Instead, the methodical, scientific, and efficient working of vast quantities of low-grade ore came to define an entirely new technological system in extracting and refining metals through the twentieth century.

Experimentation and learning were central to the delayed adaptation of cyanide to silver, pioneered in Mexico. Why did the employees in the MacArthur-Forrest laboratory in Mexico City—the "best metallurgical specialists in that process"—fail to successfully work out the application of cyaniding to silver ores before 1904?[78] Mexico's silver ores posed technical challenges that gold had not.[79] Silver often occurs in various combinations with sulfur, antimony, arsenic, and other elements, more tightly bound, and in more complicated ways, than gold. These combinations could vary widely from location to location, so that a specification of the cyanide process that extracted 80 percent from one ore sample might extract only 40 percent from another. Ores from the mines of the Real de Monte company in Pachuca, for example, presented "striking differences in the nature of the accompanying constituents of the gangue, thereby presenting an extremely complex problem from the point of view of the Cyanide Chemist."[80] Mexican ores, moreover, were reportedly "less docile" than their counterparts farther north.[81]

For nearly a decade, experiments by agents of the MacArthur-Forrest laboratory in Mexico City had "discouraged hope" in applying cyaniding to silver.[82] John Allan, a chemist at the lab, conducted extensive tests with Mexican silver ores and delivered a lukewarm report on the results at the 1904 meeting of the American Institute of Mining Engineers in Atlantic City. Commercial use of the cyanide process with silver ores, he reported, was "possible" and "merits [further] investigation" but would mostly likely serve only as a complement to other processes.[83] Although his reported calculations for yields and costs competed favorably with other processes, this was not an encouraging endorsement. Contemporary readers judged the report "skeptical," noting later that it "threw a wet blanket over the hope of many."[84] Through the 1890s "skepticism" reigned, and "many doubts were expressed as to the ability to treat [silver ores] by the cyanide process."[85]

Adapting the cyanide process to silver ores posed both chemical and mechanical problems. Early efforts sought to address the complexity of silver ores through initial roasting and chloridizing. Yet these methods still resulted in relatively low silver yields and required large amounts of fuel, and hence significant added expense in Mexico's fuel-scarce environment.[86] In contrast, the subsequent experiments in Guanajuato of Hamilton (working for the Charles Butters Company) and MacDonald (consulting for the Guanajuato Consolidated Company) soon indicated the three essential elements of effective silver cyanidation: more finely ground ore, relatively stronger cyanide solutions, and agitation and exposure of solutions to oxygen for relatively longer periods of time.[87]

Amalgamation worked best with more coarsely ground ore, or "sands," and early cyaniding mills in the gold districts treated both sands and slimes. But experimentation with Mexico's silver ores in 1904–6 increasingly found that "the finer the product, the higher the extraction."[88] This was especially true when the metal was finely dispersed through the rock and tightly bound with other minerals—more often the case for silver than for gold ores. Extremely fine grinding—"sliming"—allowed the chemical action to occur more effectively and quickly by exposing more "thoroughly every particle of the silver-compounds to the solvent action of the cyanide solution."[89] But fine grinding posed its own technological challenge; the commonly used stamp or Chilean mills were not up to the task. Only with the introduction of electricity and a new grinding technology would cyaniding become economical on a large scale. Newly developed tube mills provided that technology, and cyanide mill managers moved toward a system that used electric-powered tube mills and regrinding to produce consistent slimes for their cyanide tanks. Without electricity, tube mills would be uneconomical; without tube mills, all-slime methods could not be realized and the cyaniding of silver ores would remain inefficient and unprofitable.[90]

Once the ore was finely ground, the second key element in cyaniding was mixing the slimed pulp with the cyanide solution in large tanks. As with grinding, low-grade ores put pressure on mill managers to experiment widely with ways to increase yields while minimizing the consumption of the expensive cyanide. Mexican silver camps provided crucial innovations, most notably the "Pachuca" and "Parral" tanks designed to maximize the effect of mechanical agitation while injecting oxygen into the solution. These designs quickly became standard practice in cyaniding plants around the world.

Finally, separating the silver-rich cyanide solution from the slime also required new techniques. Earlier practices of decanting the solution did not work well with large batches and finely ground slimes.[91] The development and diffusion of the filter press (borrowed from Australian practice) proved critical to solving this mechanical problem. All three of these mechanical and procedural innovations derived from the constant experiments conducted by mill managers and metallurgical engineers, all seeking to push yields as high as possible and the costs as low as possible, ideally, toward 2.50 dollars per ton of processed ore.[92]

Once metallurgists worked out these and other elements of adapting the cyanide process to Mexico's silver ores, investments in new plants followed quickly. Miners' acceptance of silver cyaniding became widespread by 1904 or so, and by the end of 1906 most major silver camps had built or were building new cyaniding plants. By the early 1910s there would be at least 112 cyaniding plants in Mexico with a total capacity of nearly twenty-five thousand tons of ore per day.[93]

Mexico's mining sector, in other words, was a technological leader in the global adaptation of cyanide to silver ores. The initial breakthroughs in the application of the MacArthur-Forrest process to silver ores were made in Mexico, and the country's mining districts continued to produce important innovations in cyaniding and its complementary processes over the next decade. "No country," wrote one mining engineer in 1908, "has such a promising outlook for the production of silver by the cyanide process as that which Mexico promises in the next few years," and another concurred that Mexican refineries were "representative of the best practice on this continent."[94] Far from being a technological laggard in the innovation and application of new technologies, the mining sector in Mexico was a technological leader, close to and sometimes in advance of an international wave of mining innovations.

. . .

By 1910 mining in Mexico was nearly unrecognizable from the perspective of the 1870s. Not only was the industry now dominated by the production of industrial metals like copper, lead, and zinc, entirely absent thirty years earlier, but an entirely new technological system extracted and processed these industrial minerals as well as Mexico's gold and silver. The cyanide process constituted just one piece of this new system, which embraced pumping, digging, blasting, excavating, ventilating, hauling, sorting, classifying, crushing, mixing, agitating, filtering, and smelting, all fully integrated within a new infrastructure of rail transport and electrical power networks. In the production of gold and silver, the cyanide process constituted a multipart subsystem of its own, central to the transformation of Mexican mining.

With the successful adoption and diffusion of cyaniding, Mexican gold production expanded by a factor of nearly twenty-five by 1910, while silver production grew fourfold (recall figure 20). Mexico's precious metal output increased at an annual average 6.1 percent and accounted for 45 percent of Mexican exports and 6.4 percent of total GDP in 1900, more than any other single activity.[95] Technological changes nearly doubled worker productivity in the mining sector between 1890 and 1910.[96] Mining remained, as the government of Porfirio Díaz recognized, "the primary component of national wealth."[97] Yet in basic ways "Mexican" mining was not Mexican at all but part of an almost seamless North American industry.

It was foreign capital, entrepreneurship, and know-how that transformed Mexican mining. Between 1890 and 1910 new investments totaling over 300 million US dollars poured into Mexican mining and mineral refining from abroad, the equivalent of roughly 50 percent of national GDP.[98] Investors from the United States provided the lion's share of mining investment, over two-thirds, while, to take one, only slightly exaggerated view, "Not even one Mexican peso has been invested in [mining] companies."[99] Massive capital flows were accompanied by technology imports. American factories and foundries manufactured nearly all the machinery hardware destined for mine and mill sites in Mexico. Textbooks, handbooks, and journals came from New York, San Francisco, and London. Although the cyanide process itself and the MGSRC were British creations, most of the expertise that underlay its adoption, adaptation, and diffusion in Mexico came from US mining and metallurgical engineers.[100] Investors, managers, and engineers from the United States and beyond provided the entrepreneurship and know-how for new mining initiatives as they pushed experimentation with more efficient forms of organization and technology. Nearly all the new corporations that dominated mining districts in Mexico around 1900 or so were constituted in the United States. Of the 1,030 mining firms listed by John Southworth in 1910, 840 originated in the United States and only 148 in Mexico, the majority of which were small and midsized firms—those least likely to adopt cyanidation.[101] The presence of foreign personnel extended well beyond the major posts of chief consulting engineers and superintendents. As one well-traveled observer noted, "Major properties each had an American foreman, shift and level bosses, and a timekeeper, and also contractors where speed on shaft work, drifts, and raises was important."[102] Americans typically filled nearly every key management, supervising, and technical position, as well as those skilled jobs in strategic parts of the mine and refinery.[103]

Mexicans played little role in this revolution of mining and refining technologies. In a very basic sense, the mines and mills of Guanajuato, Pachuca,

El Oro, and the Sierra Madre Occidental were "Mexican" only by accident of their geographic location within that country's political borders. In all other ways, they were nearly indistinguishable from the mines and mills of California, Nevada, Colorado, and Montana. "Mexican" mining and refining had become an extension of a unified North American industry. This had not always been the case. As late as the 1870s, Mexican capital, entrepreneurship, locally developed technologies, and highly skilled and experienced Mexican mining engineers and technical workers had played a predominant role in the mining sector. A generation later, these men had been nearly entirely displaced by non-Mexican capital, technology, and skilled personnel. The demand for technical knowledge and expertise generated by Mexico's turn-of-the-century mining boom drew overwhelmingly from foreign supplies and stimulated relatively little response within Mexico.

On one level, geopolitical location mattered. Those mines and mills and workers lay within Mexican borders, extracting and processing Mexico's natural resources. Mining contributed substantially to the national economy and employed over forty thousand Mexican workers who supported several hundred thousand family members, in addition to significant backward linkages to the provision of food, fuel, and other supplies. This was the single largest sector of the Mexican economy outside traditional agriculture, fundamental to the era's economic growth. In a basic structural and economic sense, the construction of the Mexican nation, of a relatively unified national market, would not have been possible without growth in the mining sector. The most likely alternative—certainly in the minds of most contemporaries—was the landscape before 1870: low investment levels, stagnant mineral production, economic debility and backwardness, constant penury, and enduring national fragmentation. Foreign capital and the adoption of a new technological system—adapted to Mexican conditions by foreign technicians—contributed in the short term to economic growth and the consolidation of the Mexican economy. Mexican workers, mechanics, and engineers worked with the new mining and refining technologies, undoubtedly learning by seeing and by doing in cyanide plants, in the machine shops of mining companies, and underground, and we need more firm-level studies of this laboring experience. Nevertheless, the dominant experience—especially in those positions that worked most closely with new techniques—was displacement by foreign workers and engineers. The general displacement of Mexican engineers meant that there was relatively little local assimilation of new knowledge and expertise, with long-term implications for Mexican development.

PART THREE

Discussion

SEVEN

Obstacles to Adoption

BY THE TIME THAT ISAAC GARZA and his partners at the Vidriera Monterrey ran the first batch of molten glass through their newly acquired Owens machine in 1912, Mexico had imported over three hundred thousand sewing machines, and the cyanide process had reshaped gold and silver refining across most of the nation's mining districts. However, while efforts to adopt these and many other new technologies had begun to transform the Mexican landscape of labor and production in the decades after 1870, these efforts did not always go smoothly. Obstacles to successful adoption lay everywhere in the new Mexican context for imported machines, processes, and new forms of knowledge and expertise: in the physical environment, in relatively undeveloped economic markets, and in the particular social, political, and institutional contexts that imported technologies found in Mexico. Contrary to the predictions of late twentieth-century economists, adopting new knowledge from abroad was not always easy. This was certainly the case with the canonical technologies of the first industrial revolution—railroads, steam power, and ironworking, as we saw in chapters 2 and 3. Even those successful cases of technology adoption like sewing machines, glass bottle manufacturing, and the cyanide process proceeded in fits and starts, with investors, entrepreneurs, and consumers continually working to negotiate multiple obstacles. These varied widely; they were different for small-scale product technologies (like sewing machines) than for large-scale process or production technologies (like the Owens system and the cyanide process). But even when new technologies were demonstrably superior in productive capacity and efficiency in relation to the existing state of the art in Mexico, adoption did not always proceed smoothly. Technologies conceived and developed in a North Atlantic context did not necessarily find an easy local fit in Mexico.

This does not mean that they could not fit, or that they did not eventually become deeply integrated into economic markets, local social relations, and new cultural practices. Given rapid economic expansion in the North Atlantic, the resulting spillover of capital and technology washed high upon Mexico's shores, and many Mexicans proved eager and adept at integrating new technologies into their daily lives as investors, workers, and consumers. The sewing machine, glass bottle, and cyanide stories illustrate just three out of many experiences, as adopters proved able to negotiate multiple obstacles and adapt the technology to the new context, or to adapt aspects of the new contextual environment to the requisites of the imported technology. Chapter 3 argued implicitly that most obstacles to adoption across the Mexican economy were relatively malleable rather than relatively obdurate.

But obstacles to technological innovation could and did pose substantial limits to change in late-century Mexico. First, obstacles could substantially delay entrepreneurs' efforts, even though news of new advances traveled quickly across national borders and even though investors in Mexico could readily purchase the necessary hardware and know-how off North Atlantic shelves. Second, once commercialized, persistent problems of "fit" often impaired the full productive potential of newly adopted technologies. Compared to the same process in its original North Atlantic context, machines and production processes adopted in Mexico often operated at significantly lower levels of productivity or did not diffuse beyond the first adopters. Third, some technologies were not adopted at all, despite their availability in the North Atlantic. Local demand might be too weak, the magnitude of obstacles to mutually adapt imported technologies and the new context might be too great, or adopters might face concerted resistance from groups threatened by change. In these situations—relatively rare— investors perceived that the costs of adoption exceeded the potential benefits, and they abandoned (or never undertook) initial efforts.

This chapter examines the limits to technological change in late nineteenth-century Mexico. The flood of technology imports we traced in chapter 3 obscures a varied landscape of factors that delayed the adoption of new technologies, that limited or impaired their productive impact, or that prevented adoption in the first place. Why did change occur with relative ease in some activities, with greater difficulty in others, and not at all elsewhere? On one hand, the *extent* of technological change in late nineteenth-century Mexico was made possible by forces largely exogenous to the Mexican economy: the supply of new techniques and expertise available in the North

Atlantic and the interest of manufacturers and proprietors there in marketing machines around the world. In Mexico, the government of Porfirio Díaz
worked to align investment incentives with this global moment of opportunity, while economic growth and social change generated rising demand for
new products and processes. Investment in technologies quickly followed.
On the other hand, however, availability and incentives cannot fully explain
the delays, the impaired adoptions, and the persistence of older ways of doing
things. Local factors—the obstacles inherent in moving technologies across
borders, to new social contexts and new markets—fundamentally shaped the
experience of adoption and commercial use, what was adopted and what
wasn't, thus defining the *limits* to technological change. This chapter examines the limits to *adoption* before turning, in chapter 8, to the critical question of learning and assimilation.

DELAYED ADOPTION

Sewing machines, the Owens system, and cyanide treatment were each
adopted in Mexico with relatively short delays following their initial development in the North Atlantic. Mexicans were using sewing machines in the
1850s, less than a decade after Elias Howe's first US patent. Diffusion in
Mexican markets proceeded swiftly thereafter, at levels of adoption under
those in the North Atlantic but above much of the rest of the world. Likewise,
efforts to bring the Owens bottle system to Mexico began almost immediately after its US debut, although commercialization took a decade of hard
work, and one firm succeeded in monopolizing its use. Mining engineers
quickly recognized the transformative potential of cyaniding in Mexico's
precious metal sector and worked hard to adapt cyaniding to local conditions. Successful adaptation to silver ores came after a decade of intensive
experimentation, followed by rapid diffusion in the larger mining camps.
Across the economy efforts to adopt new technologies moved forward, and
delays in cross-border adoption typically amounted to months or a few years,
rather than to several decades.

But this had not always been the case. For half a century or more, efforts
to adopt the technologies of the first industrial revolution in Mexico had met
with scant success. Railroads, steam engines, and ironworking all waited
decades between initial efforts and their eventual adoption and diffusion.
Among the technologies newly available in the North Atlantic between 1820

and 1870, only modern textile factories based on imported spindles and looms established a significant foothold in Mexico. But if long delays and failed efforts dominated Mexico's first half century of independence, they did not entirely disappear during the late-century era of more rapid change.

Delays in adoption typically originated in problems of "fit" between imported technologies and new contexts. Mexico's undeveloped markets for production inputs offered the most common hurdle for new enterprises: transportation to get materials to production sites, acquisition of raw materials and intermediate inputs appropriate to the design requirements of new production technologies, the expertise and labor necessary to install and operate new production systems, and the availability of motive power to run large-scale mechanized machinery. Looming over nearly all new efforts to adopt mechanized, industrial-scale methods in mining and manufacturing was the persistently high price of fuel. Markets for all these inputs were often nonexistent or undeveloped and thus costly. Nearly anything, of course, could be had in the globalizing marketplace of the late nineteenth-century Atlantic economy, but at what price? Those who sought to adopt new technologies did not enjoy, in other words, the externalities of a developed marketplace. They had to work long and hard to explore, identify, and develop sources of transport, material inputs, expertise, and power. As a result, the costs of adoption typically ran high, raising risk, lowering incentives to invest, and hindering the efforts of new enterprises.

Transporting machinery, people, and production inputs had never been easy or cheap in Mexico. Even with falling oceanic freight rates through late century and the extension of Mexico's domestic railroad network, transport costs continued to pose substantial obstacles to the introduction of new technologies and to new enterprises generally. As late as 1909, for example, one textile manufacturer who paid 2,635 dollars for five large carding machines in Liverpool had to add 330 dollars for packing and 1,167 dollars for freight, duty, and erecting costs. Another paid 4,199 dollars for six warp frames of 336 spindles each, plus 493 dollars for packing and 1,845 dollars for transport.[1] Investors in new factories like the Vidriera Monterrey complained vigorously about the cost of transporting raw materials and lobbied federal officials to lower the rate schedules for domestic cargo. By one estimate, the cost of establishing a factory in Mexico was 55 percent higher than that of establishing the same plant in Great Britain.[2] Off the rail grid—across much of the national territory—moving machinery and goods still depended on the backs of mules and men, such as those who hauled Singer machines into villages and remote mining camps. Mexico's rugged geography continued to burden the adoption of new machinery because, even with railroads, "vast regions [were] considered almost inaccessible" into the twentieth century.[3]

Once imported, production systems required all sorts of inputs, ranging from raw materials to intermediate inputs and labor. Acquiring these at reasonable cost and sufficient quality proved a greater challenge than most entrepreneurs expected. The decade-long efforts of Juan Brittingham and his partners at the Vidriera Monterrey to locate raw materials for their glass bottle plant exemplifies the experience of many new enterprises. Textile firms constantly worked to locate adequate supplies of quality cotton at a reasonable price—sometimes from domestic planters, sometimes imported. The beer industry struggled to locate affordable supplies of hops and barley. Brewery owners made several efforts to establish local sources, with little success, and remained dependent on costly imports. Mexico's paper factories struggled for decades to locate affordable sources of linen rags and experimented with locally available agave fibers. Water always proved more difficult to acquire than investors expected. In Mexico's water-scarce environment, anyone who needed water to power mills and machinery or as part of a production process had to negotiate with local municipalities and existing rights holders, a complication that frequently led to substantial delays. And, as we will see below, firms like the Vidriera Monterrey, the Fundidora Monterrey, and many others were consistently unable to acquire fuel in the form of wood, coal, or coke at reasonable quality and cost.[4]

Semimanufactured inputs like machine parts and industrial chemicals also proved costly to acquire. Efforts to introduce machine-based production in Mexican mines and manufactories had been plagued by the high cost of metal parts since the eighteenth century. Recall that Miguel López had little hope of adopting the Newcomen steam engine to Mexico in the 1730s for precisely this reason and that he worried about Mexico's "permanent dependency" on foreign suppliers for metal parts.[5] The same challenge plagued British mining firms when they began to import steam engines in the 1820s. By the 1890s, a new generation of investors in factories and mining enterprises repeatedly lobbied the Finance Ministry to reduce import duties on intermediate inputs, especially on iron and steel manufactures and chemicals. At the same time, those interested in these lines of business lobbied for increased protection. The ministry found itself caught between competing objectives— to facilitate access to foreign sources of intermediate inputs or to incentivize their manufacture in Mexico—and initially opted for the former.[6] But whether these inputs were imported, or produced in Mexico behind protective tariffs, the result was the same: a persistently high expense that contributed to the relatively high production costs of Mexico's infant industries.

Finally, every new enterprise needed substantial sources of inanimate energy to drive the large-scale machinery that characterized most late-century production systems. In Mexico as elsewhere, water mills, steam engines, electric power, and, eventually, gasoline engines provided an essential requisite for the mechanization and modernization of economic activity across the economy. This was especially the case when mechanization depended on large-scale machinery, and for heat-intensive industrial processes like metallurgy, glassmaking, brewing, sugar refining, and brick making, all major activities in the Mexican economy. Yet the fuels necessary for inanimate power were relatively scarce in Mexico: water, wood, and coal. High power costs burdened innovators, delayed adoption, reduced operating efficiencies, and restricted the diffusion of new industrial technologies in late nineteenth-century Mexico.

Efforts to adopt inanimate power had long faced significant obstacles in Mexico, as we saw in chapters 2 and 3. Although water-driven mills were introduced soon after Europeans' arrival in the sixteenth century, they remained relatively scarce across the economic heartland of central Mexico because of the scarcity and seasonality of water. Windmills were adopted only in the Yucatan and in the cattle country of the far North in the nineteenth century, principally to draw groundwater from aquifers. Steam power had captured the minds of Mexican entrepreneurs and officials since the eighteenth century, but efforts to introduce steam engines had yielded few results for well over a century. By the 1860s, there were no more than a handful of steam engines operating in Mexico. Although steam engine imports began to rise steadily in the 1870s as the cost of machines, transportation, and expertise fell in North Atlantic markets, steam power would nonetheless remain relatively expensive because adopters in Mexico could not overcome the persistently high prices of fuel.

Centuries of cutting wood for fuel had denuded the landscape across much of Mexico's Meseta Central, and in a semiarid environment rates of reforestation could not keep up. In the nineteenth century, the increasingly voracious appetite of railroads, mines, and new industries only exacerbated what was already a long-standing problem. Anecdotal commentary on the problem of deforestation and wood-fuel scarcity abounds from the late colonial era through the nineteenth century, and what little we know about the cost of firewood and charcoal only confirms the rhetoric.[7] Prices ran well above North Atlantic levels through the century. Milled lumber, for instance, sold in central Mexico for three times the level of US prices, and charcoal prices in Mexico doubled through the second half of the century.[8] Timber scarcity affected not just fuel prices but also construction costs; Mexico imported large quantities of lumber through the late nineteenth century and would remain a net wood product importer through the twentieth.[9] Deforestation was one consequence of economic growth.

By late century, railroads and new factories increasingly demanded fuel with a higher caloric content than wood-based carbon to drive trains and machinery. But like firewood and charcoal, mineral coal and coke proved scarce and costly in Mexico. Miners and manufacturers frequently complained about the low quality and high cost of Mexican coal. Production costs ran high in the Sabinas coalfields of Coahuila—the only significant deposits in the country—and the coal itself had a high ash content and burned poorly compared to imported anthracite.[10] As a consequence, Mexico's new industrialists relied heavily on imported mineral fuel. By 1908, imports had reached about 1.3 million tons of coal and almost half a million tons of coke.[11] Imported coal and coke solved the quality but not the cost disadvantages of domestic coal, as transport could double or triple costs for consumers. At century's end, the price of coal in central Mexico ran between seven and fourteen US dollars per ton, compared to barely one-third that in the US Midwest and East.[12] Even at the Fundidora Monterrey, close to the border, fuel costs ran 50 percent higher than in the US steel industry. Other firms retrofitted their boilers—originally designed to burn coal—to run on wood, losing significant efficiencies in the process.[13] "Coal for steam power [is] too costly," noted one observer, and large factories favored water over steam when they could.[14]

Persistently high fuel costs created a powerful impediment to the adoption of power- and fuel-intensive technologies throughout Mexico. In 1898 Matías Romero declared that high fuel costs presented "the greatest and most pressing" obstacle facing the Mexican economy. Four years later *El Economista Mexicano* listed fuel costs as one of the four most important economic challenges facing Mexico (along with the monetary system, irrigation, and immigration), while the *Mexican Herald* agreed that "the quality of fuel supply in Mexico is a serious one," after earlier declaring that "Mexico's chief want from an industrial point of view is cheap fuel."[15] Investor Juan Brittingham concurred, complaining in 1910 that "fuel is the keystone of the industrial arch and high priced fuel is going to cripple generally the manufacturing end of Mexico."[16] Discovery of new coalfields, declared one US consular agent, "would make a commercial revolution in this country."[17] Yet fuel costs remained persistently high to the end of the century, despite a fivefold increase in domestic coal and coke production, and posed a powerful obstacle to the adoption of new technologies. At the same time, high fuel costs contributed to the bifurcated structure of Mexican industry: a few very large firms proved able to negotiate high fuel costs through imports or preferential rates, while small-scale artisanal workshops remained dependent on wood fuel or small lots of costly coal, with very little in the way of competitive midsized firms between.[18] Only the introduction of cheaper hydroelectric power after the turn of the century began to finally erode the persistently high cost of power. In sum, undeveloped input markets for transportation, raw materials, intermediate inputs, and motive power meant that entrepreneurs in Mexico faced consistently higher technology adoption costs than their counterparts in the North Atlantic, against whom they had to compete in product markets.

IMPAIRED ADOPTION

Obstacles not only delayed the adoption of new technologies but also impaired their use in other ways. Many investors discovered that even when they had successfully installed a new machine or process, its productivity did not match that of the same technology in its original North Atlantic context. In some cases, this was because labor issues limited the efficiency gains of new machines and processes. In others, the design of new technological systems proved poorly matched to local conditions and undermined efficiency and profitability. And some imported technologies never diffused beyond a very small number of adopters, limiting their potential productive impact in the Mexican economy.

Productive Efficiency

Innovation contributes to economic growth when it increases the productivity of production inputs like labor and land, and the wave of technology imports to Mexico after 1870 did just that. Output per worker more than doubled in Mexico's mining sector, increased by about 50 percent in manufacturing, and increased by nearly 20 percent in agriculture.[19] In the textile industry, labor productivity rose at an average annual rate of 2.4 percent between 1850 and 1913 and at 4.7 percent per year after 1891.[20] Anecdotal evidence from across the economy concurs. In the industrial center of Guadalajara, for instance, productivity per worker between 1895 and 1907 correlated closely with the introduction of power-driven machinery.[21] Analyses of productivity in the mining sector show much the same growth tendencies. Worker productivity nearly doubled between 1897 and 1907, by one estimate, while another places the increase at 250 percent over the same period.[22] These numbers represent very rough estimates based on limited data, but they indicate the direction and magnitude of technology-generated productivity gains across major sectors of the economy. The adoption of new technologies from the North Atlantic increased the productive capacity of Mexican workers and underlay Porfirian Mexico's sustained economic growth.

However, these productivity gains frequently fell well short of the productivity gains that the same new machines and processes had generated in their original North Atlantic settings. In textiles, W. A. Graham Clark observed in 1910 that Mexican employees worked fewer looms and spindles than their counterparts in the United States and England. Recent scholarship has largely confirmed this observation: in 1910, for instance, the average Mexican textile worker staffed 2.5 looms and 540 spindles, while the average British worker staffed 3.8 looms and 625 spindles and the average US worker 8.0 looms and 902 spindles. In this Mexico was little different than most late-developing countries: the first generation of industrial workers in Japan and India (for instance) were less productive than their North Atlantic counterparts working with the same machinery.[23] Historians have tended to blame low productivity on the dislocation effects of rural-to-urban migration within the first generation of industrial workers. Unfamiliar with mechanization and not yet accustomed to the tyranny of the time clock, workers who retained close ties to their home villages did not often match the productivity levels of their North Atlantic counterparts.[24] Ethnic distinctions between management and workers within Mexican plants made upward mobility on the factory floor unlikely, further diminishing incentives to prove one's worth and abilities.[25]

Inefficiencies also came when firms could not run their new, large-scale machines and production systems at full capacity. Given that these machines and systems had been designed for large markets in the North Atlantic, some historians have argued that the capacity of many imported technologies exceeded the size of Mexico's domestic market. Many of Mexico's new industries would have been, in this view, "structurally inefficient from [the] beginning."[26] However, the evidence on Mexican market size makes this a difficult argument to sustain. In nearly each case of subcapacity production—cement, steel, and glass bottles, for instance—Mexico continued to import large quantities from the United States and Europe. Imports exceeded domestic production by 100 percent for cement and by a factor of twenty for iron and steel. Market size, in other words, did not prevent Mexican firms from running at full capacity. Indeed, investors like Vicente Ferrara at the Fundidora Monterrey and Isaac Garza at the Vidriera Monterrey carefully studied market size relative to their new technological systems. The Fundidora's struggle to run at full capacity had multiple causes, including transport problems, skilled labor scarcity, fuel expense, and initial product quality.[27] Companies' failure to run their plants at full capacity typically derived from the steep challenge of wresting market share away from cheaper imports, rather than from market size. Even with substantial tariff protection (30–50 percent or more for most iron and steel products, for example, 30 percent for cement, 80–100 percent for cotton textiles, etc.), Mexican consumers frequently bought imports over domestic goods for both quality and price reasons.[28] Facing relatively high prices for machinery, transportation, material inputs, fuel, and skilled labor, and burdened by relatively lower levels of productivity per worker, Mexican producers could not easily outcompete imports even using the same technological systems. As a result, profits in import-substituting businesses were typically low and erratic.[29]

System Design

Problems also arose when new technologies, originally developed and designed within a particular social and economic context in the United States or Europe, found quite different contexts in Mexico. Sometimes these problems of fit stemmed from the new physical environment. The first Owens glass bottle machine became clogged with molten glass made from materials that cooled more quickly than those for which the machine was designed. Cyanidization faced years of experimentation with Mexico's recalcitrant silver ores before engineers developed successful adaptations. Similarly, the 120 coke ovens installed at great expense in 1907 by the Fundidora Monterrey could not produce clean coke using Mexico's Sabinas coal, and the company was forced to turn to more expensive sources of imported coal and coke.

Transporting steam engines and other machinery beyond the terminus of railway lines proved extremely difficult, given precipitous terrain and scarcity of wagon-ready roads. In Mexico's coal-scarce environment, adopters of steam power frequently adapted their boilers to burn wood, sacrificing efficiency.[30] Water scarcity presented a nearly ubiquitous obstacle, especially to miners using refining techniques developed in water-abundant regions of North America and Europe. In northern Mexico, miners turned to "dry-washing" techniques that substituted a current of air for water to flush the lighter particles of crushed ore from the heavier, metal-laden sediment. Miners used nearly a thousand dry-washing machines in one Sonoran mining district in 1909, of varying local design.[31] These kinds of challenges motivated firms to adapt the imported technologies or to develop new supply markets that would meet the requisites of the adopted technology.

While entrepreneurs worked to navigate these problems of "fit," design incompatibilities could limit the productive impact of imported technologies. Take, for instance, the installation of Mexico's first modern slaughterhouse (*rastro*).[32] In 1893 the Mexico City *cabildo* contracted with the Pauly Jail Building Company of St. Louis, Missouri, to construct Mexico's first modern slaughterhouse, modeled on North American designs (the first concessionaire had failed a year earlier). When the facility opened in September 1897 after numerous construction delays, it encountered a host of operational problems: flat cement floors did not drain blood and guts, the aerial rail system was neither integrated nor trustworthy, and heavy iron doors fell from their hinges, killing one worker. But the design of the new facility also did not fit well with the organization of Mexico City's meat distribution and retailing networks, dominated by livestock owners and meat merchants. The plant's assembly line structure had been developed in the US Midwest, where large firms like Armour and Swift used refrigerated facilities to store and transport meat, shipping it to proximate and distant markets. In Mexico City, large numbers of small to midsized meat merchants were long accustomed to picking up wagonloads of freshly butchered meat at the publicly managed slaughterhouse, and they feared the new system would undermine the competitive nature of these urban distribution markets by giving larger firms (and the new slaughterhouse owners) special advantage. Whether or not large-scale, mechanized meat processing was the most efficient long-term solution to providing sanitary meat for Mexico's rapidly growing urban populations (as Porfirian public officials argued), these early US-designed plants were plagued not only by shoddy construction but by a poor fit with the existing socioeconomic landscape. Conflicts between concessionaires, the government, livestock owners, butchers, and consumers substantially undermined their productive efficiency and profitability for over a decade. Scientific management of urban food supplies, Porfirian officials discovered, could not easily be adopted from abroad.

Diffusion

Mexico's burgeoning new industries were notoriously concentrated: a few large firms dominated the market in most fields.[33] This structure derived in part from the uncertainties inherent in adopting expensive new technologies and new firms' thin margin of profitability. Only a few entrepreneurs could access financial markets and put together the necessary investment capital and new enterprises necessary to adopt the expensive new technological systems that—for instance—constituted the Owens and cyanide processes. Even well-connected investors like Juan Brittingham and Isaac Garza struggled to construct a viable investment team. Most efforts to establish new firms based on imported technologies failed or remained barely profitable.[34] The record of new initiatives that never achieved commercial success testifies to this challenge: of 311 applications to the federal Industrias Nuevas program, many of which involved new technologies, over 80 percent were abandoned, and only 8 achieved commercial production. Investors in Mexico's new industries always sought ways to ensure profits in an environment of uncertainty, with high production costs and stiff foreign competition. Monopolizing regional or national markets provided one such strategy.[35] Government policies, moreover, did not widen access to new opportunities for most Mexicans. Investors who might have undertaken competitive small or midsized initiatives were not able to access the market opportunities available to those with substantial resources and political connections. Lending depended on personal relations, federal subsidies and tax breaks were limited to those who could invest at least 100,000 pesos, patent rights were expensive, and pervasive ethnic prejudice discouraged opportunities for a large percentage of the national population.[36]

New firms used government policies to limit competition when they could, as we saw in the Owens glass bottle story. Brittingham and his partners were not alone. For example, when the Compañía El Buen Tono adopted the Decouffle automatic cigarette-rolling machine, they achieved control over a quarter of the national cigarette market as a result of their patent battle against Tabacalera Mexicana's rival Bonsack machine.[37] In mining, the Mexican Gold and Silver Recovery Company temporarily shut down rivals' refining operations through a court injunction over patent infringement. Firms across the economy used patents to limit competition when they could. Many hundreds of firms acquired Mexican patent rights in an effort to carve out market share and limit competitive pressures—as did firms throughout the industrializing world—frequently threatening lawsuits against competitors.

Patent rights also burdened innovation by increasing the cost of acquiring new technology. By definition, patents facilitate monopoly pricing, and royalty payments proved a major obstacle for many potential investors. Juan Brittingham slowly came to understand this as he sought to commercialize the Owens system. Only when he abandoned plans to license the technology on a royalty basis was he able to establish a viable partnership with the Monterrey group. Relatively high operating costs in an underdeveloped economy challenged profitability and discouraged new investment, even with tariff protection, and royalty payments or licensing fees could easily push costs too high to justify investment. Overall, the diffusion of new technologies was limited by high acquisition costs, an institutional environment that discouraged investment by most Mexicans, and legal instruments that created barriers for subsequent adopters.

PREVENTED ADOPTION

The wave of technology imports that swept over Mexico after 1870 left indelible marks on the productive capacity of the Mexican economy, on the lives of many Mexicans, and in the ruins and remnants that survive today. More difficult to observe is what did not happen, those technologies that were not adopted in Mexico, despite availability in the North Atlantic. In households, for instance, processed foods ranging from canned meats and vegetables to dry cereals, condensed milk, and packaged crackers made a tentative appearance but were not yet the dietary staple they were becoming in the United States or would later become in Mexico. Nor did many Mexicans adopt enclosed, cast-iron cooking stoves. In the urban construction industry, some new buildings boasted steel frames and cement blocks, but these were not yet common, nor did they push above several stories, in part because of weight constraints in Mexico City's unstable lake-bed terrain. But even here the weight of tradition was not too heavy: both processed foods and construction techniques attracted more patents from Mexicans than any other two fields across the economy. Two other sectors of the Mexican economy witnessed significantly less innovation than others, with major long-term implications for both technological development and economic growth in the twentieth century: agriculture (especially food production) and iron (especially the manufacture of tools and machines).

Agriculture

More Mexicans made their living in agriculture than in any other economic activity, and no sector drew more contemporary commentary for its technological backwardness. Although we have as yet no systematic study of technology choices and agricultural production in the village economy, and only a few studies for large agricultural estates (*haciendas*), most accounts assert that village farmers were slow to adopt new techniques. The traditional digging stick and one-handled wooden plow predominated, iron or steel plowshares were rare, shovels and wheelbarrows were few, and the use of commercial fertilizer or crop rotation was often unknown.[38] Frank Tannenbaum famously noted in the 1930s that, in one study of 3,611 villages, 96 percent had no tractor and 55 percent no steel plows.[39] Nearly all accounts concur that the production of staple food crops like maize, wheat, and frijoles saw almost no technological innovation and thus no increased productivity between the 1870s and 1910.[40]

Rural Mexicans' apparent reluctance to adopt new tools, implements, and cropping systems derived from a combination of factors. First, physical and cultural isolation and the persistent poverty of many rural settings systematically discouraged innovation. Without access to markets beyond several hours' hard walk, village farmers produced for household consumption, with only a modest excess for barter and local exchange.[41] High transport costs and institutionally reinforced cultural isolation made nearly all markets local and reduced incentives to invest in productivity improvements. Rural farmers were often isolated from information markets, and poverty placed implements and draft animals out of reach for many.[42] Lives lived at the margin of subsistence created incentives to avoid the uncertainty and risk inherent in innovation. When in the 1880s railroads and creeping commercialization began to open new markets for investment in large-scale, commercial agricultural production, those with access to financial capital, political influence, or formalized property rights quickly capitalized. Many village farmers were as a consequence squeezed out by those with greater resources. Exacerbating the chronic insecurity of land tenure for villagers in places like Naranja, Michoacan, or Anenecuilco, Morelos, this further undermined incentives for productivity-enhancing investments. Unequal access to new opportunities became a fundamental characteristic of the rural landscape between 1870 and 1910, and the primary catalyst of increasing rural tensions and unrest.[43]

Second, new agricultural technologies were not always well adapted to local soil and climate conditions in Mexico. When one landowner instructed his foreman (*mayordomo*) to use an imported steel plow, for instance, the newly planted corn grew quickly. But summer storms soon destroyed the crop because the steel plow cut deep and had loosened the dry, light soil so that the plants' roots would not hold. In contrast, corn planted on neighboring plots (*milpas*) with a traditional digging stick grew more slowly but withstood the storms, their shorter stalks firmly rooted in rock-hard ground.[44] Observing a traditional one-handled wooden plow, an American observer marveled that "anything satisfactory can be accomplished with such an awkward instrument, and yet these fields in some instances show grand results."[45] He concluded that Mexican soils, often loose and full of stones, were better suited for wooden plows. Steel plows, designed to cut quickly and deeply into heavy loam, seemed poorly suited for the loose, shallow, dry, rocky, and often steeply inclined soils that characterized many of central Mexico's zones of corn agriculture.[46] Similarly, Mexico's notoriously poor roads were so hard on US-made farm wagons that it made no economic sense to buy one. Commercial farmers without rail access continued to rely on locally made carts with extra-heavy axles, no springs, and solid wooden wheels up to six feet in diameter: "well adapted to prevailing conditions here."[47] Matías Romero warned US exporters when he served as Mexico's ambassador in Washington that the "peculiar conditions of land [in Mexico] require methods especially adapted to them, and it frequently happens that agricultural implements which give a very good result in certain localities, by reason of the circumstances of the soil, do not succeed as well elsewhere. This occasions that modern appliances do not in every place bring about the results that are described, and . . . causes them sometimes to be discarded as useless."[48]

Historians have long accepted these observations: Mexican agriculturalists were slow to adopt new farming techniques, implements, and machinery, and these decisions were mainly rational rejections of technologies inappropriate to the local economic or physical environment. Recent research, however, has demonstrated that this was not true for commercial agriculturalists. Hacendados who produced for regional, national, and export markets frequently sought new technologies in order to exploit expanding market opportunities. This was true for large-scale grain producers in central Mexico as it was for tropical crop plantations in the South and vegetable growers in the Northwest.[49] Mexico's large and midscale farmers bought so many agricultural implements that imports of plows, cultivators, and harrows expanded twentyfold between 1870 and 1910.[50] Nevertheless, most Mexicans earned their living in subsistence agriculture. Peasant farmers produced a larger percentage of Mexico's total agriculture output than commercial farms, although that ratio was gradually shifting in the latter's direction. With little technological innovation among this majority, productivity remained low and agricultural production barely kept pace with population growth through the Porfiriato. Techniques of sowing and harvesting maize, beans, and other staple crops on family plots changed very little during Mexico's otherwise dramatic late nineteenth- and early twentieth-century economic transition. Because innovation was rare and productivity consequently low, average rural incomes remained close to subsistence levels, most Mexicans remained excluded from new opportunities, and new manufactured goods faced a smaller consumer market than they might have otherwise.

Iron and Steel

One of the great ironies of Mexico's late-century economic growth was that it produced Latin America's first modern steel plant in a country that, as Paolo Riguzzi has noted, lacked a substantial iron industry.[51] That steel plant, the Fundidora Monterrey, is often seen as an exemplar of Porfirian industrialization: an ultramodern firm built on global frontier technology but appearing, as it were, out of nowhere, standing alone in a landscape otherwise dominated by traditional (or artisanal) ways of doing things. Common images of Porfirian industry reinforce this view of modern factories largely isolated from the rest of the economy. Iconic images of steam-driven trains crossing a bucolic countryside, as in José María Velasco's paintings, or modern new textile factories set among the cacti and sands of an otherwise rural and undeveloped landscape have reinforced an image of imported technology as an island of modernity (figure 22).

But this is a largely inaccurate image. Although textile factories did not grow organically out of a broadly established protoindustrial foundation,

FIGURE 22. The Hercules textile mill, Querétaro. Reproduced with permission of the Library of Congress Prints and Photographs Division, Washington, D.C.

they were intimately linked to strong domestic demand for cotton cloth and a long-standing tradition of spinning and weaving, just as sewing machines were seamlessly integrated into preexisting social patterns of women's sewing. Similarly, Isaac Garza, Juan Brittingham, and others established the Vidriera Monterrey with the Owens bottling system in response to Mexico's shifting culture of alcohol consumption, with increasing numbers of middle- and working-class Mexicans choosing bottled beer over a mug of pulque. This was the case for nearly all new, mechanized industries. Increasingly through the nineteenth century, tens of thousands of men and women moved across the Mexican landscape to work in new factories and to consume their products. The Fundidora Monterrey was exceptional, but it was tightly integrated into broader patterns of economic activity and social and cultural change in late-century Mexico.

The Fundidora was just one response to a rising domestic demand for iron and steel: for steel rails and structural forms in the construction industry and in mining, for cast iron or steel parts for machines, for hardware like wire and nails, and for a wide array of tools, implements, and machinery. In the

1870s Mexico's iron industry had been nearly nonexistent, and consumers had long turned to imports from the United States or Britain for their metallurgical needs. Over the next decades rising domestic demand inspired new investments in scattered foundries, smitheries, workshops, and several industrial-scale iron and steel firms. These, including the massive Fundidora Monterrey and the Fundición de Sinaloa, acquired significant technological capabilities. Nevertheless, domestic iron and steel production did not yet put a sizable dent in the country's import dependence. All Mexican producers faced the high cost of production inputs, from fuel and iron to skilled labor. The Fundición de Sinaloa managed to survive for fifteen years only because they received a financial subsidy from the federal government. When subsidies were removed in 1906, the firm closed shop.[52] The Fundidora Monterrey struggled for a decade to sell its products to railroads and other consumers of steel because it could not quickly achieve the cost and quality profile of imported steel.[53] By 1903, small and midsized foundries were producing roughly the same amount of pig iron as the new blast furnaces at the Fundidora. However, the total value of domestic iron production constituted less than 5 percent of the total value of all iron and steel imports from the North Atlantic, as we saw in chapter 3. Although the Fundición de Sinaloa and perhaps a few other firms were able to produce steam engines and a few agricultural implements, domestic production of tools and machinery still satisfied only a very small portion of growing demand, and Mexico remained heavily dependent on imported iron and steel manufactures for decades after the revolution.

Mexico's circumstances conspired toward continued import dependence. For most of the century domestic iron production had been discouraged by low demand and high production costs. When new investors began seeking iron and steel products after 1870, they turned quickly to foreign suppliers and demanded low tariffs on imported equipment. In response, the government in Mexico City established low import duties on imported iron and steel manufactures, especially on finished products like steel rails and machinery (admitted free), pipes and fittings, wire, cable, and structural forms (dutied at 10–20 percent), while duties on many basic forms like iron and steel bars, rods, sheets, and plates ran somewhat higher, at 50 to 100 percent.[54] At the same time, however, men like Joaquín Redo, Eugenio Mier Ruben, and the founders of the Fundidora Monterrey—all interested in undertaking iron, steel, or machine construction—lobbied the government for higher tariffs on metal manufactures. In the short run, high duties on metal parts and machinery would have severely handicapped the most productive sectors of the Mexican economy, where investors argued that their activities "should not be obstructed by high duties on the materials needed for their development."[55] Yet relatively low duties and little government support meant that Mexico's iron and steel industry would remain undeveloped.

The consequences were several. Growing demand for the tools and machinery consumed by firms across the economy continued to be satisfied by imports in a self-reinforcing circle: import dependence dictated low tariffs which decreased incentives to invest locally, yielding continued dependence rather than the development of backward linkages. Even with the construction of the Fundidora Monterrey and other new iron and steel firms, Mexico's railroads, mines, and other large consumers of metal forms and parts continued to turn to imports because of price and quality considerations.[56]

Furthermore, Mexican firms, engineers, and workers had relatively few opportunities to acquire technical expertise in iron and steel work. The technological gap between the state of Mexico's domestic metal industry and the requirements of metalworking and machine tooling in the late nineteenth century proved too great for an easy transition; local blacksmithing and metalworking firms were unable to make the jump. Take the case of steam engines and boilers. Their absolute scarcity until the 1880s meant that there was little demand for the skills necessary to operate, repair, and manufacture parts, and there were few opportunities (or incentives) for local metalworkers to keep up with the global frontier. By the time demand for metallurgical and metalworking skills rose more quickly at the century's end, the gap was too large to easily cross. By then, steam engines and boilers, and parts for replacement and repair, were nearly always ordered from abroad with just a few local exceptions. As the technology imports of the late century involved ever more sophisticated machinery—embedded within, for example, sewing machines and the Owens automated bottle system—the requisites for machine tooling, precision engineering, and the capacity to manufacture finely calibrated and standardized parts became ever more important. Few Mexican artisans had significant experience in machine and tool construction, let alone in the precision boring and calibrating skills so essential in constructing industrial machinery. Without local expertise, demand turned to imports, which further undermined opportunities for local learning. Here lay the great opportunity cost of Mexico's long delay in adopting railroad, steam, and iron technologies.

Mexico's massive wave of technology imports between 1870 and 1910 stands as testimony to the depth and breadth of local investment in innovation. But technological change both creates and destroys, and those with a vested interest in the status quo—those who see their welfare threatened by dislocation or adjustment costs—may resist. Most of Mexico's rural subsistence farmers, for instance, did not widely adopt new technologies and sometimes slipped into direct resistance and violence when change threatened their access to essential resources.

The introduction of mechanized technologies also threatened the livelihood of urban artisans and inaugurated their steady downward mobility into the ranks of semiskilled factory labor. While some skilled artisanal workers proved able to take advantage of new opportunities for skilled labor in a slowly industrializing economy, many did not. As early as 1835, artisans in Puebla threatened foreign technicians working at Estevan de Antuñano's new textile factories, and they complained to the state congress that "machines are making manual work superfluous and ruining working families."[57] In Guadalajara, the appearance of new industries and the mechanization of old ones cut artisanal employment by nearly 50 percent through the middle decades of the century, while the number of unskilled factory and workshop laborers more than doubled.[58] In Mexico City, the artisanal sector also became increasingly impoverished through the century. From textile workers to leather and wood craftsmen to *tortilladoras* and launderers, early industrialization displaced traditional livelihoods.[59] Although artisans and others occasionally protested the costs of technological innovation, organized resistance among the loosely knit artisanal community was scarce and was rarely effective.[60]

While mechanization displaced artisanal livelihoods, it also created a new industrial labor force that itself could resist subsequent technological change. By 1900, workers in Mexico's modernizing industrial economy totaled many tens of thousands, a sizable, steadily growing, and increasingly organized percentage of Mexico's economically active population. Although working conditions in factories and railroads (for instance) could be difficult, wages in the modern sector typically ran 50 percent or more above the national average for both unskilled and skilled laborers. Once employed, however, industrial labor often viewed new generations of machinery and workplace demands as a threat to the status quo and to their relatively privileged positions. At the El Patriotismo mill in 1875 and at the Tlaxcalan mill San Manuel in 1898, for instance, textile workers walked out to protest the introduction of automated looms. In other textile factories, workers complained that new high-velocity machinery was more fatiguing and led to stricter (and in their view, unnecessary) work floor management.[61] They had a point. Across the industrial urban economy we can observe the paradox of high wages yet declining welfare. Recent research has shown that the average height of Mexican laborers declined through the late nineteenth century, a proxy for declining material standards of living, while the average height of upper-class Mexicans increased.[62] Early industrialization benefited workers who found jobs in new industries but apparently diminished the material welfare of the majority, just as it had in the North Atlantic countries.[63]

Resistance to technological innovation could also arise from a more generalized fear of the speed and power and scale of new machinery. Trains always posed a threat, and electric trolleys lurched and sped through crowded city streets, generating accidents and fear where pedestrians and horse-drawn carts and carriages still competed for space. José Guadalupe Posada famously portrayed these dangers in his broadsides, like one on the "terrible accident" of September 19, 1907, that killed forty train passengers (figure 23). President Díaz once referred to the popular belief that electric trolleys were "pulled by the devil."[64] Increasingly frequent factory accidents also raised concerns about the dangers presented by automated technologies. The list of men and women maimed at work is a long one, including José María Ramírez, who lost his hand when the machine he was cleaning in a cracker factory was "put in motion unexpectedly."[65] But while the dangers posed by the power and speed of mechanization elicited concern, commentary, and occasional outbursts of indignation and reproach, there was no broadly based popular or intellectual opposition to industrial innovation.

Some observers believed that Mexican culture posed the real obstacle to adopting new technologies and argued that Mexicans were generally unmechanical and resistant to technological innovation. This view was especially common among (but not limited to) foreign observers. One US consul voiced a widely held view that "[the Mexican] is uneasy over innovation which he does not value or understand."[66] Travelers reported that new technologies went unadopted because their benefits were not understood or appreciated.[67] One reported an attempt to introduce an American threshing machine that reduced labor, costs, and threshing time and improved the quality of the

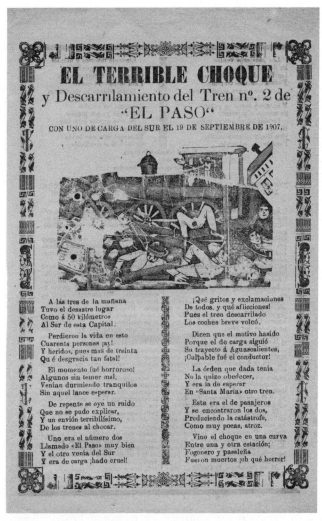

FIGURE 23. "The Terrible Crash and Derailment of Train No. 2, 'El Paso,' with a Cargo Train on September 19, 1907." Broadside. José Guadalupe Posada collection, reproduced with permission from the DeGoyler Library, Southern Methodist University.

grain but that was condemned by local priests and shipped back to the United States.[68] Many agreed that Mexico was not a nation of tinkerers or mechanics: Mexicans were "somewhat impracticable [*sic*]" and had "no genius for machinery."[69] Frequently asserting elites' disdain for mechanics and manual labor, these critiques also blamed rural Mexicans and especially the indigenous for lack of "ambition" and technological atavism.[70] To be "Mexican" meant to be dark skinned, poor, uneducated, and technologically backward, in this view. One traveler wrote that "[Mexicans] are not, in our sense, mechanics, but 'helpers' and 'handy-men.'"[71] "He is loath to lay aside the rude implements of his forefathers," wrote another in 1892, "or to take up methods of modern invention and progress."[72]

Yet these observations reveal more about observers' prejudice than they do about the innovative tendencies of most Mexicans. Alternative views are equally common. Matías Romero argued that "Mexicans are not slower than the inhabitants of other countries in adopting the use of implements and machinery to shorten and lessen labor."[73] "The average Mexican," noted one observer from the United States, "is always ready to use for his convenience these things which American genius may have developed."[74] "The peons never initiate but they are quick to imitate," wrote another; "They would . . . soon learn modern agricultural methods if placed alongside of European immigrants."[75] What Mexican workers and entrepreneurs lacked was not the inclination but rather the opportunity and incentive to adopt new methods. Mexico's villagers often saw their access to new consumer markets largely blocked by economic, geographic, and cultural distance and thus chose not to invest time or money once their subsistence needs were met. It was not aptitude or an essentialized culture that stood in the way but unequal access to education, to information, and to market opportunities and capital.[76]

Both foreign observers and Mexican elites viewed the country through an explicitly comparative North Atlantic lens. Travelers from Europe had a long history of disparaging the values, abilities, and work habits of residents of less developed societies. British and French travelers in the early modern period lambasted the Irish, Spanish, and Poles using virtually the same language of laziness, ignorance, and ineptitude used by Americans traveling in Mexico in the nineteenth century, as did European travelers in Asia and Africa.[77] While resistance and indifference to technological innovation were indeed present in late nineteenth-century Mexico, there is little to indicate that such sentiments were pervasive. Across Mexico, the introduction of new technologies brought with it substantial socioeconomic dislocation, and spaces of nonadoption were significant. Yet despite scattered skepticism and occasional resistance, these remained exceptional and were generally ineffective in slowing the adoption of new machines and processes; they were quickly overwhelmed by the strength of the spillover from the Atlantic economy and the broader social acceptance of innovation, especially, but not only, among Mexico's governing and economic elites.

. . .

Although chapter 3 and our three case studies illustrated the breadth and depth of technology adoptions across the economy, multiple factors worked to delay adoption, impair use, or sometimes prevent innovation altogether. As entrepreneurs and consumers in Mexico adopted new technologies that had been designed and developed in the North Atlantic, they confronted a new context—a new production ecology—that could hinder experiences of adoption, use, and diffusion. Within the new Mexican context of adoption, factors such as the availability of technical expertise, the development of markets for inputs and outputs, and public institutions like tariff protection and patent rights (to note just a few) could prove either permissive or constraining. These obstacles were sometimes nationally "Mexican," like those that emanated from federal laws and policies. More often, regional and especially local factors shaped possibilities for adoption. In homes, factories, and mines—always deeply embedded in local networks of markets and social relations—the daily and very human interactions of investors, engineers, workers, and consumers with newly imported technologies negotiated obstacles in the local context and translated acquisition into commercial use.

At the same time, however, the aggregate result of multiple local experiences shaped Mexico's "national" potential for economic growth in the short term, as well as the country's economic development paths in the twentieth century. While this study has traced the broad contours of technological change, we still need systematic regional and firm-based accounts. The case studies and anecdotes presented here only begin to suggest the variety of contextual elements and obstacles that entrepreneurs had to navigate to adopt new technologies from the North Atlantic. In most cases, problems of "fit" between imported technologies and the Mexican context were not sufficiently strong to hold back the wave of technological change that swept over late nineteenth-century Mexico. They did, however, limit technological change in important ways, and they also shaped possibilities for local learning and assimilation, the ways in which imported machines, foreign technicians, and other manifestations of new knowledge contributed to the development of local technological capacities—a subject to which we now turn.

EIGHT

Constraints to Learning

BETWEEN 1870 and 1910 technology imports flooded across the Mexican landscape in the form of new knowledge embodied in machines, print materials, and people. In scale and scope this wave exceeded any other in the country's history, before or since. New ways of producing goods transformed the productive capacity of the Mexican economy and laid the foundation for economic growth, even as they reshaped the everyday lives of Mexicans in profound and sometimes dislocative ways. Mexico was a technology importer at the extreme: all the hardware and new processes, along with the know-how necessary to install, operate, and repair it came from abroad, with just a few exceptions. This pattern, however, would shape development possibilities for the twentieth century. While imported technologies created new opportunities for production and profit as they undermined older ones, clear limits also emerged to the introduction, commercialization, and diffusion of technological change. More importantly, this experience offered relatively few opportunities for Mexicans to learn and assimilate new knowledge and skills, it stimulated few linkages with other economic activities, and it supported few local efforts to supply new tools and machinery. If, in the short term, this wave of creative destruction supported substantial economic growth, its long-term impact on Mexico's ability to generate sustained technological innovation, independent of foreign sources, was decidedly weak.

Continued dependence on technology imports was not universal. Individual engineers and technicians, some firms, and even entire regions successfully internalized and developed considerable technical expertise, built on local human capital and initial interaction with technology imports. The northern city of Monterrey and a handful of important industries there provide the exemplary case. But we also have hints of substantial capacities elsewhere, in Mazatlán's Fundición de Sinaloa and in a handful of other metallurgical firms, in the apparent ability of the cigarette manufacturer El Buen Tono to develop technical modifications to cigarette machinery, and in the still unexplored record of dozens or perhaps hundreds of local mechanics, engineers, and scientists who left fragmentary but tantalizing glimpses of their work in Mexico's patent records and newspapers, as well as in the more prosaic efforts of anonymous workers and tinkerers to modify existing practice. And the tens of thousands of Mexicans who worked in factories and firms that adopted new technologies—from railroads to textile mills to sewing workshops—undoubtedly acquired new expertise through the experiences of accumulated learning by doing. While important—and still very much under-researched—these experiences were exceptional or constrained. Relatively scarce and generally isolated from each other, technicians of all sorts were poorly integrated into what a century later would be called a "national innovation system" that linked business, educational institutions, and government policy.[1] First and foremost, technical jobs in new industries went overwhelmingly to foreigners. As one newspaper noted in 1899, "Every one of [the new industries] has resorted to foreigners for their installation."[2] Most Mexican workers had relatively few opportunities to use and learn technical skills beyond simple machine operation. Mexico's early dependence on foreign technologies, in other words, offered few opportunities for the *assimilation* of technical know-how, leaving a legacy of weak technological capabilities for Mexico's twentieth century and a persistent pattern of dependence.

Why was this the case? Why did the late-century wave of technological change across much of the economy leave only a weak imprint on the capabilities of Mexican engineers and skilled workers? How can we explain, in the end, Mexico's paradox of high levels of technology imports but persistently low levels of technological capabilities? Fine-grained studies of workers' interaction with machines and processes "on the shop floor" provide one way to get at these questions, but we have—as yet—few of these. This chapter takes a broader view as it examines five contextual factors that shape any local ability to learn from and assimilate new knowledge. Learning derives first and foremost from opportunities for meaningful interaction with new knowledge and expertise. Learning (and thus technology transfer) is a contact sport, resulting from direct engagement with new machinery, technical systems, and people in the classroom, the laboratory, and especially the workplace. But opportunities for interaction are themselves shaped by a set of contextual factors, including the breadth of the "technology gap" between the know-how embedded in imports and the state of expertise locally, the nature of human capital and especially the extent of technical education, the density of social networks for the diffusion of new knowledge, and incentives (or disincentives) established by government policy.

OPPORTUNITIES FOR INTERACTION

Opportunities for engineers, mechanics, and workers in Mexico to interact with and learn from newly imported technologies varied according to the characteristics of the technology in question. Sewing machines and many other small-scale, multipurpose machine and tool products diffused widely and were used intensively in Mexican homes, workshops, mines, farms, and factories. In sewing, for instance, machine use involved the mechanics of treadle motion and its translation to needle movements; the threading of bobbins and needles; the manipulation of cloth and thread; and, depending on the machine model, adjustments in needle, thread, and settings for different stitches and cloth types. Home purchasers learned the mechanics of use from the salesman himself; agents of Singer and other companies gave start-up lessons and provided some consulting and troubleshooting services in repeat visits. In sweatshops and new clothing factories, in-house foremen trained new hires, while benevolent organizations hosted classes to instruct women on machine use. The sewing machine, perhaps more than any other single technology, lay at the vanguard of a broader social acceptance of mechanization.

Hours of sewing machine use and the inevitable occurrence of jammed workings and broken parts entailed ad hoc troubleshooting and tinkering. Some users proved adept at taking apart and greasing or jury-rigging parts. This ability had limits, however, among users isolated from a broader machine culture, and especially for those in remote hamlets and villages. All had difficulty acquiring spare parts. In urban areas the widespread diffusion of sewing machines supported the eventual appearance of neighborhood machine repair shops. Although these would become a fixture of urban and small town economic life in twentieth-century Mexico, they would remain essentially artisanal in nature.

In contrast to the wide diffusion of sewing machines and other small-scale product technologies, large, factory-scale process technologies were typically concentrated in few hands. This was the case for the Owens bottle-blowing machine at the Compañía Vidriera, as well as new technologies to manufacture beer, cigarettes, cement, steel, and many other consumer and producer goods. All of Mexico's new industries faced persistently high production costs relative to foreign competitors. As a result, their directors always sought to limit competition, often using legal restrictions like patent rights and special government concessions.[3] Mexico's credit markets reinforced this tendency toward industrial concentration by restricting lending to already well-connected individuals and firms. Industrial concentration, in turn, constrained the diffusion of factory-scale technologies, and only a small number of firms and a small handful of managers, engineers, technicians, and skilled workers had the opportunity to work directly with new production technologies.

In either case, technological learning was not impossible. We can see evidence of learning with both small-scale product technologies and large-scale process technologies. In the glass industry, for example, local learning began with the efforts of Mexico's brewers to find a solution to the bottle supply problem that vexed their industry worldwide. When Juan Brittingham's investment group acquired the Owens rights, their technical knowledge extended only to a general awareness of the productive potential of the machine. Learning came in fits and starts but acquired real momentum through efforts to commercialize the technology, which required navigating Mexico's undeveloped markets for raw materials, fuel, and skilled labor. The Owens design was not inflexible, and the Toledo company provided modified machines and parts to match local conditions after extensive correspondence between the Mexican managers, resident American technicians, and the home company. But it took protracted efforts and an extensive process of exploration, feasibility studies, information gathering, dead ends, trial and error, troubleshooting, and negotiating to surmount short-term challenges. Over nearly a decade, this intensive work yielded substantial learning by both American and Mexican technicians. By the time the first bottles rolled off the factory belts in 1912, the Vidriera's investors, managers, and technicians were intimately familiar with the technical requisites of glass bottle production, the demands of their new technological system, and the nature of the Mexican context. They also learned that continued success would be more likely if they internalized these capabilities, "Mexicanized" their workforce, and reduced their "dependence on foreign workmen."[4] This effort, pursued through the middle of the twentieth century, underlay the firm's great success. Challenges inherent in negotiating the necessary adaptations may have delayed commercialization, but they provided multiple opportunities for intimate interaction and extensive local learning.

The Compañía La Vidriera was not entirely alone. The Fundidora Monterrey shut their steel mill for nearly all of 1905 to make adaptations to the plant, based on lessons learned over their first two years of halting operation.[5] Likewise, the cigarette firm El Buen Tono applied for and received over a dozen invention patents between 1890 and 1910, suggesting a level of internal research and development activity (or, perhaps, simple design-based imitation work). However, the extent of technological capabilities in these and other firms remains understudied, and we have very few examples of modernizing firms that entered the postrevolutionary period ready to locally assimilate technical capacities and move toward technological independence and innovation. Adoption of new technologies was not often accompanied by the assimilation of technical know-how.

If the diffusion of small-scale machines yielded few possibilities for local learning, and if large-scale production technologies did not diffuse widely but sometimes offered significant learning opportunities, the cyanide experience presents a third pattern. Technical information on the cyanide process was easy to obtain via print materials, and trained, experienced engineers and technicians were readily available for hire from the United States. Moreover, the sustained work of adaptation to Mexico's silver ores generated plentiful local opportunities for learning. Extensive experimentation between 1901 and 1906 succeeded in adapting the cyanide process to silver, dramatically expanding the industry's technological capabilities. However, foreign technicians held virtually all technical positions in mining and metallurgy. Nearly all viewed their time in Mexico as temporary and sooner or later took their hard-won knowledge and expertise back across the border. Despite the spillover of know-how from abroad, there was very little knowledge transfer to locally based miners and metallurgists.

Why did Mexico's long and proud tradition of formal education in precious metal mining not survive the nineteenth century? Mexican investors, entrepreneurs, engineers, and technicians had played major roles in staking claim to mine sites, investing capital, organizing companies, and managing, supervising, and conducting mine and mill site operations through midcentury and beyond. Even into the early 1890s there was still room for the Mexican engineer (*ingeniero*), formally trained or not, and for "practical mining men" to work and manage mines like La Bufa at Batopilas and many others.[6] Yet in the span of less than a decade, Mexicans virtually disappeared from significant roles in investment, leadership, management, supervision, engineering, and technical work. By 1900 there were very few who still held technical positions in the mining sector, and virtually none in the two or three dozen most important companies and districts. By then, company payrolls rarely show Mexicans employed as anything but manual laborers, carpenters, or assistants (*peones, carpinteros,* or *ayudantes*).[7] The voluminous correspondence and memoirs of US mining engineers rarely mention working alongside skilled Mexicans.[8] Beginning in the 1890s, Mexican technicians and skilled workers were effectively squeezed out of new opportunities in their country's rapidly expanding mining sector.

Globally, mining underwent a transition away from empirical, "rule-of-thumb" work and toward a more scientific and industrial approach to the extraction and refining of both precious and industrial minerals.[9] Cyaniding lay at the center of an altogether new set of technological systems in mineral refining, where formal scientific training increasingly replaced practical experience, and strictly regulated, large-scale operations became essential to profitably treat low-grade ore. Experience, experimentation, and a practiced hand still counted for a great deal, and much of the chemical basis for cyanidation was still debated and poorly understood.[10] Nevertheless, a formal education in chemistry, mineralogy, or metallurgy increasingly was prerequisite for informed, efficient, and successful experimentation. There was no universal "cyanide process" that could be explained in the classroom, outlined in a text or blueprint, and installed in any precious metal district around the world. At the heart of the process lay the knowledge that dilute cyanide solutions would selectively isolate gold and silver. But successful application to any particular body of ore depended on adapting the chemical and mechanical components of the technological system to local conditions. "Many failures," explained one of Mexico's more experienced cyanide men, "have been caused by merely imitating a neighbor's process and design of plant."[11] As another metallurgist working in Pachuca explained, even after assay tests in the lab indicated that cyaniding would work, "The exact details of the process can only be worked out by experiments run on a working scale."[12] Adaptation to local conditions was essential, and failure was nearly always, as one experienced miner noted, a matter of faulty management.[13]

Success depended on a strong foundation of formal scientific and technical education as well as learning from the experience of others. In the late nineteenth century, this was increasingly the case not just in mining and metallurgy but in many economic fields shaped by the technical innovations of the second industrial revolution. Experimentation was no longer ad hoc or trial-and-error but was informed by new chemical and metallurgical knowledge and—most importantly—by the experience of others in the international mining community.[14] Successful cyaniding engineers worked in and visited other camps, and they were prolific readers of and contributors to the major North American trade journals of the industry. Learning from others was an essential complement to learning by doing, both built on a foundation of formal scientific and technical education. And learning required speaking a common language, not simply English (in this case) but the technical language of chemistry and mineral science learned in North American mining schools like Cornell and Colorado. The adoption of the cyanide process in Mexico thus had to await the arrival of a corps of mining and metallurgical engineers with the necessary education, experience, and ready access to networks of information that would support local adaptation. Without this background, and without access to these networks, Mexican engineers and miners could not easily engage and learn from new processes.

Similar stories played out in sectors where specialized scientific and technical knowledge proved necessary to adopt and adapt radically new technological systems. In railroads, communications infrastructure, electrical plants, electric lighting and traction companies, and many public works projects, as well as in the new oil sector, positions of management and technical responsibility were largely closed to Mexicans, with only a few exceptions. The repair and construction workshops (*talleres*) of the major rail companies, mines, and factories provided one potential venue for interaction and learning by doing. Although these venues offered some opportunity for professional mobility, there is little evidence that substantial learning occurred. Railroads faced what one historian has called an "absolute scarcity" of skilled Mexican engineers, technicians, and machinists.[15] When the Revolution drove out most foreign employees, railroad workshops were left with a much greater proportion of Mexican workers but a "weak fabric of human capital" and very low levels of worker productivity.[16] The Mexican National Railroad's flagship workshop at Acámbaro, Guanajuato, did not produce its first locomotive—La Fidelita—until 1942, assembled from imported parts. The company acquired locomotive-building capacity just when freight transport shifted decisively from railroads to trucks, as the Fundición de Sinaloa had acquired the capacity to manufacture steam engines at the very moment of their obsolescence.[17] The experience of electrical companies and public works projects—all financed and managed by foreign capital and entrepreneurs, built on foreign technology, and staffed by foreign engineers and technicians—was similar.[18] And in the oil fields around Tampico and south into Veracuz, technical personnel became difficult to find after 1911. For years, Mexicans had been employed as *peones*. American or European workers held all technical positions and were "loath to transfer [technical know-how] to any Mexican."[19]

When many foreign workers fled Mexico during the Revolution, or when rebel groups appropriated railroads, factories, oil refineries, or sugar mills, Mexican workers often proved able to keep operations running. Tens of thousands of workers had, over the decades before 1911, effectively learned the mechanics of operating and sometimes troubleshooting and repairing imported equipment and technical systems. The capabilities they learned are testimony not only to the extent of interaction and engagement but to the ingenuity and talent of local workers who acquired new skills and expertise through their labor. But these kinds of *production capabilities*, acquired through the adoption of imported technologies, were insufficient to support the assimilation of deeper *technological capabilities*.

Over the last decades of the nineteenth century firms in Mexico invested millions of pesos, dollars, marks, pounds, and francs in new technologies. Imported machinery, print materials, and technicians all embodied new knowledge and expertise and carried into Mexico the potential for learning and the local development of technological capabilities. Indeed, over the course of the nineteenth century many investors believed that imported machinery and foreign mechanics (*maestros extranjeros,* as Lucas Alamán had noted) offered the most promising venue for the local dissemination of new knowledge.[20] In the end, however, opportunities for interaction proved scarce, and we can observe relatively few signs of effective local assimilation of new skills and technical knowledge. To fully understand why interactions were so rare we turn now to four factors that worked to limit those opportunities: the size of the technology gap, the poor quality of technical education (and of human capital generally), the lack of social networks for the diffusion of new knowledge, and the nature of government programs and policies.

THE TECHNOLOGY GAP

By the second half of the nineteenth century, scientific and technical know-how in the North Atlantic had increasingly diverged from that common in other parts of the world. New developments in chemicals, electricity, and metallurgical skills (for instance) had significantly widened the "technology gap" between the economies of the North Atlantic and most of the rest of the world. Jumping across the gap between the local status quo and North Atlantic models was exactly what Mexican advocates of technological progress sought: to quickly acquire the most advanced machines and ideas possible—*lo más moderno*—taking advantage of tried and tested productive capacity while avoiding the cost and uncertainty of local research, development, and invention. Sewing machines, the Owens automatic glass bottle machine, and the cyanide process all represented revolutionary, nearly overnight leaps from existing artisanal practice to large-scale mechanized production. So too did new machines, processes, and systems in construction, public works and utilities, transportation and communications, diverse manufacturing industries, and some branches of commercial agriculture.

However, imported technologies in these fields often embodied a level of technical knowledge and machine construction skills that was exceedingly scarce within late nineteenth-century Mexico's inherited human capital foundation—what Elías Trabulse has called the "severe backwardness that characterized Mexican science and technology."[21] Just how large was this gap?

Local capabilities to troubleshoot, repair, modify, provide spare parts for, and improve or adapt imported machinery typically lay out of the reach of local technicians and workers, as we have noted. Sewing machines and other types of small-scale product technologies could be operated with only brief instruction but could not be easily repaired, modified, or replicated. When José Antonio Reyes decided to build on his work experience in the Wheeler & Wilson sewing machine factory in Connecticut by setting up his own shop on Plateros Street in Mexico City in the 1860s, the services he provided were limited to assembling and disassembling machines and giving lessons.[22] Sewing machines were the product of major advances in metallurgical and machine-tooling capacities in the North Atlantic economies. Cheap steel and precision engineering achieved standardization and interchangeability at sufficiently low cost for mass marketing. In glass bottle manufacturing, not even artisanal expertise could be found locally, and the factory-scale Owens machine required two decades of dependence on foreign know-how to operate, modify, and improve before the Compañía Vidriera was able to internalize the capacity to provide those services with local workers and mechanics. In neither case, and in no other manufacturing activities, can we observe the development of backward linkages into the supply of machinery or parts. In the mining sector, very few Mexican mining engineers, trained in the National Engineering School, engaged the science and techniques of the new mining and refining practices in the field. Other new technologies in the productive economy also lay beyond the easy reach of existing scientific and technological capabilities in Mexico. From electricity, chemistry, and metallurgy to the operation of factory-scale machines, railroads, and communication networks, all depended on imported expertise to negotiate their adoption, adaptation, and use.

Two explanations for this dependence on imported expertise are possible. First, modernizing firms preferred to hire foreign expertise over domestic, even when the latter was available. Second, the latter were simply unavailable, scarce, or entirely absent, and the only way to bridge the technology gap was to acquire foreign expertise. Although it is certainly true that many firms, both Mexican and foreign, displayed a distinct preference for foreign technicians, all the evidence supports the second hypothesis. Mexico had little infrastructure for training in most fields of science, technology, and engineering outside the National Mining School before the 1870s. Few Mexicans had access to advanced training in Europe or the United States, and there was no domestic institutional base or critical mass of trained individuals who could assimilate, translate, and reproduce new technologies that were emerging out of new scientific and technical milieus abroad.

Estevan de Antuñano argued in the 1830s that without local factories to produce tools and machines Mexico would never be able to train "good machinists" who could adapt and repair the machines "which daily fall into disrepair."[23] The half century from the 1820s to the 1870s saw little borrowing and innovation, and consequently little development of technological capabilities. This was both a *know-how* gap and a *knowledge* gap. The most acute aspect of the former lay in Mexico's metallurgical, metalworking, and machine-tooling capacities. An 1853 national survey reported just five iron foundries, two of decent size but the others employing about ten workers, with an aggregate national output of just five thousand metric tons per year. At the Mexican Exposición General that same year, only two of eighty-seven display objects were machines or tools; of the ninety-one exhibits at the 1856 Exposición de Industria y Artes in Mexico City, only six were machines or implements.[24] Local blacksmiths nearly always worked with imported iron; artisans were burdened by the high cost of tools, and they substituted wood for iron whenever possible.[25] Even by the 1890s, when Mexico's new, large-scale metallurgical foundries could manufacture structural iron and steel for construction, they could not manufacture more finely tooled and engineered machine parts. Tool and machine construction remained scarce and artisanal, with little ability to replicate global frontier machinery and implements for homes, workshops, mines, and factories. This was still true when Latin America's first large-scale modern steel mill, the Fundidora Monterrey, came on line in 1903. It did not contribute to machine and tool manufacturing capacities, and it produced only basic forms like rails and structural shapes.[26] Global frontier technologies of the 1890s embodied scientific advances (in metallurgy, chemistry, and physics) and technical capabilities (in machine tooling and the scale of production) that lay increasingly beyond the capacities of individuals, firms, and societies outside the North Atlantic. Through midcentury, several generations of Mexican mechanics had little or no opportunity to engage with the already iconic technologies of mechanization. When technology imports swept across Mexico after 1870, this skill deficit yawned wide. Mexican industrial production capacities would grow substantially at century's end, but without substantial technological capabilities.

Exceptions existed, of course, and some individuals and firms acquired capabilities that enabled them to cross this gap and to work with, adapt, modify, and sometimes replicate at or near the global frontier. Glassworkers in the San Lázaro factory in Mexico City produced (in their own words) "glass and crystal, fine as well as common, whose making and quality compete advantageously with those which come to us from abroad."[27] Leandro Ramírez built his own sewing machine, which was exhibited as a product of Mexican expertise at the Paris World's Fair of 1889.[28] A handful of new scientific laboratories in Mexico City boasted the latest instruments, imported from Europe and the United States, along with capabilities for research.[29] Yet while some individuals could construct single-unit models in their laboratories and workshops, there was no domestic capacity to produce machinery for commercial sale and productive use. The Fundición de Sinaloa offered the only established exception to this, manufacturing hundreds of steam engines and boilers in Mazatlán during the 1880s and 1890s (figure 24). Yet this firm focused on technologies of the first industrial revolution and remained dependent on government subsidies, being unable otherwise to compete with the price and quality of imports. At the very moment of the Fundición's short-lived success, electricity and gasoline engines were on the verge of making steam power obsolete.

In any setting of relatively late development—nearly everywhere outside the North Atlantic in the nineteenth and twentieth centuries—the breadth

FIGURE 24. Iron and boiler works at the Fundición de Sinaloa, Mazatlán, 1898. Reproduced with permission from the DeGoyler Library, Southern Methodist University.

of the "technology gap" posed a steep challenge to the adoption and assimilation of new technologies from the global frontier (recall figure 2). When the gap was small, obstacles to adoption and use were minimized and the assimilation of know-how was relatively easy. When the gap was large, local use more likely required imported expertise, and local learning loomed both more difficult and, in the long run, more important. The first waves of "relatively late industrializers"—the United States and parts of continental Europe—faced a relatively small gap between existing artisanal practice and new industrial technologies such as textiles, steam power, and metalworking. By the late nineteenth century, however, the third wave of late industrializers (like Mexico) faced a much larger disjuncture between local capabilities and new developments abroad.[30]

A half century ago, Alexander Gerschenkron famously suggested that the existence of large technology gaps between countries favored the growth potential of latecomers, those "relatively backward."[31] The greater the gap, he argued, the larger the potential for imitation and catch-up through the rapid adoption of new technologies from abroad. Mexico's experience illustrates Gerschenkron's argument, but only in part. The country's economic growth between the 1870s and 1910—and again in the twentieth—was built squarely on the widespread adoption of new machines and processes from the technology-exporting countries in the North Atlantic. Yet the size of the technology gap also meant that learning and assimilating the knowledge and expertise embodied in late-century technologies would prove extremely difficult.

One way for Mexican technicians to surmount this hurdle might have been scientific and technical education, the subject to which we now turn.

TECHNICAL EDUCATION

Mexican officials were acutely conscious of the large gap between the rapidly advancing frontier of scientific and technical knowledge abroad and local capabilities in Mexico. Genaro Raigosa, senator from Campeche and author of the agricultural chapters in Justo Sierra's 1902–5 multivolume work on Mexico's past and present, argued for greater investment in and access to technical education for "the popular masses."[32] Others agreed that "the present greatest need in this country is the technical education of our ambitious young men."[33] The federal government responded with reform proposals and initiatives that sought explicitly to enhance local abilities to engage the global technological frontier. President Díaz himself had a particular interest in modernizing engineering education. New initiatives came on three levels—primary education, basic technical training, and advanced engineering; each, however, fell far short of initial goals.[34] Most Mexicans were poorly educated, human capital was scarce, and scientific and technical education remained difficult to acquire, except for a few. Low levels of human capital implied a perennial scarcity of skilled labor, constraining efforts to adopt and assimilate new know-how.

New investment in primary education aimed to increase basic literacy levels but achieved only limited success. Literacy rates in Mexico at the turn of the century lay not much above 20 percent, and primary school enrollment rates ran barely a quarter or a third of North Atlantic levels.[35] Low attendance and the poor quality of most education undermined government initiatives, yielding only a modest increase in literacy nationwide. In Mexico City literacy was likely closer to 50 percent, and in new industrial districts like Orizaba, Rio Blanco, and Santa Rosa literacy ran between 40 and 50 percent, about the same as in Mexico's artisanal sector at midcentury and sufficiently high to support a thriving set of penny-press newspapers for workers.[36] But basic literacy made relatively little difference to common workers' ability to operate new technologies, although there is some evidence that literacy could support upward mobility within and between firms. Mobility often brought with it increased opportunities for interaction with the technologies of production in more skilled positions.[37]

New initiatives also sought to enhance "the development of technical training for the mass of the population," to "form workers sufficiently instructed" in technical matters in order to develop national industry.[38] In 1892 the Díaz government restructured and expanded the Schools of Arts and Trades (Escuelas de Artes y Oficios), established in the 1850s to "spread instruction among artisans."[39] These adult schools featured introductory training in basic mechanical principles and skills, along with basic literacy, and offered free nighttime courses for workers. Topics included carpentry, lathe work, blacksmithing, foundry work, decorative skills, tin work, and techniques for cobblers, tailors, and seamstresses. A handful of states supported similar programs. In Guerrero, for instance, the schools offered training in the "operation and use and mechanics of the most essential tools and machines for every trade, industry, or line of work."[40] The schools complemented classroom instruction with hands-on training in workshops, often coupled with apprenticeship opportunities. Some offered English classes to facilitate employment by foreign firms. Technical training programs often targeted women, who increasingly found work in new lines of industrial labor.[41] Others took primary school students on field trips to local factories to "show the children all the departments and to give them appropriate explanations for each."[42] In 1890, President Díaz commissioned Daniel Palacios, a professor of mechanical engineering at the National Engineering School, to develop a proposal for a new School of Practical Machinists (Escuela Práctica de Maquinistas). Palacios devised a two-year curriculum and lobbied the government to provide formal support for local machine manufacturing, but the Secretaría de Fomento ultimately rejected the project, saving only courses to train railroad conductors.[43]

Federal and state support had, by 1910, established 46 Escuelas de Artes y Oficios in Mexico City (enrolling about 5,350 students) and 128 additional schools distributed throughout the states, although enrollment numbers for the state programs barely sum to the Federal District total. But enrollment levels mask attendance and graduation rates of just 25 percent or less of initial matriculation, despite the inducement of free food and clothing. Fewer than five thousand workers completed training through these schools over four decades, representing less than 0.1 percent of the labor force and just 0.6 percent of modern sector workers.[44] Likewise, the Escuela Práctica de Maquinistas (established in 1890 in response to the demand for technicians created by "the establishment of new industries," and incorporated into the Escuela de Artes y Oficios in 1896) sought to train Mexican workers to replace foreign technicians but also enrolled and graduated only very small numbers.[45] In other words, government efforts to promote basic technical training for workers produced only meager results.

Mexico boasted the oldest and most distinguished institution of advanced technical education in Latin America in its Mining College (Colegio de Minería, formerly the Real Seminario de Minería), founded in 1792. Together with the National Preparatory School (Escuela Nacional Preparatoria), the Mining College underwent major reforms in the late 1860s aimed at creating a more scientific, modern curriculum. The resulting National Engineering School, housed in the old Palacio de Minería, offered degrees in civil, mining, and mechanical engineering.[46] However, as with the Escuelas de Artes y Oficios, these engineering programs enrolled few and graduated fewer, under five hundred students over four decades.[47] The majority of these were topographical engineers, primarily trained in mapping and surveying and not in the applied work of civil, mechanical, electrical, or metallurgical engineering. Through the 1880s, for example, the National Engineering School graduated only one "industrial" engineer (and only fifty-four total before 1911).[48] "Because this country lacks industrial scientists," reported one newspaper, "this young man is the first and only one in Mexico today."[49]

The National Agricultural School likewise sought to educate and train technicians capable of introducing the latest advances in irrigation, fertilizers, seed and breed selection, and machinery.[50] In addition to a reformed agricultural curriculum, the school published a gazette and pamphlets on new methods and translated agricultural science textbooks into Spanish. However, despite the 67 students enrolled in 1907, the school graduated only 265 over its first half century, and several state-level agricultural programs closed because of lack of students.[51] Further curricular reforms and the addition of extension and experimentation stations in the last years of the Porfiriato were too little, too late.[52] The school's founding vision—to produce a new generation of agricultural technicians who could transform productivity in Mexican export and food agriculture—would go unrealized until the mid-twentieth century. In sum, high-profile reforms in Mexico's flagship technical education programs produced only meager results.[53] In 1888 there were only seventy-nine titled engineers working in the Federal District, representing fewer than one per every three thousand inhabitants.[54] By 1910 the national engineering presence had changed little. Technical engineering education had undergone modest modernization but remained the domain of a small and exclusive group, completely dwarfed by the much larger number of foreign engineers and personnel working in the country. These numbers are strikingly low in any comparative context. Mexico produced over these decades about one-half the number of engineers per capita as Brazil and Chile, one-fourth as many as Portugal and Spain, one-twelfth the number as the US South, and one-thirty-second the number as the US North.[55]

Why did efforts to promote technical education yield so little? Public officials and private investors recognized the importance of developing technical expertise. Despite recent work on technical engineering, we can still only suggest several hypotheses for future research. The curriculum at Mexican schools lagged behind the late nineteenth-century wave of global technological change. Many had long criticized the curriculum in the Mining School (for example) as too theoretical, with insufficient emphasis on practice and application, and such complaints continued despite efforts to increase the practical component at all levels through the late century.[56] This was especially important in mining and metallurgy, where the application of science to the problems of extraction and refining came together with the professionalization of engineering to transform the global industry between 1890 and 1900, effectively driving out old-school miners.[57] "They are not miners but chemists," wrote the editor of the *Mexican Mining Journal* in 1908. "The business of mining does not consist simply of taking ore out of the ground. It is much more complex and difficult and involves the science of chemistry and mechanics and delicate problems of engineering such as were not necessary in the early days of the western United States or of Mexico."[58] The old-school miner, "a gambler or an adventurer," had been replaced by the formally schooled engineer, with "specialized knowledge . . . for domesticating uncertainty."[59] In this Mexico was no different from other countries and was part of an international trend; British engineering programs in the early twentieth century also failed to keep up with those in the United States, Germany, and (increasingly) Japan.[60]

Further, the financial and administrative resources allocated by the state to technical education were likely inadequate to support an effort of sufficient scale and scope. Funding at the primary and secondary levels to funnel students toward technical careers remained low, as did funding for those experimental stations that appeared at the very end of the Porfiriato.[61] Public demand for technical education also appears to have been weak. Historians have frequently offered a cultural explanation: Mexican elites and the emerging middle class were culturally disinclined to pursue technical and mechanical professions.[62] Yet what was often expressed as a cultural disinclination can also be seen as a reaction to limited job prospects. Foreign technicians monopolized most skilled positions in modern sector firms across the economy. Whether this was because hiring firms were prejudiced against Mexicans or because it was cheaper to obtain trained foreigners than to train Mexicans on the job, the result was the same.

Individually, a few Mexicans did acquire the education and experience to work with new technologies on the global frontier. Take Claudio Juan Martínez, for example, born in 1879 and mechanically oriented as a child. He attended the Instituto Veracruzano, where he studied mathematics before attending Texas A&M. He finished a mechanical engineering degree at Cornell in 1901, doing his thesis work at the Fábrica Jabonera La Esperanza in Torreón. Subsequently, as owner of the metal foundry and workshop "Los Hornos" in that city, he hired and trained a workforce of local employees, all "born in the area."[63] The better-known Miguel Angel de Quevedo offers another example, leading a nascent interest in scientific understanding of Mexico's woodlands. He trained in France, attended international congresses (for instance, the Congress for Public Hygiene and Urban Problems, held in Paris in 1900), and helped establish new agencies and organizations in Mexico to promote and apply new scientific knowledge.[64] Throughout Mexico, many individuals established institutions and publications to disseminate their work, as Elías Trabulse has noted.[65]

But these were isolated individuals and exceptional cases, largely from privileged backgrounds. Most of the relatively few graduates from Mexico's technical schools did not work in industry but staffed government offices or held professorships at the country's universities. They were the "wizards of progress," and it was their vision of material progress and of a modern, urban, European, and industrializing Mexico that shaped most policy decisions through the Porfiriato.[66] Antonio del Castillo was perhaps the most accomplished graduate of the Mining College in the postindependence era. Immediately after graduation he was offered the chair of mineralogy. He served Mexican governments as director of the national mint and helped rewrite the country's mining laws. President Díaz later appointed him director of the School of Engineers, and he represented Mexico at various international expositions. Six years before his death in 1895 he helped establish the Geological Commission of Mexico. Except for one brief stint managing mines in Taxco during the French Intervention, his professional life was dedicated to public service in education and government. *Ingeniero* Castillo's accomplishments were exceptional; his career path was not.[67] Similarly, Amado Saavedra, more fortunate than most, perhaps, in receiving his engineering degree in the United States, returned to direct Guanajuato's engineering school.[68]

Those who obtained advanced technical education at home or abroad were an exceptionally small and elite group. Mexican technical expertise remained very scarce, unequally distributed, and largely isolated from the productive economy. With just a few exceptions, no one emerged to found a major program of basic or applied research within a university, private laboratory, or government office. Formal technical education did not produce a critical mass of technicians, let alone a national technological community, nor did it provide widespread opportunities for men in the slowly emerging middle class. Educational opportunities remained closely linked to social position, with only rare exceptions. The engineer had become "the most important professional in the Porfirian era," but newly minted Mexican engineers were scarce, as was skilled labor generally.[69] They had only limited access to new opportunities at a time when foreign expertise was both better trained and readily accessible. Investors consistently decided to hire technical expertise abroad rather than at home (recall figure 2). Formal education did not yet provide a means for social mobility, for accessing the opportunities presented by an expanding economy and a new world of technical occupations and professions.

TECHNICAL NETWORKS

The transfer of technological know-how across boundaries—between firms, regions, or countries—has been called a contact sport. It occurs most effectively through interaction and direct engagement with new knowledge embodied in people as well as in machines and processes. Engagement is facilitated by social networks that maximize the diffusion of new knowledge and expertise. These may be informal networks, centered on key "information brokers" who act as critical nodes, gathering and disseminating information via correspondence and participating in multiple enterprises and lobbying activities. Social networks may also be formally centered on associations, clubs, or societies of entrepreneurs, scientists, and technicians, established around professions or common scientific or technical themes. Institutions like firms, schools, and training or research centers also contribute to knowledge networks. Any single organization can provide a site for localized interaction and the acquisition of skills and knowledge, but the development of networks of individuals and organizations increases possibilities for exchange and enhances their impact on the development of local capacities.

In late nineteenth-century Mexico, a few individuals and organizations acquired substantial technological capabilities—at or near the global frontier. But as we have seen, their numbers were small, and there were few networks for the diffusion of knowledge and know-how beyond or even within this small community. Immigrant entrepreneurs and immigrant communities often served as brokers of new technical information, bringing with them the ability to build networks to sources of technical knowledge abroad and establishing themselves within regional and sometimes national networks within Mexico. Juan Brittingham provides one example, as he carried on an extensive daily correspondence with Mexican entrepreneurs as well as with equipment suppliers and businessmen in the United States. Men like Brittingham, Enrique Creel, Oscar Braniff, and others were not alone in acting as "intermediaries between the manufacturer and consumer."[70]

New scientific and technical societies also appeared in Mexico through the nineteenth century, with particular activity after the 1860s.[71] These included societies focused on the natural sciences such as the Sociedad Humboldt, the Sociedad de Historia Natural, the Sociedad Mexicana de Geografía y Estadística, the Instituto Nacional Geológico, and the Sociedad Mexicana de Minería. In contrast, business- and technically oriented associations for specific industries were relatively scarce. Most firms in the textile industry belonged to a national association, and groups of prominent mine and refinery owners met to discuss mutual interests and to lobby government. But few of these provided effective means for acquiring and disseminating technical information, as would many business associations by the 1940s. Local associations like the Sociedad Agrícola de Amecameca, established in 1893 among small and midsized farmers in the state of Mexico to promote the introduction of new information, seeds, and agricultural techniques in the region, offered just a few limited venues.[72]

Some professional groups supported their own technical journals like the *Anuario de la Academia Mexicana de Ciencia*, the *Boletín de Ingenieros*, *El Agricultor Mexicano*, and *El Minero Mexicano*.[73] *El Minero Mexicano* was published in Mexico City as the "voice of the Republic's mining associations," a weekly paper "dedicated to promoting the advances of the industry in general" and especially "to promoting the development of knowledge" in mining and metallurgy.[74] Through the 1870s and 1880s it ran articles on diverse extraction and refining techniques, many focused on improving the efficiency of mercury amalgamation techniques.[75] Although the paper published extensive articles and reports on Mexican mining activities, these did not match the technical detail of descriptions of metallurgical processes and techniques that could be found in the *Mining and Scientific Press* (San Francisco) and the *Engineering and Mining Journal* (New York).[76] Furthermore, the Mexican press did not provide a forum in which field engineers working in Mexican mining districts could report their results and interrogate those of others; it did little to build and support a network of applied and laboratory technicians. As late as 1903 *El Minero Mexicano* had published only a few accounts of the new cyanide separation process—first introduced in Mexico nearly a decade before. All were copies of reports published elsewhere, including a piece originally from the *Boletín de Agricultura* of El Salvador.[77]

This exemplifies the broader crisis of domestic expertise in Mexico's mining industry, where significant activity by Mexican engineers and skilled workers in the 1870s had fallen dramatically by the early 1900s, driven out by the late-century wave of foreign capital and new-generation technology. Cyanide's introduction and adaptation to Mexican conditions critically depended on technical networks through which mining and metallurgical engineers could share information. By 1905, the migration of thousands of skilled foreign technicians into Mexico's mining districts had brought not only expertise but also a distinct culture of sharing accumulated experience and knowledge, new forums for the exchange of technical information, and a dense web of professional networks. American mining engineers like T. A. Rickard, F. J. Hobson, Bernard MacDonald, and C. W. Van Law came from the same professional circles, engineered the adaptation of cyanide to Mexican ores, and socialized over drinks in Guanajuato and other centers of global mining. Mexico's large community of expat mining experts were closely linked to the global industry through US- and British-based technical publications. These papers served as forums for an international community of mining and milling engineers to describe their own operations and to query and challenge the findings of others in reports, notes, letters, and analyses.[78] But the technological transformation of the global mining industry squeezed out Mexican human as well as financial capital. Membership in the global community of mining engineers was by now determined by educational background, language, and an engineering culture that emerged from new engineering programs in US and European universities. Mexican mines and refineries had become by 1900 not simply an appendage but a vital part of a North American mining culture, which in turn was tightly integrated into a global community of information generation and sharing. Few Mexican engineers could access this network.

Social networks that might have facilitated the diffusion of new technical knowledge in Mexico were constrained by several factors. Those with training and expertise constituted only a very "small circle of men."[79] The total number of trained Mexican engineers in Mexico by 1910 constituted only a tiny fraction of those who came from the United States and Europe to find work. Furthermore, the vertical links between this small but capable elite and other social groups (technicians without formal training, skilled workers, and the literate public) were nearly nonexistent. There were, for instance, few programs to funnel promising younger students into technical and engineering programs in the way that apprenticeships had done for artisanal work a half century earlier. There was nothing like the provincial "mechanics institutes" of nineteenth-century England or San Francisco to popularize science and technology.[80] Few relationships or venues for interaction existed between Mexico's very small scientific and technical elite and the hands-on, applied productive activity in factories, mines, and elsewhere. Some have attributed this to a cultural indifference to applied mechanics as opposed to more theoretical, academic, or administrative paths. Other explanations are possible, however, especially the near-universal firm-level preference for technicians trained abroad. Either way, the result was a self-reinforcing circle: low demand for Mexican technicians yielded few entrants, which weakened demand for educational programs and only reinforced the industry preference for foreigners.

Finally, networks for information sharing were exceptional rather than typical, sparse rather than dense. The ability of the Vidriera Monterrey to acquire, install, and manage the Owens automatic glass bottle–blowing system owed much to cross-border networks initiated through Juan Brittingham, who operated as a key information broker in this enterprise and many others. The density and effectiveness of Brittingham's external network precipitated the emergence of a firm that would eventually, under Isaac Garza's leadership, internalize many of these functions. Brittingham was not alone, and both immigrant and Mexican entrepreneurs frequently played this role, but other venues for information exchange proved scarce. As a result, the learning and capacity building that we see in the Vidriera's case, or among US engineers in the cyanide case, were rare. More often, technical projects suffered from isolation, like the study of Toluca's water resources, commissioned by the city's Comisión de Aguas in 1910 and conducted by *ingeniero* Anselmo Camacho, which did not incorporate hydrological know-how learned elsewhere.[81] Despite correspondence between scientists and engineers in Mexico and the North Atlantic, Mexican technicians were scarce and were not easily integrated within broader North American networks and communities.[82]

In the business world, interrelated networks of businessmen and financiers played a crucial role in obtaining information and resources.[83] But these networks of interpersonal connections comprised a relatively small number of men, densely connected, for instance, through interlocking boards of directors. The same could be said of networks for obtaining and diffusing technical information. Only a small number of individuals acquired the requisite know-how to engage global frontier technologies. Like the closed political economy that described much of Mexican financial and business activity, technological networks tended to be highly circumscribed. Networks were few, numbers of nodes and interrelationships were small, barriers to entry were substantial, and there were few connections with groups outside the network. As a result, technological learning was constrained and remained nearly insignificant on the national level. Between 1870 and 1910, most Mexicans had little access to new opportunities in the rapidly changing economy.

GOVERNMENT POLICY

Mexico's public officials were well aware of the importance of local learning. They discussed, debated, and sometimes enacted a range of policy initiatives that aimed to support the formation of human capital, and especially "useful knowledge" and the "necessity of training mechanics."[84] At the same time, however, they adopted policies that increased Mexico's openness to new knowledge from abroad and offered strong inducements to technology imports. Over the course of the Porfiriato, efforts to open Mexico to new knowledge were more effective than efforts to encourage technical training. Technology imports grew rapidly, while there was little development of local capacities.

In addition to technical training initiatives like the Escuelas de Artes y Oficios and new engineering programs, federal policy sometimes promoted other ways to enhance technical training. For example, the government occasionally funded young men to study at foreign universities. Luis Lajous graduated from the Escuela Nacional de Ingeniería and received support to study at the Arts and Manufacturing School in Paris.[85] Yet like the graduates of Mexico's technical schools, recipients of such support numbered only a few. Large firms and elite families occasionally sent young men abroad to learn new techniques: Evaristo Madero sent family members to Manchester, England, in the 1860s to gain textile expertise, and Vicente Ferrara traveled to the United States to study the steel industry before returning to help establish the Fundidora Monterrey in 1903. Both patent law and tax incentive legislation sought to encourage or require that recipients employ Mexican students for training purposes.[86] Several legislative proposals for patent law reform in the 1880s also sought to encourage local innovation and learning by including compulsory working clauses and "introduction patents."[87] But the laws enacted in 1890 and 1903 contained neither of these clauses. Instead, legislators removed "patents of introduction," which previously had allowed Mexicans to acquire protection for new technologies if they were the first to put them into practice in Mexico. Nor did the government facilitate public access to the know-how embedded in the patent applications. Patent notices appeared publicly as only brief, three- or four-line notices, and there was no easy access to the full patent specifications in this highly centralized system. Other decrees sought to favor local learning and "the exercise of professions" by stipulating that public works projects use the "technical knowledge" of local engineers.[88] Yet there is little evidence that any of these initiatives were consistently applied or broadly effective.

Government agencies also published gazettes and pamphlets to diffuse new scientific and technical knowledge within Mexico; most of these focused on new horticultural or pastoral techniques.[89] The Secretaría de Fomento set up scientific laboratories, such as the new microscopic laboratory of the Parasitology Commission in 1902, outfitted with "the best and most modern microscopes, burners, and reactants."[90] The ministry sponsored a wide range of technical exhibitions in Mexico City and elsewhere and considered opening an "Industrial Technology Museum" (Museo Tecnológico Industrial). These exhibitions displayed new technologies—most developed abroad—and allowed Mexican hacendados, miners, and manufacturers "the opportunity of examining and comparing the various kinds of the latest machinery ... and inventions," or, as the Development Ministry stated, to "awaken incentive in the working classes and the interest of the rest."[91] Although these exhibitions might encourage some learning by seeing, they likely served to support the interests of foreign commerce, and especially the import trade, more than the local assimilation of new knowledge.[92]

In fact, the government's efforts to promote technology imports greatly overshadowed its efforts to promote local learning. Above all else, federal policy sought to reduce obstacles to the acquisition of new knowledge embodied in machinery hardware, print materials, and technicians. Foreign immigrants, investors, and workers with technical and entrepreneurial skills found open doors and welcoming arms; most enthusiastically attested to the liberal and supportive policies of the Díaz government. More concretely, the federal tariff schedule had consistently allowed free (or nearly so) entry of machinery since the first national *aranceles* of the 1820s.[93] Officials recognized that investors in new and modernizing industries faced the critical challenge of any import-substituting industry: producing goods at or below the cost of competing producers in the North Atlantic. Ready access to expertise and to technical hardware was an absolute requisite for supporting new industrial investment, and this short-term calculus trumped any interest in the development of local capabilities for the long term.

Likewise, Mexico's new patent laws of 1890 and 1903 rejected the prolearning and local-innovation provisions of both earlier law and reform proposals. Instead, new legislation strengthened the proprietary rights of original inventors, regardless of nationality, aiming above all to encourage foreign patenting and investment in the introduction of new machines and processes from abroad.[94] Similarly, the federal Industrias Nuevas program used tax exemptions to support investment in new manufacturing industries and new technologies. Here again, policy promoted the importation of technical hardware and largely neglected opportunities to promote local learning.

Finally, none of the government's efforts to promote technological modernization involved the domestic manufacture of capital equipment. Federal policy reflected a belief that investment in mechanizing and modernizing the Mexican economy demanded unencumbered access to imported technical hardware and expertise. In fact, trade policy provided a severe disincentive for any firm to manufacture capital equipment in Mexico. To do so would have required protecting those activities with high tariffs, which would have immediately compromised the short-term interests of investors in mining, manufacturing, construction, and commercial agriculture—all activities that depended heavily on imported capital goods. Even the sector with the most extensive demand for machine hardware—the large cotton textile industry—saw only occasional and frustrated efforts to initiate domestic machine manufacture. Any effort to protect machine production by taxing technology imports was a political impossibility in the short term.[95] As a result, there were few incentives to master the skills and knowledge necessary to replicate, modify, and manufacture capital equipment goods in Mexico. The Fundición de Sinaloa, the only firm that consistently produced machinery through the 1880s and 1890s, did so only with direct federal subsidies that compensated for the lack of tariff protection and closed its doors when that support was withdrawn. Furthermore, Mexico's high tariffs that protected the domestic production of many consumer goods were a response to the challenges of infant industries and the kinds of production inefficiencies we saw in chapters 5 and 7, for instance. High tariffs, in turn, lowered incentives for further investment in technological innovation. This would become increasingly true after the Revolution.[96]

In the end, government policies that directly promoted local learning and the development of local technological creativity were few and largely ineffective. Mexico's technology policy consisted of little more than consistent and concerted efforts to promote technology imports.[97] Weak state capacities—both fiscal and administrative—were partly to blame. More importantly, a short time horizon and the imperative of immediate growth in the international context of late development governed all key political decisions. In the short term, policy makers' primary objective was to ease access to the importation of new machines, tools, processes, and knowledge. Although Mexican officials and commentators voiced concern about falling "tributary" to more powerful economies—and especially to their northern neighbor—they expressed less concern about continued dependence on foreign expertise.

· · ·

As early as the 1820s, Mexican officials discussed initiatives to support local abilities to learn from the technological advances they observed in North Atlantic. They considered sending young artisans to the United States or Europe to "observe the mechanism of machines and the procedures of skilled workmen" and attracting foreign mechanics to Mexico "to teach us, [else] . . . our industry will be lost."[98] These initiatives, however, never materialized or occurred as one-off measures that failed to build local communities of skilled technicians. Low levels of technology adoption through the first half century of national independence provided very few opportunities for acquiring experience and knowledge. Little changed through late century as the technology gap between Mexico and the North Atlantic grew significantly larger. In Mexico as in most nineteenth-century nations facing a large gap between local and external capabilities, the response of both investors and government officials was to promote technology imports. Formal education programs might have helped close the gap between local and foreign capabilities, but new educational initiatives after 1870 fell well short of initial visions. Networks for the acquisition and diffusion of technical information and skills existed but remained thin, centered on a handful of individuals and organizations. And although government officials sometimes recognized the importance of local learning, few effective policies emerged. Instead, new enterprises found a ready supply of machines and technicians just across the border, pushed into Mexico by the rapidly expanding economies of the North Atlantic. Given easy access to imports, there was little domestic pressure to develop local capacities.

We can see this reflected, for instance, in Mexico's patent records. In industry after industry, the introduction of newly patented production technologies was quickly followed by a significant uptick in patenting activity. However, in nearly each case it was foreign applications that drove increased patenting, and the relatively small number of domestic patents typically focused on ancillary, relatively nontechnical aspects of new production processes.[99] When Brittingham's group first acquired rights to the Owens automatic glass bottle–blowing machine in 1903, for example, patenting in glass- and bottle-related technologies rose from an average of about one per year to nearly twenty. But nine of every ten new patents came from abroad, spillover from the increasingly active international market for glass bottles. All but one of the few Mexican glass patents after 1903 were ancillary to actual bottle manufacture and focused on less technically sophisticated aspects of the industry: bottle design, bottle capping, and processes to wash, sterilize, fill, and label bottles. The Mexican response to new opportunities proved quick and entrepreneurial but did not reflect significant technological learning.

In the cigarette industry, the introduction of the automated Bonsack and Decouffle machines between 1884 and 1894 also stimulated increased patenting in Mexico. Average annual patenting related to tobacco products rose from under one per year before 1884 to about three per year over the next decade and nearly eight annually after 1894. Again, the major increase came in foreign patents, especially after 1894, and again, Mexican participation was strongest in the least technologically sophisticated subfields, like the preparation of cigarette paper and packaging. Similarly, the domestic response to increasing imports of sewing machines was extremely modest. Mexicans took only five new patents related to sewing after 1870, all focused on low-tech aspects of sewing machine technology: modifications of the foot pedal and the seat and several accessory tools. The introduction of major new inventions from abroad, in other words, did little to stimulate technological capabilities in Mexico.

Mexico's late nineteenth-century flood of technology imports in the form of machines, print materials, and people was not accompanied by a significant transfer of knowledge and skills to local individuals, firms, and organizations. This was the technological tragedy of Porfirian growth. Both entrepreneurs and government officials found it cheaper to buy technological capabilities from abroad—in the form of engineers, mechanics, and others— than to teach and train and thus generate technological capabilities at home.[100] While incentives to import hardware were strong, incentives to train local workers and develop local capabilities remained weak, and the social and institutional contexts for technical learning in Mexico were nearly absent. Proximity to the United States' skilled labor market played a role— the decidedly mixed "advantage of proximity"—and Mexican businesses benefited from the large spillover of US engineering talent, at least in the short term.[101] However, as most opportunities for interaction fell to this group, the benefits of learning soon left the country. Because the majority of Mexicans could not easily acquire technical skills, wages for skilled positions remained high and those for most laborers very low. As a result, the distance between those few who had privileged access to new opportunities and the majority who were excluded only increased. The country lost any opportunity for technology imports to stimulate local learning, thus widening its gap from North Atlantic expertise. Mexico had accumulated much of the productive capacity offered by new technologies developed in the North Atlantic but not the knowledge and expertise that might have supported a more innovative economy and a broader distribution of economic opportunity looking forward into the twentieth century.

NINE

Conclusion

OVER THE PAST TWO CENTURIES, technology has often embodied the search for progress. Nothing so captured the aspirations and anxieties of many Mexicans as the technological manifestations of *el progreso material.* "Every machine," noted José María Landero y Cos in 1901, "is a means of conquest for the future."[1] The imperatives of progress in nineteenth-century Mexico derived from multiple sources. Intellectuals looked to Europe for models to better understand Mexico's particular history, its place in the world, and paths by which it might realize its full sovereignty and potential. Public officials studied foreign laws, debating and sometimes adopting new versions in Mexico. Investors large and small sought profits by tapping into the North Atlantic economic boom in direct and indirect ways. And consumers across a surprisingly large income range sought goods that matched new urban, industrial occupations and that they increasingly associated with an emerging middle-class culture. Many viewed material progress as the only means by which Mexico could escape its first half century of national debility and backwardness (*atraso*) and join the fraternity of modern nations.

In many ways, Mexico succeeded in achieving these positivist goals. Investors working in Mexico spent tens of millions of pesos and dollars acquiring machines and know-how of all types—new "technologies" broadly conceived. Economic growth quickly reached nearly 5 percent per year, and by the nation's centennial in 1910 many were ready to celebrate thirty-plus years of "*el paz y el trabajo,*" though they would do so prematurely.[2] In the short term, Landero y Cos was exactly right: the acquisition of new machinery (along with the expertise to install and operate production systems) underlay Mexico's sustained economic growth in the late nineteenth century. In the long term, however, he was exactly wrong. As we have seen through the preceding chapters, the flood of new technologies that swept across Mexico between roughly 1870 and 1911 did not engender a local process of learning. The diffusion of new knowledge and technique did not yield significant convergence. The principal problem lay in a continuing scarcity of human capital, and especially of technical knowledge and expertise. As *La Union* of Monterrey noted in 1899, "The scarcity of men who know how to manage the different machines that are coming with the expansion of business activity is every day more and more striking."[3] Mexico's future would remain one of persistent technological dependence precisely because of continued reliance on both imported machinery and imported expertise.

This legacy of weak technological capabilities at the end of the nineteenth century meant that it would be more difficult for firms in the twentieth century to become technologically creative—from adapting and modifying production systems, to replicating and manufacturing machinery, to generating new innovations large and small. After the Revolution, a persistent scarcity of skills, technical knowledge, and machine-building expertise meant that investors and innovators would continue to look abroad, and Mexico would continue to rely heavily on machines and know-how imported from the North Atlantic. In the first decade after the Revolution, investments in imported industrial machinery quickly recovered their upward trend of prerevolutionary growth. By 1930 machinery imports by Mexican firms had risen to fully eight times prerevolutionary numbers.[4] Nevertheless, in the 1940s both industrialists and government officials expressed concerns not only about continued "dependence" on foreign technology but also about the antiquated state of technology in many industrial sectors. Tripartite pacts between labor, industry, and the government were enacted after the Revolution and persisted into midcentury and beyond, conferring high levels of protection to industry and generally depressing incentives to invest in new technology. Mexico's "incipient economic progress will not continue," argued one analyst in 1941, "if the problems of technological modernization are not resolved."[5] These problems included continued reliance on imported materials, technical inefficiencies in many industries, and a persistent scarcity of skilled labor and supervisory personnel necessary to operate new machinery.

By the 1960s, the country's persistent "dependence" attracted increasing concern among analysts who noted a continued reliance on imported technologies.[6] Often using language that echoed the concerns of mid-nineteenth-century observers, they noted that nearly two-thirds of Mexico's machinery needs continued to be satisfied by imports and that capital goods still made up well over a third of the country's total imports—just as they had a century before.[7] One study found that 90 percent of all machine tools in Mexico were imported.[8] Mexico's mid-twentieth-century import-substituting industrialization never fully extended to the capital equipment sector. As a result, the era saw massive technology imports without a substantial development of technological capabilities. This heavy reliance on imported technology helped fuel a trade imbalance that became increasingly unsustainable and that contributed to Mexico's economic crisis of the 1980s. At the same time, low levels of technological capabilities constrained the expansion of potentially high-productivity sectors of the Mexican economy during an era of acutely high population growth. As a result, most new employment came in low-productivity and low-income sectors of the economy.[9]

As in the late nineteenth century, technological dependence was not universal in Mexico. The Banco de México and other offices worked to promote technological capabilities in firms and organizations, and universities in Mexico City, Guadalajara, and in Monterrey expanded programs in engineering and technical training. A number of firms and industries acquired substantial scientific and technological capacities, invested in research and development facilities, and generated their own streams of innovative work. Mexican trained engineers played central roles in the management and operation of massive infrastructure projects, from roads and highways to the irrigation projects that expanded agricultural potential in La Laguna and elsewhere.[10] Mexican governments made concerted efforts in the 1970s and 1990s to reform innovation policies, most notably with the creation of a national technology council (CONACYT) in the 1970s, new intellectual property laws and technology transfer policies, and more recent efforts to strengthen and decentralize the institutions that promote innovation at both national and state levels.

However, again echoing late Porfirian patterns, innovative firms and effective policies have been the exception rather than the rule. Both private and public expenditures on research and development have been well below those of other Latin American countries and less than half the average of middle-income countries globally. As a result, Mexican firms have continued to rely heavily on imported sources of innovation during the recent, post-1980s era of globalization. Mexican firms have responded to new international pressures by relying more heavily on low-cost labor, for example, and have generally invested only meager increases in research and development expenditures.[11] In the 1990s, two-thirds of Mexican contracts for technology rights had a US business partner, and many businesses remained dependent on foreign licenses. Residents of Mexico took fewer than six hundred patents yearly between 1991 and 2005, virtually the same absolute level as the late nineteenth-century peak of a century earlier, despite an almost tenfold increase in population![12]

The persistence of technological dependence through the twentieth century was not predetermined by the nineteenth-century patterns that we have examined through this book. But low levels of local capabilities have been self-reinforcing and have served to make some development paths more likely than others. In this, Mexico's experience was not unusual in any global sense. Investors and firms around the world who pursued modernizing industrial projects in the decades and centuries after England's early experience depended heavily on borrowing machinery, ideas, and often personnel from the technology exporters of the North Atlantic. In the early nineteenth century, the United States and France borrowed heavily from England, as did the Scandinavian countries and much of the rest of continental Europe. A bit later, Germany and then Russia borrowed heavily from both Britain and the United States. By the century's end and now outside Europe, Meiji Japan joined the larger countries of Latin America and then places like Egypt and India, all borrowing from North Atlantic models and manufacturers. And by the mid-twentieth century, Taiwan, South Korea, and Singapore followed suit. Mexico's early dependence on borrowed technology and expertise was in no way unusual; it has been, in fact, the global norm.

Mexican investors and officials understood that in the short run it was cheaper to buy machines from abroad than to manufacture them at home, and cheaper to import expertise than to train it locally. The former required hiring technological capabilities in the person of engineers and mechanics, readily available across the border; the latter would require confronting the challenge of developing human capital and local technological capabilities. Recall that in 1900, Mexico had one-half the number of engineers per capita as Brazil and Chile, and one-fourth as many as Portugal and Spain.[13] In the short term, this preference for imported expertise was entirely rational. The scarcity of skilled labor, technical expertise, and machine-building capabilities in Mexico meant high salaries, so shopping abroad incurred little extra. This was especially true in Mexico, where easy access to US markets has offered a steady supply of hardware and software for over a century—the double-edged "advantage of proximity" (*la ventaja de la vecindad*)—as one correspondent noted in as early as 1886.[14] This so-called advantage—*pobre México*—was reinforced by policy incentives to buy technology abroad rather than to invest in capabilities at home.[15] As a result, the pattern became self-perpetuating, and initial technological dependence became a stubbornly persistent dependence.

For some countries, early borrowing led to the development of local capabilities to imitate and replicate new technologies, and then to more deeply embedded forms of technological creativity and innovation. Through use, adaptation, and imitation, local workers and technicians engaged closely with the know-how embodied in new machines and processes, acquiring the capabilities necessary to imitate, replicate, operate, maintain, adapt, troubleshoot, and improve on imported technologies. Borrowing and imitation stimulated local capacities for subsequent innovation, and some degree of technological independence from (or, perhaps, interdependence with) the technology exporters of the world followed.[16]

In contrast, Mexico provides one case of both early and persistent technological dependence. Beginning in the early years of the nineteenth century, some in Mexico observed the early industrial activity in Britain, and soon after in the United States, and argued for the domestic adoption of steam power, tool manufacturing, and mechanized industry generally. Fausto de Elhuyar, Simón Tadeo Ortíz, Estevan de Antuñano, Lucas Alamán, and others devised policies, studied North Atlantic advances, wrote pamphlets and lobbying tracts, and invested their own resources in new projects. Not until the last third of the nineteenth century, however, were conditions in Mexico propitious for the widespread adoption of new technologies. Economic growth in the North Atlantic following the end of the US Civil War spilled outward, and machine manufacturers aggressively sought new markets for their products around the world. Young technicians and engineers from the United States and Europe sought to cut their teeth in managerial positions abroad, experience that they could later parlay into better positions back home. Within Mexico, the consolidation of a less fractured political regime by the 1870s enabled the consideration, for the first time in the nation's history, of effective policy reform. Attracting foreign investment quickly became the highest priority of federal (and often state-level) politics, first to build infrastructure and second to resuscitate the mining and resource extraction economy to meet international demand. Foreign investors responded quickly, but so did Mexican entrepreneurs as well as an increasingly influential group of first- and second-generation immigrants.[17] By the late 1880s, attention within policy-making and investing circles slowly turned toward to diversifying the Mexican economy and especially to inducing investment in domestic manufacturing. At the same time, more and more Mexicans sought jobs in new activities and began consuming new kinds of goods and services: tram and rail transport, bottled beer, and ready-made clothing, to name just a few.

In the short run, Mexico quickly accumulated the productive capacity offered by new technologies developed in the North Atlantic. Investors and entrepreneurs acquired and commercialized an impressively wide array of global frontier technologies, from sewing machines to the Owens system and the cyanide process and many others in homes, offices, factories, haciendas, and mining centers. These technologies and the personnel who helped install and operate them underlay a dramatic, "Gerschenkronian" transformation in the country's socioeconomic landscape, as dislocative and socially disruptive as it was creative. New technologies helped generate rapid economic growth over more than three decades and provided the material foundation for Mexico's substantial development of industrial capacity into the mid-twentieth century. On the other hand, however, locally assimilating the knowledge and expertise embodied in technology imports proved extraordinarily difficult. Learning by local technicians was rare, the exception rather than the rule.

This experience highlights historians' observation that technologies emerge not as abstract, universal, best-practice ways to accomplish a particular task but rather as a complex of ideas and artifacts shaped by their own historical contexts. Context includes not only technological antecedents, the technical demands of a job to be done, and the nature of economic markets for inputs and products but also political institutions, human capital and social relations, consumer markets and, arguably, cultural attributes manifest in local values and preferences.

Moved across boundaries—national or otherwise—and set down in a different production ecology, technologies designed and developed elsewhere might not quite "fit" within the new context. Overcoming the challenges of adoption requires particular kinds of human capital or production capabilities. On the one hand, much of what we observed in chapters 3 through 6 reflects the relative ease with which technologies were imported and installed in Mexican contexts. On the other hand, the limits to technological change were also manifest across the economy. The "fit" between technologies, newly available abroad, and local Mexican contexts for their installation was not automatic and often required adaptations to either imported technology or aspects of the local contextual setting, or both. Some adaptations were relatively modest and easily negotiated; others proved more difficult or intractable. Some obstacles proved malleable, others more obdurate. Problems of fit meant that imported technologies could be in some sense inappropriate for the new setting, although this does not necessarily mean that their adoption was uneconomical or irrational. Constraints could delay commercialization, limit diffusion, increase operating costs, reduce the productive capacity or operating efficiency of newly imported technologies, and even prevent adoption altogether.

But the constraints to technological *learning* were even greater and centered on five aspects of Mexico's late nineteenth-century experience that we tentatively explored in chapter 8, each pointing to important avenues for further research. First, interactions between imported technologies and local workers and technicians proved extremely limited. Given the relative scarcity of technical expertise in Mexico, it was generally cheaper and easier for investors to hire foreign expertise to install and operate new machinery than to train Mexican workers. Local workers' interaction was typically limited to relatively simple tasks of operation, the performance of ancillary activities, and perhaps simple maintenance and troubleshooting. They had few opportunities to deeply engage the black box of technological know-how embodied within sewing machines, factory production systems, and mining processes. Nor were they well prepared to do so. Very limited adoption of new technologies like steam engines, milling operations, railroads, and iron foundries (for example) in the decades before 1870 meant that very few Mexicans had acquired expertise in working with mechanized production.

After 1870, the spillover of products, technologies, and expertise embodied in thousands of young men from the North Atlantic substituted for local scarcity, but it also increasingly displaced opportunities for local engineers and workers. We need a more systematic comparison between the experiences of Mexico, Brazil, and Argentina, for instance, to better evaluate whether Mexico was, to complete President Díaz's apocryphal phrase, "[too] close to the United States." Regardless, most opportunities for interaction with new knowledge and thus for technological learning were monopolized by foreign technicians. As a consequence, Mexico lost the opportunity that technology imports might have stimulated local learning and enhanced domestic technological capabilities.

Second, the gap between technical know-how in Mexico and in the North Atlantic proved too great to easily bridge. In part, the late nineteenth-century innovations of the second industrial revolution in the United States, Great

Britain, and Germany drew heavily on new scientific knowledge and forms of technological expertise finely honed over a century of industrial growth in the North Atlantic. Metallurgy, machine tooling, the chemical industry, and the generation, distribution, and application of electricity lay at the center of this era of globalizing innovation. But Mexico had missed much of the earlier wave of industrial and mechanized technologies of the first industrial revolution. As a result, the country had only a weak foundation of experience with which to engage the new onslaught of advances it faced in the North Atlantic market. Few cases illustrate this better than the slow diffusion of steam power and ironworking capabilities through the nineteenth century. Without local expertise in the operation, adaptation, repair, and replication of these basic foundations of the industrial experience, Mexico had little capacity to assimilate the technical know-how embodied in a wholly new generation of late-century technologies, and little hope of catching up.

Third, Mexico's technical education programs did not supply the engineers and technicians who might have acquired technological capabilities and worked to bridge the gap with the North Atlantic. "We don't need scientists," argued a Monterrey newspaper in 1899, "we need men who can learn the industrial arts [based on machinery]."[18]

Despite increased investment in technical education and some curricular reforms, programs remained small and largely isolated from industry. Most importantly, graduates numbered only a relative handful and did not fill the capacity of new programs. This was true for basic training programs for workers both in the Escuelas de Artes y Oficios and in Mexico's new engineering schools. Relatively few engineering alumni played a major role in applied work, in mastering the know-how at the center of new industrial advances and working out—in the field or on the shop floor—the technical challenges of adopting and adapting imported technologies to local settings. The multiple technical challenges of adopting and assimilating new technical know-how increasingly required what Joel Mokyr has called a "knowledge economy."[19] In late-century Mexico, however, simply hiring the know-how from abroad seemed cheaper and easier in the short run. This economic logic of scarce human capital was likely reinforced by the kinds of ethnic prejudices and preferences that so frequently marked divisions between skilled and unskilled labor in Mexican mines and factories and throughout the economy.[20]

Fourth, even when Mexican entrepreneurs and technicians acquired new knowledge and expertise with foreign technologies—their capacities, their uses, and the intricacies of their inner workings—there were few venues and networks for sharing that knowledge. On the one hand, the nineteenth century witnessed a flowering of government-sponsored and privately organized societies and associations for the promotion of science and commercial enterprise—all key components of a knowledge economy. Governments and business associations sponsored scientific and technical expositions and published pamphlets that presented recent advances. Although we need further research on the nature and operation of these kinds of efforts and associations, few provided effective venues for the diffusion of knowledge and expertise in Mexico. This was especially true for the vertical diffusion of knowledge and skills through society, from the small number who acquired education and training to the majority of technicians, and especially mechanics, and workers. The glimpses we have in the secondary literature of the social relations of work within mines and factories suggest that constraints to skill sharing and to learning outweighed facilitating factors.

Finally, government policies did little to promote effective technological learning. Trade policies persistently favored ready access to capital and technical hardware from abroad instead of promoting local development at home. Although tariffs increasingly sought to protect many domestic manufacturing industries, protection was limited to consumer goods and some basic producer goods like cement, structural iron and steel, and paper. There was no sustained debate about the desirability of supporting the domestic manufacture of tools and machinery. Indeed, the principal consumers of technological hardware in all sectors of the economy made it abundantly clear that their success depended on free and easy access to the new technologies available on North Atlantic shelves. Although the Porfirian state was able to establish some degree of relative autonomy from business interests, they, like any government, depended ultimately on tax revenues derived from the most productive sectors of the economy. Furthermore, both formal policy and informal norms favored the employment of US or European engineers and technicians over their Mexican counterparts, even if the latter were available, capable, and more economical. The political economy of technological change, in other words, overwhelmingly favored borrowing and early dependence; it also substantially undermined opportunities to develop domestic expertise.

. . .

The adoption of new technologies has long been seen as the most effective way for relatively poor countries to achieve the wealth and welfare of global leaders. In late nineteenth-century Mexico, policy makers, public intellectuals, and investors repeatedly articulated this vision, and sanguine views about the transformative potential of sewing machines, factory systems, electrical power, and new production processes pervaded Mexican society, generally outweighing suspicion and resistance. This study argues that while technology imports in the form of machines, people, and print material made possible a dramatic transformation of the country's productive potential in the short run, they did not contribute to the development of sustained independent innovation in the long run. Innovational capabilities are built primarily on human capital. Beginning with the second industrial revolution of the late nineteenth century, these became increasingly based on formal scientific and technical education, knowledge, and expertise. In Mexico, the scarcity of this kind of human capital would constrain economic growth and the kinds of opportunities available to most Mexicans.

Multiple paths of technological change competed in nineteenth-century Mexico; the story was neither unilinear or deterministic. Outcomes often diverged from the visions and goals of those who promoted the importation of new techniques. Mexico did not import and innovate all that was available abroad, and technological change came slowly and incrementally, frequently fraught with difficulties. New projects produced a litany of complaints about obstacles to the installation, operation, repair, and adaptability of imported machines, parts, tools, and processes. In some cases, adoption and diffusion came quickly and easily, and in a few exceptional cases local learning could be substantial. All experiences were highly contingent on the intimate relationship between technology and contextual environment, but they were also shaped by Mexico's intimate relationship to an expanding North Atlantic economy. This relationship, and particularly Mexico's heavy reliance on imported technological hardware, knowledge, and expertise, conditioned but did not determine the long-term consequences: sometimes by displacing domestic creativity and deepening technological dependency, sometimes by creating a modern sector relatively isolated from domestic society, and occasionally by stimulating local learning and capabilities. The overall story, however, is one of persistent dependence, and the patterns established during this early transition would critically shape competing development paths for Mexico's twentieth century.

APPENDIX ONE

Sources and Notes on Mexican Patents

Because no single source contains data on all patents issued in Mexico through the long nineteenth century, I constructed a comprehensive patent database using multiple sources, cross-checking listings to separate conferred patents from applications and to fill gaps in the coverage of each source. Patent data for 1850–90 is partially based on the catalog compiled and published by Jorge A. Soberanís ("Catálogo de patentes de invención en México durante el siglo xix (1840–1900): Ensayo de interpretación sobre el proceso de industrialización del México decimonónico," Tesis de Licenciatura, UNAM, 1989), which lists all patents for which files exist in the Mexico's Archivo General de la Nación. However, this excludes the over ten thousand patents that are not retained in the AGN's *ramo* Patentes y Marcas and thus are not included in Soberanis's catalog, and for others does not distinguish between applications and conferrals. These gaps are filled using patent conferral notices published in the annual volumes of Manuel Dublán and José María Lozano's *Legislación mexicana; o, colección completa de las disposiciones legislativas expedidas desde la independencia de la república,* 37 vols. (Mexico: Imprenta de E. Dublán, 1876–1912) and those published in the various volumes of the annual *Memorias* of the Secretaría de Fomento (Development Ministry) from 1857 through the 1890s. Patent data for the period 1890 to October 1903 use conferral notices published in the daily editions of the *Diario Oficial de la Federación* (totally roughly 4,300 newspaper editions). Finally, patents for the period October 1903 to 1910 are gathered from the monthly editions of the *Gaceta oficial de patentes y marcas,* published by the Patent Office within the Development Ministry (Secretaría de Fomento). For each patent, the database includes the name(s) of the inventor(s), a brief description of the patent, the date of issue, and the patent number. Many also contain information on the residence and nationality of the patentee as well as on patent renewals, terms, fees, and classifications.

Published notices of patent conferrals before 1904 did not note the nationality of patentees, but fortunately the original letters of applications, published separately in the *Diario Oficial,* sometimes refer to nationality. After compiling this data and adding it to the database, those still lacking nationality (just over 50 percent) who had non-Spanish surnames were cross-checked with listings of patentees in the US Patent Office's *Annual Report of the Commissioner of Patents.* As a result, nationality is definitely known for roughly 85 percent of all patentees before 1904. The remainder were classified as Mexican if they had Spanish surnames, and as generically foreign if they did not. As patentees from Spain were rare, and known Mexican patentees with non-Spanish surnames were few, this gives us a rough approximation of foreign and Mexican patenting trends.

Official totals for Mexican and foreign patentees after 1904 show Mexican patenting at nearly twice the pre-1904 levels. These counts apparently designated foreigners as Mexican if they did not provide information on nationality in the patent applications. To correct this I took the percentages of Mexican and foreign patents from one sample of roughly 2,400 patents conferred between 1904 and 1910 (24.6 percent Mexican and 76.4 percent foreign) and applied these percentages to the total number of patents conceded for those years. These percentages roughly match the average distribution for the 1890–1903 period, but they hide any yearly variation in the distribution that might have existed after 1904. More information on the patent database is available from the author (ebeatty@nd.edu).

Sources and Notes on Iron, Steel, and Machinery Imports

Data on Mexico's annual imports of iron and steel manufactures (and especially of machinery and capital equipment generally) are drawn primarily from official publications of Mexico's main trading partners: the United States, Britain, France, and Germany. These include US Department of Commerce, *Foreign Commerce and Navigation of the United States* (Washington, DC: Government Printing Office, 1880–1911); Great Britain Customs Establishment, Statistical Office, *Annual Statement of the Trade and Navigation of the United Kingdom with Foreign Countries and British Possessions in the Year . . .* (London, 1883–1910); France, Direction Général des Douanes, *Tableau général du commerce de la France avec ses colonies et les puissances étrangeres pendant l'année . . .* (Paris, 1894–1911); and Germany, *Statistik des Deutschen Reichs: Auswärtiger Handel deutschen Zollgebiets im Jahre . . . , herausgegeben vom Kaiserlichen Statistischen Amte* (Berlin, 1880–1908). Other scholars have used these sources to build annual series for Mexico's foreign trade, most notably Sandra Kuntz Ficker in her two volumes *El comercio exterior de México en la era del capitalismo liberal, 1870–1929* (México: El Colegio de México, 2007) and *Las exportaciones mexicanas durante la primara globalización, 1870–1929* (México: El Colegio de México, 2010). I am deeply grateful to Sandra for sharing some of her data and wisdom with me for this project.

Establishing long-running annual series for disaggregated classes of iron and steel manufactures and machinery (from iron bars and nails to sewing machines and steam engines, for example) is difficult for several reasons: because of major differences in classification and reporting across the four countries, because of the absence of disaggregation for earlier years in the series, and because of changes in each country's "not elsewhere specified" or catch-all category. Primary subclasses in the US machinery export data include total manufacturing machines (metalworking, mining, pumps, sewing machines, shoe machines, woodworking, printing presses, windmills, typewriters, cash registers, laundry machines, and all other manufacturing machines) and total steam machines (fire, locomotive, stationary, traction, and all other, with "stationary" at 9 percent of the total, most of the rest being locomotive), as well as agricultural machines, electrical apparatus, builders' hardware, and scientific instruments. Tools and similar types of manufactures in the series include cutlery, edge tools, saws and files, scales, locks, stoves, and other tools and manufactures not elsewhere specified. Basic iron and steel forms include pig iron; bars, sheets, plates, rods, wire, and rails of iron and steel; car wheels; castings; nails; and other structural forms.

All import values are converted from national currencies to US dollars; volume series are derived by calculating unit prices when volume data are reported (in pounds, tons, kilograms, liters, etc.) or by converting value measures to constant US dollars using the price index for machinery in the foreign trade of the United States presented in Robert E. Lipsey, *Price and Quantity Trends in the Foreign Trade of the United States* (Princeton, NJ: Princeton University Press, 1963), series 071. Note that this series, "Machinery and Vehicles, except Automobiles," compares well with a similar series based on British foreign trade in C. H. Feinstein, *Statistical Tables of National Income, Expenditure, and Output of the U.K, 1855–1965* (Cambridge: Cambridge University Press, 1972), table 63, "Plant and Machinery."

NOTES

The following are abbreviations used in the notes:

AGN Archivo General de la Nacíon, Ramos

AHJB Archivo Historico de Juan Brittingham, Universidad Iberoamericana Laguna, Torreón

BLUC Bancroft Library, University of California, Berkeley

BLUT Benson Library, University of Texas, Austin

SMCA Singer Manufacturing Company Archive, Wisconsin Historical Society, Madison

TAIME *Transactions, American Institute of Mining Engineers*

TGCA Toledo Glass Company Archives, University of Toledo, Toledo, Ohio

I. INTRODUCTION

1. For one introduction to a vast literature, see Peter F. Klarén and Thomas J. Bossert, *Promise of Development: Theories of Change in Latin America* (Boulder, CO: Westview Press, 1986); also Albert O. Hirschman, *Essays on Trespassing: Economics to Politics and Beyond* (New York: Cambridge University Press, 1981), chap. 1.

2. Robert Pakenham, *The Dependency Movement: Politics and Scholarship in Development Studies* (Cambridge, MA: Harvard University Press, 1992); Stephen Haber, "Economic Growth and Latin American Historiography," in *How Latin America Fell Behind: Essays on the Economic Histories of Brazil and Mexico, 1800–1914*, ed. Stephen Haber (Stanford, CA: Stanford University Press, 1997), 1–33.

3. Gilberto Crespo y Martínez, *Las patentes de invención* (Mexico: Oficina Tip. de la Secretaría de Fomento, 1897), 5, 18.

4. Edward Beatty, "Riqueza, polémica, y política: Pensamiento y políticas económicas en México (1765–1911)," in *Historia del pensamiento económico en México: Ideas y debate en torno a la riqueza, el progreso y el auge económico de 1750 a 1900*, ed. José Enrique Covarrubias (Mexico: Universidad Nacional Autónoma de México, forthcoming); for just one example, see Mexico, Cámara de Diputados, *Dictamen presentado a la Cámara de Diputados por sus Comisiones Unidas de Minería e Industria* (1845; repr., Mexico: Librería Manuel Porrúa, 1955), 67.

5. Richard Weiner, "Battle for Survival: Porfirian Views of the International Marketplace," *Journal of Latin American Studies* 32 (2000): 645–70.

6. Mauricio Tenorio-Trillo, *Mexico at the World's Fairs: Crafting a Modern Nation* (Berkeley: University of California Press, 1996), introduction and chap. 4.

7. *El Siglo Diez y Nueve*, September 26, 1869, 3.

8. Aurora Gómez-Galvarriato, *Industry and Revolution: Social and Economic Change in the Orizaba Valley, Mexico* (Cambridge, MA: Harvard University Press, 2013), 18; Stephen Haber, Armando Razo, and Noel Maurer, *The Politics of Property Rights: Political Instability, Credible Commitments, and Economic Growth in Mexico, 1876–1929* (Cambridge: Cambridge University Press, 2003), 169; Marvin D. Bernstein, *The Mexican Mining Industry, 1890–1950: A Study in the Interaction of Politics, Economics, and Technology* (Albany: State University of New York Press, 1964), 86; Joel Alvarez de la Borda, "Transportes, negocios y política: La Compañía de Tranvías de México, 1907–1947," in *Compañías eléctricas extranjeras en México (1880–1960)*, ed. Reinhard Liehr and Mariano E. Torres Bautista (Puebla, Mexico: Benemérita Universidad Autónoma de Puebla, 2010), 77; Sandra Kuntz Ficker, *Empresa extranjera y mercado interno: El Ferrocárril Central Mexicano, 1880–1907* (Mexico: Colegio de México, 1995), 103.

9. Steven B. Bunker, *Creating Mexican Consumer Culture in the Age of Porfirio Díaz* (Albuquerque: University of New Mexico Press, 2012).

10. For one example among many, see the import manifests for the new heavy fiber weaving factory, La Compañía Industrial: pp. 251–56, box 9, folder 6, pp. 264–69; box 10, folder 3, pp. 89–96; box 10, folder 7; and boxes 13, 14, 51, and 52, all in the *ramo* Industrias Nuevas, AGN.

11. David J. Jeremy, *Transatlantic Industrial Revolution: The Diffusion of Textile Technologies between Britain and America, 1790–1830s* (Cambridge, MA: MIT Press, 1981); David J. Jeremy, ed., *International Technology Transfer: Europe, Japan and the USA, 1700–1914* (London: Edward Elgar, 1991); Sidney Pollard, *Peaceful Conquest: The Industrialization of Europe, 1760–1970* (Oxford: Oxford University Press, 1981); and Kristine Bruland, *British Technology and European Industrialization: The Norwegian Textile Industry in the Mid-nineteenth Century* (Cambridge: Cambridge University Press, 1989).

12. World Bank, "GDP per Capita," accessed July 25, 2013, http://data.worldbank.org/indicator/NY.GDP.PCAP.CD/countries/latest?display=default; also Alice Amsden, *The Rise of "The Rest": Challenges to the West from Late-Industrializing Economies* (New York: Oxford University Press, 2001).

13. Crespo y Martínez, *Patentes de invención,* 9; see also the discussion in chapter 2 below.

14. "Dictamen de la Comisión de Legislación . . . 21 de enero de 1823," in *Protección y libre cambio: El debate entre 1821 y 1836,* ed. Luis Córdova (Mexico: Banco Nacional de Comercio Exterior, 1971), 23.

15. Estevan de Antuñano, *Pensamientos para la regeneración industrial de México* (1837; repr., Mexico: Librería Manuel Porrúa, 1955), 31.

16. Mexico, *Memoria sobre el estado de la agricultura é industria de la República . . . en cumplimiento del articulo 26 del decreto orgánico de 2 de diciembre de 1842* (Mexico: Imprenta de Lara, 1843), 40, 57–58.

17. Miguel Lerdo de Tejada, *Comercio exterior de México desde la conquista hasta hoy* [Mexico, 1853], reprinted in his *Mexico in 1856, el comercio exterior desde la conquista* (Mexico: Universidad Veracruzana, 1985), 142.

18. Crespo y Martínez, *Patentes de invención,* 9.

19. Edward Beatty, *Institutions and Investment: The Political Basis of Industrialization in Mexico before 1911* (Stanford, CA: Stanford University Press, 2001), chap. 5.

20. Moses Abramovitz, "Catching Up, Forging Ahead, and Falling Behind," *Journal of Economic History* 46 (1986): 385–406; Sanjaya Lall, "Technological Capabilities and Industrialization," *World Development* 20 (1992): 165.

21. For one recent statement, see Jeffrey D. Sachs, *The End of Poverty: Economic Possibilities for Our Time* (New York: Penguin Press, 2005): "I believe that the single most important reason why prosperity spread, and why it continues to spread, is the transmission of technologies and the ideas underlying them" (41; see also 61–64).

22. Alexander Gerschenkron, *Economic Backwardness in Historical Perspective* (Cambridge: Cambridge University Press, 1962), 8.

23. Pollard, *Peaceful Conquest,* 142.

24. Robert C. Allen, *British Industrial Revolution in Global Perspective* (Cambridge: Cambridge University Press, 2009), 154–55.

25. Mexico, *Memoria sobre el estado . . . 1842,* 25.

26. Juan Nepomuceno Adorno, *Análisis de los males de México y sus remedios practicables* (Mexico: M. Muguia, 1858), 128.

27. Juan Brittingham to Juan Terrazas, November 7, 1904, doc. 0017428, AHJB.

28. Crespo y Martínez, *Patentes de invención,* 7.

29. Mexico, *Memoria sobre el estado . . . 1842,* 40, 57.

30. For an introduction to a large literature, see, on continental Europe, Pollard, *Peaceful Conquest;* on Scandinavia, Kristine Bruland, *British Technology,* and Kristine Bruland, ed., *Technology Transfer and Scandinavian Industrialization* (New York: Berg, 1991); on Japan, Tessa Morris-Suzuki, *The Technological Transformation of Japan: From the Seventeenth to the Twenty-First Century* (Cambridge: Cambridge University Press, 1994).

31. *El Correo Español,* September 1, 1891, from a speech following Mexico's participation in the 1889 Paris Exhibition; also Mauricio Tenorio-Trillo, "Stereophonic Scientific Modernisms: Social Science between Mexico and the United States,

1880s-1930s," *Journal of American History* 86 (December 1999): 1156–87, especially 1169.

32. *Diario Oficial de la Nación,* August 12, 1903.

33. José Galicia [of the Escuela Nacional de Jurisprudencia], "Conferencia sobre patentes de invención," *Revista de Legislación y Jurisprudencia,* no. 19 (1900): 453–63. See also *Diario Oficial de la Nación,* September 1, 1903; *El Economista Mexicano,* September 19, 1903, 582; and Mexico, Secretaría de Fomento, *Memoria* (1908–9) (Mexico: Imprenta de la Secretaria de Fomento, 1908–9), lxxxiii.

34. Ramón Sánchez Flores, *Historia de la tecnología y la invención en México: Introducción a su estudio y documentos para los anales de la técnica* (Mexico: Fomento Cultural Banamex, 1980); Alfonso Zamora Pérez, *Inventario crítico de las máquinas desfibradoras en México (1830–1890)* (Mexico: UAM-A, 1999).

35. Tenorio-Trillo, *Mexico at the World's Fairs,* 135; also Gerardo de la Concha and Juan Carlos Calleros, *Los caminos de la invención: Inventos e inventores en México* (Mexico: Instituto Politécnico Nacional, 1996), 14.

36. Elías Trabulse, *El círculo roto: Estudios históricos sobre la ciencia en México* (Mexico: Fondo de Cultura Económica, 1996), 23; Tenorio-Trillo, *Mexico at the World's Fairs,* 135.

37. E. Beatty, *Institutions and Investment,* chaps. 2, 4.

38. Kevin H. O'Rourke and Jeffrey G. Williamson, *Globalization and History: The Evolution of a Nineteenth-Century Atlantic Economy* (Cambridge, MA: MIT Press, 1999); A. G. Kenwood and A. L. Lougheed, *The Growth of the International Economy, 1820–1990,* 3rd ed. (London: Routledge, 1992).

39. Ian Inkster, "Technology Transfer and Industrial Transformation: An Interpretation of the Pattern of Economic Development circa 1870–1914," in *Technological Change: Methods and Themes in the History of Technology,* ed. Robert Fox (Amsterdam: Harwood Academic, 1996). On the difficult nature of international technology transfer, see W. Paul Strassmann, *Technological Change and Economic Development: The Manufacturing Experience of Mexico and Puerto Rico* (Ithaca, NY: Cornell University Press, 1968), chap. 8; Richard R. Nelson, "On Technological Capabilities and Their Acquisition," in *Science and Technology: Lessons for Development Policy,* ed. Robert E. Evenson and Gustav Ranis (Boulder, CO: Westview Press, 1990), 71–87; David J. Jeremy, introduction to Jeremy, *International Technology Transfer;* and Kristine Bruland, "The Norwegian Mechanical Engineering Industry and the Transfer of Technology, 1800–1900," in Bruland, *Technology Transfer,* 229–67. On nineteenth-century colonial contexts, see Daniel Headrick, *The Tentacles of Progress: Technology Transfer in the Age of Imperialism, 1850–1940* (New York: Oxford University Press, 1988); and Jan Todd, *Colonial Technology: Science and the Transfer of Innovation to Australia* (Cambridge: Cambridge University Press, 1995). On Meiji Japan, see Hoshimi Uchida, "The Transfer of Electrical Technologies from the United States and Europe to Japan, 1869–1914," in Jeremy, *International Technology Transfer,* 219–41; Jeffrey R. Bernstein, "Toyoda Automatic Looms and Toyota Automobiles," in *Creating Modern Capitalism: How Entrepreneurs, Companies, and Countries Triumphed in Three Industrial Revolutions,* ed.

Thomas K. McCraw (Cambridge, MA: Harvard University Press, 1997), 396–438; and Morris-Suzuki, *Technological Transformation of Japan*. On the more recent East Asian experience, see Amsden, *Rise of "The Rest,"* and Linsu Kim, *Imitation to Innovation: The Dynamics of Korea's Technological Learning* (Boston: Harvard Business School Press, 1997), and on the challenges and scant success of development policies in the second half of the twentieth century, see Clark Gibson et al., *The Samaritan's Dilemma: The Political Economy of Development Aid* (Oxford: Oxford University Press, 2005).

40. The social constructionist approach counters technological determinism: that new technologies, once available, will be commercialized and that the most economically efficient will dominate and survive. Wiebe E. Bijker, Thomas P. Hughes, and Trevor J. Pinch, eds., *The Social Construction of Technological Systems: New Directions in the Sociology and History of Technology* (Cambridge, MA: MIT Press, 1987); Wiebe E. Bijker and John Law, eds., *Shaping Technology/Building Society: Studies in Sociotechnical Change* (Cambridge, MA: MIT Press, 1992); and Donald MacKenzie and Judy Wajcman, eds., *The Social Shaping of Technology* (Philadelphia: Open University Press, 1999).

41. Jeff Horn, Leonard N. Rosenband, and Merritt Roe Smith, eds., introduction to *Reconceptualizing the Industrial Revolution* (Cambridge, MA: MIT Press, 2010).

42. Ibid., 1.

43. Lall, "Technological Capabilities"; Kim, *Imitation to Innovation;* M. Fransman and K. King, *Technological Capability in the Third World* (London: Macmillan, 1984); Bon Ho Koo and Dwight H. Perkins, eds., *Social Capability and Long-Term Economic Growth* (New York: St. Martin's Press, 1995). Both Lall and Kim identify *investment* and *production* capabilities, together with *linkage* capabilities (Lall) and *innovation* capabilities (Kim). Within this literature, concepts of technological capabilities are often vague and ambiguous.

44. For recognition of these challenges, see *El Economista Mexicano,* September 10, 1886, 62–63; for two recent illustrations, see Guillermo Guajardo, *Trabajo y tecnología en los ferrocarriles de México: Una visión histórica, 1850–1950* (Mexico: El Centauro, 2010), and John Womack Jr., *El trabajo en la Cervecería Moctezuma, 1908* (Mexico: Colegio de México, 2012).

45. Quoted in Guy P. C. Thomson, *Puebla de los Angeles: Industry and Society in a Mexican City, 1700–1850* (Boulder, CO: Westview Press, 1989), 293.

46. Nathan Rosenberg, "Economic Development and the Transfer of Technology: Some Historical Perspectives," *Technology and Culture* 11, no. 4 (1970): 550–75; Nathan Rosenberg, *Inside the Black Box: Technology and Economics* (Cambridge: Cambridge University Press, 1982), chap. 11; Vernon Ruttan and Yujiro Hayami, "Technology Transfer and Agricultural Development," *Technology and Culture* 14, no. 2 (1973): 119–51; and Jorge Katz, "Domestic Technological Innovations and Dynamic Comparative Advantages," in *International Technology Transfer: Concepts, Measures, and Comparisons,* ed. Nathan Rosenberg and Claudio Frischtak (New York: Praeger, 1985), 127–66. The concept of "absorptive capacity" was developed

primarily to explain the differential capacity of firms to assimilate and exploit external knowledge; see W. M. Cohen and D. A. Levinthal, "Absorptive Capacity: A New Perspective on Learning and Innovation," *Administrative Science Quarterly* 35 (1990): 128–52; Paola Criscuolo and Rajneesh Narula, "A Novel Approach to National Technological Accumulation and Absorptive Capacity: Aggregating Cohen and Levinthal," *European Journal of Development Research* 20, no. 1 (2008): 53–73. See also Wolfgang Keller, "Absorptive Capacity: On the Creation and Acquisition of Technology in Development," *Journal of Development Studies* 49 (1996): 199–227; Robert Solo, "The Capacity to Assimilate an Advanced Technology," *American Economic Review* 52, nos. 1–2 (1966): 91–97. For an early application to postwar Latin America, see Strassmann, *Technological Change,* chap. 8.

47. On the twentieth century, see Amsden, *Rise of "The Rest,"* chap. 1; on the nineteenth century, Inkster, "Technology Transfer."

48. Enrique Cárdenas Sánchez, *Cuando se originó el atraso económico de México: La economía mexicana en el largo siglo xix, 1780–1920* (Madrid: Biblioteca Nueva; Fundación Ortega y Gasset, 2003); Ernest Sánchez Santiró, "El desempeño de la economía mexicana tras la independencia, 1821–1870: Nuevas evidencias e interpretaciones," in *Latinoamérica y España, 1800–1850: Un crescimento económico nada excepcional,* ed. Enrique Llopis and Carlos Marichal (Madrid: Marcial Pons Historia, 2009); and Richard J. Salvucci, "Mexican National Income in the Era of Independence, 1800–40," in Haber, *How Latin America Fell Behind,* 216–42; synthesized in E. Beatty, *Institutions and Investment,* chap. 2.

49. Cárdenas Sánchez, *Cuando se originó el atraso*; E. Beatty, *Institutions and Investment,* chap. 2; Carlos Marichal and Mario Cerutti, eds., *Historia de las grandes empresas en México, 1850–1930* (Mexico: Universidad Autónoma de Nuevo León, 1997); Stephen H. Haber, *Industry and Underdevelopment: The Industrialization of Mexico, 1890–1940* (Stanford, CA: Stanford University Press, 1989). On commerce, see Sandra Kuntz Ficker, *El comercio exterior de México en la era del capitalismo liberal, 1870–1929* (Mexico: El Colegio de México, 2007); also Sandra Kuntz Ficker, ed., *Historia económica general de México: De la colonia a nuestros días* (Mexico: Colegio de México, 2010).

50. Enrique Cárdenas Sánchez, "A Macroeconomic Interpretation of Nineteenth-Century Mexico," in Haber, *How Latin America Fell Behind,* 81.

51. For the best treatments, see Sánchez Flores, *Historia de la tecnología;* Jorge A. Soberanis, "Catálogo de patentes de invención en México durante el siglo xix (1840–1900): Ensayo de interpretación sobre el proceso de industrialización del México decimonónico" (Tesis de Licenciatura, UNAM, 1989); and Mónica Blanco and María Eugenia Romero Sotelo, *Cambio tecnológico e industrialización: La manufactura mexicana y su historia, siglo xviii, xix, y xx* (Mexico: DGAPA-FE-UNAM, 1997). See Justo Sierra, *México: Su evolución social,* 3 vols. (1902–5; repr., Mexico: Miguel Angel Porrúa, 2005), for a contemporary view of technological change in agriculture, mining, manufacturing, and urban sectors. Over a half century later, the two volumes coordinated by Daniel Cosío Villegas do much the same: *El porfiriato: La vida económica,* 2 vols., Historia moderna de México 7/1 and 2

(México: Editorial Hermes, 1974). See also Leonel Corona Treviño, *La tecnología, siglos XVI al XX* (Mexico: Universidad Nacional Autónoma de México, 2004), and De la Concha and Calleros, *Caminos de la invención*. For industry-specific accounts that provide some coverage of technological change, see Dawn Keremitsis, *La industria textil mexicana en el siglo xix* (Mexico: SepSetentas, 1973) and Gómez-Galvarriato, *Industry and Revolution*, on textiles; Horacio Gutiérrez Crespo, *Historia del azúcar en México* (Mexico: Fondo de Cultura Ecónomica, 1980), on sugar; Cuauhtémoc Velasco Avila et al., *Estado y minería en México (1767–1910)* (Mexico: Fondo de Cultura Económica, 1988), and M. Bernstein, *Mexican Mining Industry*, on mining; Haber, *Industry and Underdevelopment,* on manufacturing; and Alejandro Tortolero Villaseñor, *De la coa a la máquina de vapor: Actividad agrícola e innovación tecnológica en las haciendas mexicanas, 1880–1914* (Mexico: Siglo XXI, 1995), on agriculture.

52. Victor Bulmer-Thomas, John H. Coatsworth, and Roberto Cortés Conde, eds., *The Cambridge Economic History of Latin America*, vol. 1, *The Colonial Era and the Short Nineteenth Century*, and vol. 2, *The Long Twentieth Century* (New York: Cambridge University Press, 2006); John Coatsworth and Alan Taylor, eds., *Latin America and the World Economy since 1800* (Cambridge, MA: Harvard University Center for Latin American Studies, 1999); Haber, *How Latin America Fell Behind*; Enrique Cárdenas Sánchez, José Antonio Ocampo, and Rosemary Thorpe, eds., *An Economic History of Twentieth-Century Latin America*, 3 vols. (New York: Palgrave Macmillan, 2000); Kuntz Ficker, *Historia económica general;* Cárdenas Sánchez, *Cuando se originó el atraso.*

53. Gómez-Galvarriato, *Industry and Revolution;* Womack, *Trabajo en la Cervecería Moctezuma;* and Kuntz Ficker, *Empresa extranjera.*

54. See, for instance, Arnold J. Bauer, *Goods, Power, History: Latin America's Material Culture* (Cambridge: Cambridge University Press, 2001), and Benjamin Orlove, ed., *The Allure of the Foreign: Imported Goods in Postcolonial Latin America* (Ann Arbor: University of Michigan Press, 1997); Larissa Adler Lomnitz and Marisol Perez-Lizaur, *A Mexican Elite Family, 1820–1980* (Princeton, NJ: Princeton University Press, 1987); Tenorio-Trillo, *Mexico at the World's Fairs,* 135; Jesús Gómez Serrano, "Una ciudad pujante: Aguascalientes durante el Porfiriato," in *Bienes y vivencias: El siglo XIX,* ed. Anne Staples, Historia de la vida cotidiana en México 4 (Mexico: El Colegio de México), 253–54.

55. William H. Beezley, *Judas at the Jockey Club and Other Episodes of Porfirian Mexico* (Lincoln: University of Nebraska Press, 1987), 67–88; Flavio DeRossi, *The Mexican Entrepreneur* (Paris: Development Centre for the Organization for Economic Development and Cooperation, 1971), 16.

56. Stuart Chase, *Mexico: A Study of Two Americas* (New York: Macmillan, 1931).

57. See, for instance, John Coatsworth, "Railroads, Landholding, and Agrarian Protest in the Early Porfiriato," *Hispanic American Historical Review* 54, no. 1 (1974): 48–71; Paul Vanderwood, *The Power of God against the Guns of Government* (Stanford, CA: Stanford University Press, 1998). Womack's classic study of Zapatismo in

the state of Morelos links rural unrest to the introduction of new sugar-refining technologies; John Womack Jr., *Zapata and the Mexican Revolution* (New York: Vintage Books, 1968), chap. 2.

58. Raymond Craib, *Cartographic Mexico: A History of State Fixations and Fugitive Landscapes* (Durham, NC: Duke University Press, 2004); Tenorio-Trillo, *Mexico at the World's Fairs;* Pablo Piccato, *City of Suspects: Crime in Mexico City, 1900–1931* (Durham, NC: Duke University Press, 2001).

59. Rubén Gallo, *Mexican Modernity: The Avant-Garde and the Technological Revolution* (Cambridge, MA: MIT Press, 2010); Araceli Tinajero and J. Brian Freeman, eds., *Technology and Culture in Twentieth-Century Mexico* (Tuscaloosa: University of Alabama Press, 2013); and Bunker, *Creating Mexican Consumer Culture.*

60. Haber, *Industry and Underdevelopment,* 31–34.

61. This has been most commonly argued for extractive industries; see, for instance, Jonathan Brown, *Oil and Revolution in Mexico* (Berkeley: University of California Press, 1993), and M. Bernstein, *Mexican Mining Industry.*

62. *Interest* signifies a cultural bias against inventive or innovative activity; *capacity* signifies low levels of human capital, derived from low levels of literacy and technical education. Neither has received systematic attention in the literature on nineteenth-century Mexico.

63. Mary Louise Pratt, *Imperial Eyes: Travel Writing and Transculturation* (New York: Routledge, 1992); also Ricardo Salvatore, *Imágenes de un imperio: Estados Unidos y las formas de representación de América Latina* (Buenos Aires: Editorial Sudamerica, 2006); for travelers in Porfirian Mexico, see Beezley, *Judas,* chap. 4; and Jason Ruiz, *Americans in the Treasure House: Travel to Porfirian Mexico and the Cultural Politics of Empire* (Austin: University of Texas Press, 2014).

64. For instance, Robert Redfield, *Tepotzlan, a Mexican Village: A Study of Folk Life* (Chicago: University of Chicago Press, 1930).

65. Helen Delpar, *Looking South: The Evolution of Latin Americanist Scholarship in the United States* (Tuscaloosa: University of Alabama Press, 2008), chap. 3.

66. Guillermo Bonfil Batalla, *México Profundo: Reclaiming a Civilization* (Austin: University of Texas Press, 1996).

2. TECHNOLOGY AND THE EMERGENCE OF *ATRASO*, 1820–70

1. H. G. Ward, *Mexico in 1827,* vol. 2 (London: Henry Colburn, 1828), 235–36; Joel Poinsett, *Notes on Mexico Made in the Autumn of 1822* (London: John Miller, 1825), 94–95.

2. Fanny Calderón de la Barca, *Life in Mexico* (1843; repr., Berkeley: University of California Press, 1982), 135–36; Brantz Mayer, *Mexico as It Was and as It Is* (New York: J. Winchester, 1844), 292.

3. Mariano Otero, *Consideraciones sobre la situación política y social de la República Mexicana, en el año 1847* (Mexico: Valdés y redondas, 1848).

4. Calderón de la Barca, *Life in Mexico,* 137.

5. David Landes, *The Unbound Prometheus: Technological Change and Industrial Development in Western Europe from 1750 to the Present* (Cambridge: Cambridge University Press, 1969); Joel Mokyr, *Lever of Riches: Technological Creativity and Economic Progress* (New York: Oxford University Press, 1990).

6. Mexico, *Memoria sobre el estado . . . 1842,* 40, 57.

7. For several examples, see "Voto particular del Señor Covarrubias" (February 2, 1824), in Banco Nacional de Comercio Exterior, *El comercio exterior y el artesano mexicano* (Mexico: Banco Nacional de Comercio Exterior, 1965), 162; Mexico, *Memoria sobre el estado . . . 1842,* 9–10; and E. Beatty, "Riqueza, polémica, y pólítica."

8. Alamán, quoted in Mexico, *Memoria sobre el estado . . . 1842,* 25; Lorenzo de Zavala, *Viaje a los Estados-Unidos del Norte de América* (Mérida: Castillo, 1846), 52, 299–300.

9. Haber, *How Latin America Fell Behind;* John Coatsworth, *Los orígenes del atraso: Nueve ensayos de historia económica de México en los siglos xviii y xix* (Mexico: Alianza Editorial Mexicana, 1990), table 4.1; Salvucci, "Mexican National Income"; and Cárdenas Sánchez, *Cuando se originó el atraso.*

10. Antuñano, *Pensamientos,* 33–34; "Discusión habida en la sala de sesiones del honorable congreso de la Puebla sobre el proyecto del Ciudadano José María Godoy," February 26, 1829, in Banco Nacional, *Comercio exterior,* 173; also Sánchez Flores, *Historia de la tecnología,* 349.

11. Lerdo de Tejada, *Comercio exterior,* 143.

12. Nepomuceno Adorno, *Análisis de los males,* 129.

13. Recent works include Sánchez Santiró, "Desempeño de la economía"; Cárdenas Sánchez, *Cuando se originó el atraso.*

14. See, for example, Michael Meyer, William Sherman, and Susan Deeds, *The Course of Mexican History,* 8th ed. (New York: Oxford University Press, 2007), 343.

15. Mora quoted in Richard Warren, "Elections and Popular Political Participation in Mexico, 1808–1836," in *Liberals, Power and Power: State Formation in Nineteenth-Century Latin America,* ed. Barbara Tenenbaum and Vincent Peloso (Athens: University of Georgia Press, 1996), 30.

16. Thomson, *Puebla de los Angeles,* 95–96; Amílcar Challú, "The Political Economy of Hunger in Bourbon Mexico," unpublished manuscript, 2011.

17. Richard J. Salvucci, "Agriculture and the Colonial Heritage of Latin America: Evidence from Bourbon Mexico," in *Colonial Legacies: The Problem of Persistence in Latin American History,* ed. Jeremy Adelman (New York: Routledge, 1999), 123.

18. Nepomuceno Adorno, *Análisis de los males,* 110.

19. Coatsworth, *Orígenes del atraso,* 117, table V2; and, for modest revision, Sánchez Santiró, "Desempeño de la economía," 71, table 1.

20. Leandro Prados de la Escosura, "Lost Decades? Economic Performance in Post-independence Latin America," *Journal of Latin American Studies* 41, no. 2 (2009): tables 4 and 5.

21. Amílcar E. Challú and Aurora Gómez-Galvarriato, "Further Scrutiny of a Censured Century: Real Wages in Mexico City in the Very Long Nineteenth Century

(1750s–1910s)," paper presented at the annual meeting of the Latin American Studies Aassociation, San Francisco, May 2012, table 2.

22. Mexico, *Memoria sobre el estado . . . 1842*, 3.

23. Sánchez Santiró, "Desempeño de la economía."

24. Robert W. Randall, *Real del Monte: A British Mining Venture in Mexico* (Austin: University of Texas Press, 1972); Velasco Avila et al., *Estado y minería*, chaps. 6–7.

25. Mexico, *Memoria sobre el estado de la agricultura é industria de la república en el año de 1844* (Mexico: José M. Lara, 1845), 286; also Sánchez Santiró, "Desempeño de la economía," 87 n. 46; Margaret Chowning, "Reassessing the Prospects for Profit in Nineteenth-Century Mexican Agriculture from a Regional Perspective," in Haber, *How Latin America Fell Behind*, 179–215; Thomson, *Puebla de los Ángeles,* 136, fig. 3.4; also Mexico, *Memoria sobre el estado . . . 1842*, 17–18.

26. Challú, "Political Economy of Hunger," 36, 40–41, 50–56, 137, 156; Richard J. Salvucci, "Algunas consideraciones económicas (1836): Análisis mexicano de la depresión a principios del siglo XIX," *Historia Mexicana* 55, no. 1 (July–September 2005): 76.

27. Mexico, *Memoria sobre el estado . . . 1844*, Appendixes 7 and 8.

28. Humberto Morales Moreno, "El carácter marginal y arrendatario del sistema de fábrica en paisajes agrarios mexicanos, 1780–1880," *Anuario de Estudios Americanos* 62 (2005): 163–85.

29. Richard J. Salvucci, *Textiles and Capitalism in Mexico* (Princeton, NJ: Princeton University Press, 1987), 164–66; Jesús Alvarado, "We Welcomed Foreign Fabrics and We Were Left Naked: Cotton Textile Artisans and the First Debates on Free Trade versus National Industry in Mexico" (PhD diss., University of Wisconsin–Madison, 2007), 181–82; Aurora Gómez-Galvarriato, ed., *La industria textil en México* (Mexico: Instituto Mora, 1999); Robert A. Potash, *Mexican Government and Industrial Development in the Early Republic: Banco de Avío* (Amherst: University of Massachusetts Press, 1983), 148, 159; Gómez-Galvarriato, *Industry and Revolution,* 13, figure 1.1.

30. For instance, William Bullock, *Six Months Residence and Travels in Mexico* (London: John Murray, 1824); William W. Carpenter, *Travels and Adventures in Mexico* (New York: Harper and Brothers, 1851); Sánchez Flores, *Historia de la tecnología.*

31. See Appendix 1 for a full discussion of the patent database.

32. See Appendix 2 for discussion of machine import data; also Inés Herrera Canales, *El comercio exterior de México, 1821–1875* (Mexico: El Colegio de Mexico, 1977), 26–27, table 8.

33. Randall, *Real del Monte*, 73, table 1.

34. From 1830 to 1842 the bank spent 245,271 dollars directly on machinery purchases (and 773,695 dollars in total loans), and iron and steel imports added up to 1,517,556 dollars; Potash, *Mexican Government,* 122.

35. For the first period, the growth coefficient is 0.119 and the R-squared is 0.546; for the second, 0.024 and 0.163; and for the third, 0.106 and 0.916.

36. E. Beatty, *Institutions and Investment*, chap. 4; Edward Beatty and J. Patricio Sáiz, "Propiedad industrial, patentes e inversion en tecnología en España y México (1820–1914)," ed. Rafael Dobado, Aurora Gómez-Galvarriato, and Graciela Márquez, *México y España: ¿Historias económicas paralelas?* (Mexico: Fondo de Cultura Económica, 2007).

37. I am grateful to Patricio Sáiz for sharing his data; Patricio Sáiz González, *Propiedad industrial y revolución liberal: Historia del sistema español de patentes (1759–1929)* (Madrid: Oficina Española de Patentes y Marcas, 1995).

38. Jurgen Buchenau, "Small Numbers, Great Impact: Mexico and Its Immigrants, 1821–1973," *Journal of American Ethnic History* 20, no. 3 (2001): 23–49.

39. Quoted in Salvucci, "Algunas consideraciones económicas," 77.

40. Lucas Alamán, "Representación dirigida al Exmo. señor Presidente Provisional de la República por la Junta General Directiva de la Industria Nacional sobre la importancia de esta necesidad de su Fomento" [1813], in *La industria nacional y el comercio exterior: Seis memorias oficiales sobre industria, agricultura, colonización y comercio exterior*, ed. Jan Bazant, Colección de documentos para la historia del comercio exterior de México 7 (Mexico: Banco Nacional de Comercio Exterior, 1962), 111–12.

41. John Coatsworth, "Obstacles to Economic Growth in Nineteenth-Century Mexico," *American Historical Review* 83, no. 1 (1978): 80–100; Ross Hassig, *Trade, Tribute, and Transportation: The Sixteenth-Century Political Economy of the Valley of Mexico* (Norman: University of Oklahoma Press, 1985), especially 187–207; John Coatsworth, *Growth against Development: The Economic Impact of Railroads in Porfirian Mexico* (Dekalb: Northern Illinois University Press, 1981), 17–19.

42. Hassig, *Trade, Tribute, and Transportation*, 193–95, 281–83; Challú, "Political Economy of Hunger," 69; Salvucci, *Textiles and Capitalism*, 41.

43. María Eugenia Romero Sotelo and Luis Jáuregui, *Las contingencias de una larga recuperación: La economía mexicana, 1821–1867* (Mexico: Universidad Nacional Autónoma de México, 2003), 194.

44. Coatsworth, *Growth against Development*, 33–37.

45. David Brading, *Haciendas and Ranchos in the Mexican Bajío, León, 1700–1860* (Cambridge: Cambridge University Press, 1978); Challú, "Political Economy of Hunger," 170–83, 202–10; Salvucci, *Textiles and Capitalism*, 41.

46. Richard J. Salvucci, "The Origins and Progress of U.S.-Mexican Trade, 1825–1884: 'Hoc Opus, Hic Labor Est,'" *Hispanic American Historical Review* 71, no. 4 (1991): 733; Leonidas Hamilton, *Border States of Mexico: Sonora, Sinaloa, Chihuahua and Durango* (San Francisco: Bacon, 1883), 177.

47. Antuñano, *Pensamientos*, 33–34; Alamán, "Representación," 180–81; also Potash, *Mexican Government*, and Randall, *Real del Monte*.

48. Matías Romero, *Report of the Secretary of Finance of the United States of Mexico of the 15th of January, 1879, on the Actual Condition of Mexico, and the Increase of Commerce with the United States* (New York: N. Ponce de Leon, 1880), 110; also Francisco Calderón, *La Republica restaurada: La vida económica*, Historia moderna de México 2 (Mexico: Editorial Hermes, 1955), 698–732; Nepomuceno Adorno, *Análisis de los males*, 114–15.

49. *El Economista Mexicano,* September 10, 1886, 65.

50. David Brading, *Miners and Merchants in Bourbon Mexico, 1763–1810* (Cambridge: Cambridge University Press, 1971), 134.

51. We do not have a history of water power, but see Sonya Lipsett-Rivera, *Defend Our Water with the Blood of Our Veins: The Struggle for Resources in Colonial Puebla* (Albuquerque: University of New Mexico Press, 1999), 179 n. 58; Humberto Morales Moreno, "Los molinos de trigo en los orígenes de la industrialización mexicana: Historiografía, tecnología y conservación (1780–1910)," in *Memoria del III Encuentro Nacional sobre Conservación del Patrimonio Industrial Mexicano,* ed. Belem Oviedo Gámez and Luz Carregha Lamadrid (Mexico: Comité Mexicano para la Conservación del Patrimonio Industrial, 2005), 193–211; Yolanda D. Terán Trillo, "El Castillo de la Fama," in Oviedo Gámez and Carregha Lamadrid, *Memoria del III Encuentro,* 374–86; Jane-Dale Lloyd, *Cinco ensayos sobre cultura material de rancheros y medieros del noroeste de Chihuahua, 1886–1910* (Mexico: Universidad Iberoamericana, 2001), 114–20, 152; Eric Van Young, *Hacienda and Market in Eighteenth-Century Mexico: The Rural Economy of the Guadalajara Region, 1675–1820* (Berkeley: University of California Press, 1981), 65–66; John S. Leiby, *Colonial Bureaucrats and the Mexican Economy: Growth of a Patrimonial State, 1763–1821* (New York: Peter Lang, 1986), 62–65; Vera Candiani, "Draining the Basin of Mexico: Science, Technology, and Society, 1608–1808" (PhD diss., University of California, Berkeley, 2004), 53; Sánchez Flores, *Historia de la tecnología,* 73–74, 197, 199–200; Salvucci, *Textiles and Capitalism,* 51–54; Challú, "Political Economy of Hunger," 196. Most reports of mills do not specify either their size or their source of power (animate or water); see, for instance, Morales Moreno, "Carácter marginal," 167–68, 171.

52. Quoted in Carlos Sempat Assadourian, "La bomba de fuego de Newcomen y otros artificios de desagüe: Un intento de transferencia de tecnología inglesa a la minería novohispana, 1726–1731," *Historia Mexicana* 50, no. 3 (2001): 441; see also Lerdo de Tejada, *Comercio exterior,* 142; Fernando B. Sandoval, *La industria de azúcar en Nueva España* (Mexico: Universidad Nacional Autónoma de México, 1951), 146.

53. Sánchez Flores, *Historia de la tecnología,* 211; Candiani, "Draining the Basin," 181.

54. Keremitsis, *Industria textil mexicana,* 20–24; Potash, *Mexican Government,* 149–50.

55. Landes, *Unbound Prometheus,* 95.

56. Sempat Assadourian, "Bomba de fuego," 385–457; Randall, *Real del Monte,* 18.

57. Clara Bronstein Punski, "La introducción de la máquina de vapor en México" (MA thesis, Facultad de Filosofía y Letras, UNAM, 1965), 50, 57–58; Sempat Assadourian, "Bomba de fuego," 394–95. On the Newcomen engine, see Mokyr, *Lever of Riches,* 84–85.

58. "*Son inconducibles,*" Sempat Assadourian, "Bomba de fuego," 401.

59. Ibid., 401–2.

60. Ibid., 405–6.

61. Ibid., 441–42.

62. [José Antonio Alzate], untitled article, *Diario Literario de México,* April 19, 1768, 2.

63. Bronstein Punski, "Introducción de la máquina," 3 and 78–83; Mexico, Secretaría de la Economía Nacional, *Documentos para la historia económica de México,* vol. 9 (Mexico: Secretaría de la Economía Nacional, 1934); also Sánchez Flores, *Historia de la tecnología,* 211.

64. Mexico, Secretaría de la Economía Nacional, *Documentos,* 3–4.

65. Ibid., 8–9.

66. Zavala, *Viaje a los Estados-Unidos,* 300–301.

67. Sergio Niccolai, "Algunas reflexiones sobre los orígenes de la mecanización industrial en México (1780–1850)," in *La cultura industrial Mexicana: Primer Encuentro Nacional de Arqueología Industrial,* ed. Sergio Niccolai and Humberto Morales Moreno (Puebla, Mexico: Benemérita Universidad Autónoma de Puebla, 2003); Miguel Angel Aviles-Galan, "'A Todo Vapor': Mechanisation in Porfirian Mexico Steam Power and Machine Building, 1891–1906" (PhD diss., University of British Columbia, 2010), chap. 5; Julio Sánchez Gómez, "La lenta penetración de la máquina de vapor en la minería del ámbito hispano," *Arbor* 149 (1994): 203–41; and Trabulse, *Círculo roto,* 180.

68. Randall, *Real del Monte,* 100–108; Trabulse, *Círculo roto,* 180; Sánchez Gómez, "Lenta penetración," 225–26. Potash, *Mexican Government,* 150; Mexico, *Memoria sobre el estado . . . 1844,* 20.

69. Mexico, *Memoria presentada á S.M. el Emperador por el Ministro de Fomento Luis Robles Pezuela de los trabajos ejecutados en su ramo el año de 1865* (Mexico: J.M. Andrade y F. Escalante, 1866), 420.

70. Mexico, *Memoria sobre el estado . . . 1842,* table 5; Mexico, Secretaría de Fomento, *Memoria* (1857), doc. 18–2 (twenty reported using hydropower, sixteen reported using horses or mules, and one reported using human power).

71. Machine prices for the 1830s–50s were substantially higher than for the early 1870s, when they averaged $1,266, calculated as the unit cost of steam engines imported from the United States; see also *El Siglo,* October 14, 1841, 3.

72. Mexico, *Memoria presentada,* 412.

73. Romero, *Report of the Secretary,* 110; W. Back and J.M. Lesser, "Chemical Constraints of Groundwater Management in the Yucatan Peninsula, Mexico," *Journal of Hydrology* 51 (1981): 127; also Mexico, *Memoria presentada,* 399.

74. Mexico, *Memoria presentada,* 375.

75. Antuñano, *Pensamientos,* 26; Mexico, *Memoria sobre el estado . . . 1842,* 32.

76. Mexico, Cámara de Diputados, *Dictamen,* 71–72.

77. Eric Van Young, "Material Life," in *The Countryside in Colonial Latin America,* ed. Louisa Schell Hoberman and Susan Migden Socolow (Albuquerque: University of New Mexico Press, 1996), 72.

78. Sánchez Flores, *Historia de la tecnología,* 60, 71, 86, 150, 219.

79. Besides Sánchez Flores, see Candiani, "Draining the Basin," 142–43.

80. Sánchez Flores, *Historia de la tecnología,* 69–70, 130, 174, 218; also Thomson, *Puebla de los Ángeles,* 298.

81. Candiani, "Draining the Basin," 150.

82. Sempat Assadourian, "Bomba de fuego," 394–95.

83. Bernal Díaz del Castillo, *Historia verdadera de la conquista de la Nueva España* (Madrid: Austral, 1968), 206.

84. Sánchez Flores, *Historia de la tecnología,* 183; also 59–60; on colonial blacksmith activity, see also 77, 130, 138, 143, 200, 207.

85. Ibid., 138, 190; also Candiani, "Draining the Basin," 179.

86. Sánchez Flores, *Historia de la tecnología,* 163–65, 212.

87. Bronstein Punski, "Introducción de la máquina," 67, 79.

88. We do not yet have a full study of iron and steel metallurgy; see Fernando Rosenzweig, "La industria," in Cosío Villegas, *Porfiriato,* 377–89; Sánchez Flores, *Historia de la tecnología;* Victoria Novelo, "Ferrerías y fundiciones," in *Arqueología de la industria en México,* ed. Victoria Novelo (Mexico: Museo Nacional de Culturas Populares, 1984); Potash, *Mexican Government,* 62–63, 102, 121, 124; Thomson, *Puebla de los Ángeles,* 298–99. For Lucas Alamán's assessment, see Mexico, *Memoria sobre el estado . . . 1842,* 32–34; Mexico, *Memoria sobre el estado . . . 1844,* Appendix, 11–12; Mexico, *Memoria sobre el estado de agricultura é industria de la República en el año 1845* [1846], reprinted in *La industria nacional y el comercio exterior: Seis memorias oficiales sobre industria, agricultura, colonización y comercio exterior, 1842–1851,* ed. Jan Bazant (Mexico: Banco Nacional de Comercio Exterior, 1962), 379–81.

89. Thomson, *Puebla de los Ángeles,* 299. The three other foundries included La Santa Rita of Frederick Maillard, from France, which repaired and replaced textile machinery; El Refugio of Bernardo Mier; and a large furnace at San Pablo Apetatitlán in Tlaxcala, which supplied the Mexican army. The other "iron forges" counted in the *padrones* of the 1820s and 1830s were simple blacksmith shops. Thomson, *Puebla de los Ángeles,* 294, table 8.3.

90. Henry G. Aubrey, "Deliberate Industrialization," *Social Research* 16, no. 2 (1949): 169–170; Mexico, *Memoria presentada,* 389–390. On the Ferrería de Apulco, established in 1848 and running a blast furnace by 1853, see Novelo, "Ferrerías y fundiciones," 186; Mexico, Secretaría de Fomento, *Memoria* (1865), 389.

91. Mexico, *Memoria sobre el estado . . . 1842,* 34.

92. Antuñano, *Pensamientos,* 30, 33–34.

93. Mexico, *Memoria sobre el estado . . . 1842,* 32–33; see also Mexico, *Memoria sobre el estado . . . 1844,* 31–33.

94. Mexico, Cámara de Diputados, *Dictamen,* 94–95.

95. Mexico, Secretaría de Fomento, *Memoria* (1857), doc. 18–2.

96. The 1868 *Memoria* of the Ministerio de Fomento cites national pig iron production of five thousand tons; see also the 1853 *Memoria,* doc. 18–2; Aubrey, "Deliberate Industrialization," 170. The Apulco foundry's blast furnace could produce eleven thousand pounds per day; three of these, by the mid-1860s, would yield about five thousand tons per year.

97. Lerdo de Tejada, *Comercio exterior,* 120, 142; Mexico, Cámara de Diputados, *Dictamen,* 90; Antuñano, *Pensamientos,* 30.

98. Mexico, Ministerio de Hacienda y Crédito Público, *Expediente formado en la Secretaría de Hacienda y Crédito Público sobre un proyecto de arancel* (Mexico: Imprenta del Gobierno, 1869), 152.

99. Quoted in Brígida M. von Mentz de Boege, "Tecnología minera alemana en México durante la primera mitad del siglo XIX," *Estudios de Historia Moderna y Contemporánea de México* 8 (1980): 14.

100. For instance, "Voto particular del Señor Covarrubias," in Banco Nacional, *Comercio exterior,* 162.

101. Gerschenkron, *Economic Backwardness*; for a critique of the North American obsession with Latin American backwardness, see Pedro L. San Miguel, "La representación del atraso: México en la historiografía estadounidense," *Historia Mexicana* 53, no. 1 (2003): 989–1009; Leandro Prados de la Escosura, "The Economic Consequences of Independence in Latin America," in *The Cambridge Economic History of Latin America*, vol. 1, *The Colonial Era and the Short Nineteenth Century* (Cambridge: Cambridge University Press, 2006), 470; also Coatsworth, *Orígenes del atraso;* Haber, *How Latin America Fell Behind.*

102. For example, Mexico, *Memoria sobre el estado . . . 1842*, 40, 57–58; Nepomuceno Adorno, *Análisis de los males,* 126.

103. Alvarado, "We Welcomed Foreign Fabrics," 181–82.

104. Ibid., 219; Mexico, Cámara de Diputados, *Dictamen*, 94–95; Nepomuceno Adorno, *Análisis de los males,* 129. See also Estevan de Antuñano, *Documentos para la historia de la industria en México, 1833–1846*, vol. 1 of *Obras* (Mexico: Secretaría de Hacienda y Credito Público, 1979), 12.

105. Antuñano quoted in Jesús Reyes Heroles, *El liberalismo mexicano*, vol. 3, *La integración de las ideas* (Mexico: Fondo de Cultura Económica, 1974), 481.

106. Mexico, *Memoria sobre el estado . . . 1842*, 41, 58; Nepomuceno Adorno, *Análisis de los males,* 126.

107. Ortiz quoted in Reyes Heroles, *Liberalismo mexicano,* 467; Zavala, *Viaje a los Estados-Unidos,* 300–303.

108. See E. Beatty, "Riqueza, polemica, y política," for a complete discussion.

109. Mexico, *Memoria sobre el estado . . . 1842*, 58; *Colección de artículos del Siglo XIX, sobre alzamiento de prohibiciones* (Mexico: Ignacio Cumplido, 1851), 38, 46.

110. *Colección de artículos,* 55, 56.

111. Siliceo, introduction to the Secretaría de Fomento's 1857 *Memoria,* quoted in Reyes Heroles, *Liberalismo mexicano,* 515.

112. Siliceo, quoted in Reyes Heroles, *Liberalismo mexicano,* 516; also Jaqueline Covo, *Las ideas de la Reforma en México (1855–1861)*, trans. María Francisca Mourier-Martínez (Mexico: Universidad Nacional Autónoma de México, 1983), 452.

113. *El Monitor Republicano,* July 25, 1846, October 15, 1846, and August 9, 1856. See also Covo, *Ideas de la Reforma,* 48–50.

114. For Atraso en la industria," "el atraso que tenemos," and "el perpetuo atraso de la nación," see *El Siglo Diez y Nueve,* October 8, 1841, November 21, 1841, November 7, 1843. For a sampling of other references, see *El Siglo Diez y Nueve,* April 18, 1842, 3 ("su atraso"); December 30, 1842, 4 ("el estado de atraso a que la industria se

halla reducida"); September 27, 1843, 4 ("el atraso del agricultura y la industria"); October 14, 1843, 3, and October 19, 1843, 3 ("el atraso de la agricultura, de las artes, del comercio y de la civilización"); March 22, 1852, 2 ("el atraso a la sociedad"); April 8, 1852, 3 ("el atraso y el empobrecimiento de los pueblos"); July 9, 1852 ("el estado de atraso de nuestra sociedad"); and July 15, 1852 (el atraso y los males de nuestra patria"). References to *atraso* abound also in government publications: for instance, Mexico, *Memoria sobre el estado . . . 1844*, 18, 32, 46, 55 (including "el atraso de la industria," los causas de esta atraso," and "el atraso que aumento"). For references to *atraso* in education and science, see *El Siglo Diez y Nueve*, April 19, 1842, 3 ("el atraso en las profesiones"); May 14, 1842, 2 ("atraso en . . . la enseñanza metódica y científica;" lamenting the predominance of "hombres de rutina incapaces de mejorar los métodos, máquinas e instrumentos antiguos, y más aun, de inventar otros nuevos"); March 22, 1852, 2; July 9, 1852, 1 ("el abondono con que se ha visto la educación pública"); and *El Monitor Republicano*, July 25, 1846 ("tan atrasados así nuestros conocimientos científicos"); comparing "less industrial peoples" (like Mexico) with "their skilled neighbors"—"los pueblos menos industriales" and "sus hábiles vecinos"; *El Monitor Republicano*, October 15, 1846, and August 9, 1856.

115. Mexico, Cámara de Diputados, *Dictamen*, 57, 59, 98.

116. Lucas Alamán, *Historia de México*, vol. 1 (Mexico: J. M. Lara, 1852), 142.

117. Lerdo de Tejada, *Cuadro sinóptico de la República Mexicana en 1856* [Mexico, 1853], reprinted in his *México en 1856, el comercio exterior desde la conquista* (Mexico: Universidad Veracruzana, 1985), section on "Artes y oficios," n.p.

118. Covo, *Ideas de la Reforma*, 38 calls this "circumstantial pessimism" ("pesimismo circunstancial"); see also E. Beatty, "The Impact of Foreign Trade on the Mexican Economy: Terms of Trade and the Rise of Industry, 1880–1923," *Journal of Latin American Studies* 32, no. 2 (2000): 399–433; E. Beatty, *Institutions and Investment*, chap. 2.

119. Kennett S. Cott, "Porfirian Investment Policies, 1876–1910" (PhD diss., University of New Mexico, 1979), 14, 52–55; David M. Pletcher, *Rails, Mines, and Progress: Seven American Promoters in Mexico, 1867–1911* (Ithaca, NY: Cornell University Press, 1958).

120. C. Knick Harley, "Oceanic Freight Rates and Productivity, 1740–1913: The Primacy of Mechanical Invention Reaffirmed," *Journal of Economic History* 48, no. 4 (1988): 861.

121. Antuñano, *Pensamientos*, 19, 21.

122. Mexico, *Memoria sobre el estado . . . 1842*, 34.

3. TECHNOLOGY AND THE IMPERATIVE OF *PROGRESO*,
1870–1910

1. The scene at the Casa Böker on Espíritu Santo (today, Isabela la Católica) is imagined; for Böker's sewing machine sales and store description, see Jürgen Buchenau, *Tools of Progress: A German Merchant Family in Mexico City, 1865–*

Present (Albuquerque: University of New Mexico Press, 2004), chaps. 1 and 2. See Appendix 2 for sources and discussion of machine import data.

2. Morris B. Parker, *Mules, Mines, and Me in Mexico, 1895–1932*, ed. James M. Day (Tuscon: University of Arizona Press, 1979), 94–95.

3. Cárdenas Sánchez, *Cuando se originó el atraso*.

4. Gerschenkron, *Economic Backwardness*.

5. For example, see Sachs, *End of Poverty*, 41, 61–64.

6. Antuñano, *Pensamientos*, 19, 21.

7. US Department of State, *Money and Prices in Foreign Countries*, Special Consular Report 13 (Washington, DC: Government Printing Office, 1896), 133.

8. Xavier Tafunell, "Capital Formation in Machinery in Latin America, 1890–1930," *Journal of Economic History* 69 (2009): 928–50; André Hofman and Cristián Ducoing, "Capital Goods Imports, Machinery Investment, and Economic Development in the Long Run: The Case of Chile," paper presented at the 15th World Economic History Congress, Utrecht, 2009.

9. See Appendix 2 for a discussion and sources of import data. Compare also with Kuntz Ficker's data on Mexico's import trade in *Comercio exterior*; I am grateful to Sandra for sharing unpublished data with me.

10. Xavier Tafunell and Albert Carreras, "Capital Goods Imports and Investment in Latin America in the Mid 1920s," manuscript, Universitat Pompeu Fabra, 2005, 25; also Yovanna Pineda, "Financing Manufacturing Innovation in Argentina, 1890–1930," *Business History Review* 83 (Autumn 2009): 539–62.

11. See Appendix 2; also Kuntz Ficker, *Comercio exterior*, 160, table 3.4.

12. Table 1 includes only imports from the United States, whose records allow more consistent disaggregation by classes and subclasses to 1870 than those of Britain, Germany, and France. Even in the US records, however, classification is not consistent, especially as goods move in and out of the "all other" or "not elsewhere specified" categories.

13. Armando Razo and Stephen H. Haber, "The Rate of Growth of Productivity in Mexico, 1850–1933: Evidence from the Cotton Textile Industry," *Journal of Latin American Studies* 30 (1998): 498.

14. For example, see the letters in the Daniel Burns Papers, 1890–95, BLUC, and in AHJB. Also José Alfredo Uribe Salas, "El distrito minero El Oro-Tlalpujahua entre dos siglos y el mercado internacional de tecnología," in *Five Centuries of Mexican History*, ed. Virginia Guedea and Jaime E. Rodríguez O. (Mexico: Instituto Mora, 1992), 127; Buchenau, *Tools of Progress*; and extensive advertising in the press.

15. *El Economista Mexicano*, July 27, 1907, 359.

16. *Mexican Mining Journal*, January 1908, 34; *Mexican Herald*, September 12, 1895.

17. *Boletín de la Sociedad Mexicana de Geografía y Estadística* 12, nos. 1–2 (1865–66): 23–54.

18. By the 1890s mining engineers in remote Mexican camps were posting replies by telegraph in US mining journals within days of the original article. See, for example, *Engineering and Mining Journal*, March 17, 24, 31, and April 21, 1906. The young

American mining engineer Stuart Ingram, like hundreds of others in his situation, carried notes on density factors for slime treatment at a new cyanide plant at La Cumbre mine in Chihuahua, copied from a recent edition of the *Engineering and Mining Journal*; see Stuart Ingram Notebook, BLUC, n.d., n.p.; see also the collection of technical publications in boxes 1–3, Fondo Gonzalo Robles, AGN.

19. Florence Toussaint Alcaraz, *Escenario de la prensa en el Porfiriato* (Mexico: Fundación Manuel Buendía, 1984); Carlos Forment, *Democracy in Latin America, 1760–1900*, vol. 1 (Chicago: University of Chicago Press, 2003), 194–200; Luis González y González, *San José de Gracia: Mexican Village in Transition* (Austin: University of Texas Press, 1972), 101.

20. E. Beatty and Sáiz, "Propiedad industrial"; see also Appendix 1.

21. On the uses (and abuses) of patent evidence, see K. Pavitt, "Patent Statistics as Indicators of Innovative Activities: Possibilities and Problems," *Scientometrics* 7, nos. 1–2 (1985): 77–99; K. Pavitt, "Uses and Abuses of Patent Statistics," in *Handbook of Quantitative Studies of Science and Technology,* ed. A.F.J. Van Raan (Amsterdam: Elsevier Science, 1988), 509–36; Zvi Griliches, "Patent Statistics as Economic Indicators: A Survey," *Journal of Economic Literature* 28 (December 1990): 1661–1707.

22. E. Beatty, *Institutions and Investment,* chap. 5.

23. Quote from Parker, *Mules, Mines, and Me,* 1. Parker was a twenty-four-year-old graduate of the Missouri School of Mines with some experience in New Mexican camps; see also the papers of Stuart H. Ingram (Ingram Papers, BLUC), who came to work at the Candelaria mine in Durango two years after finishing college in the United States, or the fictionalized account of Oliver Ward in Wallace Stegner's Pulitzer-winning novel *Angle of Repose* (Garden City, NY: Doubleday, 1971).

24. For a handful of examples among many, see *Mexican Herald,* October 5 and December 15, 1895; November 4, 1906; June 4, 1906; also, for instance, April 9, May 15, June 26, July 1 and 10, August 2, September 15, and November 3 and 28.

25. Harold Lane to Colonel Daniel Burns, August 13, 1901, box 3, folder 9, Daniel Burns Papers, BLUC. See also inquiries in letters of July 19 and August 31, 1891, in box 3, folders 6 and 2 respectively.

26. *Mexican Herald,* April 9 and June 6, 1906.

27. *Mining and Scientific Press,* June 29, 1907; *Engineering and Mining Journal,* April 3, 1909, 694.

28. *Mexican Herald,* June 14, 1896, 2.

29. Mexico, *Memoria sobre el estado . . . 1842,* 28, 29, 31; see also Alvarado, "We Welcomed Foreign Fabrics," 287; Sánchez Flores, *Historia de la tecnologia,* 349; and the general accounts of mining (e.g., Randall, *Real del Monte*) and textiles (e.g., Potash, *Mexican Government*). It was also the case in Querétaro at midcentury, when Cayetano Rubio contracted French specialists to operate his new Hercules textile mill, hiring "the director of the establishment, a machine operator, a card operator, a weaver, a darner, a dry clearner, and a fuller"; Blanca Estela Suárez Cortez, "Poder oligárquico y usos del agua: Querétaro en el siglo XIX (1838–1880)," in *Historia de los usos del agua en México,* ed. Luis Aboites Aguilar (Mexico: Comisión Nacional del Agua, 1998), 63.

30. Potash, *Mexican Government,* 75, 101.

31. *El Economista Mexicano,* July 1, 1899, 255. In the secondary literature, see Haber, *Industry and Underdevelopment,* 37, 82 and chap. 4; Aurora Gómez-Galvarriato, "El primer impulso industrializador de México: El caso de Fundidora Monterrey" (Tesis de Licenciatura, ITAM, 1990), and especially her *Industry and Revolution,* chap. 10; Gustavo Adolfo Barrera Pages, "Industrialización y revolución: El desempeño de la cervecería Toluca y México, S.A.: 1875–1926" (Tesis de Licenciatura, ITAM, 1999), 72; Kuntz Ficker, *Empresa extranjera;* Jeffrey Pilcher, "Mad Cowmen, Foreign Investors and the Mexican Revolution," *Journal of Iberian and Latin American Studies* 4, no. 1 (1998): 6; Juan Mora-Torres, *The Making of the Mexican Border: The State, Capitalism, and Society in Nuevo León, 1848–1910* (Austin: University of Texas Press, 2001), 193, 256; and Marichal and Cerutti, *Historia.* For contemporary anecdotal references, see *El Economista Mexicano,* January 18, 1908, 307 (cement); and *Mexican Herald,* February 2 and 19, 1896, November 24, 1895, July 29, 1898, June 8, 1902, and p. 6 or 8 of nearly every other edition of this paper through the 1890s for the comings and goings of American engineers and technicians to Mexican mines, factories, sugar refineries, and elsewhere, to "set up the new machinery" or to "erect certain machinery" (e.g., December 15, 1895, 8, and November 26, 1895, 8).

32. Victoria Novelo, "Ferrerías y fundiciones," 189.

33. John Mason Hart, *Empire and Revolution: The Americans in Mexico since the Civil War* (Berkeley: University of California Press, 2002), 236; William Schell, *Integral Outsiders: The American Colony in Mexico City, 1876–1911* (Wilmington, DE: Scholarly Resources, 2001). Senator Albert Fall estimated seventy-five thousand in Mexico in 1910; M. Bernstein, *Mexican Mining Industry,* 75.

34. Gómez-Galvarriato, *Industry and Revolution,* chap. 1.

35. Ignacio Medina, "Dinamismo frustrado: La industria metal-mecánica," in *Industria y comercio,* ed. José María Muriá and Jaime Olveda, Lecturas históricas de Guadalajara 5 (Mexico: Instituto Nacional de Antropología, 1993), 248; Theresa Alfaro-Velcamp, "Immigrant Positioning in Twentieth-Century Mexico: Middle Easterners, Foreign Citizens, and Multiculturalism," *Hispanic American Historical Review* 86, no. 1 (2006): 61–91; Von Mentz de Boege, "Tecnología minera alemana."

36. Cited in Velasco Avila et al., *Estado y minería,* 379.

37. Mexico, Secretaria de Fomento, Dirección General de Estadística a cargo a Dr. Antonio Peñafiel, *Resumen general del censo de la República Mexicana verificado el 28 de octubre de 1900* (Mexico: Imprenta de la Secretaria de Fomento, 1905); Jesús Hermosa, *Manual de geografía y estadística de la República Mejicana* (Paris: Librería de Rosa, 1857), 29.

38. Mexico, Instituto Nacional de Estadística (INEGI), *Estadísticas históricas de México,* 2 vols. (Mexico: INEGI, 1994), table 1.11; Friedrich Katz, "The Liberal Republic and the Porfiriato, 1867–1910," in *Mexico since Independence,* ed. Leslie Bethell (Cambridge: Cambridge University Press, 1991), 74.

39. Lloyd, *Cinco ensayos,* chap. 4, quotation on 161.

40. Coatsworth, *Growth against Development*, and Kuntz Ficker, *Empresa extranjera;* also Sandra Kuntz Ficker and Paolo Riguzzi, eds., *Ferrocarriles y vida económica en México (1850–1950)* (Mexico: El Colegio Mexiquense, 1996); Francisco R. Calderón, "Los ferrocarriles," in Cosío Villegas, *Porfiriato.*

41. Kuntz Ficker, *Empresa extranjera.*

42. Sierra, *México,* 31.

43. Coatsworth, *Growth against Development,* chap. 4.

44. Chapter 5 below, also Nicolás Cárdenas García, *Empresas y trabajadores en la gran minería mexicana (1900–1929)* (Mexico: Instituto Nacional de Estudios Históricos de la Revolución Mexicana, 1998), 85–86.

45. *Engineering and Mining Journal,* January 3, 1903, 36, and January 6, 1906, 39. See also Juan Manuel Romero Gil, *La minería en el noroeste de México: Utopía y realidad, 1850–1910* (Mexico: Plaza y Valdés, 2001), 129. A mule could carry 300 pounds, 150 on each side of the pack; *TAIME* 25 (1904): 23; also *Mexican Herald,* September 22, 1895 (these Durango mines "would be dividend paying properties when the required railroads are built"); Langan W. Swent, *Working for Safety and Health in Underground Mines: San Luis and Homestake Mining Companies, 1846–1988,* 2 vols. (Berkeley: Regional Oral History Office, Bancroft Library, University of California, Berkeley, 1995), 16–17; Cárdenas García, *Empresas y trabajadores,* 85–86.

46. W. A. Graham Clark, "Cotton Goods in Latin America, Part I: Cuba, Mexico and Central America," in *Special Agent Series No. 31,* ed. US Department of Commerce and Labor, Bureau of Manufacturers (Washington, DC: Government Printing Office, 1909), 26; Gómez-Galvarriato, *Industry and Revolution,* chap. 9.

47. Guillermo Guajardo Soto, "La tecnología de los Estados Unidos y la 'americanización' de los ferrocarriles estatales de México y Chile, ca. 1880–1950," *Transportes, Servicios y Telecomunicaciones* 9 (2005): 114; also Coatsworth, *Growth against Development,* chap. 5.

48. Guajardo Soto, *Trabajo y tecnología,* 163.

49. Gómez-Galvarriato, "Primer impulso," 69, table 3.2a; Kuntz Ficker, *Empresa extranjera,* 82–84.

50. John Brown, *The Baldwin Locomotive Works, 1831–1915* (Baltimore: Johns Hopkins University Press, 1995), 44–45, 84–85. Locomotive orders were concentrated in 1881–84, 1889–91, 1897, 1900, 1903–4, and 1907–8; Great Britain accounted for 16 percent, while Germany sent just a few.

51. Kuntz Ficker, *Empresa extranjera,* 99; Coatsworth, *Growth against Development,* 137–39, 146.

52. Jonathan Brown, "Foreign and Native-Born Workers in Porfirian Mexico," *American Historical Review* 98, no. 3 (1993): 786–818.

53. Guillermo Guajardo Soto, "Nuevos datos para un viejo debate: Los vínculos entre ferrocarriles e industrialización en Chile y México (1860–1950)," *El Trimestre Económico* 65, no. 2 (1998): 213–61, and Guajardo Soto, *Trabajo y tecnología,* chaps. 2 and 8.

54. Guillermo Guajardo Soto, "'A pesar de todo, se mueve': El aprendizaje tecnológico en México, ca. 1860–1930," *Iztapalapa* 43 (June–January 1998): 305–28;

Guajardo Soto, "Nuevos datos," and, especially, *Trabajo y tecnología,* 48, chap. 3, and 136, 170.

55. Coatsworth, *Growth against Development,* 141 and table 5.8.

56. Peter Temin, "Steam and Waterpower in the Early Nineteenth Century," *Journal of Economic History* 26 (June 1966): 187–205.

57. Allen H. Fenichel, *Quantitative Analysis of the Growth and Diffusion of Steam Power in Manufacturing in the United States, 1838–1919* (New York: Arno Press, 1964), 97, table 5; a fifty-horsepower engine, for example, cost 65.50 dollars per horsepower in 1870 but only 18.63 dollars per horsepower by the turn of the century.

58. Sectoral distribution estimated by sales of boilers and engines manufactured by the Fundición de Sinaloa for use in the Northwest region; see Arturo Carrillo Rojas, *Los caballos de vapor: El imperio de las máquinas durante el cañedismo* (Culiacán, Sinaloa, Mexico: Colegio de Bachilleres del Estado de Sinaloa, 1998), 233, which probably overstates the national weight of mining operations.

59. Mexico, Secretaría de Hacienda y Crédito Público, *Estadística de la República Mexicana . . . por Emiliano Busto* (Mexico: Imprenta de Ignacio Cumplido, 1880), table 2; Mexico, Secretaría de Fomento, *Boletín semestral,* foldout between 208 and 209.

60. *El Comerciante Mexicano,* February 9, 1893, 79; US Department of Commerce, *Commercial Relations of the United States with Foreign Nations* (Washington, DC: Government Printing Office, 1884–85), 670–71; Tortolero Villaseñor, *De la coa,* 215, doc. 70 and chaps. 2–3.

61. Calculated by dividing total US and British exports to Mexico by the unit price of engines. Before 1890 the average steam engine was fifty horsepower, which was roughly the average size manufactured by the Fundición de Sinaloa as well as the average employed in the United States (see Carrillo Rojas, *Caballos de vapor,* 134, 153, 167, 233; Richard B. DuBoff, "The Introduction of Electric Power in American Manufacturing," *Economic History Review* 20 [December 1967], 514), before 1890 adjusted to forty horsepower on average. Price per horsepower estimated at fifty dollars for a forty-horsepower engine in 1870–90 and twenty dollars for a fifty-horsepower engine in 1890–1910 (Fenichel, *Quantitative Analysis,* 97, table 5, and 99, table 6; see also Charles E. Emery, "Cost of Steam Power," *Transactions of the American Society of Civil Engineers* 12 [November 1883], Schedule A, col. 4). The total power capacity of this estimate is significantly above that implied by the total steam horsepower capacity reported in Colegio de México, *Estadísticas económicas del porfiriato: Fuerza de trabajo* (Mexico: Colegio de México, 1965), 130.

62. *El Comerciante Mexicano,* March 2, 1893, 118.

63. *El Comerciante Mexicano,* April 13, 1893, 217; also *Minero Mexicano,* February 6, 1890, 7–8. Rodney D. Anderson, *Outcasts in Their Own Land: Mexican Industrial Workers, 1906–1911,* The Origins of Modern Mexico (Dekalb: Northern Illinois University Press, 1976), 92–93.

64. Ernesto Galarza, *La industria eléctrica en México* (Mexico: Fondo de Cultura Económica, 1941); Reinhard Liehr and Mariano E. Torres Bautista, eds.,

Compañías eléctricas extranjeras en México (1860–1960) (Puebla, Mexico: Benemérita Universidad Autónoma de Puebla, 2010); also M. Bernstein, *Mexican Mining Industry,* 42, 44; *Engineering and Mining Journal,* July 6, 1905, 9–10; Keremitsis, *Industria textil mexicana,* 99.

65. *Mexican Herald,* June 17 and June 20, 1906; also Uribe Salas, "Distrito minero," 134; Percy F. Martin, *Mexico of the XXth Century,* vol. 1 (London: Edward Arnold, 1907), 297; *Mexican Herald,* June 17 and 20, 1906; *Engineering and Mining Journal,* January 5, 1907; John R. Southworth, *Las minas de México (edición ilustrada)* (Liverpool: Blake and MacKenzie, 1905), 110–12.

66. Mexico, Secretaría de Fomento, *Memoria* (1865), 389; *El Monitor Republicano,* August 13, 1873. We do not yet have a careful study of Mexico's early iron and steel industry.

67. Mexico, Secretaría de Fomento, *Memoria* (1865), 390; Patent #483 for a "procedimiento para la fabricación de acero por medio de ceniza de soza, sal común, barro plástico seco, óxido de manganezo y escorna," April 15, 1859; Jecker's application was opposed by J. S. Whithead, representing the Ferreterías de Encarnación and Guadalupe in Zimapan, Hidalgo.

68. *The Mexican Year Book 1908, Comprising Historical, Statistical and Fiscal Information* (London: McCorquodale, n.d.), 537–39; *El Economista Mexicano,* November 7, 1903; also L. Hamilton, *Border States,* 175–81.

69. L. Hamilton, *Border States,* 175–76.

70. *El Economista Mexicano,* November 7, 1903; *Mexican Herald,* Feburary 11, 1905.

71. Gómez-Galvarriato, "Primer impulso"; Haber, *Industry and Underdevelopment,* 44–46, 85.

72. Compare with the arguments in Haber, *Industry and Underdevelopment,* 45; Paolo Riguzzi, "Los caminos del atraso: Tecnología, instituciones e inversión en los ferrocarriles mexicanos, 1850–1900," in Kuntz Ficker and Riguzzi, *Ferrocarrilees y vida económica,* 31–98.

73. Box 54, folder 2, *ramo* Industrias Nuevas, AGN; also, the author's patent database; US Department of State, *Monthly Consular and Trade Reports,* no. 316 (Washington, DC: Government Printing Office, January 1907), 58; Dithridge to Brittingham, February 21, 1904, AHJB; John R. Southworth and Percy G. Holms, *El directorio oficial minero de México* (Liverpool: Blake and MacKenzie, 1910), 43–44; *Mexican Herald,* March 2, 1906, and July 4, 1906.

74. Gómez Serrano, "Ciudad pujante," 259; *El Comerciante Mexicano,* March 23, 1893, 174; 188BROD and 93WIRE, *ramo* Industrias Nuevas, AGN; US Department of State, *Monthly Consular and Trade Reports,* no. 340 (Washington, DC: Government Printing Office, January 1909), 212.

75. Guillermo Guajardo Soto, "Between the Workshop and the State: Training Human Capital in Railroad Companies in Mexico and Chile, 1850–1930," *MPRA* Paper No. 16135, July 2009, http://mpra.ub.uni-muenchen.de/16135/.

76. Southworth, *Minas de México,* 208, on Tajo; *Mining and Scientific Press,* May 26, 1906, on El Oro. Charles Butters reported that the plates made at El Oro

"wear much longer than Krupp plates, and cost just half as much." See also T. A. Rickard, *Journeys of Observation* (San Francisco: Dewey, 1907), 66, 69; *Mexican Herald,* September 26, 1895, on the Pachuca Foundry and Machine Shops.

77. *Mexican Herald,* July 4, 1906, 11, and July 20, 11. Also *El Comerciante Mexicano,* February 2, 1893, 58; Dithridge to Juan Brittingham, February 21, 1904, AHJB.

78. Edward J. Howell, *Mexico: Its Progress and Commercial Possibilities* (London: W. B. Whittingham, 1892), 56.

79. Gómez Serrano, "Ciudad pujante," 259; *El Monitor Repúblicano,* August 13, 1873, 4.

80. For other reports of local production of diverse machinery, see Graziella Altamirano and Guadalupe Villa, eds., *Chihuahua: Textos de su historia, 1824–1921,* vol. 2 (Mexico: Instituto José María Luis Mora, 1988), 256; Rosenzweig, "Industria," 372–73, refers to a steam engine, circa 1881, "designed and constructed in the country," installed at the match factory of Alfonso Labet.

81. *El Comerciante Mexicano,* January 19, February 2, and March 2, 1893.

82. Southworth and Holms, *Directorio oficial,* 43–44.

83. Ireneo Paz, *Álbum de la paz y trabajo* (Mexico: I. Paz, 1911), 101–4.

84. Miguel Angel Aviles-Galan, "'A Todo Vapor,'" and Carrillo Rojas, *Caballos de vapor.* See also company's files in box 14, folders 4–6, and boxes 15–17, *ramo* Industrias Nuevas, AGN. Aviles-Galan suggests that there were originally two foundries in Mazatlán with significant technological capabilities, later combined (95 n. 113).

85. Carillo Rojas, *Caballos de vapor,* 177–78; only 17 percent of the machines were shipped out of the state.

86. *El Minero Mexicano,* December 14, 1876, 417.

87. *The Mexican Year Book, 1912: A Financial and Commercial Handbook, Compiled from Official and Other Returns* (London: McCorquodale, 1912), 114–15.

88. Haber, *Industry and Underdevelopment,* 33, table 3.1; *El Economista Mexicano,* November 7, 1903; also *Mexican Mining Journal,* February 1908, 34. Compare with the list of US foundries published in the 1888 *Railroad, Telegraph and Steamship Builders' Directory* (New York: Railway Directory Publishing, 1888), running twenty pages of two-column, small-print, single-spaced company names.

89. Guajardo Soto, *Trabajo y tecnología,* 163.

90. Price from US Department of State, *Monthly Consular and Trade Reports,* no. 316 (Washington, DC: Government Printing Office, January 1907), 58; see Appendix 2 for total import value.

4. SEWING MACHINES

1. Luis Tablada, of Texcoco (not José Juan Tablada, the Mexican poet, writer, and columnist for *El Imparcial* [1871–1945]), *Diario del Hogar,* August 17, 1902.

2. *El Socialista,* June 11, 1876, 1, reprinted in Centro de Estudios Históricos del Movimiento Obrero Mexicano, *La mujer y el movimiento obrero mexicano en el siglo*

XIX: Antología de la prensa obrera (Mexico: Centro de Estudios Historicos del Movimiento Obrero Mexicano, 1975), 141–43.

3. Luís González y González, *Pueblo en vilo: Microhistoria de San José de Gracia* (Mexico City: Colegio de México, 1972), 99; US Department of Commerce, *Commercial Relations* (1896–97), 472.

4. Robert Bruce Davies, *Peacefully Working to Conquer the World: Singer Sewing Machines in Foreign Markets, 1854–1920* (New York: Arno Press, 1976).

5. Sarmiento quoted in Roberto Cortés Conde, "Sarmiento and Economic Progress: From Facundo to the Presidency," in *Sarmiento: Author of a Nation*, ed. Tulio Halperín Donghi et al. (Berkeley: University of California Press, 1994), 120.

6. *El Monitor Republicano,* April 25, 1874, though it is not entirely clear whether the writer means this as a testament to eloquence or not; *Diario del Hogar,* August 17, 1902.

7. Francis Hopkinson Smith, *A White Umbrella in Mexico* (New York: Houghton, Mifflin, 1889), 109; Carl Lumholtz, *New Trails in Mexico: An Account of One Year's Exploration in North-Western Sonora, Mexico, and South-Western Arizona, 1909–1910* (New York: Charles Scribners, 1912), 125.

8. Karl Marx, *Capital: A Critique of Political Economy,* vol. 1 (New York: Modern Library, 1906), 516.

9. For example, *El Socialista,* June 11, 1876; *La Convención Radical Obrera,* May 27, 1894, 3, both in Centro de Estudios Históricos, *Mujer y el movimiento,* 141–47.

10. Both periodicals quoted in Marguerite Connolly, "The Disappearance of the Domestic Sewing Machine, 1890–1925," *Winterthur Portfolio* 34, no. 1 (Spring 1999): 31; see also Harvey Green, *The Light of the Home: An Intimate View of the Lives of Women in Victorian America* (New York: Pantheon, 1983); Barbara Burman, ed., *The Culture of Sewing: Gender, Consumption, and Home Dressmaking* (Oxford: Berg, 1999).

11. *El Correo de Chihuahua,* April 25, 1902, in Altamirano and Villa, *Chihuahua,* 259.

12. Fred V. Carstensen, *American Enterprise in Foreign Markets: Studies of Singer and International Harvester in Imperial Russia* (Chapel Hill: University of North Carolina Press, 1984); Davies, *Peacefully Working;* Andrew Godley, "The Global Diffusion of the Sewing Machine, 1850–1914," *Research in Economic History* 20 (2001): 1–45, and "Selling the Sewing Machine around the World: Singer's International Marketing Strategies, 1850–1920," *Enterprise and Society* 7, no. 2 (2006): 266–300.

13. Carstensen, *American Enterprise,* 5; also Marie Eileen Francois, "Vivir de prestado: El empeño en la ciudad de México," in Staples, *Bienes y vivencias,* 107. For an estimate of 500 percent over hand sewing, see Mokyr, *Lever of Riches,* 142.

14. Outworkers were women who worked from their home, subcontracted by merchants who supplied cloth; David Hounshell, *From the American System to Mass Production: The Development of Manufacturing Technology in the United States* (Baltimore: Johns Hopkins University Press, 1984), 17.

15. David Arnold, *Everyday Technology: Machines and the Making of India's Modernity* (Chicago: University of Chicago Press, 2013).

16. Juan Nepomuceno Almonte, *Guía de forasteros de México y repertorio de conocimientos útiles* in 1852, as cited in Francois, "Vivir de prestado," 105.

17. See, for instance, *The Two Republics,* June 3, 1868. In the decades following, nearly every daily paper in Mexico typically carried advertisements from competing companies.

18. *El Monitor Repúblicano,* April 26, 1874, and *El Siglo Diez y Nueve,* March 12, 1883, among many others.

19. Buchenau, *Tools of Progress,* 25–28; *El Monitor Repúblicano,* June 11, 1870, and August 13, 1878, which advertised both "máquinas para familia" and "máquinas MEDIUM para taller."

20. Romero, *Report of the Secretary,* 111.

21. *El Monitor Repúblicano,* April 26, 1874, or *Diario del Hogar,* April 25 or July 15, 1883, among many others. See also letters of L. O. Harnecker to Singer Co. of February 4, 1893, and December 12, 1893, both in box 103, folder 7, SMCA.

22. John C. Campbell of the Davis Company, quoted in *Mexican Herald,* June 10, 1905.

23. For instance: *Diario del Hogar,* January 4, 1884, February 17, 1886, March 6, 1886 (the "Frister and Rossmann" company of Berlin); Great Britain, Board of Trade, *Board of Trade Journal* 39 (October-December 1902): 448.

24. Correspondence with the company headquarters in New York can be found in boxes 103–4, SMCA, and scattered in their microfilm collection. All managers of the central and branch offices were American or European, often with previous experience with the Singer Company. Sales agents were both foreigners and Mexicans, judging from the surnames; see Harnecker to Liskow, March 30, 1893, box 103, folder 6, SMCA. On sales strategies, see Carstensen, *American Enterprise;* also General Consul Barlow's report in US Department of Commerce, *Commercial Relations* (1902); *Mexican Herald,* June 10, 1905; and Mexico, Secretaría de Fomento, *Boletín semestral,* 57.

25. Patricia Arias, *Los vecinos de la Sierra: Microhistoria de Pueblo Nuevo* (Guadalajara: Universidad de Guadalajara, 1996), 87; Solomon Bulkley Griffin, *Mexico of To-day* (New York: Harper and Brothers, 1886), 163.

26. Oscar R. Graham to Singer Company, September 11, 1887, box 103, folder 5, SMCA.

27. Lucas to Graham, November 21, 1888, box 103, folder 5, SMCA.

28. National Reporter System, *Federal Reporter* 99 (March–April 1900): 232–34; Griffin, *Mexico of To-day,* 163.

29. Outside the Western Hemisphere, scholars have estimated Singer's share at 90 percent. In the United States and Latin America, Singer controlled only about 75 percent of the market; Godley, "Global Diffusion," 19. See also US Department of State, *Monthly Consular and Trade Reports,* no. 40 (1892), 407; *El País,* August 4, 1909; and *El Imparcial,* April 24, 1909.

30. See Appendix 2.

31. George McKenzie to Roberto Boker, November 19, 1879, box 103, folder 5, SMCA.

32. Compare with Godley, "Global Diffusion," figure 1. The other downturns in the Mexican import series correspond closely to economic conditions, including the recessions of 1893–94 and 1907–8. For the sensitivity of imports to economic conditions, see *Diario del Hogar,* July 5, 1908.

33. US State Department, *Monthly Consular and Trade Reports,* no. 330 (March 1908), 19, and US Department of Commerce, *Commercial Relations* (1896–97), 60.

34. Paterson to Singer Company, June 9, 1879, box 103, folder 5, SMCA; *El Monitor Republicano,* January 19, 1875; and Susie Porter, *Working Women in Mexico City: Public Discourses and Material Conditions, 1879–1931* (Tucson: University of Arizona Press, 2003), 33.

35. *El Imparcial,* May 14, 1905, March 19, 1906, June 7, 1906, May 9, 1910, and September 10, 1910; in *Diario del Hogar,* August 16, 1908; and in *El País,* August 14, 1910. There is some evidence that machines continued to be sold at somewhat higher prices. One company sold machines through an exclusive agent in San Luis Potosí and elsewhere for $125, of which $30 covered shipping costs. *Federal Reporter* 99 (March-April 1900): 232–34.

36. Hill to Singer Company, September 10, 1892, box 103, folder 6, SMCA; Graham to the Singer Company, September 11, 1887, and Hill to the Singer Company, August 3, 1889, both in box 103, folder 5, SMCA; also Marie Eileen Francois, *A Culture of Everyday Credit: Housekeeping, Pawnbroking, and Governance in Mexico City, 1750–1920* (Lincoln: University of Nebraska Press, 2006), 185, 253, 391 n. 120.

37. *El Monitor Repúblicano,* July 5, 1873, 3; also *El Monitor Republicano,* March 1, 1872, and March 5, 1884. See also advertisements for auctions in *Diario del Hogar,* April 8, 1883, May 8, 1892, and February 12, 1897.

38. Hill to Singer Company, September 10, 1892, box 103, folder 6, SMCA; Graham to the Singer Company, September 11, 1887, and Hill to the Singer Company, August 3, 1889, both in box 103, folder 5, SMCA.

39. My estimated price series for 1870–1910 begins at sixty-five dollars per machine in 1870 and falls to fifty dollars by 1878 and forty dollars by 1884. Godley, in "Selling the Sewing Machine" (272), argues that the global price after 1880 was about thirty dollars per machine and that prices changed little if at all from the end of the US patent pool (1877) to World War I. By 1910, Singer machines sold in Mexico for one hundred pesos or fifty dollars, while other firms were selling machines for fifty-five pesos, or US$27.50. In the United States, a machine could be bought in 1899 through John Wanamaker for twenty-five dollars and in 1902, from Sears, for just ten dollars; see M. Connolly, "Disappearance," 32, 36. I weighted the unit prices for Mexico on the high side, given Singer's market dominance and anecdotal data that suggest a somewhat higher average than Godley's thirty dollars. Thus the total cumulative machine imports of 328,000 is likely a conservative estimate. See also Hill to Singer Company, March 16, 1892, box 103, folder 6, SMCA.

40. On household size (urban at a 3.6 person average and rural at 4.5 people), see Lanny Thompson, "Artisans, Marginals, and Proletarians: The Households of the Popular Classes in Mexico City, 1876–1950," and Alejandro Solís Matías, "Organización familiar rural en el siglo XIX: La Barca, Jalisco," both in Guedea and Rodríguez

O., *Five Centuries*, 307–24, and 300–306, respectively; also Thomson, *Puebla de los Angeles*, 165. It is not clear whether family household size is the most appropriate measurement unit; extended families, neighborhoods, or entire villages might conceivably substitute as the most appropriate consumption unit for a single sewing machine.

41. Godley, "Global Diffusion," 20–23.

42. Ibid.; also Joan Perkin, "Sewing Machines: Liberation or Drudgery for Women," *History Today*, December 2002, 35–41.

43. US Department of State, *Monthly Consular and Trade Reports* no. 40 (1892), 407.

44. S. M. Lee, *Glimpses of Mexico and California* (Boston: Geo H. Ellis, 1887), 33.

45. Toussaint Alcaraz, *Escenario de la prensa*.

46. Gustavo Curiel et al., eds., *Pintura y vida cotidiana en México, 1650–1950* (Mexico: Fondo Cultura Banamex, 1999), 204.

47. Romero, *Report of the Secretary*, 111.

48. Sources for cost-of-living estimates include Aurora Gómez-Galvarriato, "The Evolution of Prices and Real Wages in Mexico from the Porfiriato to the Revolution," in *Latin America and the World Economy*, ed. John H. Coatsworth and Alan M. Taylor (Cambridge, MA: Harvard University Press, 1998), appendix table 12.1; Francois, *Culture of Everyday Credit*, 406 n. 102; Mexico, Secretaría de Industria, Comercio, y Trabajo, *Boletín* 1, nos. 1–2 (1918): 56; and Mexico, Instituto Nacional de Estadística, *Estadísticas históricas,* vol., table 20.1.

49. Data on average wage earners per family from Thompson, "Artisans, Marginals," 310. Sources for wage levels per occupational group come from archival sources for the mining sector (BL), from payroll records in urban factories (*ramo* Departamento de Trabajo, AGN), in public surveys (e.g., US Department of Commerce, *Commercial Relations* [1895–96], 408–9; [1896–97], 475; [1902], 525, 538), and in Gómez-Galvarriato, *Industry and Revolution*, figure 7.1.

50. Susie Porter disagrees with this analysis: "The cost of a sewing machine proved to be prohibitive for most women," citing wages of fifty centavos or so per day and machine costs between fifty and seventy pesos; *Working Women*, 33. For a vivid portrait of a young housekeeper saving for a machine a generation later, see Katherine Anne Porter, "Leaving the Petate," *New Republic*, February 4, 1931, 318–20.

51. Morris B. Parker, *Mules, Mines, and Me in Mexico, 1895–1932*, ed. James M. Day (Tucson: University of Arizona Press, 1979), 94–95. In many parts of the developing world today it is not uncommon to see machines set up on dirt streets or along rural roads to capture the sewing and repair trade in the neighborhood and from passersby.

52. John Lear, *Workers, Neighbors, and Citizens: The Revolution in Mexico City* (Lincoln: University of Nebraska Press, 2001), 75.

53. Joaquín García Icazbalceta, *Vocabulario de Mexicanismos* (Mexico: Tip. Y Lit. "La Europea" de J. Aguilar Vera, 1899), 205. We don't have a study of outworking arrangements in Mexico, but see, for example, Lear, *Workers, Neighbors, and Citizens,* 73–75.

54. *National Geographic*, June 1919, 311. John Reed, *Insurgent Mexico* (New York: International Publishers, 1969), 42, 270.

55. US Department of Commerce, *Commercial Relations* (1871), 911; Patton to the Singer Company, April 6, 1888, box 103, folder 5, SMCA; Hill to Singer Company, March 16, 1892, August 18, 1892, and September 10, 1892, box 103, folder 6, SMCA; Harnecker to Singer Company, May 23, 1893, box 103, folder 7, SMCA.

56. Hill to Singer Company, December 12, 1888, box 103, folder 5, SMCA.

57. Hill to Singer Company, March 16, 1892, box 103, folder 6, SMCA.

58. Graham to Singer Company, August 17, 1887, box 103, folder 5, SMCA.

59. Graham to Singer Company, August 17, 1887, box 103, folder 5, SMCA; also Harnecker to Singer Company, June 9, 1892, box 103, folder 6, SMCA.

60. Parker, *Mules, Mines, and Me*, 94–95.

61. US Department of State, *Monthly Consular and Trade Reports*, no. 40 (1992), 407. See also Harry Alverson Franck, *Trailing Cortez through Mexico* (New York: Frederick A. Stokes, 1935), 12; and Lumholtz, *New Trails*, 365.

62. General Consul Barlow's report in US Department of State, *Commercial Relations* (1896–97), 427.

63. González y González, *San José de Gracia*, 99.

64. Redfield, *Tepotztlan*, 39.

65. Andrew Godley, "Homeworking and the Sewing Machine in the British Clothing Industry, 1850–1905," in Burman, *Culture of Sewing*.

66. Kuntz Ficker, *Comercio exterior*, figure 5.5.

67. Advertisement for Uhink y Cía., in *El Monitor Repúblicano,* October 8, 1882. Also José María Muría and Angélica Peregrina, *Viajeros Anglosajones por Jalisco* (Mexico: Siglo XIX, 1992), 362; David Ames Wells, *A Study of Mexico* (New York: D. Appleton, 1887), 138; and Mary Elizabeth Blake and Margaret Frances Sullivan, *Mexico: Picturesque, Political, and Progressive* (Boston: Lee and Shepard, 1888), 221.

68. Lear, *Workers, Neighbors, and Citizens,* 66–67, 73–74.

69. Ignacia Torres Viuda de Alvarez, quoted in S. Porter, *Working Women,* 4, also 33–35.

70. S. Porter, *Working Women*, 18. See also *Siglo Diez y Nueve*, November 19, 1888.

71. Forment, *Democracy in Latin America, 1760–1900,* 1:272.

72. Oscar R. Graham to Singer Company, October 28, 1887, box 103, folder 6, SMCA. See also *El Correo de Chihuahua,* April 25, 1902, quoted in Altamirano and Villa, *Chihuahua*, 259–61; and Mark Wasserman, *Capitalists, Caciques, and Revolution: The Native Elite and Foreign Enterprise in Chihuahua, Mexico, 1854–1911* (Chapel Hill: University of North Carolina Press, 1984), 59.

73. US Department of Commerce, *Commercial Relations* (1898), 579. For other notices of clothing factories, see US Department of Commerce and Labor, *Special Agent Series*, no. 14 (1907), 37.

74. Ford to the Singer Company, November 21, 1891, box 103, folder 6, SMCA.

75. *Mexican Herald,* October 30, 1893, 6.

76. Lear, *Workers, Neighbors and Citizens,* 75; also *La Convención Radical Obrera,* February 24 and March 3, 1901, printed in Centro de Estudios Históricos, *Mujer y el movimiento,* 145–47.

77. Gómez-Galvarriato, *Industry and Revolution,* table 1.3; Bunker, *Creating Mexican Consumer Culture,* chap. 3.

78. Lear, *Workers, Neighbors and Citizens,* 74.

79. S. Porter, *Working Women,* 33–35, 44–45; Moramay López-Alonso, *Measuring Up: A History of Living Standards in Mexico, 1850–1950* (Stanford, CA: Stanford University Press, 2012); see also *El Siglo Diez y Nueve,* December 23, 1882, on workers' health; Inspector Medico Campos, July 22, 1922, box 1211, folder 2, *ramo* Departamento de Trabajo, AGN.

80. Graciela Márquez, "Tariff Protection in Mexico, 1892–1909: Ad Valorem Tariff Rates and Sources of Variation," in Coatsworth and Taylor, *Latin America,* table 14.2; on textile imports, see Kuntz Ficker, *Comercio exterior de México,* figure 5.5.

81. Hart, *Empire and Revolution,* 258.

82. US Department of Commerce, *Commercial Relations* (1896–97), 427.

83. For example, see letter of Ramon Torres Cordero representing seamstresses, November 4, 1914, box 101, folder 23 (1915), *ramo* Departamento del Trabajo, AGN, though compare with the language in *El Socialista,* June 11, 1876; also S. Porter, *Working Women,* 87–90.

84. Parker, *Mules, Mines, and Me,* 94–95.

85. Reed, *Insurgent Mexico,* 270.

86. M. Connolly, "Disappearance."

87. Parker, *Mules, Mines, and Me,* 94–95.

88. Harnecker to Singer Company, June 14, 1892, box 103, folder 6, SMCA. See also Hill to Singer Company, January 12, 1892, March 5, 1892, March 16, 1892, May 5, 1892, August 13, 1892, and September 10, 1892, and Harnecker's reports of January 14, 1893, and February 4, 1893, all box 103, folder 6, SMCA.

89. Harnecker to Singer Company, March 5, 1893, box 103, folder 6, SMCA. By midsummer 1893, conditions were beginning to improve, although the office warned New York that while "business should be up, [recovery of revenues will] really take a year as the fall crop will go toward old indebtedness." Harnecker to Singer Company, June 26, 1893, box 103, folder 6, SMCA.

90. Harnecker to Singer Company, June 26, 1893, box 103, folder 6, SMCA.

91. He would stay until at least 1904, the longest-serving Singer administrator in Mexico; Harnecker to Singer Company, December 12, 1892, box 103, folder 6, SMCA, and January 14, 1893, and February 4, 1893, box 103, folder 7, SMCA.

92. Hill to Singer Company, September 10, 1892, box 103, folder 6, SMCA. See also Francois, *Culture of Everyday Credit,* 185, 253, 391 n. 120.

93. Gómez-Galvarriato, *Industry and Revolution,* chap. 3.

94. Graham to the Singer Company, September 11, 1887, and Hill to the Singer Company, August 3, 1889, in box 103, folder 5, SMCA.

95. This was especially true for the first generation of advertisements through the 1860s and 1870s. See, for instance, Lohse y Compañía's ad for La Nueva Americana, *El Monitor Republicano,* April 26, 1874.

96. Juan Brittingham, letter, February 14, 1910, doc. 33–587, AHJB.

97. US Department of Commerce, *Commercial Relations* (1896–97), 427; Hill to Singer Company, December 19, 1888, box 103, folder 5, SMCA.

98. US Department of Commerce, *Commercial Relations* (1896–97), 427; Singer trained its agents in the field to do nearly all necessary repairs and adjustments; see Paterson to Singer Company, June 9, 1879, and Boker to Singer Company, February 7, 1882, box 103, folder 5, SMCA; also González y González, *San José de Gracia,* 99.

99. Ignacia Torres Viuda de Alvarez, quoted in S. Porter, *Working Women,* 4.

100. *El País,* September 22, 1909; *El Siglo Diez y Nueve,* February 8, 1890, and July 14, 1894; *La Convención Radical Obrera,* May 27, 1894, 3.

101. The life span of a turn-of-the-century sewing machine has been estimated at twenty to thirty years, and many survived heavy use well beyond that span; Godley, "Selling the Sewing Machine," 276; also Thomas H. Becker, *Doing Business in the New Latin America: A Guide to Cultures, Practices, and Opportunities* (Westport, CT: Praeger, 2004), 143.

102. For example, *Mexican Herald,* January 1, 1896, 7, for a new "general repair shop" opened at Cinco de Mayo No. 6.

103. Medina, "Dinamismo frustrado," 253–55.

104. Oscar R. Graham to Singer Co., October 28, 1887, U.S. Mss A1, box 103, folder 5, SMCA.

105. Parker, *Mules, Mines, and Me,* 94–95.

106. Stuart H. Ingram Notebook, n.p., MSS 81/40pm, BLUC.

107. Tenorio-Trillo, *Mexico at the World's Fairs,* 134; Leandro Ramírez does not show up in Mexico's patent records. In 1921, Pedro Filippinni, an Italian national residing in Mazatlán, would take a US patent for a "fan attachment for sewing machines"; US Patent #1,366,776.

108. Saucedo to Singer Company, June 30, 1900, box 104, folder 1, SMCA.

109. *Diario del Hogar,* date unknown, 1902; *El Economista Mexicano,* April 26, 1902, 61; also Rosenzweig, "Industria," 384.

110. *El Socialista,* June 11, 1876, 1.

111. Schell, *Integral Outsiders,* 23, citing Ramon Eduardo Ruíz, *The Great Rebellion: Mexico, 1905–1924* (New York: W. W. Norton, 1980), 168. See also Charles W. Hamilton, *Early Day Oil Tales of Mexico* (Houston: Gulf, 1966), 92.

112. Sewing machines would not be produced in Mexico until the 1950s; Mario Velarde, *Directorio de empresas industriales beneficiadas con exenciones fiscales, 1940–1960* (Mexico: Banco de México, 1961), 255–56.

5. BEER AND GLASS BOTTLES

1. Susan M. Gauss and Edward Beatty, "The World's Beer: The Historical Geography of Brewing in Mexico," in *The Geography of Beer: Regions, Environment, and Societies,* ed. Mark Patterson and Nancy Hoalst-Pullen (New York: Springer, 2014), 57–66.

2. Miguel Angel Fernández, *El vidrio en México* (Mexico: Centro de Arte Vitro, 1990), 176; Werner P. Sutton, "Malt and Beer in Spanish America," in *Special Con-*

sular Report No. 1, ed. US Department of State, Bureau of Statistics (Washington, DC: Government Printing Office, 1890), 331; Martin, *Mexico of the Twentieth Century*, 2:235. On the beer industry, see Gabriela Recio, "El nacimiento de la industria cervecera en México, 1880–1910," in *Cruda realidad: Producción, consumo y fiscalidad de las bebidas alcohólicas en México y América Latina, siglos XVII–XX*, ed. Ernest Sánchez Santiró (Mexico: Instituto Mora, 2007), 155–85; Gustavo Adolfo Barrera Pages, "Industrialización y revolución: El desempeño de la cervecería Toluca y México, S.A.: 1875–1926" (Tesis de Licenciatura, ITAM, 1999).

3. For prices, see Sutton, "Malt and Beer," 331, 336; and Mario Barbosa Cruz, "La persistencia de una tradición: Consumo de pulque en la ciudad de México, 1900–1920," in Sánchez Santiró, *Cruda realidad*, 24. Jane-Dale Lloyd notes that many rancheros in Chihuahua preferred beer to pulque and could afford it; *Cinco ensayos*, 88; Howell, *Mexico*, 55.

4. Calculated using the adult male population of Mexico's seventeen largest cities; Mexico, INEGI, *Estadísticas históricas de México*. Import data from Colegio de México, *Estadísticas económicas del Porfiriato: Comercio exterior de México, 1877–1911* (Mexico: Colegio de México, 1960), 208, for total bottled beer imports, and US Department of Commerce, *Foreign Commerce and Navigation of the United States* (Washington, DC: Government Printing Office, 1880–1911), for US unbottled beer exports to Mexico; national production calculated from Cervecería Cuauhtémoc production in Haber, *Industry and Underdevelopment*, table 4.3, as 28–30 percent of national production; see also work in progress by Susan M. Gauss.

5. *Monterrey News*, August 29, 1905, quoted in Steven Bunker, "Consumers of Good Taste: Marketing Modernity in Northern Mexico, 1890–1910," *Mexican Studies/Estudios Mexicanos* 13, no. 2 (1997): 233.

6. Calculations based on annual production of the Cervecería Cuauhtémoc in Monterrey at 28 to 30 percent of the national market; see Haber, *Industry*, table 4.3 and *passim*.

7. Sutton, "Malt and Beer," 330–31.

8. One new glass factory in Puebla sent its manager to France in 1902 to hire experienced glassworkers; *Mexican Herald*, June 8, 1902, 7, also July 2, 1896, 8 and July 29, 1898, 4. See the applications of Thomas y Compañía and Carlos Banoni to the Ministry of Development for tax exemptions; papers in box 53, folder 6, and box 35, folder 4, *ramo* Industrias Nuevas, AGN.

9. Isidro Vizcaya Canales, *Los orígenes de la industrialización de Monterrey* (Monterrey: Archivo General del Estado de Nuevo León, 2001), 89.

10. Calculated as the ratio of total bottle imports [from US Department of Commerce, *Foreign Commerce and Navigation* (various years), and Rosenzweig, "Industria," 374, to Mexican beer consumption, assuming roughly 88 percent of consumption was in bottles rather than barrels.

11. Quoted in Mora-Torres, *Making of the Mexican Border*, 242.

12. Beatty, *Institutions and Investment*, 63–66, adjusted with data from Romero, *Report of the Secretary*, 132–33; US Census Office, *Census Reports of the United States* [1900, 1905, 1910] (Washington, DC: US Census Office, 1900, 1905, 1910); Warren

C. Scoville, *Revolution in Glassmaking: Entrepreneurship and Technological Change in the American Industry, 1880–1920* (Cambridge, MA: Harvard University Press, 1948), 230, 250; and Mexico, Secretaría de Hacienda de Hacienda y Crédito Público, *Boletín del Ministerio de Hacienda* (Mexico: Imprenta de la Secretaría de Hacienda, various years).

13. Fernández, *Vidrio en México*, and Gonzalo López Cervantes, "Notas para el estudio del vidrio en la Nueva España," Cuadernos de Trabajo No. 19, Instituto Nacional de Antropología e Historia, Departamento de Prehistoria, 1979.

14. Barrera Pages, "Industrialización," 66–69. See also Juan Manuel Romero Gil, "Las bebidas espirituosas en Sonora: Notas sobre su producción, consumo e impuestos (1850–1920)," in Sánchez Santiró, *Cruda realidad*, 16; Mora-Torres, *Making of the Mexican Border*, 242; Nora Hamilton, *The Limits of State Autonomy: Post-Revolutionary Mexico* (Princeton, NJ: Princeton University Press, 1982), 310–11.

15. US Bureau of the Census, *Twelfth Census of Manufacturers, 1900*, vol. 9, pt. 3 (Washington, DC: Government Printing Office, 1901–3), 975. See also Scoville, *Revolution in Glassmaking*, 103.

16. E. William Fairfield, *Fire and Sand: The History of the Libbey-Owens Sheet Glass Company* (Cleveland, OH: Lezius-Hiles, 1960), chaps. 5–9, and Scoville, *Revolution in Glassmaking*, chap. 4. This section is based on these works as well as the record books in TGCA.

17. Scoville, *Revolution in Glassmaking*, 154–62; Pearce Davis, *The Development of the American Glass Industry* (Cambridge, MA: Harvard University Press, 1949), 208–9; T. K. Derry and Trevor I. Williams, *A Short History of Technology from the Earliest Times to A.D. 1900* (1960; repr., New York: Dover, 1993), 598; Fairfield, *Fire and Sand*, 48.

18. Scoville, *Revolution in Glassmaking*, 103 n. 64; also record book #1, p. 263, TGCA.

19. Libbey and Owens formed the Owens Bottle Machine Company in September, 1903, to market rights to US bottle producers only. For the US Owens patents, see box 2, record book #1, pp. 33, 270–77, 285; record book #2, pp. 1–19; and box 6, folder 10, all in TGCA. For the European patent negotiations, see record book #2. The Owens patents in Mexico are #2904 on March 10, 1903, for "Machine for and method of shaping glass"; #3271 on October 1, 1903, for "Glass tank or pot"; and #4832 on August 19, 1905, for "Improvements relating to the production of articles of glass and apparatus therefore"; Mexico, Secretaría de Fomento, *Gaceta oficial de patentes y marcas*, various months.

20. The Owens machine cost just under 10,000 dollars in 1904 and between 35,000 and 40,000 dollars by 1914. Installing the machine also required the acquisition of new furnaces, lehrs (temperature-controlled kilns), feeders, and other equipment—essentially the construction of an entirely new physical plant, running to several hundred thousand dollars. Box 2, record book #2, pp. 39 ff., TGCA; Scoville, *Revolution in Glassmaking*, 103, 165 n. 60.

21. Davis, *Development*, 213; Scoville, *Revolution in Glassmaking*, 104–7. Royalties lay between fifty and fifty-four cents per gross from 1904 to 1909 and declined

to around fifteen to twenty-five cents per gross over the next decade. See Scoville, *Revolution in Glassmaking,* 107 n. 85; also Fairfield, *Fire and Sand,* 55.

22. Box 2, record book #2, pp. 47–58, 124–26, 195–99, 259, TGCA. Also US Bureau of Foreign and Domestic Commerce, *Commercial Reports,* nos. 1–75 (Washington, DC: Government Printing Office, 1910), 173.

23. Davis, *Development,* table 19, 223.

24. Recio, "Nacimiento," table 5; Haber, *Industry,* 52–55; Vizcaya Canales, *Orígenes,* 76–77.

25. Doc. 20–0096, AHJB.

26. Brittingham to Belden, June 28, 1905, doc. 19A-401, AHJB; for the contract, see box 2, record book #3, p. 29, TGCA; box 6, record book #13, June 13, 1905, TGCA.

27. Juan Ignacio Barragán and Mario Cerutti, *Juan F. Brittingham y la industria en México, 1859–1940* (Monterrey, Mexico: n.d.). After Brittingham established himself in Mexico he went exclusively by "Juan" in all correspondence, whether in English or Spanish. He was not a "foreign investor" but an immigrant who never naturalized but had little intention of returning to the United States. Although he sent his children to high school and college in New England, they too pursued professional opportunities in Mexico. Only the violence of the 1910 revolution drove Brittingham temporarily back to the United States, after which he returned to Gómez Palacio and eventually to Mexico City, before dying in Los Angeles in 1940.

28. See, for example, docs. 19-B140, 0020123, 0020190, 0020272, 0020562, 0021206, 0024505, and 0024–148, AHJB.

29. Brittingham to Terrazas, November 7, 1904, and to Creel, November 16, 1904, docs. 0017428 and 0017507, AHJB.

30. Creel's letters to Brittingham in 1902, docs. 02–0518 and 0519, AHJB. Also Creel to Brittingham, November 15, 1904, and March 6, 1905, docs. 02–0221 and 0222, AHJB. See also Mario Cerutti, "La Compañía Industrial Jabonera de La Laguna: Comerciantes, agricultores e industria en el norte de México (1880–1925)," in *Historia de las grandes empresas en México, 1850–1930,* ed. Carlos Marichal and Mario Cerutti (Mexico: Colegio de México, 1997), 167–200.

31. Terrazas to Brittingham, March 9 and March 17, 1905, docs. 20–0096 and 06–0083, AHJB.

32. Terrazas to Brittingham, March 17, 1905, doc. 06–0083, AHJB.

33. Fairfield, *Fire and Sand,* ch. 6; Scoville, *Revolution in Glassmaking,* 288 n. 54.

34. These included (among others) inquiries from a Mr. Pedrazo (August 1905, doc. 20–0138, AHJB); from a J. A. Bolton of Montclair, New Jersey (November 1905, doc. 20–0107, AHJB); from George W. Dithridge (November 1906, doc. 20–0109, AHJB); from a Dr. Corkrell of Mexico City, with a letter from Pittsburgh (April 1907, doc. 20–0049, AHJB); and from Hermann Heye of Germany, a principal in the ownership of the Owens European rights (April 1908, doc. 63-A126, AHJB).

35. Terrazas to Brittingham, March 9, 1905, doc. 20–0096, AHJB.

36. Brittingham to Creel, May 27, 1905, doc. 19A-274, AHJB.

37. Beatty, *Institutions and Investment,* chap. 4.

38. Contract of incorporation (copy), 1905, doc. 20–0153, AHJB. The company's capital was set at 400,000 pesos, divided equally among the four investors. Brittingham and Terrazas were joined by Francisco Belden, a friend and Monterrey businessman, and by Arthur Fowle.

39. Contract with Option of June 13, 1905, docs. 20–0020 and 0021, AHJB. See also box 6, record book #13, June 13, 1905, TGCA.

40. Walbridge to Roever, February 14, 1907, doc. 20–0064, AHJB.

41. See, for instance, Brittingham to Walbridge, July 7, 1906, doc. 022229, AHJB.

42. Brittingham to the Toledo Glass Company, August 31, 1905, doc. 19B-217, AHJB.

43. Brittingham to Terrazas, August 3, 1905, doc. 19-B028, AHJB; Walbridge to Brittingham, August 31, 1905, doc. 20–0138, AHJB, and Brittingham to Walbridge, September 6, 1905, doc. 19-B278, AHJB; and regarding Julio Limantour, see Brittingham to Terrazas, December 6, 1905, doc. 0020218, AHJB.

44. See, for instance, Walbridge to Brittingham, August 31, 1905, doc. 20–0138, AHJB.

45. Bolton to Brittingham, November 9, 1905, doc. 20–0107, AHJB.

46. Walbridge to Brittingham, September 29, 1905, doc. 20–0130, AHJB.

47. Brittingham to Belden, November 13, 1905, doc. 0020071, AHJB; also Brittingham to Terrazas, August 24, 1905, doc. 19-B162, AHJB; Walbridge to Brittingham, September 18, 1905, doc. 20–0131 AHJB.

48. Brittingham to Terrazas, December 6, 1905, doc. 0020071, AHJB; also Brittingham to Belden, December 22, 1905, doc. 63-A004, AHJB.

49. Brittingham to Belden, December 22, 1905, February 16, 1906, and March 8, 1906, in docs. 63-A004, 63-A012, and 0021164 respectively, AHJB.

50. Brittingham to Walbridge, December 22, 1905, doc. 63-A002, AHJB.

51. Brittingham to Belden, December 22, 1905, doc. 63-A004, AHJB.

52. Brittingham to Terrazas, July 17, 1905, doc. 19-A574, AHJB.

53. Brittingham to Belden, December 22, 1905, doc. 63-A004, AHJB; Brittingham to Walbridge, January 4, 1906, doc. 63-A007, AHJB; Brittingham to Belden, June 11, 1906, doc. 0022077, AHJB.

54. Brittingham to Belden, March 9, 1906, doc. 63-A016, AHJB.

55. Brittingham to Walbridge, December 22, 1905, doc. 63-A002, AHJB, January 4, 1906, doc. 63-A007, AHJB, and March 9, 1906, doc. 63-A013, AHJB. Brittingham offered a royalty of fifty cents gold per gross to both the American Bottle Company and the Cervecera Toluca y México, plus the machinery itself at cost (roughly 8,000 dollars). See Brittingham to Terrazas, September 12, 1906, doc. 022602, AHJB.

56. Walbridge to Brittingham, September 22, 1906, doc. 20–0115, AHJB.

57. Brittingham to Walbridge, March 9, 1906, doc. 63-A013, AHJB.

58. Brittingham to Belden, June 9, 1906 and Walbridge to Brittingham, July 2, 1906, in docs. 63-A027 and 20–0119, respectively, AHJB. See also Brittingham to Walbridge, July 7, 1906, doc. 0022229, AHJB; Brittingham to Terrazas, September

19, 1906, doc. 0022602, AHJB; Brittingham to Walbridge, September 14, 1906, doc. 0022634, AHJB.

59. It is not clear whom Negovetich and Roever represented. Their goal was to establish a large-scale bottle factory in Mexico City, perhaps with a secondary plant in Chihuahua. They referred to their financial backers "back east," and some of their letters were postmarked in Providence, Rhode Island, and New York City. Roever claimed close ties with European glass producers, and both men were socially connected to Mexico City's American colony; see *Mexican Herald,* May 28, 1905, and August 19, 1910. Negovetich had first contacted the Toledo Glass Company in September 1905. Walbridge identified him to Brittingham as "of the British Club" and reported that he wanted to open a bottle factory in Toluca with a capacity of one hundred thousand gross per year. Brittingham in turn assumed that Negovetich represented the Cervecería Toluca y México. There was no further contact until February 1907.

60. Negovetich to Mills, February 6, 1907, doc. 20–0063, AHJB; Walbridge to Roever, February 14, 1907, doc. 20–0064, AHJB; Brittingham to Walbridge, February 19, 1907, doc. 63-A055, AHJB, and February 23, 1907, doc. 63-A057, AHJB.

61. Mexico imported bottles from Germany, where relatively cheaper labor costs than the United States meant that high royalties in Mexico would leave its industry uncompetitive with German products; Walbridge to Brittingham, March 28, 1907. Royalties to licensees in the United States were initially set as a percentage (e.g., 50 percent) of the reduction in labor costs made possible by the Owens machine; Scoville, *Revolution in Glassmaking,* 107.

62. Brittingham to Walbridge, February 23, 1907, doc. 63-A057, AHJB; Walbridge to Brittingham, March 6, 1907, doc. 20–0055, AHJB, and March 18, 1907, doc. 20–0058, AHJB.

63. Brittingham to Walbridge, March 28, 1907, doc. 63-A062, AHJB.

64. Negovetich to Toledo Glass, August 12, 1907, doc. 20–0020, AHJB; Geddes to Brittingham, August 13, 1907, doc. 20–0011, AHJB, and August 14, 1907, doc. 20–0008, AHJB; Negovetich to Geddes, August 14, 1907, doc. 20–0010, AHJB; Negovetich to Geddes, August 15, 1907, doc. 20–0089, AHJB, and August 16, 1907, doc. 20–0093, AHJB. See also Roever to Brittingham, September 5, 1907, doc. 20–0078, September 17, 1907, doc. 20–0079, AHJB, and October 15, 1907, doc. 20–0083, AHJB. Also Brittingham to Roever, September 19, 1907, doc. 63-A099, AHJB, and October 18, 1907, doc. 63-A110, AHJB.

65. See Terrazas to Brittingham, August 1, 1905, doc. 06–0100, AHJB, and March 5, 1906, doc. 06–0129, AHJB; Brittingham to Terrazas, March 16, 1906, doc. 0021204, AHJB; Brittingham to Walbridge, July 7, 1906, doc. 0022229, AHJB.

66. Brittingham to Walbridge, September 14, 1906, doc. 022634, AHJB.

67. Brittingham to Belden, March 28, 1906, doc. 63A-021, AHJB; Brittingham to Terrazas, March 28, 1906, doc. 63A-023, AHJB.

68. Brittingham to Walbridge, October 12, 1906, doc. 63A-038, AHJB. Sand (or crushed quartz rock) provides the silica that, melted and fused, constitutes the primary ingredient for glass. However, silica melts at such a high temperature (just over

3,000 degrees Fahrenheit), that it is impractical and unprofitable to use alone. Adding an alkali such as sodium carbonate (soda ash) to the silica reduces its melting point to a more reasonable level (about 850 degrees), thus reducing expensive fuel requirements. Lime to reduce the solubility of the silica-soda combination usually constitutes the third major ingredient, with a typical ratio among these of roughly 75 percent silica, 15 percent soda, and 10 percent lime. On glass production, see Davis, *Development*, 41–42; Scoville, *Revolution in Glassmaking*, 14–17, 39–40.

69. Brittingham to Belden, July 31, 1905, doc. 19-B003, AHJB, who heard reports that the earlier failure of the old Monterrey glass factory was due not to labor problems but to a failure to secure an adequate supply of raw materials.

70. Brittingham to Lawton, November 8, 1906, doc. 63-A040, AHJB. Brittingham received overly optimistic reports of Chihuahua River sand from George Dithridge, recommended by Toledo. Dithridge was a US engineer who invested in several mining ventures in Chihuahua. His brother worked for the Toledo Glass Company as an engineer, and their family had a long history of involvement with the glass industry in the United States and England. The Toledo Company had recommended him to Brittingham as a source of expertise after Dithridge had earlier inquired about the Mexican rights to the Owens machine; see box 2, record book #1, p. 131, TGCA; also Dithridge to Brittingham, January 25, 1907, doc. 20–0061, AHJB.

71. Brittingham to Dithridge, January 21, 1907, doc. 63A-050, AHJB.

72. Brittingham to Walbridge, March 24, 1909, doc. 63A-196, AHJB.

73. Dithridge to Brittingham, January 18, 1907, doc. 20–0067, AHJB.

74. Dithridge to Brittingham, February 21, 1907, doc. 20–0060, AHJB; also Agusto Genin to Brittingham, September 1, 1906, doc. 20–0103, AHJB.

75. Naomi R. Lamoreaux and Kenneth L. Sokoloff, "Inventive Activity and the Market for Technology in the United States, 1840–1920," NBER Working Paper #7107, National Bureau of Economic Research, Cambridge, MA, 1999, 4–6; Scoville, *Revolution in Glassmaking*, 88–89.

76. Limantour to Brittingham, November 18, 1908, doc. 06–0013, AHJB; Dithridge to Brittingham, December 15, 1906, doc. 20–0070, AHJB; *El Economista Mexicano*, December 6, 1902, 200; also Mora-Torres, *Making of the Mexican Border*, 236.

77. Dithridge to Brittingham, January 18, 1907, doc. 20–0067, AHJB.

78. Brittingham to Garza, March 17, 1909, doc. 63A-193, AHJB.

79. Dithridge to Brittingham, December 15, 1906, doc. 20–0072, AHJB; January 18, 1907, doc. 20–0067, AHJB; and February 21, 1907, doc. 20–0060, AHJB.

80. Travis to Brittingham, August 4, 1907, doc. 20–0023, AHJB; Dithridge to Brittingham, February 21, 1907, doc. 20–0060, AHJB.

81. See Limantour to Brittingham, November 18, 1908, doc. 06–0013, AHJB; Brittingham to Garza, May 4, 1909, doc. 63A-204, AHJB.

82. Correspondence with C.B. Cleveland of the Chicago, Rock Island and Pacific Railroad, November 5, 1906, doc. 20–0110, AHJB, and with H. Lawton of the Ferrocarril Central Mexicano, December 1, 1906, doc. 20–0097, AHJB; Dithridge to Brittingham, January 25, 1907, doc. 20–0061, AHJB.

83. Brittingham to Garza, May 4, 1909, doc. 63A-204, AHJB.

84. Dithridge to Brittingham, December 15, 1906, doc. 20–0072, AHJB, and January 25, 1907, doc. 20–0061, AHJB.

85. Brittingham to Walbridge, March 17, 1908, doc. 63A-118, AHJB.

86. Brittingham to Garza, March 25, 1908, doc. 63A-122, AHJB.

87. Brittingham to Walbridge, November 8, 1908, doc. 63A-127, AHJB.

88. Brittingham to Walbridge, April 8, 1909, doc. 63A-199, AHJB; Garza to Brittingham, May 13, 1909, doc. 09–0321, AHJB; Arbuckle Ryan Company to Brittingham, August 4, 1909, doc. 09–0336, AHJB.

89. Both were valued at 200,000 dollars; Brittingham to Isaac Garza, April 20, 1909, doc. 63A-212, AHJB. Also Barragán and Cerutti, *Juan Brittingham;* box 6, record book #30, January 20 and February 23, 1909, TGCA. Its directors included Juan Brittingham, Isaac Garza, Juan Terrazas, Mariano Hernández, Francisco Garza, Manuel Cantú Treviño, José Belden, and Roberto G. Sada.

90. Brittingham to Walbridge, November 8, 1908, doc. 63A-127, AHJB.

91. Brittingham to José Yves Limantour, December 22, 1909, doc. 0033127, AHJB; Brittingham to Walbridge, December 27, 1909, doc. 0033155, AHJB; Brittingham to Creel, February 15, 1910, doc. 0033592, AHJB.

92. Brittingham to Garza, March 17, 1909, doc. 63A-193, AHJB. For more on the high price of imported coal to produce gas, see, for instance, Brittingham to Niggli, April 24, 1909, doc. SN07–414, AHJB; also May 4, 1909, doc. 63-A193 and 63-A204, AHJB.

93. Brittingham to Garza, May 20, 1909, and July 21, 1909, docs. 63-A212 and 63-A216, AHJB.

94. Garza to Brittingham, August 7, 1909, doc. 09–0232, AHJB.

95. Limantour to Brittingham, November 18, 1908, doc. 06–0013, AHJB.

96. Travis to Brittingham, August 4, 1907, doc. 20–0023, AHJB; Dithridge to Brittingham, February 21, 1907, doc. 20–0060, AHJB.

97. Limantour to Brittingham, November 18, 1908, doc. 06–0013, AHJB.

98. Brittingham to Walbridge, March 9, 1909, Brittingham to Overa, March 19, 1909, and Brittingham to Kemff, February 20, 1909, docs. 63-A191, 63-A195, and 63-A172 respectively, AHJB. One typical inquiry began, "The writer is a clean cut young business man of thirty with five years banking and eight years practical experience with the above concern [the Mannington Glass Works Company]." See Layton to Terrazas, November 30, 1908, doc. 20–0101, AHJB. While most job applicants from abroad sought salaries on par with US wage scales, those hired in Mexico had to settle for less. William Travis, a former glass plant manager from West Virginia, sought 6,000 dollars per year for his services but was offered only 3,500; Travis to Walbridge, June 23, 1907; Walbridge to Travis, July 6, 1907; Travis to Brittingham, August 4, 1907; and Brittingham to Travis, August 5, 1907, docs. 20–0031, 20–0034, 20–0023, and 20–0030 respectively, AHJB. See also March 1909 exchange between Brittingham and Isaac Garza concerning the high cost of foreign engineers in letter book 63-A.

99. Sada to Brittingham, May 27, 1911, doc. 09–0359, AHJB.

100. Mora-Torres, *Making of the Mexican Border*, 250.

101. Walbridge to Brittingham, November 8, 1910, doc. 09–0240, AHJB.

102. Walbridge to Brittingham, November 8, 1910, doc. 09–0240, AHJB.

103. Box 2, record book #3, p. 68, TGCA; also the memo of November 10, 1910, in doc. 09–0276, AHJB.

104. Walbridge to Vidriera Monterrey, November 11, 1910, doc. 09–0239, AHJB. For a fluxing alkali Monterrey chose to use soda ash imported from Britain. They discussed using sulphate of soda instead and disagreed about the relative benefits of the two alkalis, but most attention was devoted to reducing the cost of the input. The Toledo engineers suggested reducing the formula from 58 percent to 48 percent soda ash, while a British glassmaker said that cutting the soda ash with salt cake reduced costs and yielded quality glass. By late 1911, moreover, the directors had some promising leads on sources of sodium sulfate in San Luis Potosí and felt that this would reduce the necessary adaptations to the imported machines and connections. On this and related issues, see Walbridge to Brittingham, June 22, 1907, doc. 20–0040, AHJB; Toledo Glass to Brittingham, December 5, 1910, doc. 09–0290, AHJB; Livaudais to Brittingham, March 28, 1911, and April 19, 1911, docs. 09–0372 and 09–0370, AHJB; Roberto Sada to Brittingham, October 27, 1911, doc. 09–0347, AHJB.

105. See Mariano Hernández to Brittingham, November 5, 1910, doc. 09–0272, AHJB, and November 11, 1910, doc. 09–0273, AHJB; Barragán and Cerutti, *Juan Brittingham*, 175.

106. Barbara Hibino, "Cervecería Cuauhtémoc: A Case Study of Technological and Industrial Development in Mexico," *Mexican Studies/Estudios Mexicanos* 8, 1 (1992): 33–34; Barragán and Cerutti, *Juan Brittingham*, 175–76.

107. For 1923 production figures, see the annual report of Roberto Garza Sada, manager of the factory, December 31, 1923, doc. 09–0149, AHJB. For 1924 production figures, see the Dunn & Company report of July 30, 1924, doc. 09–0148, AHJB. For comparative numbers, see Mora-Torres, *Making of the Mexican Border*, 250, and Fairfield, *Fire and Sand*, 53.

108. Barragán and Cerutti, *Juan Brittingham*, 184, 197; Hibino, "Cervecería Cuauhtémoc"; Michael Snodgrass, *Deference and Defiance in Monterrey: Workers, Paternalism, and Revolution in Mexico, 1890–1950* (Cambridge: Cambridge University Press, 2003), 16, 257–61; N. Hamilton, *Limits of State Autonomy*, 306–17.

109. Fernández, *Vidrio en México*, n.p.

110. Gauss and Beatty, "World's Beer."

111. Noel Maurer, "Rents in Early Industrializing Economies: The Case of Porfirian Mexico, 1898–1911," unpublished manuscript, Stanford University, 1997; Haber, *Industry and Underdevelopment*, chaps. 5 and 7.

112. Roever to Brittingham, July 9, 1907, doc. 20–0039, AHJB.

113. Dithridge to Brittingham and Terrazas, November 15, 1906, doc. 20–0073, AHJB.

114. Arbuckle Ryan Company to Brittingham, August 4, 1909, doc. 09–0336, AHJB.

6. CYANIDE AND SILVER

1. Teodoro Flores, *Estudio geológico-minero de los distritos de El Oro y Tlalpuja-hua*, Instituto Geológico de México, Boletín No. 37 (Mexico: Secretaria de Gobernación, 1920), 12.

2. Todd, *Colonial Technology*, 111.

3. Joaquín Muñoz, "La minería en México: Bosquejo histórico," *Quinto Centenario* 11 (1986): 149.

4. Peter Bakewell, *Silver Mining and Society in Colonial Mexico: Zacatecas, 1546–1700* (Cambridge: Cambridge University Press, 1971); Brading, *Miners and Merchants*.

5. Alan Probert, "Bartolomé de Medina: The Patio Process and the Sixteenth-Century Silver Crisis," *Journal of the West* 8, no. 1 (1969): 90–124; Peter Bakewell, *Miners of the Red Mountain: Indian Labor in Potosí, 1545–1650* (Albuquerque: University of New Mexico Press, 1984), chap. 1; Alma Parra, "Experiencia, destreza e innovaciones en la minería de Guanajuato en el siglo XIX," *Historias* 58 (May–August 2004): 74–75.

6. For descriptions, see Allen T. Bird, *The Land of Nayarit: An Account of the Great Mineral Region South of the Gila River and East from the Gulf of California to the Sierra Madre* (Nogales: Arizona and Sonora Chamber of Mines, 1904); Maturin M. Ballou, *Aztec Land* (Boston: Houghton, Mifflin, 1890), 99–101; Parker, *Mules, Mines, and Me*, 25–29; Charles B. Dahlgren, *Historic Mines of Mexico: A Review of the Mines of That Republic for the Past Three Centuries* (New York, 1883), 16–18, 168 ff.; Langan W. Swent, *Working for Safety and Health in Underground Mines: San Luis and Homestake Mining Companies, 1846–1988*, 2 vols. (Berkeley: Regional Oral History Office, Bancroft Library, University of California, 1995), 31–32; and the reports of C. A. Hamilton, December 2, 1885, and March 26, 1886, Greene Gold-Silver Company Papers, BLUC. *Azogueros* still managed the amalgamation process in a few places on the eve of the Revolution in 1910. On the technology of colonial mining, see Trabulse, *Círculo roto*, chap. 8.

7. Muñoz, "Minería en México," 150; Dahlgren, *Historic Mines of Mexico*, 18; Marshall C. Eakin, *British Enterprise in Brazil: The St. John d'el Rey Mining Company and the Morro Velho Gold Mine, 1830–1960* (Durham, NC: Duke University Press, 1989); Raymond E. Dumett, *El Dorado in West Africa: The Gold-mining Frontier, African Labor, and Colonial Capitalism in the Gold Coast, 1875–1900* (Athens: Ohio University Press, 1998).

8. Parra, "Experiencia," 70.

9. *Engineering and Mining Journal*, November 24, 1908, 808 (air hammers); *Mexican Herald*, March 15, 1896, 2 (rock drills), and January 31 and March 31, 1896 (pumping engines); also Dahlgren, *Historic Mines of Mexico*, 20; Swent, *Working for Safety*, 35; box 7, folder 5, Probert Papers, BLUT; Rafael Montejano y Aguiñaga, *La minería en San Luis Potosí* (San Luis Potosí: Archivo Histórico del Estado, 1994), 51–54.

10. On variations to amalgamation, see Parra, "Experiencia"; also Von Mentz de Boege, "Tecnología minera alemana."

11. *Mexican Mining Journal,* January 1908, 22–23; *Mexican Herald,* July 4, 18, and 20 and August 4, 1906; *Engineering and Mining Journal,* January 5, 1907, 41–42; April 4, 1908, 708; October 3, 1908, 670; *El Minero Mexicano,* December 4, 1902, 26; and C. A. Hamilton Report on La Mina Candelaria, 1889, 32, BL; also Cárdenas García, *Empresas y trabajadores,* 80.

12. Report on Pachuca Tailings Property, box 7, folder 2, Probert Papers, BLUT; *Engineering and Mining Journal,* January 5, 1907, 41–42; April 4, 1908, 708. American companies often bought properties "more for their dumps than anything else"; *Mexican Herald,* July 20, 1906. Processed ore—tailings—were often used to backfill mined-out spaces underground—"stopes."

13. Mexican mining engineer Manuel Bustamante, writing in *El Minero Mexicano,* October 31, 1901, 207; also Southworth, *Minas de México,* 178.

14. *Engineering and Mining Journal,* January 18, 1890, 82.

15. Julio Bazdresch, quoted in Cárdenas García, *Empresas y trabajadores,* 79.

16. Louis Lejeune, *Tierras mexicanas* (México: Mirada Viajera, 1995). On the increasing prevalence of low-grade ores in Mexican mines, see Mexico, Secretaría de Fomento, *Memoria* (1901–4), lxxxviii; *Mexican Mining Journal,* March 1908, 19–20; *Mexican Herald,* September 22, 1895, and June 17, 1906; and Dalhgren, *Historic Mines,* 15, 41. Also Velasco Avila et al., *Estado y minería,* 263, 338, 392, and Cárdenas García, *Empresas y trabajadores,* 69, 78–79.

17. Oscar Sánchez Rangel, "La última etapa de una empresa familiar en Guanajuato: La antigua casa Rul," *Legajos,* no. 4 (April–June 2010): 14, 33.

18. Cárdenas García, *Empresas y trabajadores,* 90. For the best account of patio process innovation, see Parra, "Experiencia"; also Sánchez Rangel, "Última etapa," 17–18, 31. On chlorination and lixiviation, see M. Bernstein, *Mexican Mining Industry,* 20.

19. *Mexican Mining Journal,* March 1908, 19; Mark R. Lamb, "Present Cyanide Practice in Mexico," *Engineering and Mining Journal,* April 4, 1908, 703. On decline in Guanajuato, see Sánchez Rangel, "Última etapa"; on the Pozos district, see *Engineering and Mining Journal,* May 7, 1910, 961–64; on Real de Monte in Pachuca, see Rocío Ruiz de la Barrera, "La empresa de Minas del Real del Monte (1849–1906). Medio siglo de explotación minera: ¿Casualidad o desarrollo estratégico?," in Marichal and Cerutti, *Historia,* 313.

20. Bernard MacDonald, "Development of the Cyanide Process for Silver Ores in Mexico," *Engineering and Mining Journal,* April 18, 1908, 802; Velasco Avila et al., *Estado y minería,* chap. 14.

21. Manuel Dublán and José Maria Lozano, *Legislación mexicana; o, colección completa de las disposiciones legislativas expedidas desde la independencia de la república, 1687–1910,* vol. 18 (Mexico: Imprenta de E. Dublán, 1876–1912), 287–88.

22. *El Hijo del Pueblo* (Guanajuato), March 11, 1906, 1.

23. On the Rae and Simpson patents, see Alan Lougheed, "The Discovery, Development, and Diffusion of New Technology: The Cyanide Process for the Extraction of Gold, 1887–1914," *Prometheus* 7, no. 1 (June 1989): 72 n. 10. The Cassel Company was a subsidiary of the Tharsis Company, which had extensive mining

properties in Spain and refining plants in Britain, and was itself a subsidiary of the St. Rollox Alkali Company of Glasgow.

24. For descriptions of the process developed by John Stewart MacArthur and William Forrest, see Todd, *Colonial Technology*, 113–14; Lougheed, "Discovery"; and Robert L. Spude, "Cyanide and the Flood of Gold: Some Colorado Beginnings of the Cyanide Process of Gold Extraction," *Essays and Monographs in Colorado History* 12 (1991): 1–35, as well as R. Chadwick, "New Extraction Processes for Metals," in *A History of Technology: The Late Nineteenth Century*, ed. Charles Singer and Trevor Williams (London: Oxford University Press, 1965), vol. 5.

25. Roger Burt, "Innovation or Imitation? Technological Dependency in the American Nonferrous Mining Industry," *Technology and Culture* 41, no. 1 (2000): 321–47; Lougheed, "Discovery"; Alan Lougheed, "The Cyanide Process and Gold Extraction in Australia and New Zealand, 1888–1913," *Australian Economic History Review* 27 (March 1987): 44–60; Sybil M. Jack, "The Introduction of Cyaniding in New Zealand: A Case Study in the Role of Technology in History," *Prometheus* 2, no. 1 (June 1984): 17–37; and Todd, *Colonial Technology*, chap. 7. The British patents are dated October 19, 1887, July 14, 1888, and July 16, 1888.

26. Burt, "Innovation or Imitation," 334.

27. Mexico, Secretaría de Hacienda y Crédito Público, *Estadística de la República Mexicana*, 2:8.

28. *El Minero Mexicano*, March 20, 1890, 79. For brief histories of the MacArthur-Forrest process in Mexico, see Velasco Avila et al., *Estado y minería*, chaps. 17–18; Sánchez Flores, *Historia de la tecnología*, 314–15; M. Bernstein, *Mexican Mining Industry*, 44–46.

29. *El Minero Mexicano*, March 20, 1890, 79.

30. See Bertram Hunt's letter to the editor of *Mining and Scientific Press*, August 28, 1908; also A. W. Allen, "Early History of the Cyanide Process," *Engineering and Mining Journal*, October 8, 1927, 569–74, who suggests that their work came in 1898.

31. Mexican patents #399 (conceded on January 20, 1893), #511 and #515 (November 30, 1893). The company later solicited and received #846 (April 21, 1896) and #925 (November 10, 1896). MGSRC agents in the field included George Williamson at the El Oro camp, Edward Halse in Sonora, and Loftos J. Nunn in Zacatecas; see *Mexican Herald*, September 1 and October 12, 1895, and March 17, 1896. The records of the Cassel Company are held in the Cheshire County Records Office, England. However, surviving records are limited to board minutes and reports; Todd, *Colonial Technology*, chaps. 8–9. I have been told by the Records Office archivist that there is no surviving correspondence or discussion related to Cassel's work in Mexico and the subsidiary Mexican company.

32. According to Hunt, the company was floated in 1892–93 (*Mining and Scientific Press*, August 28, 1908), although other sources place this later in the decade (see *The Mexican Year Book, 1914: A Financial and Commercial Handbook, Compiled from Official and Other Returns* [London: McCorquodale, 1914], 72). W.H. Trewartha-James managed the new company in the 1890s; *Mexican Herald*, October 17, 1895, 8. See also letters on the company's letterhead, dated 1891 and 1892: "The

Mexican Gold and Silver Recovery Company, Ltd., *Procedimiento privilegiado de cianuro. Sistema MacArthur-Forrest*," located at 2a Calle de la Providencia, No. 7, found in box 3, folder 4, D-E Miscellany, and box 3, folder 6, F-H Miscellany, Daniel M. Burns Papers, BLUC. For the Sinaloa office in Mazatlán, see the letter of its agent, J. W. Edwards, to Daniel Burns on March 27, 1902, box 3, folder 6, F-H Miscellany, Burns Papers, BLUC; see also correspondence in the Probert Papers, BLUT.

33. Uribe Salas, "Distrito minero," 52–56, and José Alfredo Uribe Salas, "El desarrollo de la minería michoacana en el siglo XIX," manuscript, n.d., accessed September 18, 2009, http://morgan.iia.unam.mx/usr/Industrial/BOL06/URIBE. html. See also Probert Papers, E60–E62, BLUT; T. A. Rickard, *Journeys of Observation* (San Francisco: Dewey, 1907), 54–56; *Mining and Scientific Press,* September 29, 1906; and *Mexican Herald,* September 1, 1895, which reported that the plant "now satisfactory [*sic*] worked." Compare, however, *TAIME* 37 (1906): 5, which reported that El Oro's cyanide mill no. 1 had been completed in 1899 and no. 2 in 1905. See also *El Minero Mexicano,* January 1, 1908, 9; *Engineering and Mining Journal,* October 8, 1927, 572; *Mining and Scientific Press,* September 29 and October 6, 1906. El Oro's early practice combined amalgamation at the stamping stage with subsequent cyanidation. On the Dos Estrellas mine, see Uribe Salas, "Desarrollo."

34. See the work of Juan Manuel Romero Gil, especially *Minería* and "La modernización de la minería Sonorense en el Porfiriato," in *Noroeste minero: La minería en Sonora, Baja California y Baja California Sur durante el Porfiriato,* ed. Francisco Altable (Mexico: Instituto Sudcaliforniano de Cultura, 2002), 17–90; also Mexico, Secretaria de Fomento, *Anales del Ministerio de Fomento,* vol. 5 (1881), 449, cited in Velasca Avila et al., *Estado y minería,* 370.

35. See *El Minero Mexicano,* December 8, 1902, 278–81, December 11, 1902, 301–3, and January 1, 1903, 3–5; also February 1, 1900, 63. See also Francis J. Hobson, "Cyanidation in Mexico" [1908], reprinted in *More Recent Cyanide Practice,* ed. H. Foster Bain (San Francisco: Mining and Scientific Press, 1910), 169, as well as *TAIME* 32 (1902): 179–215. However, see Southworth, *Minas de México,* 202, who in 1905 does not mention this mine but reports on the "relatively small hacienda and smelted with amalgamation and cyanide" of the Anglo-Mexican's Jesus-María mine. A report in the *Mexican Herald* (June 5, 1905, 7) places these plants a bit later, with the Charles Butters company supervising cyaniding plants (of Butters's own patented design) at Minas Prietas and Copala closer to 1905. Data from various primary and secondary sources on these early cyaniding plants are often ambiguous and sometimes contradictory. Sources often do not give full details of district, company, mine, mill, and supervising engineer. Romero Gil presents the best work on Porfirian mining in the Northwest (e.g., *Minería,* 189, 194–200, and "Modernización"). By 1898 there were three large companies operating cyaniding plants in the region: Creston-Colorado, Charles Butters, and Grand Central, the last of British capital.

36. Southworth, *Minas de México,* 219–21; also *El Minero Mexicano,* February 1, 1900, 63; *Engineering and Mining Journal,* January 3, 1903, 36; Romero Gil, *Minería,* 194–200, and "Minería y sociedad en el Noreste Porfiriana," *El Siglo Diez y Nueve* 1 (October 1991): 56–57; and Velasco Avila et al., *Estado y minería,* 382.

Charles Butters played a major role in diffusing and modifying the cyanide process (beginning in the Virginia City mines in Nevada) and invested in a number of mines in Sonora and Sinaloa (Romero Gil, "Modernización," 60). On the Palmarejo mill, see *TAIME* 36 (1905): 234–87.

37. Southworth and Holms, *Directorio oficial minero*, 26.

38. See also ibid., 23–24.

39. Mexico, Secretaría de Fomento, *Memoria* (1897–1900), 99–111, 523–74.

40. Calculated from Mexican production and price data in Christopher J. Schmitz, *World Non-ferrous Metal Production and Prices, 1700–1976* (London: Frank Cass, 1979), tables 5.18, 12.20, and 33.4.

41. In practice, metal-bearing ores were rarely exclusively gold or silver. Both minerals are typically found together, in widely varying ratios. Mineral-bearing veins in some regions were heavily gold dominant, as in the El Oro–Tlalpujahua district (one sample there assayed, per ton, 225 grams of gold and 2.5 grams of silver; M. Bernstein, *Mexican Mining Industry*, 67). But most ores in Mexico were heavily silver dominant. Often there were paying quantities of both metals in mined ore, making the choice of refining techniques very complicated and subject to extensive experimentation.

42. *TAIME* 36 (1905): 234–87.

43. Southworth and Holms, *Directorio oficial minero*, 23–24.

44. Mexico, Secretaría de Fomento, *Memoria* (1901–4), xc; *Mexican Herald*, September 8, 1895, and February 27, 1896. Also Velasco Avila et al., *Estado y minería*, 388.

45. *TAIME* 25 (1904): 13; *TAIME* 40 (1909): 764–65.

46. *Mining and Scientific Press*, August 1, 1908.

47. *El Minero Mexicano*, January 16, 1902.

48. MacDonald, "Development," 802.

49. Quote is from the "Preface to the Fourth English Edition" (1906), reproduced in the fifth edition of James Park's *The Cyanide Process of Gold Extraction: A Text-Book for the Use of Mining Students, Metallurgists, and Cyanide Operators* (London: Charles Griffin, 1913), vii.

50. Southworth, *Minas de México*, 109–15, 132; and for another survey with the same view, Mexico, Secretaría de Fomento, *Memoria* (1897–1900), 99–111, 523–74. See also Velasco Avila, *Estado y minería*, 388.

51. *Mining and Scientific Press*, August 29, 1908, and January 6, 1906; *Engineering and Mining Journal*, October 8, 1927, 572.

52. *Mining and Scientific Press*, August 1 and 8, 1908. In this retrospective self-authored article, the date is printed as 1906, but the relationship of these experiments with the installation of cyanide plants explained later in the piece implies a typographic error. See also T. A. Rickard's comments in *Mining and Scientific Press*, May 18, 1907. On Hobson, see Francisco Javier Meyer Cosío, *La minería en Guanajuato (1892–1913)* (Mexico: Colegio de Michoacán y la Universidad de Guanajuato, 1998), 204. Hobson's explanation of the process: "The importance of the tests lay in the discovery that silver could be successfully extracted from its ores . . . if ground

sufficiently fine, by subjecting the sand to a leach, wherein the silver was brought into contact with 30 times its weight of potassium cyanide, and that silver could be extracted from the slime if the latter was agitated with 16 times its weight of potassium cyanide." Hobson, "Cyanidation in Mexico," 168. The Durango mill was likely for the Candelaria Consolidated Mexican Mining Company; see C. P. Furry to D. M. Burns, August 8, September 14, November 11, and December 16, 1901, box 3, folder 39, and Genaro Escobar to Burns, November 10, 1900, box 4, folder 11, Burns Papers, BL.

53. A. Allen, "Early History," 573. Allen argues here that this was "the first successful commercial demonstration of the MacArthur-Forrest invention on a large scale in the treatment of a raw material in which silver predominated in quantity and value"; see also *Engineering and Mining Journal,* November 28, 1903, 826.

54. Bernard MacDonald, "How Cyanidation Was First Applied to Silver Ores," *Engineering and Mining Journal,* June 20, 1925, 1003–4, and "Development," 802–3; also *Mining and Scientific Press,* January 6, 1906, May 18, 1907, and June 29, 1907; *Engineering and Mining Journal,* May 3, 1902, 612; January 3, 1903, 35; October 3, 1908, 670; and October 8, 1927, 573; also Martin, *Mexico of the XXth Century,* chap. 70; Rafael Orozco, *La industria minera de México: Distrito de Guanajuato* (México: Talleres Gráficos de la Nación, 1922), chap. 8. See also *Hijo del Pueblo,* August 30 and November 29, 1903, and June 17, 1906. Velasco Avila et al., *Estado y minería,* 389, write that the first *experimental* cyanide plant in Guanajuato was erected by Charles Butters in 1902.

55. MacDonald, "How Cyanidation Was First Applied," 1003.

56. An account by Francis J. Hobson ("The Cyanide Process at Guanajuato," *Mining and Scientific Press,* January 6, 1906) places an earlier test in 1899, yielding poor results (a silver yield of only 40–85 percent of assayed value). He concurs that the 1902 tests conducted by E. M. Hamilton (of the Charles Butters Company, contracted by Guanajuato Consolidated through the MGSRC, testing ore from the Sirena mine) produced excellent results with over 90 percent yield, adding that Hobson himself replicated these results in the MacArthur-Forrest lab in Mexico City in 1904. See *Mining and Scientific Press,* January 6, 1906; MacDonald, "Development," 802–3; and T. A. Rickard in *Mining and Scientific Press,* May 18, 1907. MacDonald's article "How Cyanidation Was First Applied" clearly constructs its account to enhance his role in this innovation. His tests indicated that "fine grinding" meant passing through 200 mesh and the use of a 2.5 percent cyanide solution.

57. For accounts of the Guanajuato mining renaissance of 1904–7, see Meyer Cosío, *Minería en Guanajuato;* Southworth, *Minas de México;* as well as *Mexican Mining Journal,* January 1908, 22–23; *Engineering and Mining Journal,* September 23, 1905, 529; January 5, 1907, 41–42; April 4, 1908, 703–20; September 26, 1908, 615–20; October 3, 1908, 669–71; October 24, 1908, 806–8; November 14, 1908, 947–50; November 21, 1908, 997–1001; April 3, 1909, 691–94; and May 7, 1910, 961–63.

58. See the photographs of these in *Engineering and Mining Journal,* April 4, 1908, 705–70, as well as detailed process description; also September 26, 1908,

613–20; November 14, 1908, 947–50. The Nayal and San Próspero mills treated custom ore from regional mines; the Peregrina and Pinguico mills treated ores from the Development Company's own mines.

59. *El Hijo del Pueblo*, March 11, 1906, 1; *Mexican Herald*, August 4, 1906; Orozco, *Industria minera*, 74. Also *Mining and Scientific Press*, January 6, 1906; M. Bernstein, *Mexican Mining Industry*, 46. Hobson states in "Cyanidation in Mexico" that by 1908 Guanajuato's cyanide mills were treating collectively 2,500 tons daily, soon to be increased to 6,000 tons, divided among ten mills (most "of my own design").

60. MacDonald, "Development," 803; Lamb, "Present Cyanide Practice," 703.

61. On El Oro–Tlalpujahua, see José Alfredo Uribe Salas, "Empresas y empresarios en la minería michoacana de la segunda mitad del siglo xix," in *Minería regional mexicana: Primer Reunión de Historiadores de la Minería Latinoamericana (IV)*, ed. Dolores Avila Herrera and Rina Ortiz (Mexico: Instituto Nacional de Antropologia e Historia, 1994), 41–58. On Pachuca (and for the quote), *Mexican Herald*, November 24, 1906; see also *Engineering and Mining Journal*, January 5, 1907, 42; Sánchez Rangel, "Última etapa."

62. *Mexican Mining Journal*, March 1908, 19; A. Allen, "Early History," 573. The Pachuca district had suffered a great setback in early efforts of revival when nearly all its major mines flooded in early 1896, shutting down the district for some time; see the *Mexican Herald*, various articles through January and February 1896. However, this crisis forced the rapid adoption of new high-powered machinery, beginning with engines and pumps. *Engineering and Mining Journal*, July 27, 1907, 160, for the *hacienda de beneficio* San Francisco and La Union Hacienda.

63. *Engineering and Mining Journal*, January 5, 1907, 42. On Zacatecas, see Armando Márquez Herrera, "Las transformaciones de la minería zacatecana durante el porfiriato," in Avila Herrera and Ortiz, *Minería regional mexicana*, 59–76.

64. *Mexican Herald*, November 24, 1906. See also *Mexican Mining Journal*, March 1908, 19. For contemporary reference to the importance of the 1904–6 period, see *Engineering and Mining Journal*, January 6, 1906, 37.

65. *Mexican Mining Journal*, March 1908, 19. Also Romero Gil, "Modernización," 53.

66. *El Hijo del Pueblo*, March 11, 1906, 1.

67. *Engineering and Mining Journal*, January 5, 1907, 41.

68. *Mexican Mining Journal*, March 1908, 19; also *Mexican Herald*, June 17 and September 14, 1906, among many others.

69. MacDonald, "Development," 802; Andrés Villafana, *Reseña minera de la region central y sureste del estado de Jalisco* (Mexico: Imprenta de la Secretaría de Fomento, 1916), 92; Velasco Avila et al., *Estado y minería*, 282. Also *Mexican Mining Journal*, March 1908, 19; *Mining and Scientific Press*, August 1, 1908.

70. T. A. Rickard, "Old and New Methods at Guanajuato, Mexico," *Mining and Scientific Press* 94 (June 29, 1907): 824–25. Percentages estimated by multiplying the national count of refineries for each process published in Colegio de México, *Estadísticas económicas del Porfiriato: Fuerza del trabajo*, by the average annual production of plants for each process in a 1906 survey of Sonoran refineries (from

Romero Gil, "Modernización," 239, table 42). The cyanide process was just one part of a broader revolution in mineral refining that included lixiviation, large-scale smelting operations, and the flotation process.

71. Cárdenas García, *Empresas y trabajadores*, 12–13.

72. *Engineering and Mining Journal*, April 4, 1908, 706, 717; *TAIME* 36 (1905): 240; *Mining and Scientific Press*, May 18, 1907, 257, and references nearly ubiquitous in the articles and reports published in the major industry journals. See also Todd, *Colonial Technology*, 191–92.

73. Charles George Warnford Lock, *Gold Milling: Principles and Practice* (London: E. and F. N. Spon, 1901), xiii–xiv. Once the central elements of the chemical process and parameters for both amalgamation and cyanidation were established, local variations were predominantly mechanical and organizational; on amalgamation, see report by Manager A. J. Bowie, April 12, 1882, in Greene Gold and Silver Papers, BL. See also table of contents of John Edward Clennell, *The Cyanide Handbook* (New York: McGraw-Hill, 1910).

74. Logan Hovis and Jeremy Mouat, "Miners, Engineers, and the Transformation of Work in the Western Mining Industry, 1880–1930," *Technology and Culture* 37, no. 3 (1996): 450–54; also *Mining and Scientific Press*, June 8, 1907.

75. *Mexican Herald*, March 11, 1906; also Cárdenas García, *Empresas y trabajadores*, chap. 2; Velasco Avila et al., *Estado y minería*, 275.

76. Lamb, "Present Cyanide Practice," 703.

77. Romero quoted in Velasco Avila et al., *Estado y minería*, 392.

78. MacDonald, "How Cyanidation Was First Applied"; also Bertram Hunt in *Mining and Scientific Press*, August 29, 1908.

79. *TAIME* 40 (1909): 764.

80. "Preliminary Metallurgical Report on Ores from the Compañía de Real Del Monte y Pachuca," box 7, folder 3, p. 1, Probert Papers, BLUT.

81. Lamb, "Present Cyanide Practice," 703.

82. *Mining and Scientific Press*, May 18, 1907, 260.

83. *TAIME* 25 (1904): 12–31.

84. A. Allen, "Early History," 572; MacDonald, "How Cyanidation Was First Applied," 1003.

85. *Engineering and Mining Journal*, January 5, 1907, 41, and October 8, 1927, 572; *Mining and Scientific Press*, August 1, 1908. Skepticism about the viability of new processes was not confined to Mexico. Historians have noted the "skepticism" of miners in New Zealand and the United States—"outright incredulity"; see Jack, "Introduction of Cyaniding," 24; Lougheed, "Discovery," 66; Burt, "Innovation or Imitation," 335. Also MacDonald, "Development," 803; Ingeniero de Minas Manuel Bustamante, "Estudio sobre los métodos de amalgamación," *El Minero Mexicano*, October 31, 1901.

86. Southworth and Holms, *Directorio oficial minero*, 23–24; and chapter 7, below.

87. See T. A. Rickard's comments in *Mining and Engineering Press*, May 18, 1907, and Bernard MacDonald, "How Cyanidation Was First Applied," 1003–4. See also MacDonald, "Development," 802–3; and A. Allen, "Early History," 572–73.

88. See *Mining and Scientific Press,* December 15, 1906, also October 6, 1906, for a sampling among many such affirmations of the importance of fine grinding and sliming.

89. "Preliminary Metallurgical Report on Ores from the Compañía Real del Monte," box 7, folder 2, p. 16, Probert Papers, BLUT; "Preliminary Report on Ores from Mr. France," box 7, folder 2, Probert Papers, BLUT. *Slimes* refers to the most finely ground ore, capable of passing through wire screens of 150 to 200 mesh. Traditionally, grinding (in stamp mills, Chilean mills, *arrastres,* etc.) had always produced both sands and slimes but could not produce consistent slimes alone. Slimes resisted both concentrating and amalgamating treatment and were not effectively processed until the development of the cyanide process. One miner described the "jelly-like mass" of slimes, recalling that "a hog, running at full speed, jumped over the ridge one day and went out of sight [into the slime pit], never to appear again." *TAIME* 32 (1908): 208.

90. A. Allen, "Early History," 572. The tube mill—a cylindrical or conical barrel filled with hard pebbles—was first introduced in western Australia in 1898 by A. Trewartha-James, who had undertaken the first cyanide tests in Mexico seven years earlier. Tube mills produced an all-slime product (about 95 percent through 150 mesh). On tube mills in Mexico, see also *Mining and Scientific Press,* May 26, 1906; *TAIME* 32 (1906): 3–35 (on experiments at the El Oro mills); and *Engineering and Mining Journal,* April 4, 1908, 704–8, on their introduction in Guanajuato and Pachuca. Also on "all-slime" plants, see *Engineering and Mining Journal,* April 4, 1908, 717; June 20, 1925; and October 8, 1927. Francis Hobson gives a detailed account of ore-grinding issues during this period in "Cyanide Process at Guanajuato."

91. *Engineering and Mining Journal,* October 8, 1927, 572.

92. Techniques to facilitate fine grinding, pulp agitation, and solution filtering were not the only efficiency-improving innovations in cyaniding through these years, only the most important in the adaptation of cyaniding to silver ores. Others included experiments to substitute zinc dust for zinc shavings in the final stages; *Mining and Scientific Press,* December 15, 1906, and January 5, 1907; substituting sodium cyanide for potassium cyanide when miners found that the former would yield a sufficiently strong solution at nearly 25 percent less weight than potassium cyanide, reducing freight charges, especially for those mines a long mule-ride distance from rail stations; *TAIME* 36 (1905): 250.

93. Mexico, Secretaria de Industria, Comercio y Trabajo, *Anuario de estadística minera 1922* (1924), 101, quoted in Haber, Razo, and Mauer, *Politics of Property Rights,* 268, table 7.4.

94. J. Leslie Mennell, of *Mining World* (Mennell had some professional interest in this statement, as a chemist of the MGSRC; see J. L. Mennell to the chief metallurgist at the Real de Monte Company, August 21, 1906, Probart Papers, box 7, folder 2, BLUT); F. L. Bosqui, "Recent Improvements in the Cyanide Process," *Mining and Scientific Press,* December 15, 1906.

95. Production data from Schmitz, *World Non-ferrous Metal Production,* tables 5.18 and 12.20, also figures 6.1–3; export data from Kuntz Ficker, *Comercio exterior,*

473, table A.4; GDP data from Mexico, Instituto Nacional de Estadística, *Estadísticas historicas*, 1:401, table 8.1; see also Cárdenas García, *Empresas y trabajadores*, 67.

96. Moisés Gámez, *De negro brillante a blanco plateado: La empresa minera mexicana a finales del siglo XIX* (San Luis Potosí: Colegio de San Luis, 2001), 92, table 13; also Cárdenas Garcia, *Empresas y trabajadores*, 67, and Uribe Salas, "Distrito minero," 134.

97. Mexico, Secretaría de Fomento, *Memoria* (1901–4), lxxv.

98. H. A. C. Jenison's "Mining History of Mexico," *Engineering and Mining Journal*, March 3, 1923, 402; *Mexican Year Book, 1912*, 279. Contemporary estimates range from 323 to 363 million dollars. However, these represent simply the summed total of the capitalization of new firms. Actual dollars invested were likely lower; how much lower is difficult to estimate.

99. Quoted from Orozco, *Industria minera*, 131. US consul Letcher placed Mexican ownership at 2.6 percent; M. Letcher, "Wealth of Mexico," July 18, 1912, in US Department of Commerce and Labor, *Daily Consular and Trade Reports* (Washington, DC: Government Printing Office, 1912), 316.

100. Velasco Avila et al., *Estado y minería*, 397.

101. Southworth and Holms, *Directorio oficial minero*, 242, cited in Velasco Avila et al., *Estado y minería*, 368; Cárdenas García, *Empresas y trabajadores*, 75.

102. Parker, *Mules, Mines, and Me*, 33.

103. Swent, *Working for Safety*, 20. American's presence in key technical positions was not, however, universal. In Pachuca, for example, Francisco Narvaez managed the Hacienda La Union while Edmond Girault supervised the Mexican-owned San Rafael mines. Both oversaw new plants that showed "excellent results"; Southworth, *Minas de México*, 138; *Engineering and Mining Journal*, April 4, 1908, 708.

7. OBSTACLES TO ADOPTION

1. W. Clark, "Cotton Goods," 26.

2. Gregory Clark, "Why Isn't the Whole World Developed? Lessons from the Cotton Mills," *Journal of Economic History* 47, no. 1 (1987): 145–46.

3. *El Economista Mexicano*, September 10, 1886, 64.

4. Gómez-Galvarriato, *Industry and Revolution*, chap. 2; Barrera Pages, "Industrialización y revolución," chap. 3; also Sutton, "Malt and Beer"; Mexico, *Memoria sobre el estado . . . 1842*, 29–31, and *Memoria sobre el estado . . . 1844*, appendixes 17–19; J. Bazant, *Industria nacional*, 178–81, 299–300, 370; also see the cases of the Mexican Powder Company along the Río Hondo in the State of Mexico, box 1, folder 5, pp. 3–38, and folder 6, p. 23, and Los Altos Hornos Mexicanos, box 8, folder 9, p. 23, both in *ramo* Industrias Nuevas, AGN.

5. Sempat Assadourian, "Bomba de fuego," 401–2.

6. E. Beatty, *Institutions and Investment*, table 6. For chemical inputs, see the files of the Roessler and Hasslacher Chemical Company, box 31, folders 7–10, espe-

cially folder 8, pp. 55–57, *ramo* Industrias Nuevas, AGN; also *Boletín de la Sociedad Financiera Internacional,* January 1908.

7. For a sampling of contemporary commentary, see J. R. Flippin, *Sketches from the Mountains of Mexico* (Cincinnati, OH: Standard Publishing, 1889), 292; Southworth and Holms, *Directorio oficial minero,* 23–24; *Mining and Scientific Press,* June 8, 1907; Limantour to Brittingham, November 18, 1908, doc. 06–0013, AHJB; Dithridge to Brittingham, December 15, 1906, doc. 20–0070, AHJB; *El Economista Mexicano,* December 6, 1902, 200; *Mining and Scientific Press,* June 8, 1907; Lionel Carden, *Report on the Cotton Manufacturing Industry in Mexico,* British Diplomatic and Consular Reports, Miscellaneous Series, no. 453 (London: HMSO, 1898), 8; W. Clark, "Cotton Goods," 26; *Mexican Year Book, 1912,* 52; US Department of State, Bureau of Statistics, *Special Consular Report No. 5* (1891), 4 (for Sonora); US Department of Commerce, *Commercial Relations,* 444; Parker, *Mules, Mines, and Me,* 79; A. A. Graham, *Mexico with Comparisons and Conclusions* (Topeka: Crane, 1907), 15–16; *El Comerciante Mexicano,* March 9, 1883, 142, also chapter 5 above, notes 75–78. Secondary references include Lane Simonian, *Defending the Land of the Jaguar: A History of Conservation in Mexico* (Austin: University of Texas Press, 1995), 42–43, 56–58, 63–64, and chap. 4; M. Bernstein, *Mexican Mining Industry,* 36; Beezley, *Judas,* 69; Niccolai, "Algunas reflexiones," 205–6; Kuntz Ficker, *Empresa extranjera,* 86–87 (who notes that Mexico's wood supply was insufficient to satisfy the demands of railroad construction); Rosenzweig, "Industria," 363, 377; Mario Trujillo Bolio, *Operarios fabriles en el Valle de México 1864–1884* (Mexico: Colegio de Mexico, 1997), 53, 59; Randall, *Real del Monte,* 162–63; Keremitsis, *Industrial textil mexicana,* 20; Von Mentz de Boege, "Tecnología minera alemana," 5.

8. US Bureau of Foreign and Domestic Commerce, *Commercial Reports* (1901), 444; Challú and Gómez-Galvarriato, "Further Scrutiny."

9. W. Neil Adger et al., "Total Economic Value of Forests in Mexico," *Ambio* 24, no. 5 (1995): 287.

10. M. Bernstein, *Mexican Mining Industry,* 34–36; also *Engineering and Mining Journal,* April 18, 1908, 802; US Department of State, Bureau of Statistics, *Special Consular Report No. 5* (1891), 9; W. Clark, "Cotton Goods," 26 ("an inferior grade" compared to imported coal); US Department of Commerce and Labor, Bureau of Manufactures, *Special Consular Report No. 43,* pt. I (1910): 13; also Aurora Gómez-Galvarriato, "El desempeño de la Fundidora de Hierro y Acero de Monterrey durante el Porfiriato," in Marichal and Cerutti, *Historia,* 205; Keremitsis, *Industria textil mexicana,* 99.

11. US Department of State, Bureau of Statistics, *Special Consular Report No. 5* (1891), 3, and *Special Consular Report No. 6* (1891), 80; *Mexican Herald,* April 13, 1897, 5; Kuntz Ficker, *Comercio exterior,* table 5.3; the report of the US consul in Piedras Negras, US Department of State, Bureau of Statistics, *Special Consular Report No. 5* (1891), 12, and also US Department of Commerce, Bureau of Manufactures, *Special Consular Report No. 43,* pt. I (1910), 8. See also W. Clark, "Cotton Goods," 26; US Department of State, Bureau of Foreign Commerce, *Special Consular Report No. 21,* pt. I (1900), 242. In 1910 about 18 percent of Mexico's coal imports

came from Germany and 5 percent from Australia. See also Mexico, Secretaría de Fomento, *Memoria* (1897–1900), 532–33.

12. On coal prices, see Matías Romero, *Geographical and Statistical Notes on Mexico* (New York: G. P. Putnam's Sons, 1898), 533–34; US Department of State, Bureau of Statistics, *Special Consular Report No. 5* (1891), 3; *Mexican Herald,* April 13, 1897, 5; Matías Romero, *Report of the Secretary,* 23; Carden, *Report on the Cotton,* 8; and US Department of State, Bureau of Statistics, *Special Consular Report No. 21,* pt. 1 (1900), 243–45; *Engineering and Mining Journal,* April 18, 1908, 802; W. Clark, "Cotton Goods," 26; US Department of Commerce, Bureau of Manufactures, *Special Consular Report No. 43,* pt. 1 (1910), 10; box 28, folder 6, pp. 53–54, and folder 7, pp. 63–54, and box 31, folder 8, pp. 55–57, *ramo* Industrias Nuevas, AGN; *Diario oficial de la Federación,* October 11, 1909; also Jeremy Atack, Fred Bateman, and Thomas Weiss, "The Regional Diffusion and Adoption of the Steam Engine in American Manufacturing," *Journal of Economic History* 40, no. 2 (1980): 281–308.

13. Aviles-Galan, "'A Todo Vapor,'" 65; US Department of Commerce, Bureau of Manufactures, *Special Consular Report No. 43,* pt. 1 (1910), 14.

14. Quote from W. Clark, "Cotton Goods," 21; also Gómez-Galvarriato, "Desempeño," 228–30. Late twentieth-century reports still judged Mexico's coal resources to be small and of low quality; Robert-Bruce Wallace, "Coal in Mexico," 2008, www.economia.unam.mx/publicaciones/econinforma/pdfs/359/brucelish.pdf.

15. Matías Romero, *Mexico and the United States; A Study of Subjects Affecting Their Political, Commercial, and Social Relations, Made with a View to Their Promotion* (New York: G. P. Putnam, 1898), 23; *El Economista Mexicano,* December 6, 1902, 200; *Mexican Herald,* March 14, 1896, 7, October 19, 1906, and April 13, 1897, 5; Mexico, Ministerio de Hacienda y Crédito Público, *Expediente,* 152; J. A. Robertson to José Yves Limantour, February 27, 1895, in José Yves Limantour Papers, 1:12, Condumex, Mexico.

16. Brittingham to C. R. Hudson, January 6, 1910, doc. 33–279, AHJB.

17. US Department of State, Bureau of Statistics, *Special Consular Report No. 5* (1891), 9.

18. US Department of State, Bureau of Foreign Commerce, *Special Consular Reports,* no. 21, pt. I (1900), 246; Suárez Cortez, "Poder oligárquico"; Rocío Castañeda González, "Esfuerzos públicos y privados para el abasto de agua a Toluca (1862–1910)," in *Historia de los usos del agua en México; oligarquías, empresas y ayuntamientos (1840–1940),* ed. Blanca Estela Cortez (Mexico: Comisión Nacional de Agua, 1998), 107–82; and Trujillo Bolio, *Operarios fabriles,* 50–51.

19. Margaret Towner, "Monopoly Capitalism and Women's Work during the Porfiriato," *Latin American Perspectives* 4, nos. 1–2 (1977), table 2, calculated from data in Colegio de México, *Estadísticas económicas del porfiriato: Fuerza de trabajo.* See also Donald B. Keesing, "Structural Change Early in Development: Mexico's Changing Industrial and Occupational Structure from 1895 to 1950," *Journal of Economic History* 29, no. 4 (1969): 725.

20. Armando Razo and Stephen H. Haber, "The Rate of Growth of Productivity in Mexico, 1850–1933: Evidence from the Cotton Textile Industry," *Journal of Latin American Studies* 30 (1998): 496–99, tables 1, 2, and 6.

21. Rodney D. Anderson, "Guadalajara's Artisans and Shopkeepers, 1842–1907: The Origins of a Mexican Petite Bourgeoisie," in Guedea and Rodríguez O., *Five Centuries*, 299.

22. Gámez, *De negro brillante*, 92; Velasco Avila et al., *Estado y minería*, 163; Cárdenas García, *Empresas y trabajadores*, 67, 88. Also Uribe Salas, "Distrito minero," 134.

23. W. Clark, "Cotton Goods," 21–26. See also Haber, *Industry and Underdevelopment*, 34–35; Gómez-Galvarriato, *Industry and Revolution,* chap. 10.

24. Novelo, "Ferrerías y fundiciones," 189; Haber, *Industry and Underdevelopment*, 34–37.

25. Jonathan Brown, "Foreign and Native-Born Workers."

26. Haber, *Industry and Underdevelopment*, 34; In contrast, see Gómez-Galvarriato, *Industry and Revolution,* chap. 10, and Gómez-Galvarriato, "Desempeño," 228.

27. Mora-Torres, *Making of the Mexican Border*, 254–55; *Mexican Year Book, 1908*, 537; Gómez-Galvarriato, "Desempeño."

28. Mexican producers also faced dumping by US firms; Mora-Torres, *Making of the Mexican Border*, 258–61. On tariff levels, E. Beatty, *Institutions and Investment*, table 6.

29. Haber, *Industry and Underdevelopment*, chap. 7; Maurer, "Rents."

30. Gómez-Galvarriato, "Desempeño," 232–34; Aviles-Galan, "'A Todo Vapor,'" 95 n. 113.

31. US Bureau of Foreign and Domestic Commerce, *Commercial Reports*, nos. 1–75 (1910), 519, reporting that the air currents were produced by crude bellows or fans, nearly always run by hand, with the simple iron parts constructed by local blacksmiths.

32. Based on Pilcher, "Mad Cowmen," and Jeffrey M. Pilcher, "Fajitas and the Failure of Refrigerated Meatpacking in Mexico: Consumer Culture and Porfirian Capitalism," *Americas* 60, no. 3 (2004): 411–29. In addition, see box 6, folders 1–3, *ramo* Industrias Nuevas, AGN; *El Economista Mexicano*, April 19, 1902, 43, June 7, 1902, 167, July 5, 1902, 259, September 27, 1902, 512–13, November 8, 1902, 123, March 28, 1903, 566, August 6, 1904, 409, and February 8, 1908, 366; also the files of the company in the Missouri Historical Society.

33. Haber, *Industry and Underdevelopment*, chap. 4; Juan Carlos Moreno-Brid and Jaime Ros, *Development and Growth in the Mexican Economy: A Historical Perspective* (New York: Oxford University Press, 2009), chap. 3.

34. Noel Maurer, "Rents"; Haber, *Industry and Underdevelopment*, chaps. 5 and 7.

35. E. Beatty, *Institutions and Investment*, chap. 6; Haber, *Industry and Underdevelopment*, chap. 6.

36. Haber, Razo, and Maurer, *Politics of Property Rights*; E. Beatty, *Institutions and Investment*, chaps. 4, 6, and 7.

37. E. Beatty, *Institutions and Investment*, 121–22.

38. US Department of Commerce, *Commercial Relations* (1886–87), 335, and (1896–97), 486, among others. For anthropological accounts, see Artemio Cruz León, *Los instrumentos agrícolas en la zona central de Veracruz* (Chapingo, Mexico: Universidad Autónoma de Chapingo, 1989), and Guy Stresser-Pean, "El arado criollo en México y en América Central," in *Homenaje a Isabel Kelly*, ed. Yólotl González (Mexico: INAH, 1989), 197–226.

39. Frank Tannenbaum, *The Struggle for Peace and Bread* (New York: Knopf, 1950). Another 1930s study reported just 0.9 cultivators and 0.3 sowing machiners per every hundred villagers; Chase, *Mexico*, 211; also US Department of Commerce and Labor, *Special Consular Report No. 27* (1903), xxvii, 109–13.

40. Coatsworth, *Orígenes del atraso*, chap. 7; Tortolero Villaseñor, *De la coa*, chap. 2; also González y González, *San José de Gracia*, 107.

41. See, for one example, Emilio Kourí, *A Pueblo Divided: Business, Property, and Community in Papantla, Mexico* (Stanford, CA: Stanford University Press, 2004), 67, chap. 2, and 319 n. 89.

42. Stresser-Pean, "Arado criollo," 211; US Department of Commerce, *Commercial Relations* (1896–97), 114.

43. Paul Friedrich, *Agrarian Revolt in a Mexican Village* (Chicago: University of Chicago Press, 1977); Womack, *Zapata*; John Tutino, *From Insurrection to Revolution in Mexico: Social Bases of Agrarian Violence, 1750–1940* (Princeton, NJ: Princeton University Press, 1986), among many others.

44. Beezley, *Judas*, 84, from an account by Henry Howard Harper, *A Journey in Southeastern Mexico: Narrative of Experiences and Observations on Agricultural and Industrial Experiences* (Boston, 1910).

45. Beezley, *Judas*, 86.

46. Cruz León, *Instrumentos agrícolas*, 43; also Stresser-Pean, "Arado criollo," 203, 212, 219.

47. US Department of Commerce and Labor, *Special Consular Report No. 27* (1903), xxvii, 117.

48. Romero, *Report of the Secretary*, 111.

49. Tortelero Villaseñor, *De la coa*, chaps. 2–3.

50. Machine import data; see Appendix 2.

51. Riguzzi, "Caminos del atraso," 31–98.

52. Box 14, folders 4–6, and boxes 15–17, Industrias Nuevas, AGN; José Yves Limantour Papers, series 1, roll 12, April 24, 1897, Condumex, Mexico.

53. Gómez-Galvarriato, "Primer impulso industrializador."

54. E. Beatty, *Institutions and Investment*, 72–73; Guajardo, *Trabajo y tecnología*, 118–19.

55. Quoted in Guajardo, *Trabajo y tecnología*, 119.

56. Ibid., 163.

57. Quoted in Alvarado, "We Welcomed Foreign Fabrics," 299–300.

58. Anderson, "Guadalajara's Artisans," 198.

59. Keesing, "Structural Change"; in Aguascalientes, see Gómez Serrano, "Ciudad pujante," 256.

60. Vanessa E. Teitelbaum, *Entre el control y la movilización: Honor, trabajo y solidaridades artesanales en la Ciudad de México a mediados del siglo XIX*, Estudios históricos (Mexico: Colegio de México, 2008); and Sonia Pérez Toledo, *Los hijos del trabajo: Los artesanos de la Ciudad de México, 1780–1853* (Mexico: Colegio de México, 2011).

61. Coralia Gutiérrez Alvarez, "La penosa existencia en las fábricas textiles de Puebla y Tlaxcala," in Staples, *Bienes y vivencias*, 541; Anderson, *Outcasts in Their Own Land*, 94–95.

62. López-Alonso, *Measuring Up*.

63. Robert Fogel, "The Persistence of Misery in Europe and America before 1900," in *The Escape from Hunger and Premature Death, 1700–2100* (Cambridge: Cambridge University Press, 2004).

64. Patrick Frank, *Posada's Broadsheets: Mexican Popular Imagery, 1890–1910* (Albuquerque: University of New Mexico Press, 1998), 187–90.

65. *El Imparcial*, June 20, 1902, 2.

66. Cited in Cott, "Porfirian Investment Policies," 297.

67. Beezley, *Judas*, 126–28.

68. Ballou, *Aztec Land*, 38–39; see also 72–73 and Christopher R. Boyer, *Becoming Campesinos: Politics, Identity, and Post-Revolutionary Struggle in Michoacán, 1920–1935* (Stanford, CA: Stanford University Press, 2003), 52.

69. *Mexican Trader*, March 30, 1893, 189; General Lew Wallace in Chihuahua, 1867, quoted in *The Mexican Year Book: The Standard Authority on Mexico, 1920–21* (Los Angeles: Mexican Year Book Co., 1922), 270.

70. Covo, *Ideas de la Reforma*, 36; also *Economista Mexicano*, September 10, 1886, 64; Ballou, *Aztec Land*, 73, for one of many examples.

71. Charles Fletcher Lummis, *The Awakening of a Nation: Mexico of To-day* (New York: Harper, 1898), 75.

72. Howell, *Mexico*, 45; also Beezley, *Judas*, especially 126–28; US Department of Commerce and Labor, *Special Consular Report No. 27* (1903), xxvii, 110.

73. Romero, *Report of the Secretary*, 111.

74. C. P. Bond, of Massachusetts, quoted in *Mexican Herald*, December 12, 1895, 7.

75. *Mexican Trader*, February 23, 1893, 107; see also Parker, *Mules, Mines, and Me*, 92–93; T. A. Rickard, *Journeys of Observation* (San Francisco: Dewey, 1907), 101; *El Hijo del Pueblo* (Guanajuato), September 30, 1906.

76. Vizcaya Canales, *Orígenes de la industrialización*, 40; also *El Comerciante Mexicano*, April 6, 1898, 206.

77. Antoni Maczak, "Observations on Wealth and Economic Development in Renaissance and Baroque Travel Literature," in *State and Society in Europe from the Fifteenth Century to the Eighteenth Century*, ed. Jaroslaw Pelenski (Warsaw: Warsaw University Press, 1985), 237; compare, for instance, with the discussion in Beezley, *Judas*, 68–76; also Arnold, *Everyday Technology*, 23–24.

1. Richard R. Nelson, ed., *National Innovation Systems: A Comparative Analysis* (Oxford: Oxford University Press, 1993).

2. *La Union* (Monterrey), quoted in *El Economista Mexicano*, July 1, 1899, 255.

3. Haber, *Industry and Underdevelopment*, chap. 4.

4. Mora-Torres, *Making of the Mexican Border*, 249–52; Hibino, "Cervecería Cuauhtémoc." See also Dithridge to Brittingham and Terrazas, November 15, 1906, doc. 20–0073, AHJB. On Monterrey's business culture, see Mario Cerutti, *Burguesía, capitales e industria en el norte de México, Monterrey y su ámbito regional (1850–1910)* (Mexico: Alianza Editora, 1992).

5. Rosenzweig, "Industria," 381.

6. *Mexican Herald,* October 30, 1895. See also, for example, recent work by Juan Manuel Romero Gil, José Alfredo Uribe Sales, Alma Parra, and Moisés Gámez (see bibliography for full citations), and Orozco, *Industria minera de México*, 139 ff.

7. Payrolls can be found in BLUC: for instance, the *Memoria de Raya* from the Cuyutlan Gold Mining Company, MSS M-M 1700:60.

8. Published accounts include Rickard, *Journeys of Observation*, and Parker, *Mules, Mines, and Me*, among others. Unpublished accounts can be found in BLUC and BLUT, as in the case of the Daniel Burns Papers, the Santa Rosa de Ures Mining Company Papers, the Edward Otho Cresap Ord Papers, and the Minas Nuevas Mining Company Papers, all at BLUC.

9. On the oil industry, see Myrna I. Santiago, *The Ecology of Oil: Environment, Labor, and the Mexican Revolution, 1900–1938* (Cambridge: Cambridge University Press, 2006), 150.

10. See the correspondence of engineers from Mexico, the US West, and South Africa to the *Mining and Scientific Press* between August 1908 and February 1909, collected in Bain, *More Recent Cyanide Practice*, 176–89. See also Bertram Hunt, "Cyanidation in Mexico," *Mining and Scientific Press,* August 29, 1908; Jeremy Mouat, "The Development of the Flotation Process: Technological Change and the Genesis of Modern Mining, 1898–1911," *Australian Economic History Review* 36, no. 1 (1996): 5.

11. Hobson, "Cyanidation in Mexico"; Robert L. Spude, "Cyanide," 10.

12. "Preliminary Report on Ores from Mr. France," July 4, 1906, box 7, folder 2, Probert Papers, BLUT.

13. *Mexican Mining Journal,* March 1908, 20.

14. The field notebooks carried by mining engineers illustrate their constant search for more effective and efficient methods; see, for example, the notebook of Stuart Ingram (MSS 81/40 pm, BLUC), with its "Notes for cyanide plant" and "Stope costs Cuyutlan Gold Mines Co."

15. Riguzzi, "Caminos del atraso," 77–78.

16. Guajardo Soto, *Trabajo y tecnología*, chaps. 3 and 7, "Between the Workshop and the State," 16, 26, 33, and "Tecnología de los Estados Unidos."

17. C. López-Cajún et al., "Steam Locomotives in the History of Technology of Mexico," *International Symposium on History of Machines and Mechanisms: Proceed-*

ings of HHM 2008, ed. Hong-Sen Yan and Marco Ceccarelli (Dordrecht: Springer, 2009), 151–64.

18. On electrical companies, see Galarza, *Industria eléctrica en México*; Liehr and Torres Bautista, *Compañías eléctricas extranjeras*. On public works, see Patricia Connolly, *El contratista de don Porfirio: Obras públicas, deuda y desarrollo desigual* (Mexico: Fondo de Cultura Económico, 1997), and Sandra Kuntz Ficker and Patricia Connolly, *Ferrocarrilles y obras públicas* (Mexico: Instituto Mora, 1999). On Weetman Pearson's dependence on imported expertise, see also *Mexican Herald,* February 19, 1896, 8.

19. Jonathan Brown, *Oil and Revolution in Mexico* (Berkeley: University of California Press, 1993), 110, 145; Guajardo Soto, *Trabajo y tecnología,* 151; Santiago, *Ecology of Oil,* 185; also Medina, "Dinamismo frustrado," 246.

20. Alamán, "Representación," 190–91.

21. Trabulse, *Círculo roto,* 23.

22. *La Sociedad,* June 1, 1865, 4.

23. Antuñano, *Pensamientos,* 17.

24. Mexico, Secretaría de Fomento, *Memoria* (1857), doc. 18–2, pp. 73–77, 152–54; *Memoria* (1876–77), 535.

25. Mexico, Ministerio de Hacienda y Crédito Público, *Expediente,* 152; Von Mentz de Boege, "Tecnología minera alemana," 14.

26. Gómez-Galvarriato, "Primer impulso industrializador," 44–46.

27. Quoted in Rosenzweig, "Industria," 374.

28. Tenorio-Trillo, *Mexico at the World's Fairs,* 134. On skill development at the Fundición del Gobierno in Mexico City, see Rosenzweig, "Industria," 385.

29. *Mexican Herald,* February 8, 1896, 8.

30. William F. Maloney and Felipe Valencia Caicedo, "Engineers, Innovative Capacity and Development in the Americas," IZA Discussion Paper No. 8271, Institute for the Study of Labor, Bonn, June 2014; also Jeremy, *Transatlantic Industrial Revolution* and *International Technology Transfer.*

31. Gerschenkron, *Economic Backwardness.*

32. Genaro Raigosa, "Agricultura," in Sierra, *México,* vol. 2.

33. *Mexican Herald,* August 17, 1896, 4.

34. *Boletín de Instrucción Pública,* December 1, 1911. On science education, see Elías Trabulse, *Historia de la ciencia en México: Estudios y textos* (Mexico: Fondo de Cultura Económica, 1983).

35. Mexico, Instituto Nacional de Estadística (INEGI), *Estadísticas históricas de México,* vol. 1, table 2.5; Richard Easterlin, "Why Isn't the Whole World Developed?" *Journal of Economic History* 41, no. 1 (1981): 1–19; Forment, *Democracy in Latin America,* 1:243–44.

36. Gómez-Galvarriato, *Industry and Revolution,* chap. 3; Toussaint Alcaraz, *Escenario de la prensa,* chaps. 3 and 6. Also Mexico, INEGI, *Estadísticas históricas de México,* table 2.5. In Monterrey, literacy was nearly 60 percent in 1921; Snodgrass, *Deference and Defiance,* 113.

37. Gómez-Galvarriato, *Industry and Revolution,* chap. 2; Keesing, "Structural Change," 729.

38. *Boletín de Instrucción Pública* 1 (1903): 356, 360–61, quoted in Mílada Bazant, *Historia de la educación durante el porfiriato* (Mexico: Colegio de México, 1993), 116. The following paragraphs are based on the work of Mílada Bazant unless otherwise noted. See especially her *Historia de la educación,* in particular chap. 5, as well as her chapters "La enseñanza y la práctica de la ingeniería durante el porfiriato," in *La educación en la historia de México,* ed. Josefina Zoraida Vázquez (Mexico: Colegio de México, 1992), and "La educación técnica durante el porfiriato," in *La ciudad y el campo en la historia de México: Memoria de la VII Reunión de Historiadores Mexicanos y Norteamericanos 1985* (México: UNAM, 1992), 915–25.

39. Lerdo de Tejada, *Comercio exterior,* 143; also Sánchez Flores, *Historia de la tecnología,* 288–89.

40. M. Bazant, *Historia de la educación,* 108; also *El Hijo del Pueblo* (Guanajuato), August 23, 1903.

41. M. Bazant, *Historia de la educación,* Anexo 1.

42. *El Imparcial,* June 20, 1902, 2.

43. Guajardo Soto, *Trabajo y tecnología,* 55–57, 147–49.

44. On the numbers, see M. Bazant, *Historia de la educación,* Appendix 1, and also 110, 112. The labor force was calculated in 1895 at about 4.5 million, of which about 17 percent worked in the modern sector (manufacturing, mining, transportation, and construction); see also Guajardo Soto, *Trabajo y tecnología,* table 3.1.

45. *Diario de los Debates,* 15th Legislature (1890), 1, 78–79. See also *Mexican Herald,* August 17, 1896, 4, and September 5, 1897, 4, for calls to establish a polytechnic institute. See also F. Katz, "Liberal Republic," 76.

46. M. Bazant, *Historia de la educación,* 241–42.

47. Ibid., 243, and "Enseñanza," Appendix 1.

48. Riguzzi, "Caminos del atraso," table 3.

49. *El Minero Mexicano,* September 22, 1887, 299.

50. M. Bazant, *Historia de la educación,* 248–53, also Tortolero Villaseñor, *De la coa*; and María Cecilia Zuleta, "La Secretaría de Fomento y el fomento agrícola en México, 1876–1910: La invención de una agricultura próspera que no fue," *Mundo Agrario: Revista de Estudios Rurales* 1, no. 1 (2000): n.p.

51. *Boletín de Instrucción Pública,* July 20, 1907, 700; M. Bazant, "Educación técnica," 918. Mexico's first forestry school was founded in 1908 with support from the French government, arranged by Miguel Angel de Quevedo. It soon had thirty-two students but fell victim to the revolutionary turmoil; Simonian, *Defending the Land,* 25.

52. Sierra, *México,* 2:42–44.

53. The *Colegio Militar* also trained military officers in civil and mechanical engineering. Its curriculum underwent substantial reform during the Porfiriato, upgrading standards and promoting more practical education and training. However, the impact of reform on military capabilities and technical expertise was limited to a small core of newly professionalized officers. James R. Kelley, "The Education and Training of Porfirian Officers: Success or Failure?" *Military Affairs* 39, no. 3 (October 1975): 124–28.

54. Mexico, Secretaría de Fomento, *Boletín Semestral de la República Mexicana, 1889, á cargo del Dr. Antonio Peñafiel* (1890), 61. UNESCO would recommend a goal of nine per thousand for developing countries in 1970; Strassmann, *Technological Change*, 275. This would have implied over 10,000 engineers in Mexico in 1910, rather than the roughly 450 produced by the engineering schools over the previous thirty-five years.

55. Maloney and Valencia Caicedo, "Engineers," appendix.

56. M. Bazant, "Educación técnica," 917–18; Juan José Saldaña, "The Failed Search for 'Useful Knowledge': Enlightened Scientific and Technological Policies in New Spain," in *Cross Cultural Diffusion of Science: Latin America*, vol. 5, *Acts of the XVII International Congress of History of Science*, edited by Juan José Saldaña, Cuadernos de Quipu 2 (Berkeley: Sociedad Latinoamericana de Historia de las Ciencias y la Tecnología, 1987), 49–50.

57. On this transition in the western United States, see Kathleen H. Ochs, "The Rise of American Mining Engineers: A Case Study of the Colorado School of Mines," *Technology and Culture* 33, no. 2 (1992): 278–301; Logan Hovis and Jeremy Mouat, "Miners, Engineers"; Burt, "Innovation or Imitation"; and Spude, "Cyanide."

58. *Mexican Mining Journal*, January, 1908, 10.

59. Cárdenas García, *Empresas y trabajadores*, 16.

60. William Lazonick, "What Happened to the Theory of Economic Development?" in *Favorites of Fortune: Technology, Growth, and Economic Development since the Industrial Revolution*, ed. Patrice Higonnet, David S. Landes, and Henry Rosovsky (Cambridge, MA: Harvard University Press, 1991), 283–84.

61. Zuleta, "Secretaría de Fomento."

62. See, for example, Lomnitz and Peréz-Lizaur, *Mexican Elite Family*, 220.

63. Paz, *Álbum de la paz*, 101–4. See also the entries on Mexico's exhibitions in several world's fairs in Tenorio-Trillo, *Mexico at the World's Fairs*, chap. 8.

64. Simonian, *Defending the Land*, chap. 4.

65. Trabulse, *Círculo roto*, 21.

66. On the scarcity of *industriales científicos* in Mexico, see *El Minero Mexicano*, September 22, 1887, 299. See also M. Bazant, "Educación técnica," 918; Edward Beatty, "Visiónes del futuro: La reorientación de la política económica en México (1867–1893)," *Signos Históricos* 10 (July–December 2003): 39–56; and Tenorio-Trillo, *Mexico at the World's Fairs*, chap. 2 on the "wizards of progress."

67. Ezequiel Ordoñez, "Memoir of Antonio del Castillo," in *Bulletin of the Geological Society of America, Vol. 7*, edited by Joseph Stanley Brown (Rochester, NY: Geological Society of America, 1896), 486–87.

68. *Hijo del Pueblo* (Guanajuato), August 23, 1903.

69. M. Bazant, "Educación técnica," 920.

70. Henry Ewing, of Chihuahua's Mormon colony, ran *La Unión Mercantil* and distributed technical information from the United States concerning irrigation and agriculture; *Utah since Statehood: Historical and Biographical*, vol. 4 (Chicago: S.J. Clarke, 1920), 587. See also Haber, *Industry and Underdevelopment*, chap. 5; on Creel, see Mark Wasserman, "Enrique Creel: Business and Politics in Mexico,

1880–1930," *Business History Review* 59, no. 4 (1985): 645–62; on Braniff, see Martin, *Mexico of the XXth Century*, 2:234–35.

71. Trabulse, *Historia de la ciencia;* also Forment, *Democracy in Latin America,* chap. 11; Alvarado, "We Welcomed Foreign Fabrics," 285 n. 73.

72. *El Tiempo,* January 31, 1893, 2.

73. Elsa Barberena Blázquez and Carmen Block Iturriaga, "Publicaciones periódicas científicas y tecnológicas mexicanas del siglo XIX: Un proyecto de bases de datos," *Quipu* 3, no. 1 (January–April 1986): 7–26.

74. *El Minero Mexicano,* December 14, 1876.

75. For example, *El Minero Mexicano,* December 10, 1874, September 22, 1887, and February 6, 1890.

76. See, for example, *El Minero Mexicano,* February 1, 1900, 52; February 15, 1900, 74; and February 22, 1900, 88. For a similar critique, see Trabulse, *Círculo roto,* 178–80.

77. *El Minero Mexicano,* January 8, 1903, 15–17, January 15, 1903, 27–29, and January 22, 1903, 38–40.

78. See issues of *Mining and Scientific Press* and *Engineering and Mining Journal* between 1890 and 1910, especially A. Allen, "Early History," 574; also Lamb, "Present Cyanide Practice," 703. C. W. Van Law, superintendent of the cyanide plant of the Guanajuato Reduction and Mining Company, ended one of his many published reports with a collegial "trusting that the above data may be of interest to some of your readers"; *Engineering and Mining Journal,* July 14, 1907.

79. Trabulse, *Círculo roto,* 21.

80. Ian Inkster, "Science and the Mechanics' Institutes, 1820–1850: The Case of Sheffield," *Annals of Science* 32 (1975): 451–74, or, for instance, the Franklin Institute of Philadelphia or the *Scientific American.*

81. Castañeda González, "Esfuerzos públicos y privados," 178.

82. Tenorio Trillo, "Stereophonic Scientific Modernisms."

83. Aldo Musacchio and Ian Read, "Bankers, Industrialists, and Their Cliques: Elite Networks in Mexico and Brazil during Early Industrialization," *Enterprise and Society* 8, no. 4 (2007): 842–80.

84. Mexico, Secretaría de Fomento, *Memoria* (1887), 538–57, quoted in M. Bazant, "Educación técnica," 916; *Diario de los Debates,* 15th Legislature (1890, vol. 1), 78–79; also the letter of José Yves Limantour of September 20, 1898, box 1, folder 12, *ramo* Industrias Nuevas, AGN.

85. M. Bazant, "Enseñanza," 186–96. See also *El Minero Mexicano,* September 22, 1887, 299; Tenorio Trillo, "Stereophonic Scientific Modernisms," 1167.

86. E. Beatty, *Institutions and Investment,* chap. 4 on patent law and chap. 6 on Industrias Nuevas contracts; on the terms of extraction concessions, see *Engineering and Mining Journal,* December 31, 1910, 1312; also Cárdenas García, *Empresas y trabajadores,* 66.

87. Article 4 of the 1882 Proyecto de Ley, Mexico, Secretaría de Fomento, *Memoria* (1877–82), 1:435; *Memoria:* (1901–4), cxxxvi; also Sánchez Flores, *Historia de la tecnología,* 382.

88. *Boletín de Instrucción Pública,* July 20, 1907, 699–700.

89. Among many others, see Carlos F. Landero, *Exámen termoquímico de algunas reacciones relativas a la formación del cloruro de plata* (Mexico: Oficina Tipográfica de la Secretaría de Fomento, 1889).

90. *El Imparcial,* June 20, 1902, 2.

91. Mexico, Secretaría de Fomento, *Memoria* (1876–77), 530; *Mexican Herald,* October 26, 1895.

92. On the exhibitions, see *Mexican Herald,* January 28, 1896, March 21, 1896, April 17, 1896, and January 1, 1903; also Dublán y Lozano, *Legislación mexicana,* 35:491–95, 698. On municipal and state support, see *Mexican Herald,* March 10, April 18, and August 16, 1902; also the prospectus of the 1896 Mexican International Exposition, in SMRC, 104:1.

93. Potash, *Mexican Government,* 21; Alvarado, "We Welcomed Foreign Fabrics," 189, 236. Also see E. Beatty, *Institutions and Investment,* chap. 3; Márquez, "Tariff Protection." Machinery entered Mexico tariff free until 1897 and was taxed at about 5 percent of its invoice value thereafter.

94. E. Beatty, *Institutions and Investment,* chap. 4; Sánchez Flores, *Historia de la tecnología,* 382.

95. See, for instance, the letter of José Yves Limantour on February 27, 1895, box 1, folder 12, *ramo* Industrias Nuevas, AGN.

96. Gómez-Galvarriato, *Industry and Revolution,* chap. 9.

97. For partial exceptions, see Castañeda González, "Esfuerzos públicos," and the *Boletínes* published by the agricultural experimentation station in San Juan Bautista, Tabasco, 1910, and in Ciudad Juárez, Chihuahua, 1907–9.

98. Alvarado, "We Welcomed Foreign Fabrics," 185–86, 196, 216; Potash, *Mexican Government,* 112, 206.

99. Based on analyses of patent streams in the author's patent database; see Appendix 2.

100. Riguzzi, "Caminos del atraso," 78.

101. Quote from *Economista Mexicano,* September 10, 1886, 63.

9. CONCLUSION

1. Landero y Cos to the Ministerio de Fomento, January 10, 1901, box 29, folder 1, *ramo* Industrias Nuevas, AGN.

2. Paz, *Álbum de la paz.*

3. *La Unión* (Monterrey), quoted in *El Economista Mexicano,* July 1, 1899, 255.

4. Haber, Razo, and Maurer, *Politics of Property Rights,* table 5.13.

5. Marcelo G. Aramburu, "El desarrollo de las industrias de transformación en México," *Revista de Economía* 4, no. 5 (May 1941): 409. See also Jaime Aboites, *Breve historia de un invento olvidado* (Mexico: UAM, 1989), 53; Susan M. Gauss, *Made in Mexico: Regions, Nation, and the State in the Rise of Mexican Industrialism, 1920s–1940s* (University Park: Pennsylvania State University Press, 2010), 152, 169,

184; Gómez-Galvarriato, *Industry and Revolution*, chap. 9; Moreno-Brid and Ros, *Development and Growth*, 117; and Clark W. Reynolds, *The Mexican Economy: Twentieth Century Structure and Growth* (New Haven, CT: Yale University Press, 1970), 181, 300.

6. For the quotes on "dependence" and on "weak," "scarce," "restricted," and "backward" technological capabilities, as well as a broader discussion, see Nacional Financiera, Comisión Económica para la América Latina, *La política industrial en el desarrollo económico de México* (Mexico: Nacional Financiera, 1971); Nacional Financiera, *México: Los bienes de capital en la situación económica presente* (Mexico: Nacional Financiera, 1985), 19, 139–42, 215, 279–80; Kurt Unger, "El desarrollo industrial y tecnológico mexicano: Estado actual de la integración industrial y tecnológica," in *Aspectos tecnológicos de la modernización industrial de México,* ed. Pablo Mulás del Pozo (Mexico: Academia de la Investigación Científica y Fondo de Cultura Económica, 1995), 49.

7. Nacional Financiera, *México,* 19; Roger D. Hansen, *The Politics of Mexican Development* (Baltimore: Johns Hopkins University Press, 1971), 56.

8. Moreno-Brid and Ros, *Development and Growth,* 117.

9. Ibid., 235–38.

10. See, for instance, chap. 1 of Mikael Wolfe, *Watering the Revolution: The Technopolitical Success and Socioecological Failure of Agrarian Reform in La Laguna, Mexico* (Durham, NC: Duke University Press, forthcoming).

11. Kurt Unger, "La globalización del sistema innovativo Mexicano: Empresas extranjeras y tecnología importada," Documento de Trabajo No. 175, Centro de Investigación y Docencia Económicas, 1999.

12. Kenneth C. Shadlen, "The Puzzling Politics of Patents and Innovation Policy in Mexico," *Law and Business Review of the Americas* 16, no. 4 (2010): 823–38; Patricia Graf, "Research and Development in Mexican-American Relations Post-NAFTA," *Journal für Entwicklunhspolitic* 29, no. 2 (2013): 12, 14, 20.

13. Maloney and Caicedo, "Engineers."

14. M. Zapata Vera in *La Economista Mexicano,* September 10, 1886, 63.

15. The full phrase, attributed to President Díaz, runs: "Poor Mexico, so close to the United States but so far from God."

16. Among others, Amsden, *Rise of "the Rest,"* chap. 1.

17. E. Beatty, *Institutions and Investment,* chap. 2.

18. *La Unión,* quoted in *El Economista Mexicano,* July 1, 1899, 255.

19. Joel Mokyr, *The Gifts of Athena* (Princeton, NJ: Princeton University Press, 2002).

20. Luis Avelino Sánchez Graillet, "Tecnología, trabajo y raza en la industria petrolera en México" (PhD diss. in progress, UNAM).

BIBLIOGRAPHY

MAJOR ARCHIVAL SOURCES

Archivo General de la Nación, Mexico City

Departamento de Trabajo
Fondo Gonzalo Robles
Industrias Nuevas
Jorge Vera Estañol
Patentes y Marcas

Archivo Historico de Juan Brittingham, Universidad Iberoamericana Laguna, Torreón

Archivo Histórico de la Ciudad de Guanajuato

Bancroft Library, University of California, Berkeley

Daniel M. Burns Papers
Reports on the property of the Candelaria Mining Co.
Cuyutlan Gold Mining Company
Greene Gold-Silver Company, Mulatos Reports
C. A. Hamilton Report on La Mina Candelaria
Stuart H. Ingram Notebook
Minas Nuevas Mining Co. Records
Edward Otho Cresap Ord Papers
Santa Rosa de Ures Mining Co. Papers
James Jerome Smith Correspondence

Benson Library, University of Texas, Austin

Minas de Sombrerete Papers
Alan & Lillie M. Probert Collection

Condumex, Mexico

Archivo Bernardo Reyes
Archivo José Yves Limantour

Missouri State Historical Society, Vertical Files, Pauly Company

Roberto Garza Mexican Textile Archive, Hesburgh Library, University of Notre Dame

Singer Manufacturing Company Archive, Wisconsin Historical Society, Madison

Toledo Glass Company Archives, University of Toledo, Toledo, Ohio

PERIODICALS

Board of Trade Journal
Boletín de Instrucción Pública
Boletín de la República Mexicana
Boletín de la Sociedad Financiera Internacional
Boletín de la Sociedad Mexicana de Geografía y Estadística
Boletín Financiero y Minero de México
El Comerciante Mexicano
La Convención Radical Obrera
El Correo Español
Diario del Hogar
Diario de los Debates
Diario Literario de México
Diario Oficial de la Nación
El Economista Mexicano
Engineering and Mining Journal
The Federal Reporter
El Foro
Gaceta de Literatura de México
El Hijo del Pueblo (Guanajuato)
El Imparcial
The Mexican Herald

The Mexican Mining Journal
El Minero Mexicano
Mining and Scientific Press
El Monitor Repúblicano
Monterrey News
The National Federal Reporter
National Geographic
El País
El Siglo Diez y Nueve
El Socialista
La Sociedad
El Tiempo
Transactions, American Institute of Mining Engineers
The Two Republics

BOOKS AND ARTICLES

Aboites, Jaime. *Breve historia de un invento olvidado.* Mexico: UAM, 1989.
Abramovitz, M. "Catching Up, Forging Ahead, and Falling Behind." *Journal of Economic History* 46 (1986): 385–406.
Adger, W. Neil, Katrina Brown, Raffaello Cervigni, and Dominic Moran. "Total Economic Value of Forests in Mexico." *Ambio* 24, no. 5 (1995): 286–96.
Alamán, Lucas. *Historia de México.* Vol. 1. Mexico: J. M. Lara, 1852.
———. "Representación dirigida al Exmo. señor Presidente Provisional de la República por la Junta General Directiva de la Industria Nacional sobre la importancia de esta necesidad de su Fomento" [1813]. In *La industria nacional y el comercio exterior: Seis memorias oficiales sobre industria, agricultura, colonización y comercio exterior,* edited by Jan Bazant, Colección de documentos para la historia del comercio exterior de México 7. Mexico: Banco Nacional de Comercio Exterior, 1962.
Alfaro-Velcamp, Theresa. "Immigrant Positioning in Twentieth-Century Mexico: Middle Easterners, Foreign Citizens, and Multiculturalism." *Hispanic American Historical Review* 86, no. 1 (2006): 61–91.
Allen, A. W. "Early History of the Cyanide Process." *Engineering and Mining Journal,* October 8, 1927, 569–74.
Allen, Robert C. *The British Industrial Revolution in Global Perspective.* Cambridge: Cambridge University Press, 2009.
Altable Fernández, Francisco, ed. *Noroeste minero: La minería en Sonora, Baja California y Baja California Sur durante el porfiriato.* Mexico: Instituto Sudcaliforniano de Cultura, 2002.
Altamirano, Graziella, and Guadalupe Villa, eds. *Chihuahua: Textos de su historia, 1824–1921.* Vol. 2. Mexico: Instituto José María Luis Mora, 1988.

Alvarado, Jesús. "We Welcomed Foreign Fabrics and We Were Left Naked: Cotton Textile Artisans and the First Debates on Free Trade versus National Industry in Mexico." PhD diss., University of Wisconsin-Madison, 2007.

Alvarez de la Borda, Joel. "Transportes, negocios y política: La Compañía de Tranvías de México, 1907–1947." In *Compañías eléctricas extranjeras en México (1880–1960)*, edited by Reinhard Lierh and Mariano E. Torres Bautista, 67–106. Puebla, Mexico: Benemérita Universidad Autónoma de Puebla, 2010.

Amsden, Alice. *The Rise of "the Rest": Challenges to the West from Late-Industrializing Economies*. Oxford: Oxford University Press, 2001.

Anderson, Rodney D. "Guadalajara's Artisans and Shopkeepers, 1842–1907: The Origins of a Mexican Petite Bourgeoisie." In *Five Centuries of Mexican History / Cinco siglos de historia de México*, edited by Virginia Guedea and Jaime E. Rodríguez O., 286–99. Mexico: Instituto Mora, 1992.

———. *Outcasts in Their Own Land: Mexican Industrial Workers, 1906–1911*. The Origins of Modern Mexico. Dekalb: Northern Illinois University Press, 1976.

Antuñano, Estevan de. *Documentos para la historia de la industria en México, 1833–1846*. Vol. 1 of *Obras*. Mexico: Secretaría de Hacienda y Credito Público, 1979.

———. *Pensamientos para la regeneración industrial de México*. 1837. Reprint, Mexico: Librería Manuel Porrúa, 1955.

Aramburu, Marcelo G. "El desarrollo de las industrias de transformación en México." *Revista de Economía* 4, no. 5 (May 1941): 409–16.

Arias, Patricia. *Los vecinos de la Sierra: Microhistoria de Pueblo Nuevo*. Guadalajara: Universidad de Guadalajara, 1996.

Arnold, David. *Everyday Technology: Machines and the Making of India's Modernity*. Chicago: University of Chicago Press, 2013.

Atack, Jeremy, Fred Bateman, and Thomas Weiss. "The Regional Diffusion and Adoption of the Steam Engine in American Manufacturing." *Journal of Economic History* 40, no. 2 (1980): 281–308.

Aubrey, Henry G. "Deliberate Industrialization." *Social Research* 16, no. 2 (1949): 158–82.

Avila Herrera, Dolores, and Rina Ortiz, eds. *Minería regional mexicana: Primer Reunión de Historiadores de la Minería Latinoamericana (IV)*. Mexico: Instituto Nacional de Antropología e Historia, 1994.

Aviles-Galan, Miguel Angel. "'A Todo Vapor': Mechanisation in Porfirian Mexico Steam Power and Machine Building, 1891–1906." PhD diss., University of British Columbia, 2010.

Back, W., and J. M. Lesser. "Chemical Constraints of Groundwater Management in the Yucatan Peninsula, Mexico." *Journal of Hydrology* 51 (1981): 119–30.

Bain, H. Foster, ed. *More Recent Cyanide Practice*. San Francisco: Mining and Scientific Press, 1910.

Bakewell, Peter. *Miners of the Red Mountain: Indian Labor in Potosí, 1545–1650*. Albuquerque: University of New Mexico Press, 1984.

———. *Silver Mining and Society in Colonial Mexico: Zacatecas, 1546–1700*. Cambridge: Cambridge University Press, 1971.

Ballou, Maturin M. *Aztec Land*. Boston: Houghton Mifflin, 1890.

Banco Nacional de Comercio Exterior. *El comercio exterior y el artesano mexicano (1825–1830)*. Mexico: Banco Nacional de Comercio Exterior, 1965.

Barberena Blázquez, Elsa, and Carmen Block Iturriaga. "Publicaciones periódicas científicas y tecnológicas mexicanas del siglo XIX: Un proyecto de bases de datos." *Quipu* 3, no. 1 (1986): 7–26.

Barbosa Cruz, Mario. "La persistencia de una tradición: Consumo de pulque en la ciudad de México, 1900–1920." In *Cruda realidad: Producción, consumo y fiscalidad de las bebidas alcohólicas en México y América Latina, siglos XVII–XX,* edited by Ernest Sánchez Santiró, 213–42. Mexico: Instituto Mora, 2007.

Barragán, Juan Ignacio, and Mario Cerutti. *Juan F. Brittingham y la industria en México, 1859–1940*. Monterrey, Mexico: n.p., n.d.

Barrera Pages, Gustavo Adolfo. "Industrialización y revolución: El desempeño de la cervecería Toluca y México, S.A.: 1875–1926." Tesis de Licenciatura, ITAM, 1999.

Bauer, Arnold J. *Goods, Power, History: Latin America's Material Culture*. New Approaches to the Americas. Cambridge: Cambridge University Press, 2001.

Bazant, Jan, ed. *La industria nacional y el comercio exterior: Seis memorias oficiales sobre industria, agricultura, colonización y comercio exterior, 1842–1851*. Mexico: Banco Nacional de Comercio Exterior, 1962.

Bazant, Mílada. "La educación técnica durante el porfiriato." In *La ciudad y el campo en la historia de México: Memoria de la VII Reunión de Historiadores Mexicanos y Norteamericanos 1985*, 915–25. México: UNAM, 1992.

———. "La enseñanza y la práctica de la ingeniería durante el porfiriato." In *La educación en la historia de México,* edited by Josefina Zoraida Vázquez, 167–210. Mexico: Colegio de México, 1992.

———. *Historia de la educación durante el porfiriato*. Mexico: Colegio de México, 1993.

Beatty, Charles. "Untangling the Beattys: A Hundred Years of Edge-Tool Makers." *Chronicle of the Early American Industries Association* 60, no. 2 (2007): 49–67, and 60, no. 3 (2007): 99–111.

Beatty, Edward. "The Impact of Foreign Trade on the Mexican Economy: Terms of Trade and the Rise of Industry, 1880–1923." *Journal of Latin American Studies* 32, no. 2 (2000): 399–433.

———. *Institutions and Investment: The Political Basis of Industrialization in Mexico before 1911*. Stanford, CA: Stanford University Press, 2001.

———. "Riqueza, polémica, y política: Pensamiento y políticas económicas en México (1765–1911)." In *Historia del pensamiento económico en México: Ideas y debate en torno a la riqueza, el progreso y el auge económico de 1750 a 1900,* edited by José Enrique Covarrubias. Mexico: Universidad Nacional Autónoma de México, forthcoming.

———. "Visiones del futuro: La reorientación de la política económica en México (1867–1893)." *Signos Históricos* (Mexico) 10 (July–December 2003): 39–56.

Beatty, Edward, and J. Patricio Sáiz. "Propiedad industrial, patentes e inversión en tecnología en España y México (1820–1914)." In *México y España ¿Historias económicas paralelas?*, edited by Rafael Dobado, Aurora Gómez-Galvarriato, and Graciela Márquez, 425–70. Mexico: Fondo de Cultura Económica, 2007.

Becker, Thomas H. *Doing Business in the New Latin America: A Guide to Cultures, Practices, and Opportunities.* Westport, CT: Praeger, 2004.

Beezley, William H. *Judas at the Jockey Club and Other Episodes of Porfirian Mexico.* Lincoln: University of Nebraska Press, 1987.

Bernstein, Jeffrey R. "Toyoda Automatic Looms and Toyota Automobiles." In *Creating Modern Capitalism: How Entrepreneurs, Companies, and Countries Triumphed in Three Industrial Revolutions,* edited by Thomas K. McCraw, 396–438. Cambridge, MA: Harvard University Press, 1997.

Bernstein, Marvin D. *The Mexican Mining Industry, 1890–1950: A Study in the Interaction of Politics, Economics, and Technology.* Albany: State University of New York Press, 1964.

Bijker, Wiebe E., Thomas P. Hughes, and Trevor J. Pinch, eds. *The Social Construction of Technological Systems: New Directions in the Sociology and History of Technology.* Cambridge, MA: MIT Press, 1987.

Bijker, Wiebe, and John Law, eds. *Shaping Technology/Building Society: Studies in Sociotechnical Change.* Cambridge, MA: MIT Press, 1992.

Bird, Allen T. *The Land of Nayarit: An Account of the Great Mineral Region South of the Gila River and East from the Gulf of California to the Sierra Madre.* Nogales: Arizona and Sonora Chamber of Mines, 1904.

Blake, Mary Elizabeth, and Margaret Frances Sullivan. *Mexico: Picturesque, Political and Progressive.* Boston: Lee and Shepard, 1888.

Blanco, Mónica, and María Eugenia Romero Sotelo. *Cambio tecnológico e industrialización: La manufactura mexicana y su historia, siglo xviii, xix, y xx.* Mexico: DGAPA-FE-UNAM, 1997.

Bonfil Batalla, Guillermo. *México Profundo: Reclaiming a Civilization.* Austin: University of Texas Press, 1996.

Bronstein Punski, Clara. "La introducción de la máquina de vapor en México." MA thesis, Facultad de Filosofía y Letras, UNAM, 1965.

Boyer, Christopher R. *Becoming Campesinos: Politics, Identity, and Post-Revolutionary Struggle in Michoacán, 1920–1935.* Stanford, CA: Stanford University Press, 2003.

Brading, David. *Haciendas and Ranchos in the Mexican Bajío: León, 1700–1860.* Cambridge: Cambridge University Press, 1978.

———. *Miners and Merchants in Bourbon Mexico, 1763–1810.* Cambridge: Cambridge University Press, 1971.

Brown, John K. *The Baldwin Locomotive Works, 1831–1915.* Baltimore: Johns Hopkins University Press, 1995.

Brown, Jonathan. "Foreign and Native-Born Workers in Porfirian Mexico." *American Historical Review* 98, no. 3 (1993): 786–818.

———. *Oil and Revolution in Mexico.* Berkeley: University of California Press, 1993.

Bruland, Kristine. *British Technology and European Industrialization: The Norwegian Textile Industry in the Mid-nineteenth Century.* Cambridge: Cambridge University Press, 1989.

———. "The Norwegian Mechanical Engineering Industry and the Transfer of Technology, 1800–1900." In *Technology Transfer and Scandinavian Industrialization*, edited by Kristine Bruland, 229–67. New York: Berg, 1991.

———, ed. *Technology Transfer and Scandinavian Industrialization.* New York: Berg, 1991.

Buchenau, Jurgen. "Small Numbers, Great Impact: Mexico and Its Immigrants, 1821–1973." *Journal of American Ethnic History* 20, no. 3 (2001): 23–49.

———. *Tools of Progress: A German Merchant Family in Mexico City, 1865–Present.* Albuquerque: University of New Mexico Press, 2004.

Bullock, William. *Six Months Residence and Travels in Mexico.* London: John Murray, 1824.

Bulmer-Thomas, Victor, John H. Coatsworth, and Roberto Cortés Conde, eds. *The Cambridge Economic History of Latin America.* Vol. 1. *The Colonial Era and the Short Nineteenth Century.* New York: Cambridge University Press, 2006.

Bunker, Steven B. "Consumers of Good Taste: Marketing Modernity in Northern Mexico, 1890–1910." *Mexican Studies/Estudios Mexicanos* 13, no. 2 (1997): 227–70.

———. *Creating Mexican Consumer Culture in the Age of Porfirio Díaz.* Albuquerque: University of New Mexico Press, 2012.

Burman, Barbara, ed. *The Culture of Sewing: Gender, Consumption, and Home Dressmaking.* Oxford: Berg, 1999.

Burt, Roger. "Innovation or Imitation? Technological Dependency in the American Nonferrous Mining Industry." *Technology and Culture* 41, no. 1 (2000): 321–47.

Calderón, Francisco R. "Los ferrocarriles." In *El Porfiriato: La vida económica,* 2 vols., edited by Daniel Cosío Villegas, Historia moderna de México 7/1 and 2, 483–634. Mexico: Editorial Hermes, 1974.

———. *La República restaurada: La vida económica.* Historia moderna de México 2. Mexico: Editorial Hermes, 1955.

Calderón de la Barca, Fanny. *Life in Mexico.* 1843. Reprint, Berkeley: University of California Press, 1982.

Candiani, Vera. "Draining the Basin of Mexico: Science, Technology, and Society, 1608–1808." PhD diss., University of California, Berkeley, 2004.

Carden, Lionel. *Report on the Cotton Manufacturing Industry in Mexico.* British Diplomatic and Consular Reports, Miscellaneous Series, no. 453. London: HMSO, 1898.

Cárdenas García, Nicolás. *Empresas y trabajadores en la gran minería mexicana (1900–1929).* Mexico: Instituto Nacional de Estudios Históricos de la Revolución Mexicana, 1998.

Cárdenas Sánchez, Enrique. *Cuando se originó el atraso económico de México: La economía mexicana en el largo siglo xix, 1780–1920.* Madrid: Biblioteca Nueva; Fundación Ortega y Gasset, 2003.

———. "A Macroeconomic Interpretation of Nineteenth-Century Mexico." In *How Latin America Fell Behind,* edited by Stephen Haber, 65–92. Stanford, CA: Stanford University Press, 1997.

Cárdenas Sánchez, Enrique, José Antonio Ocampo, and Rosemary Thorpe, eds. *An Economic History of Twentieth-Century Latin America.* 3 vols. New York: Palgrave Macmillan, 2000.

Carpenter, William W. *Travels and Adventures in Mexico.* New York: Harper and Brothers, 1851.

Carrillo Rojas, Arturo. *Los caballos de vapor: El imperio de las máquinas durante el cañedismo.* Culiacán, Sinaloa: Colegio de Bachilleres del Estado de Sinaloa, 1998.

Carstensen, Fred V. *American Enterprise in Foreign Markets: Studies of Singer and International Harvester in Imperial Russia.* Chapel Hill: University of North Carolina Press, 1984.

Castañeda González, Rocío. "Esfuerzos públicos y privados para el abasto de agua a Toluca (1862–1910)." In *Historia de los usos del agua en México: Oligarquías, empresas y ayuntamientos (1840–1940)*, edited by Blanca Estela Cortez, 107–82. Mexico: Comisión Nacional de Agua, 1998.

Centro de Estudios Históricos del Movimiento Obrero Mexicano. *La mujer y el movimiento obrero mexicano en el siglo XIX: Antología de la prensa obrera.* Mexico: Centro de Estudios Historicos del Movimiento Obrero Mexicano, 1975.

Cerutti, Mario. *Burguesía, capitales e industria en el norte de México, Monterry y su ámbito regional (1850–1910).* Mexico: Alianza Editorial, 1992.

———. "La Compañía Industrial Jabonera de La Laguna: Comerciantes, agricultores e industria en el norte de México (1880–1925)." In *Historia de las grandes empresas en México, 1850–1930*, edited by Carlos Marichal and Mario Cerutti, 167–200. Mexico: Colegio de México, 1997.

Chadwick, R. "New Extraction Processes for Metals." In *A History of Technology: The Late Nineteenth Century,* vol. 5, edited by Charles Singer and Trevor Williams. London: Oxford University Press, 1965.

Challú, Amílcar. "The Political Economy of Hunger in Bourbon Mexico." Unpublished manuscript, 2011.

Challú, Amílcar E., and Aurora Gómez-Galvarriato. "Further Scrutiny of a Censured Century: Real Wages in Mexico City in the Very Long Nineteenth Century (1750s-1910s)." Paper presented at the annual meeting of the Latin American Studies Association, San Francisco, 2012.

Chase, Stuart. *Mexico: A Study of Two Americas.* New York: Macmillan, 1931.

Chowning, Margaret. "Reassessing the Prospects for Profit in Nineteenth-Century Mexican Agriculture from a Regional Perspective." In *How Latin America Fell Behind,* edited by Stephen Haber, 179–215. Stanford, CA: Stanford University Press, 1997.

Clark, Gregory. "Why Isn't the Whole World Developed? Lessons from the Cotton Mills." *Journal of Economic History* 47, no. 1 (1987): 145–46.

Clark, W. A. Graham. "Cotton Goods in Latin America, Part I: Cuba, Mexico and Central America." In *Special Agent Series No. 31*, edited by US Department of Commerce and Labor, Bureau of Manufacturers, 19–41. Washington, DC: Government Printing Office, 1909.

Clennell, John Edward. *The Cyanide Handbook*. New York: McGraw-Hill, 1910.

Coatsworth, John. *Growth against Development: The Economic Impact of Railroads in Porfirian Mexico*. Dekalb: Northern Illinois University Press, 1981.

———. "Obstacles to Economic Growth in Nineteenth-Century Mexico." *American Historical Review* 83, no. 1 (1978): 80–100.

———. *Los orígenes del atraso: Nueve ensayos de historia económica de México en los siglos xviii y xix*. Mexico: Alianza Editorial Mexicana, 1990.

———. "Railroads, Landholding, and Agrarian Protest in the Early Porfiriato." *Hispanic American Historical Review* 54, no. 1 (1974): 48–71.

Coatsworth, John, and Alan Taylor, eds. *Latin America and the World Economy since 1800*. Cambridge, MA: Harvard University Center for Latin American Studies, 1999.

Cohen, W. M., and D. A. Levinthal. "Absorptive Capacity: A New Perspective on Learning and Innovation." *Administrative Science Quarterly* 35, no. 1 (1990): 128–52.

Colección de artículos del Siglo XIX, sobre alzamiento de prohibiciones. Mexico: Ignacio Cumplido, 1851.

Colegio de México. *Estadísticas económicas del porfiriato: Comercio exterior de México, 1877–1911*. Mexico: Colegio de México, 1960.

———. *Estadísticas económicas del porfiriato: Fuerza de trabajo*. Mexico: Colegio de México, 1965.

Connolly, Marguerite. "The Disappearance of the Domestic Sewing Machine, 1890–1925." *Winterthur Portfolio* 34, no. 1 (Spring 1999): 31–48.

Connolly, Patricia. *El contratista de don Porfirio: Obras públicas, deuda y desarrollo desigual*. Mexico: Fondo de Cultura Económico, 1997.

Corona Treviño, Leonel. *La tecnología, siglos XVI al XX*. Mexico: Universidad Nacional Autónoma de México, 2004.

Cortés Conde, Roberto. "Sarmiento and Economic Progress: From Facundo to the Presidency." In *Sarmiento: Author of a Nation*, ed. Tulio Halperín Donghi, Iván Jaksic, Gwen Kirkpatrick, and Francine Masiello, 114–26. Berkeley: University of California Press, 1994.

Cosío Villegas, Daniel, ed. *El Porfiriato: La vida económica*. 2 vols. Historia moderna de México 7/1 and 2. México: Editorial Hermes, 1974.

Cott, Kennett S. "Porfirian Investment Policies, 1876–1910." PhD diss., University of New Mexico, 1979.

Covo, Jaqueline. *Las ideas de la Reforma en México (1855–1861)*. Translated by María Francisca Mourier-Martínez. Mexico: Universidad Nacional Autónoma de México, 1983.

Craib, Raymond. *Cartographic Mexico: A History of State Fixations and Fugitive Landscapes*. Durham, NC: Duke University Press, 2004.

Crespo, Horacio Gutiérrez. *Historia del azúcar en México*. Mexico: Fondo de Cultura Ecónomica, 1980.

Crespo y Martínez, Gilberto. *Las patentes de invención*. Mexico: Oficina Tip. de la Secretaría de Fomento, 1897.

Criscuolo, Paola, and Rajneesh Narula. "A Novel Approach to National Technological Accumulation and Absorptive Capacity: Aggregating Cohen and Levinthal." *European Journal of Development Research* 20, no. 1 (2008): 53–73.

Cruz León, Artemio. *Los instrumentos agrícolas en la zona central de Veracruz.* Chapingo, Mexico: Universidad Autónoma de Chapingo, 1989.

Curiel, Gustavo. *Pintura y vida cotidiana en México, 1650–1950.* Mexico: Fondo Cultura Banamex, 1999.

Dahlgren, Charles B. *Historic Mines of Mexico: A Review of the Mines of That Republic for the Past Three Centuries.* New York, 1883.

Davies, Robert Bruce. *Peacefully Working to Conquer the World: Singer Sewing Machines in Foreign Markets, 1854–1920.* New York: Arno Press, 1976.

Davis, Pearce. *The Development of the American Glass Industry.* Cambridge, MA: Harvard University Press, 1949.

De la Concha, Gerardo, and Juan Carlos Calleros. *Los caminos de la invención: Inventos e inventores en México.* Mexico: Instituto Politécnico Nacional, 1996.

Delpar, Helen. *Looking South: The Evolution of Latin Americanist Scholarship in the United States.* Tuscaloosa: University of Alabama Press, 2008.

DeRossi, Flavio. *The Mexican Entrepreneur.* Paris: Development Centre for the Organization for Economic Development and Cooperation, 1971.

Derry, T. K., and Trevor I. Williams. *A Short History of Technology from the Earliest Times to A.D. 1900.* 1960. Reprint, New York: Dover, 1993.

Díaz del Castillo, Bernal. *Historia verdadera de la conquista de la Nueva España.* Madrid: Austral, 1968.

"Dictamen de la Comisión de Legislación . . . 21 de enero de 1823." In *Protección y libre cambio: El debate entre 1821 y 1836,* edited by Luis Córdova, 23. Mexico: Banco Nacional de Comercio Exterior, 1971.

Dublán, Manuel, and José María Lozano. *Legislación mexicana; o, colección completa de las disposiciones legislativas expedidas desde la independencia de la república . . . 1687–1910.* 37 vols. Mexico: Imprenta de E. Dublán, 1876–1912.

Duboff, Richard B. "The Introduction of Electric Power in American Manufacturing." *Economic History Review* 20 (December 1967): 509–18.

Dumett, Raymond E. *El Dorado in West Africa: The Gold-Mining Frontier, African Labor, and Colonial Capitalism in the Gold Coast, 1875–1900.* Athens: Ohio University Press, 1998.

Eakin, Marshall C. *British Enterprise in Brazil: The St. John d'el Rey Mining Company and the Morro Velho Gold Mine, 1830–1960.* Durham, NC: Duke University Press, 1989.

Easterlin, Richard. "Why Isn't the Whole World Developed?" *Journal of Economic History* 41, no. 1 (1981): 1–19.

Emery, Charles E. "The Cost of Steam Power." *Transactions of the American Society of Civil Engineers* 12 (November 1883): 425–35.

Evenson, Robert E., and Gustav Ranis, eds. *Science and Technology: Lessons for Development Policy.* Boulder, CO: Westview Press, 1990.

Fairfield, E. William. *Fire and Sand: The History of the Libbey-Owens Sheet Glass Company.* Cleveland, OH: Lezius-Hiles, 1960.

Feinstein, Charles. *Statistical Tables of National Income, Expenditure and Output of the U.K., 1855–1965.* Cambridge: Cambridge University Press, 1972.

Fenichel, Allen H. *Quantitative Analysis of the Growth and Diffusion of Steam Power in Manufacturing in the United States, 1838–1919.* New York: Arno Press, 1964.

Fernández, Miguel Ángel. *El vidrio en México.* Mexico: Centro de Arte Vitro, 1990.

Flippin, J. R. *Sketches from the Mountains of Mexico.* Cincinnati, OH: Standard Publishing, 1889.

Flores, Teodoro. *Estudio geológico-minero de los distritos de El Oro y Tlalpujahua.* Instituto Geológico de México, Boletín No. 37. Mexico: Secretaria de Gobernación, 1920.

Fogel, Robert. "The Persistence of Misery in Europe and America before 1900." In *The Escape from Hunger and Premature Death, 1700–2100,* 1–19. Cambridge: Cambridge University Press, 2004.

Forment, Carlos. *Democracy in Latin America, 1760–1900.* Vol. 1. Chicago: University of Chicago Press, 2003.

France. Direction Général des Douanes. *Tableau général du commerce de la France avec les colonies et les puissances étrangeres pendant l'année . . .* Paris, 1894–1911.

Franck, Harry Alverson. *Trailing Cortez through Mexico.* New York: Fredrick A. Stokes, 1935.

Francois, Marie Eileen. *A Culture of Everyday Credit: Housekeeping, Pawnbroking, and Governance in Mexico City, 1750–1920.* Lincoln: University of Nebraska Press, 2006.

———. "Vivir de prestado: El empeño en la ciudad de México." In *Bienes y vivencias: El siglo XIX,* edited by Anne Staples, 81–117. Historia de la vida cotidiana en México 4. Mexico: Colegio de México, 2005.

Frank, Patrick. *Posada's Broadsheets: Mexican Popular Imagery, 1890–1910.* Albuquerque: University of New Mexico Press, 1998.

Fransman, M., and K. King. *Technological Capability in the Third World.* London: Macmillan, 1984.

Friedrich, Paul. *Agrarian Revolt in a Mexican Village.* Chicago: University of Chicago Press, 1977.

Galarza, Ernesto. *La industria eléctrica en México.* Mexico: Fondo de Cultura Económica, 1941.

Galicia, José. "Conferencia sobre patentes de invención." *Revista de Legislación y Jurisprudencia,* no. 19 (1900): 453–63.

Gallo, Rubén. *Mexican Modernity: The Avant-Garde and the Technological Revolution.* Cambridge, MA: MIT Press, 2010.

Gámez, Moisés. *De negro brillante a blanco plateado: La empresa minera mexicana a finales del siglo XIX.* San Luis Potosí: Colegio de San Luis, 2001.

García Icazbalceta, Joaquín. *Vocabulario de Mexicanismos.* México: Tip. y Lit. "La Europea" de J. Aguilar Vera, 1899.

Gauss, Susan. *Made in Mexico: Regions, Nation, and the State in the Rise of Mexican Industrialism, 1920s–1940s.* University Park: Pennsylvania State University Press, 2010.

Gauss, Susan M., and Edward Beatty. "The World's Beer: The Historical Geography of Brewing in Mexico." In *The Geography of Beer: Regions, Environment, and Societies,* edited by Mark Patterson and Nancy Hoalst-Pullen, 57–66. New York: Springer, 2014.

Germany. *Statistik des Deutschen Reichs: Auswärtiger Handel deutschen Zollgebiets im Jahre . . . , herausgegeben vom Kaiserlichen Statistischen Amte.* Berlin, 1880–1908.

Gerschenkron, Alexander. *Economic Backwardness in Historical Perspective.* Cambridge: Cambridge University Press, 1962.

Gibson, Clark, Elinor Ostrom, Krister Anderson, and Sujai Shivakumar. *The Samaritan's Dilemma: The Political Economy of Development Aid.* Oxford: Oxford University Press, 2005.

Godley, Andrew. "The Global Diffusion of the Sewing Machine, 1850–1914." *Research in Economic History* 20 (2001): 1–45.

———. "Homeworking and the Sewing Machine in the British Clothing Industry, 1850–1905." In *The Culture of Sewing: Gender, Consumption and Home Dressmaking,* edited by Barbara Burman, 255–68. Oxford: Oxford University Press, 1999.

———. "Selling the Sewing Machine around the World: Singer's International Marketing Strategies, 1850–1920." *Enterprise and Society* 7, no. 2 (2006): 266–300.

Gómez-Galvarriato, Aurora. "El desempeño de la Fundidora de Hierro y Acero de Monterrey durante el Porfiriato." In *Historia de las grandes empresas en México, 1850–1930,* edited by Carlos Marichal and Mario Cerutti, 201–44. Mexico: Fondo de Cultura Económica, 1997.

———. "The Evolution of Prices and Real Wages in Mexico from the Porfiriato to the Revolution." In *Latin America and the World Economy,* edited by John H. Coatsworth and Alan M. Taylor, 347–78. Cambridge, MA: David Rockefeller Center for Latin American Studies, Harvard University, 1998.

———, ed. *La industria textil en México.* Mexico: Instituto Mora, 1999.

———. *Industry and Revolution: Social and Economic Change in the Orizaba Valley, Mexico.* Cambridge, MA: Harvard University Press, 2013.

———. "El primer impulso industrializador de México: El caso de Fundidora Monterrey." Tesis de Licenciatura, ITAM, 1990.

Gómez Serrano, Jesús. "Una ciudad pujante: Aguascalientes durante el porfiriato." In *Bienes y vivencias: El siglo XIX,* edited by Anne Staples, 253–86. Historia de la vida cotidiana en México 4. Mexico: Colegio de México, 2005.

González y González, Luís. *Pueblo en vilo: Microhistoria de San José de Gracia.* Mexico City: Colegio de México, 1972.

———. *San José de Gracia: Mexican Village in Transition.* Austin: University of Texas Press, 1972.

Graf, Patricia. "Research and Development in Mexican-American Relations Post-NAFTA." *Journal für Entwicklunhspolitic* 29, no. 2 (2013): 11–30.

Graham, A. A. *Mexico with Comparisons and Conclusions.* Topeka: Crane, 1907.

Great Britain Customs Establishment. Statistical Office. *Annual Statement of the Trade and Navigation of the United Kingdom with Foreign Countries and British Possessions in the Year . . .* London, 1883–1910.

Green, Harvey. *The Light of the Home: An Intimate View of the Lives of Women in Victorian America.* New York: Pantheon, 1983.

Griffin, Solomon Bulkley. *Mexico of To-day.* New York: Harper and Brothers, 1886.

Griliches, Zvi. "Patent Statistics as Economic Indicators: A Survey." *Journal of Economic Literature* 28 (December 1990): 1661–1707.

Guajardo Soto, Guillermo. "'A pesar de todo, se mueve': El aprendizaje tecnológico en México, ca. 1860–1930." *Iztapalapa* 43 (June–January 1998): 305–28.

———. "Between the Workshop and the State: Training Human Capital in Railroad Companies in Mexico and Chile, 1850–1930." MPRA Paper No. 16135, July 2009. http://mpra.ub.uni-muenchen.de/16135/.

———. "Nuevos datos para un viejo debate: Los vínculos entre ferrocarriles e industrialización en Chile y México (1860–1950)." *El Trimestre Económico* 65, no. 2 (1998): 213–61.

———. "La tecnología de los Estados Unidos y la 'americanización' de los ferrocarriles estatales de México y Chile, ca. 1880–1950." *Transportes, Servicios y Telecomunicaciones* no. 9 (December 2005): 110–30.

———. *Trabajo y tecnología en los ferrocarriles de México: Una visión histórica, 1850–1950.* Mexico: El Centauro, 2010.

Guedea, Virginia, and Jaime E. Rodríguez O., eds. *Five Centuries of Mexican History / Cinco siglos de historia de México.* Mexico: Instituto Mora, 1992.

Gutiérrez Alvarez, Coralia. "La penosa existencia en las fábricas textiles de Puebla y Tlaxcala." In *Bienes y vivencias: El siglo XIX,* edited by Anne Staples, 527–62. Historia de la vida cotidiana en México 4. Mexico: Colegio de México, 2005.

Gutiérrez Crespo, Horacio. *Historia del azúcar en México.* Mexico: Fondo de Cultura Ecónomica, 1980.

Haber, Stephen H. "Economic Growth and Latin American Historiography," in *How Latin America Fell Behind: Essays on the Economic Histories of Brazil and Mexico, 1800–1914,* ed. Stephen Haber, 1–33. Stanford, CA: Stanford University Press, 1997.

———, ed. *How Latin America Fell Behind: Essays on the Economic Histories of Brazil and Mexico, 1800–1914.* Stanford, CA: Stanford University Press, 1997.

———. *Industry and Underdevelopment: The Industrialization of Mexico, 1890–1940.* Stanford, CA: Stanford University Press, 1989.

Haber, Stephen H., Armando Razo, and Noel Mauer. *The Politics of Property Rights: Political Instability, Credible Commitments, and Economic Growth in Mexico, 1876–1929.* Cambridge: Cambridge University Press, 2003.

Hamilton, Charles W. *Early Day Oil Tales of Mexico.* Houston: Gulf, 1966.

Hamilton, Leonidas. *Border States of Mexico: Sonora, Sinaloa, Chihuahua and Durango.* San Francisco: Bacon, 1883.

Hamilton, Nora. *The Limits of State Autonomy: Post-revolutionary Mexico.* Princeton, NJ: Princeton University Press, 1982.

Hansen, Roger D. *The Politics of Mexican Development.* Baltimore: Johns Hopkins University Press, 1971.

Harley, C. Knick. "Oceanic Freight Rates and Productivity, 1740–1913: The Primacy of Mechanical Invention Reaffirmed." *Journal of Economic History* 48, no. 4 (December 1988): 851–76.

Harper, Henry Howard. *A Journey in Southeastern Mexico: Narrative of Experiences and Observations on Agricultural and Industrial Experiences.* Boston, 1910.

Hart, John Mason. *Empire and Revolution: The Americans in Mexico since the Civil War.* Berkeley: University of California Press, 2002.

Hassig, Ross. *Trade, Tribute, and Transportation: The Sixteenth-Century Political Economy of the Valley of Mexico.* Norman: University of Oklahoma Press, 1985.

Headrick, Daniel R. *The Tentacles of Progress: Technology Transfer in the Age of Imperialism, 1850–1940.* New York: Oxford University Press, 1988.

Hermosa, Jesús. *Manual de geografía y estadística de la República Mejicana.* Paris: Librería de Rosa, 1857.

Herrera Canales, Inés. *El comercio exterior de México, 1821–1875.* Mexico: Colegio de Mexico, 1977.

Hibino, Barbara. "Cervecería Cuauhtémoc: A Case Study of Technological and Industrial Development in Mexico." *Mexican Studies/Estudios Mexicanos* 8, no. 1 (1992): 23–43.

Hirschman, Albert O. *Essays on Trespassing: Economics to Politics and Beyond.* New York: Cambridge University Press, 1981.

Hobson, Francis J. "Cyanidation in Mexico." In *More Recent Cyanide Practice,* edited by H. Foster Bain, 167–76. San Francisco: Mining and Scientific Press, 1910.

Hofman, André, and Cristián Ducoing. "Capital Goods Imports, Machinery Investment, and Economic Development in the Long Run: The Case of Chile." Paper presented at the 15th World Economic History Congress, Utrecht, 2009.

Horn, Jeff, Leonard N. Rosenband, and Merritt Roe Smith, eds. *Reconceptualizing the Industrial Revolution.* Cambridge, MA: MIT Press, 2010.

Hounshell, David. *From the American System to Mass Production, 1800–1932: The Development of Manufacturing Technology in the United States.* Baltimore: Johns Hopkins University Press, 1984.

Hovis, Logan, and Jeremy Mouat. "Miners, Engineers, and the Transformation of Work in the Western Mining Industry, 1880–1930." *Technology and Culture* 37, no. 3 (1996): 429–56.

Howell, Edward J. *Mexico: Its Progress and Commercial Possibilities.* London: W. B. Whittingham, 1892.

Hunt, Bertram. "Cyanidation in Mexico." *Mining and Scientific Press,* August 29, 1908.

Inkster, Ian. "Patents as Indicators of Technological Change and Innovation: An Historical Analysis of the Patent Data, 1830–1914." Paper presented at the Meeting of the Newcomen Society, London, 2002.

———. "Science and the Mechanics' Institutes, 1820–1850: The Case of Sheffield." *Annals of Science* 32 (1975): 451–74.

———. "Technology Transfer and Industrial Transformation: An Interpretation of the Pattern of Economic Development circa 1870–1914." In *Technological Change: Methods and Themes in the History of Technology,* edited by Robert Fox, 177–200. Amsterdam: Harwood Academic, 1996.

Jack, Sybil M. "The Introduction of Cyaniding in New Zealand: A Case Study in the Role of Technology in History." *Prometheus* 2, no. 1 (June 1984): 17–37.

Jeremy, David J. ed. *International Technology Transfer: Europe, Japan, and the USA, 1700–1914.* London: Edward Elgar, 1991.

———. Introduction to *International Technology Transfer: Europe, Japan and the USA, 1700–1914,* edited by David J. Jeremy. London: Edward Elgar, 1991.

———. *Transatlantic Industrial Revolution: The Diffusion of Textile Technologies between Britain and America, 1790–1830s.* Cambridge, MA: MIT Press, 1981.

Katz, Friedrich. "The Liberal Republic and the Porfiriato." In *Mexico since Independence,* edited by Leslie Bethell, 49–124. Cambridge: Cambridge University Press, 1991.

Katz, Jorge. "Domestic Technological Innovations and Dynamic Comparative Advantages." In *International Technology Transfer: Concepts, Measures, and Comparisons,* edited by Nathan Rosenberg and Claudio Frischtak, 127–66. New York: Praeger, 1985.

Keesing, Donald B. "Structural Change Early in Development: Mexico's Changing Industrial and Occupational Structure from 1895 to 1950." *Journal of Economic History* 29, no. 4 (1969): 716–38.

Keller, Wolfgang. "Absorptive Capacity: On the Creation and Acquisition of Technology in Development." *Journal of Development Studies* 49 (1996): 199–227.

Kelley, James R. "The Education and Training of Porfirian Officers: Success or Failure?" *Military Affairs* 39, no. 3 (October 1975): 124–28.

Kenwood, A. G., and A. L. Lougheed. *The Growth of the International Economy, 1820–1990.* 3rd ed. London: Routledge, 1992.

Keremitsis, Dawn. *La industria textil mexicana en el siglo xix.* Mexico: SepSetentas, 1973.

Kim, Linsu. *Imitation to Innovation: The Dynamics of Korea's Technological Learning.* Boston: Harvard Business School Press, 1997.

Klarén, Peter F., and Thomas J. Bossert. *Promise of Development: Theories of Change in Latin America.* Boulder, CO: Westview Press, 1986.

Koo, Bon Ho, and Dwight H. Perkins, eds. *Social Capability and Long-Term Economic Growth.* New York: St. Martin's Press, 1995.

Kourí, Emilio. *A Pueblo Divided: Business, Property, and Community in Papantla, Mexico.* Stanford, CA: Stanford University Press, 2004.

Kuntz Ficker, Sandra. *El comercio exterior de México en la era del capitalismo liberal, 1870–1929.* Mexico: Colegio de México, 2007.

———. *Empresa extranjera y mercado interno: El Ferrocarril Central Mexicano, 1880–1907.* Mexico: Colegio de México, 1995.

———. *Las exportaciones mexicanas durante la primera globalización, 1870–1929.* Mexico: Colegio de México, 2010.

———, ed. *Historia económica general de México: De la colonia a nuestros días.* Mexico: Colegio de México, 2010.

Kuntz Ficker, Sandra, and Patricia Connolly. *Ferrocarriles y obras públicas.* Mexico: Instituto Mora, 1999.

Kuntz Ficker, Sandra, and Paolo Riguzzi, eds. *Ferrocarriles y vida económica en México (1850–1950).* Mexico: Colegio Mexiquense, 1996.

Lall, Sanjaya. "Technological Capabilities and Industrialization." *World Development* 20, no. 2 (1992): 165–86.

Lamb, Mark R. "Present Cyanide Practice in Mexico." *Engineering and Mining Journal,* April 4, 1908, 703–9.

Lamoreaux, Naomi R., and Kenneth L. Sokoloff. "Inventive Activity and the Market for Technology in the United States, 1840–1920." NBER Working Paper #7107, National Bureau of Economic Research, Cambridge, MA, 1999.

Landero, Carlos F. de. *Exámen termoquímico de algunas reacciones relativas a la formación del cloruro de plata.* Mexico: Oficina Tipográfica de la Secretaría de Fomento, 1889.

Landes, David S. *The Unbound Prometheus: Technological Change and Industrial Development in Western Europe from 1750 to the Present.* Cambridge: Cambridge University Press, 1969.

Lazonick, William. "What Happened to the Theory of Economic Development?" In *Favorites of Fortune: Technology, Growth, and Economic Development since the Industrial Revolution,* edited by Patrice Higonnet, David S. Landes, and Henry Rosovsky, 267–96. Cambridge, MA: Harvard University Press, 1991.

Lear, John. *Workers, Neighbors and Citizens: The Revolution in Mexico City.* Lincoln: University of Nebraska Press, 2001.

Lee, S. M. *Glimpses of Mexico and California.* Boston: Geo. H. Ellis, 1887.

Leiby, John S. *Colonial Bureaucrats and the Mexican Economy: Growth of a Patrimonial State, 1763–1821.* New York: Peter Lang, 1986.

Lejeune, Louis. *Tierras mexicanas.* Mexico: Mirada Viajera, 1995.

Lerdo de Tejada, Miguel. *Comercio exterior de México desde la conquista hasta hoy.* Mexico, 1853. Reprinted in his *Mexico en 1856, el comercio exterior desde la conquista.* Mexico: Universidad Veracruzana, 1985.

———. *Cuadro sinóptico de la República Mexicana en 1856* [Mexico, 1856]. Reprinted in his *Mexico en 1856, el comercio exterior desde la conquista.* Mexico: Universidad Veracruzana, 1985.

Liehr, Reinhard, and Mariano E. Torres Bautista, eds. *Compañías eléctricas extranjeras en México (1880–1960).* Puebla, Mexico: Benemérita Universidad Autónoma de Puebla, 2010.

Lipsett-Rivera, Sonya. *Defend Our Water with the Blood of Our Veins: The Struggle for Resources in Colonial Puebla.* Albuquerque: University of New Mexico Press, 1999.

Lipsey, Robert E. *Price and Quantity Trends in the Foreign Trade of the United States.* Princeton, NJ: Princeton University Press, 1963.

Lloyd, Jane-Dale. *Cinco ensayos sobre cultura material de rancheros y medieros del noroeste de Chihuahua, 1886–1910.* Mexico: Universidad Iberoamericana, 2001.

Lobato, F. *A los señores profesores ingenieros de minas e hidro-agrimensores, Don Ignacio Alcocer y Don Manuel Contreras, en testimonio de aprecio.* Guanajuato: Tipografía de la Reforma, 1863.

Lock, Charles George Warnford. *Gold Milling: Principles and Practice.* London: E. and F. N. Spon, 1901.

Lomnitz, Larissa Adler, and Marison Perez-Lizaur. *A Mexican Elite Family, 1820–1980.* Translated by Cinna Lomnitz. Princeton, NJ: Princeton University Press, 1987.

López-Alonso, Moramay. *Measuring Up: A History of Living Standards in Mexico, 1850–1950.* Stanford, CA: Stanford University Press, 2012.

López-Cajún, C., M. Rafael-Morales, J. Cervantes-de-Gortari, and R. Colás-Otiz. "Steam Locomotives in the History of Technology of Mexico." In *International Symposium on History of Machines and Mechanisms: Proceedings of HHM 2008,* edited by Hong-Sen Yan and Marco Ceccarelli (Dordrecht: Springer, 2009), 151–64.

López Cervantes, Gonzalo. "Notas para el estudio del vidrio en la Nueva España." Cuadernos de Trabajo No. 19, Instituto Nacional de Antropología e Historia, Departamento de Prehistoria, 1979.

Lougheed, Alan. "The Cyanide Process and Gold Extraction in Australia and New Zealand, 1888–1913." *Australian Economic History Review* 27 (March 1987): 44–60.

———. "The Discovery, Development, and Diffusion of New Technology: The Cyanide Process for the Extraction of Gold, 1887–1914." *Prometheus* 7, no. 1 (June 1989): 61–74.

Lumholtz, Carl. *New Trails in Mexico: An Account of One Year's Exploration in North-Western Sonora, Mexico, and South-western Arizona, 1909–1910.* New York: Charles Scribners, 1912.

Lummis, Charles Fletcher. *The Awakening of a Nation: Mexico of To-day.* New York: Harper, 1898.

MacDonald, Bernard. "Development of the Cyanide Process for Silver Ores in Mexico." *Engineering and Mining Journal,* April 18, 1908, 802.

MacKenzie, Donald, and Judy Wajcman, eds. *The Social Shaping of Technology.* Philadelphia: Open University Press, 1999.

Maczak, Antoni. "Observations on Wealth and Economic Development in Renaissance and Baroque Travel Literature." In *State and Society in Europe from the Fifteenth Century to the Eighteenth Century,* edited by Jaroslaw Pelenski, 231–44. Warsaw: Warsaw University Press, 1985.

Maloney, William F., and Felipe Valencia Caicedo. "Engineers, Innovative Capacity and Development in the Americas." IZA Discussion Paper No. 8271, Institute for the Study of Labor, Bonn, Germany, June 2014.

Marichal, Carlos, and Mario Cerutti, eds. *Historia de las grandes empresas en México, 1850–1930.* Mexico: Universidad Autónoma de Nuevo León, 1997.

Márquez, Graciela. "Tariff Protection in Mexico, 1892–1909: Ad Valorem Tariff Rates and Sources of Variation." In *Latin America and the World Economy since 1800*, edited by John H. Coatsworth and Alan M. Taylor, 407–42. Cambridge, MA: Harvard University Press, 1998.

Márquez Herrera, Armando. "Las transformaciones de la minería zacatecana durante el porfiriato." In *Minería regional mexicana,* edited by Dolores Avila Herrera and Rina Ortiz, 59–76. Mexico: Instituto Nacional de Antropología e Historia, 1994.

Martin, Percy F. *Mexico of the XXth Century.* 2 vols. London: Edward Arnold, 1907.

Marx, Karl. *Capital: A Critique of Political Economy.* Vol. 1. New York: Modern Library, 1906.

Maurer, Noel. "Rents in Early Industrializing Economies: The Case of Porfirian Mexico, 1898–1911." Unpublished manuscript, Stanford University, 1997.

Mayer, Brantz. *Mexico as It Was and as It Is.* New York: J. Winchester, 1844.

Medina, Ignacio. "Dinamismo frustrado: La industria metal-mecánica." In *Industria y comercio,* edited by José María Muría and Jaime Olveda, Lecturas históricas de Guadalajara 5. Mexico: Instituto Nacional de Antropología, 1993.

The Mexican Year Book, 1908, Comprising Historical, Statistical and Fiscal Information. London: McCorquodalen.d.

The Mexican Year Book, 1912: A Financial and Commercial Handbook, Compiled from Official and Other Returns. London: McCorquodale, 1912.

The Mexican Year Book, 1914: A Financial and Commercial Handbook, Compiled from Official and Other Returns. London: McCorquodale, 1914.

The Mexican Year Book: The Standard Authority on Mexico, 1920–21. Los Angeles: Mexican Year Book Co., 1922.

Mexico. Cámara de Diputados. *Dictamen presentado a la Cámara de Diputados por sus Comisiones Unidas de Minería e Industria.* [1845]. Mexico: Librería Manuel Porrúa, 1955.

Mexico. *Memoria presentada a S. M. el Emperador por el Ministro de Fomento Luis Robles Pezuela de los trabajos ejecutados en su ramo el año de 1865.* Mexico: J. M. Andrade y F. Escalante, 1866.

Mexico. *Memoria sobre el estado de agricultura é industria de la República … en cumplimiento del articulo 26 del decreto orgánico de 2 de diciembre de 1842.* Mexico: Imprenta de Lara, 1843.

Mexico. *Memoria sobre el estado de agricultura é industria de la República en el año de 1844.* Mexico: José M. Lara, 1845.

Mexico. *Memoria sobre el estado de agricultura é industria de la República en el año 1845.* [1846]. Reprinted in *La industria nacional y el comercio exterior: Seis memo-*

rias oficiales sobre industria, agricultura, colonización y comercio exterior, 1842–1851, ed. Jan Bazant. Mexico: Banco Nacional de Comercio Exterior, 1962.

Mexico. Instituto Nacional de Estadística (INEGI). *Estadísticas históricas de México*. 2 vols. Mexico: INEGI, 1994.

Mexico. Ministerio de Hacienda y Crédito Público. *Expediente formado en la Secretaría de Hacienda y Crédito Público sobre un proyecto de Arancel*. Mexico: Imprenta del Gobierno, 1869.

Mexico. Secretaría de Fomento. *Boletín semestral de la República Mexicana, 1888, á cargo del Dr. Antonio Peñafiel*. Mexico: Oficina Tip. de la Secretaría de Fomento, 1890.

———. *Gaceta oficial de patentes y marcas*. Mexico: Imprenta de la Secretaría de Fomento, (monthly) 1903–11.

———. *Memoria*. Volumes for various years. Mexico: Imprenta de la Secretaría de Fomento, 1857–1911.

Mexico. Secretaria de Fomento. Dirección General de Estadística a cargo a Dr. Antonio Peñafiel. *Resumen general del censo de la República Mexicana verificado el 28 de octubre de 1900*. Mexico: Imprenta de la Secretaria de Fomento, 1905.

Mexico. Secretaría de Hacienda y Crédito Público. *Boletín del Ministerio de Hacienda*. Volumes for 1889–1911. Mexico: Imprenta de la Secretaría de Hacienda, 1889–1911.

———. *Estadística de la República Mexicana . . . por Emiliano Busto*. Mexico: Imprenta de Ignacio Cumplido, 1880.

Mexico. Secretaría de Industria, Comercio y Trabajo. *Boletín*.

Mexico. Secretaría de la Economía Nacional. *Documentos para la historia económica de México*. Vol. 9. Mexico, Secretaría de la Economía Nacional, 1934.

Meyer, Michael, William Sherman, and Susan Deeds. *The Course of Mexican History*. 8th ed. New York: Oxford University Press, 2007.

Meyer Cosío, Francisco Javier. *La minería en Guanajuato (1892–1913)*. Mexico: El Colegio de Michoacán y la Universidad de Guanajuato, 1998.

Mokyr, Joel. *The Gifts of Athena*. Princeton, NJ: Princeton University Press, 2002.

———. *Lever of Riches: Technological Creativity and Economic Progress*. New York: Oxford University Press, 1990.

Montejano y Aguiñaga, Rafael. *La minería en San Luis Potosí*. San Luis Potosí: Archivo Histórico del Estado, 1994.

Morales Moreno, Humberto. "El carácter marginal y arrendatario del sistema de fábrica en paisajes agrarios mexicanos, 1780–1880." *Anuario de Estudios Americanos* 62 (2005): 163–85.

———. "Los molinos de trigo en los orígenes de la industrialización mexicana: historiografía, tecnología y conservación (1780–1910)." In *Memoria del III Encuentro Nacional sobre Conservación del Patrimonio Industrial Mexicano,* edited by Belem Oviedo Gámez and Luz Carregha Lamadrid, 193–211. Mexico: Comité Mexicano para la Conservación del Patrimonio Industrial, 2005.

Mora-Torres, Juan. *The Making of the Mexican Border: The State, Capitalism, and Society in Nuevo León, 1848–1910*. Austin: University of Texas Press, 2001.

Moreno-Brid, Juan Carlos, and Jaime Ros. *Development and Growth in the Mexican Economy: A Historical Perspective.* New York: Oxford University Press, 2009.

Morris-Suzuki, Tessa. *The Technological Transformation of Japan: From the Seventeenth to the Twenty-First Century.* Cambridge: Cambridge University Press, 1994.

Mouat, Jeremy. "The Development of the Flotation Process: Technological Change and the Genesis of Modern Mining, 1898–1911." *Australian Economic History Review* 36, no. 1 (March 1996): 3–31.

Muñoz, Joaquín. "La minería en México: Bosquejo histórico." *Quinto Centenario* 11 (1986): 145–56.

Muría, José María, and Angélica Peregrina. *Viajeros Anglosajones por Jalisco.* Mexico: Siglo XIX, 1992.

Musacchio, Aldo, and Ian Read. "Bankers, Industrialists, and Their Cliques: Elite Networks in Mexico and Brazil during Early Industrialization." *Enterprise and Society* 8, no. 4 (2007): 842–80.

Nacional Financiera. *México: Los bienes de capital en la situación económica presente.* Mexico: Nacional Financiera, 1985.

Nacional Financiera. Comisión Económica para la América Latina. *La política industrial en el desarrollo económico de México.* Mexico: Nacional Financiera, 1971.

Nelson, Richard R., ed. *National Innovation Systems: A Comparative Analysis.* Oxford: Oxford University Press, 1993.

———. "On Technological Capabilities and Their Acquisition." In *Science and Technology: Lessons for Development Policy,* edited by Robert E. Evenson and Gustav Ranis, 71–87. Boulder, CO: Westview Press, 1990.

Nepomuceno Adorno, Juan. *Análisis de los males de México y sus remedios practicables.* Mexico: M. Muguia, 1858.

Niccolai, Sergio. "Algunas reflexiones sobre los orígenes de la mecanización industrial en México (1780–1850)." In *La cultura industrial Mexicana: Primer Encuentro Nacional de Arqueología Industrial,* edited by Sergio Niccolai and Humberto Morales Moreno, 191–215. Puebla, Mexico: Benemérita Universidad Autónoma de Puebla, 2003.

Novelo, Victoria. "Ferrerías y fundiciones." In *Arqueología de la industria en México,* edited by Victoria Novelo. Mexico: Museo Nacional de Culturas Populares, 1984.

Ochs, Kathleen H. "The Rise of American Mining Engineers: A Case Study of the Colorado School of Mines." *Technology and Culture* 33, no. 2 (1992): 278–301.

Ordoñez, Ezequiel. "Memoir of Antonio del Castillo." In *Bulletin of the Geological Society of America, Vol. 7,* edited by Joseph Stanley-Brown, 486–87. Rochester, NY: Geological Society of America, 1896.

Orlove, Benjamin, ed. *The Allure of the Foreign: Imported Goods in Postcolonial Latin America.* Ann Arbor: University of Michigan Press, 1997.

O'Rourke, Kevin H., and Jeffrey G. Williamson. *Globalization and History: The Evolution of a Ninteenth-Century Atlantic Economy.* Cambridge, MA: MIT Press, 1999.

Orozco, Rafael. *La industria minera de México: Distrito de Guanajuato*. México: Talleres Gráficos de la Nación, 1922.

Otero, Mariano. *Consideraciones sobre la situación política y social de la República Mexicana, en el año 1847*. Mexico: Valdés y redondas, 1848.

Pakenham, Robert. *The Dependency Movement: Politics and Scholarship in Development Studies*. Cambridge, MA: Harvard University Press, 1992.

Park, James. *The Cyanide Process of Gold Extraction: A Text-Book for the Use of Mining Students, Metallurgists, and Cyanide Operators*. 5th ed. London: Charles Griffin, 1913.

Parker, Morris B. *Mules, Mines, and Me in Mexico, 1895–1932*. Edited by James M. Day. Tucson: University of Arizona Press, 1979.

Parra, Alma. "Experiencia, destreza e innovaciones en la minería de Guanajuato en el siglo XIX." *Historias* 58 (May-August 2004): 69–82.

Pavitt, K. "Patent Statistics as Indicators of Innovative Activities: Possibilities and Problems." *Scientometrics* 7, nos. 1–2 (1985): 77–99.

———. "Uses and Abuses of Patent Statistics." In *Handbook of Quantitative Studies of Science and Technology*, edited by A. F. J. Van Raan, 509–36. Amsterdam: Elsevier Science, 1988.

Paz, Ireneo. *Álbum de la paz y el trabajo*. Mexico: I. Paz, 1911.

Pérez Toledo, Sonia. *Los hijos del trabajo: Los artesanos de la Ciudad de México, 1780–1853*. Mexico: Colegio de México, 2011.

Perkin, Joan. "Sewing Machines: Liberation or Drudgery for Women." *History Today*, December 2002, 35–41.

Piccato, Pablo. *City of Suspects: Crime in Mexico City, 1900–1931*. Durham, NC: Duke University Press, 2001.

Pilcher, Jeffrey M. "Fajitas and the Failure of Refrigerated Meatpacking in Mexico: Consumer Culture and Porfirian Capitalism." *Americas* 60, no. 3 (2004): 411–29.

———. "Mad Cowmen, Foreign Investors and the Mexican Revolution." *Journal of Iberian and Latin American Studies* 4, no. 1 (1998): 1–15.

Pineda, Yovanna. "Financing Manufacturing Innovation in Argentina, 1890–1930." *Business History Review* 83 (Autumn 2009): 539–62.

Pletcher, David M. *Rails, Mines, and Progress: Seven American Promoters in Mexico, 1867–1911*. Ithaca, NY: Cornell University Press, 1958.

Poinsett, Joel. *Notes on Mexico Made in the Autumn of 1822*. London: John Miller, 1825.

Pollard, Sidney. *Peaceful Conquest: The Industrialization of Europe, 1760–1970*. Oxford: Oxford University Press, 1981.

Porter, Katherine Anne. "Leaving the Petate." *New Republic*, February 4, 1931, 318–20.

Porter, Susie. *Working Women in Mexico City: Public Discourses and Material Conditions, 1879–1931*. Tucson: University of Arizona Press, 2003.

Potash, Robert A. *Mexican Government and Industrial Development in the Early Republic: The Banco de Avío*. Amherst: University of Massachusetts Press, 1983.

Prados de la Escosura, Leandro. "The Economic Consequences of Independence in Latin America." In *The Cambridge Economic History of Latin America,* vol. 1, *The Colonial Era and the Short Nineteenth Century,* 463–504. Cambridge: Cambridge University Press, 2006.

———. "Lost Decades? Economic Performance in Post-independence Latin America." *Journal of Latin American Studies* 41, no. 2 (2009): 279–307.

Pratt, Mary Louise. *Imperial Eyes: Travel Writing and Transculturation.* New York: Routledge, 1992.

Probert, Alan. "Bartolomé de Medina: The Patio Process and the Sixteenth Century Silver Crisis." *Journal of the West* 8, no. 1 (1969): 90–124.

Railroad, Telegraph and Steamship Builders' Directory. New York: Railway Directory Publishing, 1888.

Randall, Robert W. *Real del Monte: A British Mining Venture in Mexico.* Austin: University of Texas Press, 1972.

Razo, Armando, and Stephen H. Haber. "The Rate of Growth of Productivity in Mexico, 1850–1933: Evidence from the Cotton Textile Industry." *Journal of Latin American Studies* 30 (1998): 481–517.

Recio, Gabriela. "El nacimiento de la industria cervecera en México, 1880–1910." In *Cruda realidad: Producción, consumo y fiscalidad de las bebidas alcohólicas en México y América Latina, siglos XVII–XX,* edited by Ernest Sánchez Santiró, 155–85. Mexico: Instituto Mora, 2007.

Redfield, Robert. *Tepotzlan, a Mexican Village: A Study of Folk Life.* Chicago: University of Chicago Press, 1930.

Reed, John. *Insurgent Mexico.* New York: International Publishers, 1969.

Reyes Heroles, Jesús. *El liberalismo mexicano.* Vol. 3. *La integración de las ideas.* Mexico: Fondo de Cultura Económica, 1974.

Reynolds, Clark W. *The Mexican Economy: Twentieth Century Structure and Growth.* New Haven, CT: Yale University Press, 1970.

Rickard, T. A. *Journeys of Observation.* San Francisco: Dewey, 1907.

———. "Old and New Methods at Guanajuato, Mexico." *Mining and Scientific Press,* June 29, 1907, 824–25.

Riguzzi, Paolo. "Los caminos del atraso: Tecnología, instituciones e inversión en los ferrocarriles mexicanos, 1850–1900." In *Ferrocarriles y vida económica en México (1850–1950),* edited by Sandra Kuntz Ficker and Paolo Riguzzi, 31–98. Mexico City: Colegio de México, 1996.

Romero, Matías. *Geographical and Statistical Notes on Mexico.* New York: G. P. Putnam's Sons, 1898.

———. *Mexico and the United States; A Study of Subjects Affecting Their Political, Commercial, and Social Relations, Made with a View to Their Promotion.* New York: G. P. Putnam, 1898.

———. *Report of the Secretary of Finance of the United States of Mexico of the 15th of January, 1879, on the Actual Condition of Mexico, and the Increase of Commerce with the United States.* New York: N. Ponce de Leon, 1880.

Romero Gil, Juan Manuel. "Las bebidas espirituosas en Sonora: Notas sobre su producción, consumo e impuestos (1850–1920)." In *Cruda realidad: Producción, consumo y fiscalidad de las bebidas alcohólicas en México y América Latina, siglos XVII–XX,* edited by Ernest Sánchez Santiró, 106–33. Mexico: Instituto Mora, 2007.

———. *La minería en la noroeste de México: Utopía y realidad, 1850–1910.* Mexico: Plaza y Valdés, 2001.

———. "Minería y sociedad en el Noreste Porfiriana." *Siglo XIX* 1 (October 1991): 37–73.

———. "La modernización de la minería Sonorense en el Porfiriato." In *Noroeste minero: La minería en Sonora, Baja California y Baja California Sur durante el Porfiriato,* edited by Francisco Altable, 17–90. Mexico: Instituto Sudcaliforniano de Cultura, 2002.

Romero Sotelo, María Eugenia, and Luis Jáuregui. *Las contingencias de una larga recuperación: La economía mexicana, 1821–1867.* Mexico: Universidad Nacional Autónoma de México, 2003.

Rosenberg, Nathan. "Economic Development and the Transfer of Technology: Some Historical Perspectives." *Technology and Culture* 11, no. 4 (1970): 550–75.

———. *Inside the Black Box: Technology and Economics.* Cambridge: Cambridge University Press, 1982.

Rosenzweig, Fernando. "La industria." In *El Porfiriato: La vida económica,* edited by Daniel Cosío Villegas, 2 vols., Historia moderna de México 7/1 and 2, 311–481. Mexico: Editorial Hermes, 1965.

Ruiz, Jason. *Americans in the Treasure House: Travel to Porfirian Mexico and the Cultural Politics of Empire.* Austin: University of Texas Press, 2014.

Ruíz, Ramon Eduardo. *The Great Rebellion: Mexico, 1905–1924.* New York: W. W. Norton, 1980.

Ruiz de la Barrera, Rocío. "La empresa de Minas del Real del Monte (1849–1906). Medio siglo de explotación minera: ¿Casualidad o desarrollo estratégico?" In *Historia de las grandes empresas en México, 1850–1930,* edited by Carlos Marichal and Mario Cerutti, 291–316. Mexico: Colegio de México, 1997.

Ruttan, Vernon, and Yujiro Hayami. "Technology Transfer and Agricultural Development." *Technology and Culture* 14, no. 2 (1973): 119–51.

Sachs, Jeffrey D. *The End of Poverty: Economic Possibilities for Our Time.* New York: Penguin Press, 2005.

Sáiz González, J. Patricio. *Propiedad industrial y revolución liberal: Historia del sistema español de patentes (1759–1929).* Madrid: Oficina Española de Patentes y Marcas, 1995.

Saldaña, Juan José. "The Failed Search for 'Useful Knowledge': Enlightened Scientific and Technological Policies in New Spain." In *Cross Cultural Diffusion of Science: Latin America,* vol. 5, *Acts of the XVII International Congress of History of Science,* edited by Juan José Saldaña, Cuadernos de Quipu 2. Berkeley: Sociedad Latinoamericana de Historia de las Ciencias y la Tecnología, 1987.

Salvatore, Ricardo. *Imágenes de un imperio: Estados Unidos y las formas de representación de América Latina.* Buenos Aires: Editorial Sudamerica, 2006.

Salvucci, Richard J. "Agriculture and the Colonial Heritage of Latin America: Evidence from Bourbon Mexico." In *Colonial Legacies: The Problem of Persistence in Latin American History,* edited by Jeremy Adelman, 107–33. New York: Routledge, 1999.

——. "Algunas consideraciones económicas (1836): Análisis mexicano de la depresión a principios del siglo XIX." *Historia Mexicana* 55, no. 1 (July-September 2005): 67–97.

——. "Mexican National Income in the Era of Independence, 1800–40." In *How Latin American Fell Behind: Essays on the Economic Histories of Brazil and Mexico, 1800–1914,* edited by Stephen Haber, 216–42. Stanford, CA: Stanford University Press, 1997.

——. "The Origins and Progress of U.S.-Mexican Trade, 1825–1884: 'Hoc Opus, Hic Labor Est.'" *Hispanic American Historical Review* 71, no. 4 (1991): 697–735.

——. *Textiles and Capitalism in Mexico.* Princeton, NJ: Princeton University Press, 1987.

Sánchez Flores, Ramón. *Historia de la tecnología y la invención en México: Introducción a su estudio y documentos para los anales de la técnica.* Mexico: Fomento Cultural Banamex, 1980.

Sánchez Gómez, Julio. "La lenta penetración de la máquina de vapor en la minería del ámbito hispano." *Arbor* 149 (October-November 1994): 203–41.

Sánchez Graillet, Luis Avelino. "Tecnología, trabajo y raza en la industria petrolera en México." PhD diss. in progress, UNAM.

Sánchez Rangel, Oscar. "La última etapa de una empresa familiar en Guanajuato: La antigua casa Rul." *Legajos,* no. 4 (April–June 2010): 13–42.

Sánchez Santiró, Ernest, ed. *Cruda realidad: Producción, consumo y fiscalidad de las bebidas alcohólicas en México y América Latina, siglos XVII-XX.* Mexico: Instituto Mora, 2007.

——. "El desempeño de la economía mexicana tras la independencia, 1821–1870: Nuevas evidencias e interpretaciones." In *Latinoamérica y España, 1800–1850: Un crecimiento económico nada excepcional,* edited by Enrique Llopis and Carlos Marichal, 65–110. Madrid: Marcial Pons Historia, 2009.

Sandoval, Fernando B. *La industria de azúcar en Nueva España.* México: Universidad Nacional Autónoma de México, 1951.

San Miguel, Pedro L. "La representación del atraso: México en la historiografía estadounidense." *Historia Mexicana* 53, no. 1 (2003): 989–1009.

Santiago, Myrna I. *The Ecology of Oil: Environment, Labor, and the Mexican Revolution, 1900–1938.* Cambridge: Cambridge University Press, 2006.

Schell, William. *Integral Outsiders: The American Colony in Mexico City, 1876–1911.* Wilmington, DE: Scholarly Resources, 2001.

Schmitz, Christopher J. *World Non-ferrous Metal Production and Prices, 1700–1976.* London: Frank Cass, 1979.

Scoville, Warren C. *Revolution in Glassmaking: Entrepreneurship and Technological Change in the American Industry, 1880–1920.* Cambridge, MA: Harvard University Press, 1948.

Sempat Assadourian, Carlos. "La bomba de fuego de Newcomen y otros artificios de desagüe: Un intento de transferencia de tecnología inglesa a la minería novohispana, 1726–1731." *Historia Mexicana* 50, no. 3 (2001): 385–457.

Shadlen, Kenneth C. "The Puzzling Politics of Patents and Innovation Policy in Mexico." *Law and Business Review of the Americas* 16, no. 4 (2010): 823–38.

Sierra, Justo. *México: Su evolución social.* 3 vols. 1902–5. Reprint, Mexico: Miguel Angel Porrúa, 2005.

Simonian, Lane. *Defending the Land of the Jaguar: A History of Conservation in Mexico.* Austin: University of Texas Press, 1995.

Smith, Francis Hopkinson. *A White Umbrella in Mexico.* New York: Houghton, Mifflin, 1889.

Snodgrass, Michael. *Deference and Defiance in Monterrey: Workers, Paternalism, and Revolution in Mexico, 1890–1950.* Cambridge: Cambridge University Press, 2003.

Soberanis, Jorge A. "Catálogo de patentes de invención en México durante el siglo xix (1840–1900): Ensayo de interpretación sobre el proceso de industrialización del México decimonónico." Tesis de Licenciatura, UNAM, 1989.

Solís Matías, Alejandro. "Organización familiar rural en el siglo XIX: La Barca, Jalisco." In *Five Centuries of Mexican History / Cinco siglos de historia de México,* edited by Virginia Guedea and Jaime E. Rodríguez O., 300–306. Mexico: Instituto Mora, 1992.

Solo, Robert. "The Capacity to Assimilate an Advanced Technology." *American Economic Review* 52, nos. 1–2 (1966): 91–97.

Southworth, John R. *Las minas de México (edición ilustrada).* Liverpool: Blake and Mackenzie, 1905.

Southworth, John R., and Percy G. Holms. *El directorio oficial minero de México.* Liverpool: Blake and Mackenzie, 1910.

Spude, Robert L. "Cyanide and the Flood of Gold: Some Colorado Beginnings of the Cyanide Process of Gold Extraction." *Essays and Monographs in Colorado History* 12 (1991): 1–35.

Staples, Anne, ed. *Bienes y vivencias: El siglo XIX.* Historia de la vida cotidiana en México 4. Mexico: Colegio de México, 2005.

Stegner, Wallace. *Angle of Repose.* Garden City, NY: Doubleday, 1971.

Strassmann, W. Paul. *Technological Change and Economic Development: The Manufacturing Experience of Mexico and Puerto Rico.* Ithaca, NY: Cornell University Press, 1968.

Stresser-Pean, Guy. "El arado criollo en México y en América Central." In *Homenaje a Isabel Kelly,* edited by Yólotl González, 197–226. Mexico: INAH, 1989.

Suárez Cortez, Blanca Estela. "Poder oligárquico y usos del agua: Querétaro en el siglo XIX (1838–1880)." In *Historia de los usos del agua en México,* edited by Luis Aboites Aguilar, 17–106. Mexico: Comisión Nacional del Agua, 1998.

Sutton, Werner P. "Malt and Beer in Spanish America." In *Special Consular Reports No. 1*, edited by US Department of State, Bureau of Statistics, 329–38. Washington, DC: Government Printing Office, 1890.

Swent, Langan W. *Working for Safety and Health in Underground Mines: San Luis and Homestake Mining Companies, 1846–1988.* 2 vols. Western Mining in the Twentieth Century Oral History Series. Berkeley: Regional Oral History Office, Bancroft Library, University of California, Berkeley, 1995.

Tafunell, Xavier. "Capital Formation in Machinery in Latin America, 1890–1930." *Journal of Economic History* 69 (2009): 928–50.

Tafunell, Xavier, and Albert Carreras. "Capital Goods Imports and Investment in Latin America in the Mid 1920s." Manuscript, Universitat Pompeu Fabra, 2005.

Tannenbaum, Frank. *The Struggle for Peace and Bread.* New York: Knopf, 1950.

Teitelbaum, Vanessa E. *Entre el control y la movilización: Honor, trabajo y solidaridades artesanales en la Ciudad de México a mediados del siglo XIX.* Estudios históricos. Mexico: El Colegio de Mexico, 2008.

Temin, Peter. "Steam and Waterpower in the Early 19th Century." *Journal of Economic History* 26 (June 1966): 187–205.

Tenorio-Trillo, Mauricio. *Mexico at the World's Fairs: Crafting a Modern Nation.* Berkeley: University of California Press, 1996.

———. "Stereophonic Scientific Modernisms: Social Science between Mexico and the United States, 1880s-1930s." *Journal of American History* (December 1999): 1156–87.

Terán Trillo, Yolanda. "El Castillo de la Fama." In *Memoria del III Encuentro Nacional sobre Conservación del Patrimonio Industrial Mexicano,* edited by Belem Oviedo Gámez and Luz Carregha Lamadrid, 374–86. Mexico: Comité Mexicano para la Conservación del Patrimonio Industrial, A.C., 2005.

Thompson, Lanny. "Artisans, Marginals, and Proletarians: The Households of the Popular Classes in Mexico City, 1876–1950." In *Five Centuries of Mexican History / Cinco siglos de historia de México,* edited by Virginia Guedea and Jaime E. Rodríguez O., 307–24. Mexico: Instituto Mora, 1992.

Thomson, Guy P. C. *Puebla de los Angeles: Industry and Society in a Mexican City, 1700–1850.* Boulder, CO: Westview Press, 1989.

Tinajero, Araceli, and J. Brian Freeman, eds. *Technology and Culture in Twentieth-Century Mexico.* Tuscaloosa: University of Alabama Press, 2013.

Todd, Jan. *Colonial Technology: Science and the Transfer of Innovation to Australia.* Cambridge: Cambridge University Press, 1995.

Tortolero Villaseñor, Alejandro. *De la coa a la máquina de vapor: Actividad agrícola e innovación tecnológica en las haciendas mexicanas, 1880–1914.* Mexico: Siglo XXI, 1995.

Toussaint Alcaraz, Florence. *Escenario de la prensa en el Porfiriato.* Mexico: Fundación Manuel Buendía, 1984.

Towner, Margaret. "Monopoly Capitalism and Women's Work during the Porfiriato." *Latin American Perspectives* 4, nos. 1–2 (1977): 90–105.

Trabulse, Elías. *El círculo roto: Estudios históricos sobre la ciencia en México*. Mexico: Fondo de Cultura Económica, 1996.

———. *Historia de la ciencia en México: Estudios y textos*. Mexico: Fondo de Cultura Económica, 1983.

Trujillo Bolio, Mario. *Operarios fabriles en el Valle de México, 1864–1884*. Mexico: Colegio de México, 1997.

Tutino, John. *From Insurrection to Revolution in Mexico: Social Bases of Agrarian Violence, 1750–1940*. Princeton, NJ: Princeton University Press, 1986.

Uchida, Hoshimi. "The Transfer of Electrical Technologies from the United States and Europe to Japan, 1869–1914." In *International Technology Transfer: Europe, Japan and the USA, 1700–1914*, edited by David J. Jeremy, 219–41. Edward Elgar, 1991.

Unger, Kurt R. "El desarrollo industrial y tecnológico mexicano: Estado actual de la integración industrial y tecnológica." In *Aspectos tecnológicos de la modernización industrial de México,* edited by Pablo Mulás del Pozo, 44–80. Mexico: Academia de la Investigación Científica y Fondo de Cultura Económica, 1995.

———. "La globalización del sistema innovativo Mexicano: Empresas extranjeras y tecnología importada." Documento de Trabajo No. 175, Centro de Investigación y Docencia Económicas, 1999.

Uribe Salas, José Alfredo. "El desarrollo de la minería michoacana en el siglo XIX." Manuscript. n.d. Accessed September 18, 2009. http://morgan.iia.unam.mx/usr/Industrial/BOL06/URIBE.html.

———. "El distrito minero El Oro-Tlalpujahua entre dos siglos y el mercado internacional de tecnología." In *Five Centuries of Mexican History,* edited by Virginia Guedea and Jaime E. Rodríguez O., 119–35. Mexico: Instituto Mora, 1992.

———. "Empresas y empresarios en la minería michoacana de la segunda mitad del siglo xix." In *Minería regional mexicana: Primer Reunión de Historiadores de la Minería Latinoamericana (IV),* edited by Dolores Avila Herrera and Rina Ortiz, 41–58. Mexico: Instituto Nacional de Antropología e Historia, 1994.

US Bureau of the Census. *Twelfth Census of Manufacturers, 1900*. Vol. 9, pt. 3. Washington, DC: Government Printing Office, 1901–3.

US Bureau of Foreign and Domestic Commerce. *Commercial Reports,* nos. 1–75. Washington, DC: Government Printing Office, 1910.

US Census Office. *Census Reports of the United States* [1900, 1905, 1910]. Washington, DC: US Census Office, various years.

US Department of Commerce [1903–12, Commerce and Labor]. *Commercial Relations of the United States with Foreign Nations*. Washington, DC: Government Printing Office, various dates.

———. *Daily Consular and Trade Reports*. Washington, DC: Government Printing Office, various years.

———. *Foreign Commerce and Navigation of the United States*. Washington, DC: Government Printing Office, annual 1880–1911.

———. *Special Agent Series*. Washington, DC: Government Printing Office, various dates.

US Department of State. *Money and Prices in Foreign Countries.* Special Consular Report 13. Washington, DC: Government Printing Office, 1896.

———. *Monthly Consular and Trade Reports.* Washington, DC: Government Printing Office, various years.

US Department of State/Department of Commerce and Labor. Bureau of Manufactures [continued by Department of State, Bureau of Statistics and Bureau of Foreign Commerce]. *Special Consular Reports.* Washington, DC: Government Printing Office, various dates.

Utah since Statehood: Historical and Biographical. Vol. 4. Chicago: S. J. Clarke, 1920.

Vanderwood, Paul. *The Power of God against the Guns of Government.* Stanford, CA: Stanford University Press, 1998.

Van Young, Eric. *Hacienda and Market in Eighteenth-Century Mexico: The Rural Economy of the Guadalajara Region, 1675–1820.* Berkeley: University of California Press, 1981.

———. "Material Life." In *The Countryside in Colonial Latin America,* edited by Louisa Schell Hoberman and Susan Migden Socolow, 49–74. Albuquerque: University of New Mexico Press, 1996.

Velarde, Mario. *Directorio de empresas industriales beneficiadas con exenciones fiscales, 1940–1960.* Mexico: Banco de México, 1961.

Velasco Avila, Cuauhtémoc, Eduardo Flores Clair, Alma Parra Campos, and Edgar Gutiérrez López. *Estado y minería en México (1767–1910).* Mexico: Fondo de Cultura Económica, 1988.

Villafana, Andrés. *Reseña minera de la región central y sureste del estado de Jalisco.* Mexico: Imprenta de la Secretaría de Fomento, 1916.

Vizcaya Canales, Isidro. *Los orígenes de la industrialización de Monterrey.* Monterrey: Archivo General del Estado de Nuevo León, 2001.

Von Mentz de Boege, Brígida M. "Tecnología minera alemana en México durante la primera mitad del siglo XIX." *Estudios de Historia Moderna y Contemporánea de México* 8 (1980): 85–95.

Wallace, Robert-Bruce. "Coal in Mexico." 2008. www.economia.unam.mx/publicaciones/econinforma/pdfs/359/brucelish.pdf.

Ward, H. G. *Mexico in 1827.* Vol. 2. London: Henry Colburn, 1828.

Warren, Richard. "Elections and Popular Political Participation in Mexico, 1808–1836," In *Liberals, Power and Power: State Formation in Nineteenth-Century Latin America,* edited by Barbara Tenenbaum and Vincent Peloso. Athens: University of Georgia Press, 1996.

Wasserman, Mark. *Capitalists, Caciques, and Revolution: The Native Elite and Foreign Enterprise in Chihuahua, Mexico, 1854–1911.* Chapel Hill: University of North Carolina Press, 1984.

———. "Enrique Creel: Business and Politics in Mexico, 1880–1930." *Business History Review* 59, no. 4 (1985): 645–62.

Weiner, Richard. "Battle for Survival: Porfirian Views of the International Marketplace." *Journal of Latin American Studies* 32 (2000): 645–70.

Wells, David Ames. *A Study of Mexico.* New York: D. Appleton, 1887.

Wolfe, Mikael. *Watering the Revolution: The Technopolitical Success and Socioeco-logical Failure of Agrarian Reform in La Laguna, Mexico.* Durham, NC: Duke University Press, forthcoming.

Womack, John, Jr. *El trabajo en la Cervecería Moctezuma, 1908.* Mexico: Colegio de México, 2012.

———. *Zapata and the Mexican Revolution.* New York: Vintage Books, 1968.

Zamora Pérez, Alfonso. *Inventario crítico de las máquinas desfibradoras en México (1830–1890).* Mexico: UAM-A, 1999.

Zavala, Lorenzo de. *Viaje a los Estados-Unidos del Norte de América.* Mérida: Castillo y Compañía, 1846.

Zuleta, María Cecilia. "La Secretaría de Fomento y el fomento agrícola en México, 1876–1910: La invención de una agricultura próspera que no fue." *Mundo Agrario: Revista de Estudios Rurales* 1, no. 1 (2000): s.n.

INDEX

absorptive capacity, 227–28n43
Acámbaro, Guanajuato, 187
accidents, 177, 178f23
acquisition costs, 169
adaptations, 209; of agricultural technologies, 171; challenges, 184–85; cyanide process, 134, 185; cyanide process to silver ores, 142–43, 146, 149, 159, 269n92; "dry-washing" techniques, 167; economic aspects, 150; glass industry, 127; global adaptation of cyanide, 151; of imported machines, 260n104; imported technicians, 128; levels of difficulty, 213–14; local conditions effects on, 171; local learning opportunities, 185; Owens bottle system, 127, 129, 184; of production systems, 208–9; system design, 166
adoption, delayed. *See* delayed adoption
adoption of technology, 4, 18, 79–80, 267n62; in agriculture sector, 170–72; automative bottle production, 131; barriers to, 72; challenges of, 14, 108, 213; conditions for, 212; constraints to, 24; cost of, 160; cyanidation and gold, 142; cyanide process, 134, 145, 146, 151–52; dynamite, 146; economic growth, 153; electric power, 73, 146; entrepreneurs on, 10; experiences, variety of, 8; and factory-scale production, 108; and freight cost, 69–70; and glass bottle-blowing production systems, 108; government officials on, 10;

impact on technological capabilities, 102; importance of, 29; and industries, 8; investment in technology, 96; investors on, 10; limitations of, 57–58, 159; and low assimilation of knowledge, 8; and market structure, 168; need for, 4; from North America, 7; obstacles to, 16, 74, 126–27, 157–72, 180; and Owens machine, 108; pace of, 217; and patents, 113; plows, 171; pneumatic drills, 146; post-1870 economic expansion and, 57; pre-1870s Mexico and, 57; prevented adoption, 7–8, 169–72; production capabilities and imported technology, 188; and production systems, 108; and rail system, 57; and rapid economic growth, 7; reluctance towards, 170; sewing machines, 84, 87, 96, 100, 105; and steam technology, 72; technology transfer, 11, 17; transformative potential of, 217; trends and patterns, 8; and use rights, 113; and village economy, 170; and wealthy nations, 9
Adorno, Juan, 12, 31
"advantage of proximity" (*la ventaja de la vecindad*), 206, 210–11
advertisements, newspaper, 7, 88f11, 91–92, 247n17
agave fibers, 161
agents, foreign, 85
agents, Singer, 183
agricultural conditions, and sewing machine consumption, 100

agricultural implements, 170, 174

agriculturalists, commercial, and adoption of technology, 172

agricultural machinery imports, 61t1

agricultural technology, 22, 170

agricultural workers, 170

agriculture, 27, 78t2, 170–72; adaptations, effects of local conditions on, 171; and backwardness (*atraso*), 170; cultivators, number of, 274n39; information, 279n70; innovation capabilities, 170; labor productivity, rising, 164–65; large-scale commercial production, 170; output, 172; perceived future of, 3; productivity, 172; and steam technology, 72; technological innovations, 172; threshing machine technology, 177–78; worker output, 164–65

Aguascalientes, 71, 91

Alamán, Lucas, 29, 33, 38, 188, 212; on material progress, 50, 51–52; quotes on iron, 46, 49; on steam power, 44; textile financing, 45

Alamogordo, New Mexico, 123

Álbum de la paz y el trabajo (Paz), 4

alcohol culture, 109

alkali chemicals, 111, 124, 260n104

Allan, John, 149

Allen, A., on the MacArthur-Forrest invention, 266n53

Allen, Robert C., 11

alluvial deposits, 136

Alzate, José Antonio, 42–43, 44

amalgamation process, 137, 264n33, 268n73, 269n89; abandonment of, 146; amalgamation plants, 143, 144, 146; *Azogueros,* 261n6; costs of, 139; and cyanide experimentation, 147; and cyanide process, 142; modifications to, 138; and silver depreciation, 139

American Bottle Company, 119, 256n55; and Owens machine Mexican patent rights, 120–21

American colony in Mexico City, 257n59

American Institute of Mining Engineers, 149

Anenecuilco, Mexico, 171

Angle of Repose (Stegner), 240n23

Anglo-Mexican Mining Company, 141

Anheuser Busch Company, 119

anthracite, 127, 163

antiguas, 148

Antuñano, Estevan de, 10, 33, 40, 49, 50, 51, 53, 58, 190, 212; *grito* of, 29–30; textile factories, 176

apparel, imported. *See* clothing imports

Arbuckle Ryan Company, 126

Argentina, 10, 85, 214

Armour company, 167

arrieros, 69

artisanal workers, 12, 27, 103, 110f14, 111, 165, 175, 176

artisanal workshops, 27, 97, 99, 110f14; fuel dependency of, 164

artisans, Mexican, 12, 27, 103, 110f14, 111, 175, 176

assembly line, 167

assimilation of expertise, displacement, Mexican worker, 153

assimilation of knowledge, 18, 188, 213; capacity for, 215; challenges of, 14; displacement, Mexican worker, 153; opportunity access, unequal, 182; overview of constraints to, 24; and sewing machine consumption, 84, 105; transfer as, 17; and wealthy nations, 9

Atlantic City, New Jersey, 149

Atlantic context, 9

Atlantic economy: and demand for gold and silver, 134; expansion of, 2; and glass making industry, 112; and Mexican natural resource exploitation/trade, 29, 69; Mexico's integration into, 130; post-1870, 59

Atlantic recession of 1892–93, 89

atraso (backwardness), 27–54; agriculture sector, 170; Antuñano on, 58; economy, 11, 21, 22, 28, 153; effects on production technologies, 153; emergence of, 50–52; iron and steel industry, 46–49; and material progress, 12–13, 208; power and, 41–45; references to, 238n114; transportation and, 38–41

Australia, 91, 140, 269n90

automation: accidents, 177; bottle production, 112, 131; domestic production, 114; effects of on skilled glass workers, 114;

and labor needs, 128; North Atlantic, 58, 112; purchase of, 131; walkout protests, 177; and wood-based fuels, 124
Aviles-Galan, Miguel Angel, 78f10, 78t1, 245n84
azogueros (mercury men), 137, 261n6
Aztec precious metals, 136

backward linkages, 175
backwardness (*atraso*), 27–54; agriculture sector, 170; Antuñano on, 58; economy, 11, 21, 22, 28, 153; effects on production technologies, 153; emergence of, 50–52; iron and steel industry, 46–49; and material progress, 12–13, 208; power and, 41–45; references to, 238n114; transportation and, 38–41
Bajío, 40
Baldwin Works, 70
Balkans, 91
barter networks, 93, 170
basic forms, iron and steel, 61t1
Batcheller, Henry R., 141
Batopilas, Mexico, 185
Bazant, Mílada, 278n38
beer consumption, 130, 131f17, 253n10; and bottle supply constraint, 116; changes in, 109; and demand for glass bottles, 131; replacing pulque, 6; as symbol of modernity, 130
beer industry, 107–33, 213; competitive dynamics of, 117–18; consumption changes, 173; data reports, 109; and demand for glass bottles, 107; exports, Mexican, 109; imports, foreign, 109, 130; markets, Mexican, 117, 118; in Mexico, 107; and raw materials acquisition, 161
Belden, Francisco, 118–19, 122, 256n38
Belden, José, 259n89
Belgium, 64
Bernard, Pedro Marí, 47
Bernstein, Marvin D., 147f20
bisulfate of soda, 124
bituminous coal, 127
black box technologies, 84, 214
blacksmith shops, 71, 175, 236n89, 273n31
boiler and engine manufacture, 61t1, 78t2, 175, 192f24, 243n58

Böker, Roberto, 55
Bolton, J. A., 119, 255n34
Bonsack machine, 169, 206
books, 62–64
border crossing factor of knowledge exchange, 14–15
borrowed technology/expertise, 210, 212, 216
bottle blowing mechanization, 113
bottle company, first, 127
bottle imports, 110, 111, 131, 253n10, 257n61
bottle market, Mexican, 119, 125
bottle production, domestic, 107, 122–23; costs of, 114; economics of, 118; and foreign competition, 123; local learning opportunities, 184; negotiations, 125; and Owens machine, 114; uncertainties of, 123
bottle supply constraint, 116, 119
bottles vs. barrels, 253n10
bottle tariffs, 131–32
Boudoüin, Emilio, 75
Bourbon modernization projects, 20, 27, 135
Braniff, Oscar, 199
Brazil, 10, 210, 214
Brehme, Hugo, 95
breweries, domestic, 6, 107, 108; brewing, 162; *cervecerías* (large-scale breweries), 109, 118; expansion of, 111; and local supply sources, 161; and refrigerated railcars, 111; and regional markets, 130
brewers, domestic, 125
brewers, foreign, 109
brick making, 162
Britain, 214–15; and adoption of sewing machines, 87; alkali chemicals imports from, 124; beer exports, 109; diffusion rate of sewing machines, 91; economic growth, 28; and global patents, 64; industrialization, 8–9, 212; locomotives orders, 242n50; Mexico's view of, 9; and Owens machine, 113; as technology exporter, 9; as technology producer, 9
British exports, 243n61; alkali chemicals, 124; beer, 109; cyanide process, 152; and sewing machine exports, 86; sewing machines, 83, 88; soda ash (sodium carbonate), 260n104; steam engine export, 72; steel rail exports, 70

British investors, 135; first railroad concession, 68–69
British technicians, 8–9
Brittingham, Juan F., 67, 127–28, 132–33, 161, 163, 168, 173, 184, 199, 202, 206, 255n27, 256n38, 256n55, 257n59; Chihuahua river sand, 258n70; as director, 259n89; and Enrique Creel, 115–16; on fuel costs, 163–64; and Juan Terraza, 114–25; and Negovetich & Roever, 121–22; and Owens machine, 114–25; patent rights, Mexican, 206; and royalty issue, 121–22, 169; and Toledo Glass Company, 114–25; and Vidriera Monterrey, 173
Burns, Daniel, 66
Busch, Adolfo, 119–20
Bustamante Valdés, J., 137f18
Bustos mill, 145
butchers, 167–68
Butters, Charles, 244–45n76, 264n35, 265n36, 266n54

cabildo, 167
Calle de Manrique, 55
Calle Espíritu Santo, 55
Camacho, Anselmo, 202
Campeche, Mexico, 94
camps, Mexican, 239n18
Canada, 122
Candelaria Consolidated Mexican Mining Company, 266n52
Candelaria mine, 240n23
capabilities, technological, 15–16, 16f2, 188, 206, 227n43, 245n84
capacity, production: of cyanide plants, 151; and market size, 166; significance of, 230n62; and skilled worker scarcity, 166
capital, 4, 153, 170
capital, foreign, 6, 135, 152, 153
capital equipment, 9, 59, 210
capital goods, imports of, 79, 210
capital investment, fixed, 79, 152
capitalization estimates, 270n98
cargo transport costs, 69
Carillo Rojas, Arturo, 78t1
carriers, human cargo (tamemes), 38
carts (carro), mule-drawn transport, 38

carts, locally made, and local conditions, 171
Casa Böker, 55, 238n1
Cassel Gold Extraction Company, 139, 140, 141, 144, 262–63n23, 263n31
Castillo, Antonio del, 197
cast-iron, 169, 173
"catch up" industrialization, 11
Celaya, Mexico, 111
cement, 6, 166
cement block construction, 169–70
Cementos Hidalgos, 108
Centennial, Mexican, 4, 208
Central (rail system), 71, 131f17
Central Europe, 87
central Mexico, 118, 172
Cerro Colorado mines, 142
Cervecera Toluca y México, 256n55, 257n59
Cervecería Cuauhtémoc, 110, 118–20
Cervecería Moctezuma, 112f15
cervecerias (large-scale breweries), 109
Cervecería Sonora, 111
Cervecería Toluca y México, 111, 118–19
Chalco, 73
charcoal, 163
Charles Butter company, 142, 150, 264n35, 266n56
chemicals, North Atlantic, 58
Cheshire County Record Office archives, 263n31
Chihuahua, Mexico, 56, 94, 240n18, 279n70; bottle factory plans, 257n59; Brittingham & Terrazas, 117–18; cervecerias (large-scale breweries), 109, 118; clothing manufactories, 98; Jesús María mine, 69; milling facilities, 142; mining engineers, 258n70; Palmarejo plant, 142; rail system, 71; ready-made clothing factories, 98; and Singer sewing machine office, 103
Chihuahua River sand, 123, 258n70
Chile, 210
Chilean mills, 150
Chilpancingo, Guerrero, 95
chlorination, 138
cigarette manufacturing, 6, 168–69, 182, 206
cigarette market, national, 168–69

cigarette-rolling machine, Decouffle, 168–69
cities, and electric power, 73
civil engineering, *Colegio Militar* and, 278n53
civil unrest (1911), 128
civil unrest (1912), 129
Civil War, U.S., 13, 19
Clark, W. A. Graham, 165
clothing, ready-made. *See* ready-made clothing
clothing imports, 83–84, 99
clothing industry, 6, 84, 91, 98, 99, 246n14. *See also* garment industry; ready-made clothing; textile industry
clothing production, economics, 97
Coahuila, Mexico, 124, 163
coal: domestic, 127, 163; imports, 124–25, 271–72n11, 272n14; mines, 124; scarcity of, 162
coke ovens, system design, 166
Colegio Militar, 278n53
colonial economy, 27; wood-fuel scarcity, 162–63
colonial mining technology, 27, 261n6
Colorado mining school, 187
commercial agriculture, 19, 27, 72, 172
commercialization of new technologies, 213, 227n40; agricultural sector, 170; Brittingham, Juan F., 169; commercial practices, 14; cyaniding with silver ores, 149; in glass bottle manufacture, 111–12; local learning opportunities, 184; obstacles to, 132; Owens bottle system, 159; Owens system, 126–27; and production uncertainty, 122; and royalty issue, 122
communication technology, 22, 187
Compañía de Tranvías de México, 6
Compañía El Buen Tono, 168–69
Compañía Hidroelétrica *e* Irrigadora de Chapala, 73
Compañía La Vidriera. *See* Vidriera Monterrey
Compañía Vidriera Monterrey. *See* Vidriera Monterrey
Compañí La Jabonera La Laguna, 108, 116
comparative advantage, 29
competition limits, 169, 184

competitive pricing, 118, 119, 132
CONACYT (national technology council), 210
constraints, 14; adoption of technology, 214; and beer industry, 110; on expansion of high-productivity sectors, 210; and industrial concentration, 184; to learning, 181–207; skill sharing and learning, 216; technological learning, 214; weight constraints, 169
construction industry, 169, 170, 173
consumer demand. *See* demand, consumer
consumer goods, 6, 71, 216
consumer markets: expansion of, 6; *falta de consumo,* 19; for manufactured goods, 172; and sewing machine consumption, 84, 100; and transportation, 41
consumers, 213; and adoption of technology, 18, 84; beer preferences, 109; choice of imports over domestic goods, 166; consumption increases, 6; demand and beer industry, 107; and emerging middle-class culture, 208; and productive efficiency, 168; of sewing machines, 91, 92f12
context, Mexican, 217; and "fit" problems, 160, 213; imported technologies, 84, 161, 217; and imported technology, 160; and local learning, 184; and technology component fit, 129
context of adoption, 16
context of origin, 16
contextual factors, 182, 217
"convergent" industrialization, 11
Copala cyanide plants, 264n35
copper sulfate (*magistral*), 137
core technologies, adoption and diffusion of, 79
Corkrell, Dr., 255n34
Cornell mining school, 187
Cortés, Hernán, 47
cost of living estimates, 249n48
costs, fixed, and Owens machine, 108
cotton textiles, and tariff protections, 166
creativity, technological, 2, 9, 13, 14, 17, 205, 212, 213, 217
credit markets, Mexican, 184
Creel, Enrique, 115–16, 199

steam power, 73, 215; summary of limitations to, 169; vertical diffusion, 216
digging sticks, 170
dislocation effects, 179, 213
displacement, 153, 176, 217
disposable income, and sewing machine consumption, 84
distribution of wealth and knowledge, 14
Dithridge, George W., 124, 255n34, 258n70
domestic goods, imports chosen over, 166
domestic markets, 69, 108, 165–66
Dos Estrellas mines, 141
dressmakers, 98
drought, 89, 100
"dry-washing" techniques, 167
Dublán, Manuel, 219
Durango, Mexico, 104, 144, 240n23
Durango mill, 266n52
Durango mines, 242n45
duty-free machine imports, 85, 174
dynamite, 6, 138, 146

early industrialization, 177
economic backwardness(*atraso*), 11, 21, 22, 28, 153
economic context of technological change, 14
economic crisis (1980s), 210
economic growth, 3, 4, 9, 164–65, 208; and adoption of technology, 7, 18, 153; and assimilation of technology, 18; backwardness (*atraso*), 11, 21, 22, 28, 153; central paradox of, 24; constraints on, 217; and deforestation, 163; economic contraction, 122; economic expansion, 20, 69; and foreign capital, 153; and global knowledge, 13–14; Great Britain, 28; growth era of 1870–1910, 56; and imported human capital, 18; and imported technology, 57; and innovations, 164; late-century, 71; and mining industry, 153; new technologies, 213; North Atlantic, 28, 212; patterns of, 173; Porfirian Mexico, 165; pre-1870s Mexico, 56; railroads and, 71; recovery (1860–1870), 19; and sewing machine consumption, 84; stagnation of, 18–19; sustainability of, 13–14; and technologi-

cal innovation, 181; and technology imports, 164; United States, 28
economic incentives, and bottle production, 131
economic malaise, 28, 68
economic power, North Atlantic, 9, 11–12
economic theory, 10
economies of scale, increased, and electric power, 98
economists, viewpoint of, 10
economy: aspirations for economic independence, 3; diversification, 213; duality of, 21; and high fuel costs, 163–94; and inanimate power sources, 162; and new technologies, 227n40; productive capacity, 169; recessions, 248n32; and social constructionist approach, 227n40; underdevelopment, 169; village economy, 170
Edison General Electric, 112
education, unequal access to, 179
education, engineering, 185–86, 210, 215, 278n53
education, technical, 210, 215, 217
educational initiatives, 205–6
educational institutions, "national innovation system", 182
Egypt, 10, 210
1870 watershed, 20, 59
El Buen Tono, 181–82, 185
El Centro Mercantil, 98
El Correo de Chihuahua, 86
El Economista Mexicano, 163
electrical industry: electrification, 146; foreign financing of, 187–88; and garment factories, 97; investors, 73; North Atlantic, 58; opportunity access, unequal, 187; and power costs, 97; as principle source of motive power, 73; replacing men and mules, 6; and sweatshops/workshops, 97
electrical machinery imports, 61t1, 73
electric power, 73, 98, 124, 150, 162, 217
electric power plants, 73, 124–25
Elhúyar, Fausto de, 42, 44
Elhúyar, Fausto de, 212
El Imparcial, 89
elites, Mexican, 178–80

factory systems, transformative potential of, 217
Fall, Albert, 241n33
falta de consumo (weak consumer markets), 19
Fernández Leal, Manuel, 12
Ferrara, Vicente, 166, 203
Ferreterías de Encarnación and Guadalupe, 244n67
Ferrocarril Central Mexicano, 70
fertilizer, commercial, 170
Ficker, Sandra Kuntz, 61f7, 221
Filippinni, Pedro, 252n107
filter press, development and diffusion of, 150
finance capital, 170
firms, new. *See* initiatives, new
first generation industrial workers, 165
first industrializers, 10
"fit" problems of adoption, 160, 166, 180, 213
fixed capital investment, 79
Flores mill, 145
flotation process, 268n70
food crops, staple, 170
Ford, H.W., 98
foreign agents, 85
foreign capital, 6, 135, 152, 153
foreign engineers, 16, 259n98. *See* engineers, imported
foreign expertise, 16. *See* expertise, imported
foreign imports, 122, 124. *See* imports, foreign
foreign interventions, 9–10; and effects on Mexico, 9–10
foreign investment, 59
foreign investors. *See* investors, foreign
foreign knowledge/expertise, 58
foreign laws, 208
foreign management, in metallurgical industry, 135
foreign mechanics, and local learning, 188
foreign patent rights, 117, 206
foreign skilled workers, 16, 72, 128, 152, 182
foreign technicians, 16, 70
foreign technology, 21–22, 58
foreign trade, 19

foreign worker dependency, 184
forestry schools, 278n51
formal education, 185–86
foundational technologies. *See also* iron; railroads; steam power
foundries, 71, 236n89, 245n84
Fowle, Arthur, 116, 256n38
France: and adoption of sewing machines, 87; borrowed technology/expertise, 210; glassworkers from, 253n8; and global patents, 64; investors, 98; Mexico's view of, 9; support of first Mexican forestry school, 278n51
freight costs, 69–70, 160
freight transport, 187
French occupation (1862–1867), 28
"frozen throat" problem, 128
fuel costs, 124; and adoption of technology, 160; as impediment to adoption of technologies, 163–64; and industrial-scale mining/manufacturing, 160; and production capacity, 166; roasting and chloridization of silver ores, 149; and steam power, 162–63
fuel oil engines, 73–74, 97
fuel oil imports, 124
fuel sources, 24, 118, 124; cost and accessibility of, 123, 161; and glass industry, 127; local sources, 111; Owens system, 127; scarcity of, 162; wood-based, 124. *See also* deforestation; wood
Fundición de Sinaloa, 104, 192f24; boiler and engine manufacture, 78t2, 243n58; government subsidy, 174; horizontal double-acting cylinder steam engine, 78f10; and learning capacities, 181–82; and steam engine horsepower, 243n61; steam engine manufacture capacity, 187; technological capabilities, 174
Fundidora Monterrey, 70, 108, 132, 172; adaptations, 185; cultural integration, 173; fuel cost and accessibility at, 161; fuel costs, 163; and imports, 175; lobbying for higher tariffs, 174; and market size studies, 166; sales difficulties, 174; system design, 166; technological capabilities, 174

hydroelectric power, 73, 164
hydropower. *See* water power

immigrants, 37, 67, 179, 199, 201, 204, 212
impaired adoption, 7–8, 164–69; diffusion,
    168–69; limitations of adoption, 164;
    productive efficiency, 164–66; and
    profitability, 164; system design, 166–68
imperialist expansion, North Atlantic, 59
import data, 35f4, 59–64, 239n12; clothing
    imports, 99; downturns, 248n32; glass
    bottles, 110; as measure of investment
    and capacity of economy, 59; sewing
    machines, 89–90, 157; steam engines,
    72, 73; supplies in 1910, 71–72
import dependence, 174, 175
import duties, on iron and steel manufac-
    tures, 174
imported bottles, 131; displacement by
    Vidriera Monterrey, 129
imported clothing. *See* clothing imports
imported expertise: cyanide process, 185;
    dependence on, concern about, 209;
    late-century reliance on, 17; and local
    capabilities, 58–59; preference for, 210
imported fuel sources, 124
imported goods, 132, 174
imported technology, 210; dependence on,
    concern about, 3, 14, 209; design incom-
    patibility limitations, 167; and effects of
    early reliance/dependence on, 17; and
    "fit" problems, 160; and late developers,
    17; and Mexican context, 160; and
    production system capacity, 165; reli-
    ance/dependence on, 217; summary of,
    79–80
import expertise, 117
import machinery, dependence on, concern
    about, 209
imports, foreign: alkali chemicals, 124;
    chosen over domestic goods, 166; and
    domestic production costs, 122; metal
    forms, 175; metal manufactures, 175;
    and sewing machines, 102
imports, hardware and expertise, 3
imports, iron, steel and machinery, 221–22
import-substituting industrialization,
    109–10, 166, 210

import trade, effects of ready-made cloth-
    ing production on, 96
inaccessibility, and adoption of technology,
    161
inanimate power, 29, 162
incentives, 14, 111, 171, 175, 179, 183
income, disposable, and sewing machine
    consumption, 84
independence, Mexican, 4
India, 87, 91, 102, 165, 210
"Industria" (Rosenzweig), 245n80
industrial approach to mining, 6
industrial capacity, foundational technolo-
    gies, 213
industrial concentration, 73, 184
industrial growth, 13, 130
industrialists, views on dependence on
    foreign technology, 209
industrialization, early: benefits to workers,
    177; and British machinery, 8–9;
    decreased standard of living, 177; Por-
    firian Mexico, 172; in U.S. and western
    Europe, 8–9
industrialization, history of, 8–9
industrializers, 10
industrial labor force, and resistance to
    adoption, 176–77
industrial machinery, importation of, 175
industrial metals, global demand for, 6
industrial processes, heat-intensive, 162
industrial production, North Atlantic, 58
industrial revolution, first, 28; adoption of
    technology, 159; core technologies of, 9;
    and industrialization, 57; and Mexican
    economic troubles, 19; Mexico, 215;
    Mexico's isolation from technologies of,
    58; of North Atlantic, 28
industrial revolution, second, 13, 214–15,
    217; characteristics of, 59; effects on
    technological imports, 57; technical
    education after, 186–87
industrial workers, first generation, 165
Industrias Nuevas program, 168
industry sector, 8, 78t2, 209
inefficiencies, 165, 166
"inevitable law of progress", 3
informal economy sector, 93
information: information markets, 170;

information networks, 187, 215–16; unequal access to, 179

infrastructure, 4, 71, 79, 210, 212

Ingram, Stuart, 240n18, 240n23

injuries, 177

Inkster, Ian, 65f9

innovation capabilities, 209, 210, 212, 227n43; agriculture, 170; built on human capital, 217; burdened by patent rights, 169; in cyanide process, 147; and cyanide process adaptations, 150–51; of cyaniding to silver ores, 146; iron, 170

innovations: avoidance, 170; cultural bias against, 230n62; in cyaniding, 151; and economic growth, 164; investments, 176; lack of sustained, 217; limitations of, 7–8; local investment, 176; originations of technological, 8–9; poverty effects on, 170; and production inputs productivity, 164; promotion of, 210; technological innovations, 181

innovators, 162, 209

input markers, undeveloped, effects on adoption of technology, 164

installment plans, 87, 90

institutional environment, as limit to diffusion, 169

institutional reform, 20

integration, of new technologies, 158

intellectual property laws, 210

intellectuals, 4, 9

interaction with technology, 8, 182, 183–88, 214

intermediate inputs, 15, 79, 160–62, 164

international expositions, 11–12, 104, 115–16, 216

inventions, process, 130

invention vs. adoption, 10

inventive activity, 4, 9, 64; coverage of, 22; cultural bias against, 230n62; domestic, 12–13; flow of, 10; origins and determinants of, 9

inventors, Mexican, 12–13, 64

investments, 19; in agricultural production, large-scale commercial, 170; attraction of foreign, 212; capabilities, 227n43; capital investments and market structure, 168; capital investments in bottle

production, 131–32; in cyanide plants, 151; estimates, 270n98; fixed capital investment, 79; in glass bottle manufacture, 118; government incentives, 159; in Guanajuato mines, 144; imported industrial machinery, 209; incentives, undermining of, 171; little pressure for, 3; and local capabilities, 72; local investments, 176; in local technological capabilities, 212; low level of, 153; in manufacturing, 213; in Mexican mining, 138; in mining sector, 152; in new technology systems, 188; North Atlantic capital investments, 13; as response to social change, 56; sewing machines, 96; in technology imports, 8, 56

investors, 6, 7, 9; and adoption of technology, 18, 79; and beer industry, 109; Brittingham, Juan F., 168; challenges to, 132; commercialization of new technologies, 213; and commercialization of technology, 122; domestic, 59, 98, 210; electrical industry, 73; and flow of investment capital, 13; foreign, 6, 59, 98, 152, 212; and foreign engineers, 16; garment factories, 96; Garza, Isaac, 168; look abroad, 209; and market size studies, 166; and Owens machine, 107; and production capabilities, 16; profitability, 208; royalties as obstacle for, 169; and sewing machine consumption, 96; on technology imports, 10; US in mining sector, 152

iron, 3, 46–49, 74–79, 172–75. *See also* boiler and engine manufacture

iron and steel industry, 79, 172–75, 244n66; adoption and diffusion of, 79; and backwardness (*atraso*), 46–49; domestic production, 174; duties on, 174; Fundición de Sinaloa, 174; Fundidora Monterrey, 174; history of, 174; and import dependence, 174; innovation capabilities, 170; iron and steel imports, 61t1, 174; iron forges, 236n89; iron imports, 79, 221–22, 232n34; iron technologies, 17; ironworking, 236n88; and production capabilities, 17, 19; *Progreso*, 74–80; and tariff protections, 166

manufacturing *(continued)*
  perceived future of, 3; worker output,
  164
maritime sector, 78t2
market competition, 9
market identification, 118
marketing strategies: Singer Sewing
  Machine Company, 87; Toledo Glass
  Company, 113
market opportunities, unequal access to, 179
market rights, bottle producers, 254n19
markets, information, 170
markets, Mexican: access to, 170; and
  capital flow, 72; and foreign investment,
  59; for production inputs, 160; and
  production system capacity, 165–66;
  railroads and, 71; and rail system, 69;
  size of, 166; and transportation, 41
markets, undeveloped, 132, 160
markets, US, accessibility of, 210
market share competition, 166, 169
market size, and production capacity, 166
market structure, 168
Martínez, D. Claudio Juan, 77, 197
Martínez de los Ríos, Ramón Esteban, 10
Marx, Karl, 85–86
material culture, 95–96
material progress *(progreso material)*, 3, 4,
  5f1, 11, 12–13, 20, 28–29, 208
Maximilian, 52, 59
Mazatlán, Mexico, 94, 104, 181–82; *cervecerías* (large-scale breweries), 109; Filippinni, Pedro, 252n107; foundries,
  192f24, 245n84
meat industry, 167
mechanical engineering, 278n53
mechanics, foreign, and local learning, 188
mechanics, Mexican, 12; and mining industry, 153; and rail system, 70–71
mechanization of production: accidents,
  177; and bottle production feasibility,
  131; domestic adoption of, 212; fear of
  physical dangers, 177; history of, 8–9;
  industrial displacement of traditional
  livelihoods, 176; and labor costs reduction, 128; machinery, large-scale, 160;
  meat processing, 167
Médanos de Samalayuca, sand, 123

Medina, Bartolomé de, 135, 137
Memoria of the Ministerio de Fomento,
  236n96
Memoria of the Secretaría de Fomento, 142
Méndez Vallesteros, Nicolás, 46
Mendirichaga, Tomás, 114, 119–20
Mennell, J. Leslie, 269n94
mercury amalgamation system, 135, 137, 143
mercury men *(azogueros)*, 137
Mérida, Mexico, 109
Mesata Central, 72, 162
metal-bearing ores, 265n41
metal forms, 174, 175
metallurgical industry, 134, 175, 187. *See also*
  iron and steel industry
metal manufactures, 174–75
metal refinement, coverage of, 22
metalworking, 9, 71; firms, new, 175; and
  inanimate power sources, 162; industrial
  revolution, first, 28
Mexican army, foundries and, 236n89
Mexican Central railroad, 71, 131f17
Mexican civil war (1857–59), 28
Mexican context. *See* context, Mexican
Mexican culture, and foreign technology,
  21–22
Mexican Gold & Silver Recovery Com-
  pany, Ltd. (MGSRC), 141, 142, 144, 152,
  169, 263–64n32; field agents, 263n31;
  Mennell, J. Leslie, 269n94; and ore
  testing, 266n56
Mexican Goldfields Ltd., 142
Mexican Herald, 163
Mexican independence (1821), 27–28
"Mexicanized" workforce, 184
Mexican Light and Power Company, 73
Mexican National Railroad, 70, 187
Mexican ownership, Letcher, M., 270n99
Mexican patent rights. *See* patent rights,
  Mexican
Mexican patents. *See* patents, Mexican
Mexican Philanthropic Society (Sociedad
  Filantrópica Mexicana], 103
Mexico City: artisanal sector, 176; and beer
  industry, 111; bottle factory plans, 257n59;
  and Cassel Company, 141; Cervecería
  Toluca y México, 111; and clothing indus-
  try, 97, 98; colonial travel routes to, 40;

cost of living estimates, 93; *Diario del Hogar,* 83; garment factories, 96, 97f13; MacArthur-Forrest laboratory, 143, 149, 266n56; newspaper advertisements, 90; railroad concession, first, 69; sewing machines, 87, 89, 96; Singer Sewing Machine Company, 55, 100; slaughterhouse (*rastro*), 167; and workforce, 96

México: Su evolución social, 4, 5f1

MGSRC (Mexican Gold & Silver Recovery Company, Ltd.), 141, 142, 144, 152, 169, 263–64n32; field agents, 263n31; Mennell, J. Leslie, 269n94; and ore testing, 266n56

Michoacán, Mexico, 85, 95, 123, 141, 171

middle class culture, 91–93, 97–98, 208

Middle East, 87

Mier, Bernardo, 236n89

migration, North Atlantic, 13

military, Mexican, 98

military power, North Atlantic, 9, 11–12

milling facilities, 141

Mills, James E., 141

Minas Prietas mines, 142, 264n35

mineral fuel, imported, 163

mineral production, stagnation of, 153

mineral refining, 72, 186, 268n70

Mining College, 27

mining industry, 6, 19, 212; bonanzas of high-paying ores, 52, 135, 138, 147–48; and cyanide process, 135, 140; demand, consumer, 173; displacement of Mexicans by foreigners, 152–53; "dry-washing" techniques, 167; and economic growth, 153; and electric power, 73; floods, 267n62; history of, 38, 135; labor productivity, rising, 164–65; and local learning in mining industry, 153; and Mexican worker displacement, 153; mineral-bearing veins, 265n41; miners, 268n85; mining engineers, 6, 239–40n18, 277n14; mining facilities, 141; mining firms, 152, 161; mining machinery imports, 61t1; national wealth (*riqueza nacional*), 153; natural resources, 153; as North American industry, 152–53; scientific and industrial approach, 186; and steam technol-

ogy, 72; summary of transformation of, 151–54; technical education, 187; worker output, 164

Mining School, 196–97

mining schools, 65, 187, 196

mining sector, global adaptation of cyanide to silver ores, 151

mining sector, Mexican, 78t2; as technological leader, 151; worker productivity, 152

Missouri School of Mines, 240n23

mobility, worker, and ethnic distinctions, 165

Moctezuma brewerey, 111, 119

modernity, symbols of, 130, 172, 173f22

"modernization", as label for material progress, 7

modernization projects, Bourbon, 20

modern sector vs. traditional sector, 21, 93, 217

Mokyr, Joel, 215

monopolies, market, 168

monopoly positions, 132

monopoly pricing, from patent rights, Mexican, 169

monopoly rights, 117, 123

Monterrey, Mexico: and beer industry, 110, 118; and bottle production feasibility, 125; *cervecerias* (large-scale breweries), 109, 120; Cuauhtémoc brewery, 111, 114; and industry fuel use, 127; and learning capacities, 181; and sewing machine manufacture, 104

Monterrey glass factory, 16, 18, 55; and commercialization of bottle technology, 107–8; early failure, 258n69; fluxing alkali, 260n104; "frozen throat" problem, 128; and Owens machine, 116

Mora, José María Luis, 29, 30

Morelos, Mexico, 171, 229–30n57

Mormon colony in Chihuahua, 279n70

mules, 38, 87, 160; mules trains, 40; mule transport, 95, 103; in railway age, 69

Mules, Mines, and Me (Parker), 240n23

Murphy, Tomás, 44

Museo Tecnológico Industrial, 12

Naranja, Mexico, 171

national fragmentation, effects on production technologies, 153

industrial concentration as constraint for, 184; and interactions, 183–88; in learning and assimilation, 181; for Mexican engineers and technicians, 185–86; in new technology systems, 187; and technology transfer, 182

oral histories, 102–3

ore grinding, 266n56

ores, Mexican, 134, 149

ore testing, 266n56

ore treatment, custom, 267n58

Orizaba, Mexico, 43, 112f15; *cervecerias* (large-scale breweries), 109; and clothing industry, 98, 102; Moctezuma brewerey, 111, 119

Ortiz, Simón Tadeo, 44, 212

Otero, Mariano, 27

Ottoman Empire, 91

output data, agriculture, 172

outworking arrangements, 86, 97

overland transport, 40, 59, 160

Owens, Michael J., 107–8, 112–13, 129, 254n19

Owens bottle system, machine manufacture, 175

Owens European Bottle-Machine Company, 113

Owens European rights, 255n34

Owens machine, 55–56, 107, 126f16; and adoption of technology, 108; and consumer demand, 111; contrast to sewing machine adoption, 108; cost, 254n20; development of, 113; and diffusion of technology, 108; and domestic market, 108; installation, 254n20; and investors, 107; and labor cost reduction, 257n61; legal rights for use of, 131; licensing contracts, 119; local adoption of, 114; local learning opportunities, 184; Mexican rights, 258n70; and obstacles to commercialization, 114; patent rights, Mexican, 206; production capacity of, 113–14; productive capacity, 118; system design, 166; and technology transfer, 108

Owens Mexican Bottle Machine Company (La Owens de México), 117, 254n19, 256n38

Owens Mexican patent rights, investors interest, 119

Owens system, 128–29; and adaptation problems, 129; adjustments to Mexican context, 128; commercialization of, 126–27; commercialization of new technologies, 213; and delayed adoption, 159; diffusion of technology, 159; licensing contracts, 118, 119; and monopoly rights, 117; obstacles to adoption, 107–8; and obstacles to commercialization, 132; and unskilled labor, 128

Pachuca, Hidalgo, 137, 137f18; and cyanide experimentation, 186; *haciendas de beneficio,* 143; and mercury amalgamation system, 143; milling facilities, 152–53; mines, 152–53; mining industry, 139, 149; Real de Monte, 149; and silver cyaniding, 145; tailings (processed ore), 138

Pachuca district, 136; flooding of 1896, 267n62; managers, 270n103; and precious metal mining, 135; and transportation, 40

Pachuca tanks, 150

padrones, and blacksmith shops, 236n89

Palacio de Hierro, 98

Palacios, Daniel, 194

Palafox y Calva Gálvez, Juan de, 48

Palmarejo plant, 142

Pan-American Mining Company, 142

papermaking industry, 40, 161

Paris Exposition (1889), 104

Parral, Chiuhuahua, 124–25

Parral tanks, 150

parts, imports, 187

patent applications, 64

patent battles, 168–69

patent laws, Mexican, 117

patent records, Mexican, 182, 206

patent rights, Mexican, 119, 168–69, 184; Brittingham, Juan F., 206; as burden on innovation, 169; cigarette manufacturing, 206; competition for, 116–17; cost of, 168, 169; as limit to diffusion, 169; Mexican Gold & Silver Recovery Company, Ltd. (MGSRC), 169; monopoly pricing from, 169; Owens machine, 206 patents: fan attachment patent, 252n107; MacArthur-Forrest cyanide separation process, 140

patents, foreign, 206; Owens machine, 113

patents, global, 64, 65f9

patents, Mexican, 12–13, 132, 219–20; 1991–2005, 210; construction techniques, 170; cyanide process, 141; processed foods, 170; transportation, 40

patents, US, Owens machine, 113

patents rights, Mexican: as competition limiter, 169; as market share tool, 169

patio process, 137, 137f18, 139, 140, 146

Patterson, Mr., 95

Pauly Jail Building Company, 167

pawned sewing machines, 100–101

pax porfiriana, 19, 57

peasant farmers, 172

Pedrazo, Mr., 255n34

Peimbert, Cecilia K., 5f1, 39f5

Perigrina mill, 145, 267n58

petroleum production, domestic, 74

Philippines, 91

pig iron production, 236n96

Pinguico mill, 145, 267n58

plantations, tropical crop, 172

plow adaptations, 171

plows, wooden, 170, 171

plowshares, iron/steel, 170, 171

pneumatic drills, 138, 146

policy incentives, and technology imports, 212

policy makers, 9

political environments, 14

political influence, 170

political institutions, 14

political organizational structures, 14

political power, North Atlantic, 11–12

politics, foreign investment as priority for, 212

Pollard, Sidney, 11

polytechnic institute, 278n45

population growth, 98–99, 172

porcelain factories, 16

Porfirian government. *See* Porfirian Mexico

Porfirian Mexico: dependence on businesses, 216; economic growth, 165; government, 167; industrialization, 172;

patterns of, 210; relative autonomy of, 216; technology tragedy of, 206

Porfiriato, 70, 172, 278n53. See also *pax porfiriana;* Porfirian Mexico

Porrúa, Miguel Angel, 5f1, 39f5

Porter, Susie, 249n50

porters, 55

Portugal, 210

Posada, José Guadalupe, 177, 178f23

positivist goals, 208

postindependence depression, 30–38

potassium cyanide, 139–40, 266n52, 269n92

poverty, 11, 170, 176

power, 41–46, 72–74; and backwardness (*atraso*), 41–45; costs, 73, 97, 162; electrical industry, 97; motive, availability of, 160; and ready-made clothing production, 97; steam, 72

power, North Atlantic, 13, 59

practical experience, replaced by scientific and industrial approach, 186

precious metal mining, 6; economics of, 146; education, 185–86; output data, 151–52; processing systems, 134

prevented adoption, 7–8, 169–72, 214; agriculture, 170–72; cast-iron stoves, 169; cement block construction, 169; construction industry, urban, 169; processed foods, 169; steel frame construction, 169; urban construction industry, 169

prices, changing relative, 7

primary agents of technological change, 6–7

principle source of motive power, electrical industry as, 73

print materials, 62–64, 152, 181, 216; cyanide process, 185; and knowledge transfer, 206; and local learning capabilities, 188

processed foods, 169–70

processed ore (tailings), as backfill for stopes, 262n12

producer goods, basic, and tariff protections, 216

producers, Mexican, and import competition, 166

trade records, 90
trading partners, leading, 61f7
traditional (artisanal) ways, 172
traditional household production, 96
traditional livelihoods, replacement of, 7; industrial displacement of, 176
traditional machines, replaced by new technologies, 6
traditional technological systems, and refineries, 139
train accidents, 177, 178f23
trains. *See* railroads
Transactions of the Institute of Mining and Metallurgy, 143
transfer, and relation to capabilities and technology imports, 15–16, 16f2
transport, and gasoline engines, 74
transport, freight, 187
transport, human, 38, 95, 160
transport, mule, 95
transport, overland, 40, 95, 131
transportation, 213; 1870 watershed, 59; and backwardness (*atraso*), 38–41; cargo transport costs, 69; challenges of, 38, 95; colonial period, 38–40; and consumer markets, 41; costs and accessibility, 18–19, 123; effects on production technologies, 38; industrial revolution, first, 28; mid-century costs, 40; relative statis of, 29; systems of, 84; technologies, new, 9
transport costs, 118, 160; and bottle production feasibility, 123; and coal imports, 125; effects on agriculture, 170; effects on production technologies, 69–70; manufacturing firms and, 132; and railroad negotiations, 125
transport issues, 160, 166
Transvaal gold district, 140
Travis, William, 259n98
trends and patterns, and adoption of technology, 8
Treviño, Manuel Cantú, 259n89
Trewartha-James, W. H., 141, 142, 144, 263n32, 269n90
tripartite pacts, 209
trolleys, 177
Tron, Enrique, 98
truck transport, 187

tube mills, 73, 150, 269n90
"turnkey" operations, 15, 129, 131
twentieth century, late, 207, 209, 210, 211, 213, 217
typhus epidemic (1893), and Singer sewing machine repossession, 100–101

Uhink y Compañía agency, 87
underdevelopment, 11
UNESCO, educational goals, 279n54
Union sewing machines, 87
United States: 1870 watershed, 59; and adoption of sewing machines, 87; Baldwin Works, 70; beer exports, 109; borrowed technology/expertise, 210; Civil War, 13, 19, 59, 212; clothing exports, 83; and cyanidation, 140; and decline of ready-made clothing imports, 99; dependence on, concern about, 4; diffusion rate of sewing machines, 91; economic growth, 28; expansion, threats of, 4; expertise, exported, 152; glass industry fuel costs, 124; globalization era, 13; and global patents, 64; Guanajuato mines purchases, 144; industrialization, pattern of, 59; industrial revolution, second, 13; invasion of 1847–48, 28; investors, 152; and licensing contracts, 122; locomotive exports, 70; market accessibility, 210; and Mexican metalllurgical industry, 135; Mexico's view of, 9; and mining industry, 152, 268n85; patent pool, 90, 248n39; power, 59; rail investors, 69; sewing machine exports, 83–84, 86, 87, 88; sewing machine salesmen, 85; steam engine export, 72; steel industry fuel costs, 163; steel rail exports, 70; and supply links, 104; as technology exporter, 9; as technology producer, 9
unrest, rural, 229–30n57
unskilled labor, 128, 132, 176
upper-class Mexicans, 177
urban markets: beer industry, 130; clothing manufactories, 97–98; investors, 98; meat industry, 167; urban construction industry, 169
use rights, 113

Valenciana mine, 139
values, tastes and habits, 14
Van Law, C. W., 200, 280n78
Velasco, José María, 4, 172
Veracruz, Mexico, 40, 55, 69, 87
vertical diffusion, of knowledge, 216
Vidriera Monterrey, 56, 108, 132, 183–84;
    adjustments at, 129–30; and American
    engineers, 128; benefits of "Mexi-
    canized" workforce, 184; capitalization
    of, 126, 129; crystal and flat glass, 130;
    cultural change, 173; and displacement
    of bottle importation, 129; factory
    investors in, 160; Garza-Sada ownership
    team, 130; and internal capacities, 130;
    and local learning capabilities, 184; and
    market size studies, 166; Owens system
    at, 107, 129; raw materials, 130, 161;
    reduction of foreign worker depend-
    ency, 184
Villa, Pancho, 94
village economy, adoption of technology
    by, 170
Virginia City mines, 265n36
Virgoe, Walter H., 143
Vocabulario de Mexicanismos, 94

wages, 176, 210, 259n98
wagons, US farm, and local conditions, 171
Waite, Charles B., 112, 112f15
Walbridge, William, 118, 120, 121–22,
    257n59
walkout protests, 177
Wanamaker, John, sewing machine prices,
    248n39
Ward, Oliver, 240n23
warehouse sector, 78t2
waste rock accumulations (tailings), 138
water mills, 162
Water Pierce Oil Company, 127
water power, 234n51, 235n70; as alternative
    to steam, 72–73; vs. electric power, 73;
    limitations of, 74; North Atlantic, 28;
    resources for, 161; water-driven mills,
    162
water scarcity, 162; adaptations of refining
    techniques, 167
wealth: achievement of, 216; generation of

new, 4; North Atlantic, 13; per capita,
    27–28
welfare, achievement of, 216
welfare decline/high wage paradox, 177
Wheeler & Wilson sewing machine com-
    pany, 87, 88f11, 98
White sewing machines, 87
Whithead, J. S., 244n67
Whittemore, C. W., 89
Wiechers, H. L., 119
Wilcox, Mr. (American engineer), 126
Williamson, George, 263n31
windmills, 162
Womack, John, Jr., 229–30n57
women: and clothing industry, 83–84, 96,
    97f13, 102–3; and commercial outwork,
    93–94, 246n14; consumer demands of,
    6; and garment factories, 96, 97f13,
    102–3; and labor activism, 99; and labor
    issues, 86; occupations, 96; oral histo-
    ries of garment factory workers, 102–3;
    and sewing machine consumption, 91,
    93–94, 105, 249n50; and sewing
    machine proficiency, 102; in sewing
    workshops, 97f13; and "sweated" labor,
    93–94; women's welfare, 99
wood: craftsmen of, 176; fuels from, 124,
    162–63; scarcity of, 162; supply, 271n7.
    See also deforestation; fuel sources
worker displacement, Mexican, in mining
    sector, 153
worker productivity, in mining sector, 152
workers, artisanal, 12, 27, 103, 110f14, 111,
    165, 175, 176
workers, foreign, dependence on, concern
    about, 184
workers, Mexican, 6; injuries, 177; and
    mining industry, 153; organized, 176;
    productive capacity of, 165, 166; resist-
    ance of, 176–77; scarcity of, 166; textile
    industry, 99–100, 165; training of, 132;
    women, 96
working class, growth of: and accessibility
    of sewing machines, 100; and beer
    preference, 107; and consumer demand,
    97–98; and ready-made clothing pro-
    duction, 97–98
working conditions, 176